Ida Maddalena was born in Catailli, Southern Italy in 1935. She settled in England in the mid fifties and has lived for many years in Maidstone, Kent with her husband Aldo. In between a career caring for the sick and elderly she has found time to bring up three children and is now a grandmother three times over.

From Monte Cassino to Maidstone

Ida Maddalena

Published in 2006 by Ida Maddalena

ISBN 0-9554922-0-3

978-0-9554922-0-4

This book is dedicated to my beautiful grandchildren: Fabio, James and Gabriella

PREFACE

The reason I decided to write my life story was because I wanted my family, friends and future generations to appreciate how important it is to have faith and to be honest. I believe I have been guided along the road of my life. I put my trust in God and have been rewarded.

As a child I witnessed the ravages of war in my native Italy, an appalling chapters of history. The countryside around Monte Cassino was devastated and my extended family and neighbours suffered terribly during the conflict and for long afterwards.

Since I was little I had wanted to be educated and to be able to help people less fortunate than myself. The Second World War made that difficult for me, but God knew my desires and helped me to achieve my dreams. I left my village and spent my adolescence in Rome, the Eternal City, a world away from my simple childhood home. I lived and worked in the Vatican before going to live in London and qualify as a nurse. The caring profession gave me a wealth of experience in hospitals in Kent, while I brought up my own family. Eventually I ran my own residential home in Maidstone looking after older people, which had always been the very heart of my ambition.

I have been poor but never hungry, never homeless, never completely destitute. God always provided for me. Above all, I have met many good people and have been given a lot of love and support. All the events described in this book really happened, although I have changed some people's names. So here is an account of those people and the places, jobs, trials and traumas, pleasures and sorrows that have made up my life.

CHAPTER ONE - THE BEGINNING

Conca Della Campania, a small corner of Italy, is a lovely valley sheltered by mountains. The time has gone past, but if I close my eyes I can still visualise the place as it was - a group of villages. Frazione Cave and Catailli were two of them. Catailli was the place I was born. It was on a hillside. The villas there were owned by rich people. They had beautiful gardens surrounded by high walls. When I was about six years old my cousins, my friends and I climbed the walls to admire the beautiful flowers.

The countryside was also beautiful with many trees of all kinds. In spring the fresh air, the violets and the daisies along the road made a lovely scene, and there was the smell of the flowers: oranges, lemons and figs, the apples and everything that was in bloom. We took long walks to enjoy their fragrances.

In middle of the main village, Conca, stood a sixteenth century castle. We used to explore it. Our teacher owned the castle and she told us a story. In a corner of the castle was a deep hole at the bottom of which were many sharp, iron spikes. I was told that, in mediaeval times, the Count who ruled the area used to throw men and women who displeased him down this hole to die a horrible death.

The war changed all that. Many villas were destroyed and all the villages were damaged by bombs and shells. Frazione Cave was completely destroyed. Some have been reconstructed but quite few have been abandoned - just a few derelict walls and bricks looking forlornly at the sky. The gardens, too, were abandoned and the flowerbeds choked by weeds. Some villages were completely destroyed. Some houses have been rebuilt and are now inhabited, but others are woodland. What surprised me was that the castle, the highest building in the place, survived the bombs and shells and the damage to it was minimal.

My grandfather and grandmother owned one of the many farms and my uncle and my aunt, with their seven children, lived there too. I liked it there because I enjoyed playing with my cousins. I could run in the fields with them after the butterflies.

One morning I looked out of the window and saw the cows. They were ploughing the soil by themselves!

"Look!" I said to my grandmother, "the cows are ploughing the soil by themselves!"

"Oh, don't be silly, girl!" she said, "Gennaro is there."

I was very curious and ran downstairs to see what was going on. He was so little that the cows were hiding him. I couldn't understand; I heard his voice but I couldn't see him. I went nearer and saw a dwarf. I went back and asked grandmother,

"Who is he?"

"He's Gennaro," she said, "your mother's cousin and my nephew."

"So what is he to me?"

"Well, he's your second cousin."

Later he came up and grandmother told him what had happened and they had a good laugh.

One day I went to the farm where there were all kinds of animals including one very aggressive cockerel. I called out to my cousin Tony to lock him up but instead he threw a stone and killed it.

"Oh, no!" I said, "Look what you have done! What shall we say to grandmother? Tell me!"

"We can't tell her!" he said, "If only we could, we would have a lovely roast dinner!"

"She will be very upset."

He said there was only one thing to do: to make a hole, put it in and cover it up and that would be the end of the cockerel. But grandmother said,

"Children, I haven't heard or seen the cockerel."

What could we say? Tony said,

"Who knows where he is, grandmother? Maybe the gypsies have had him!"

"Well, now you're talking nonsense! How could that be? That cockerel would certainly peck the eyes out of anybody trying to go near him!"

Then my cousin said,

"The foxes must have had him. I'm sure they must have made a good meal out of him!"

"This problem will never be resolved. It will stay with us."

Not too far from the house there was a pool of spring water that we used for drinking. The water was always cool in summer but in winter it was almost warm. One day I asked granddad about it.

"Spring water never changes temperature," he said, "because in winter the air is very cold so the water seems to be warm, and in

summer it is very warm and the water seems to be very cold."
I didn't get it, but when I went to school I asked the teacher and she said exactly the same as granddad.

On one side of the yard there was a big pond. The water was rather muddy and was only good for the cows and other livestock to drink. There were frogs and even a few fish in it. Often I went there to watch the fish. I tried to catch some a few times but they were too quick for me. One day I went there looking for fish and saw something move. I stood back petrified. Near me, staring, its body lifted ready to strike, was a snake, a viper, one of the most poisonous ones. I just stood there, not knowing what to do. Fortunately, the snake was more scared than I was. It hissed a few times and went away. It was a long time before I could move.

A month before, a boy had been bitten in the arm by a snake. He was quite a way away from the village and by the time the doctor saw him the poisoning was well advanced. He saved his life, but had to amputate his arm.

Another day I was walking along the road near the farm when I felt a whispering wind in my face. I realised what it was. What a shock! A snake had come from the other side of the road. When we met, she was in such rush she was almost upright, head to tail. I can tell you, that wasn't very funny! Afterwards I thought that the snake must be blind and that was the reason she didn't see me. I was shocked and went in and told grandmother. She laughed and laughed, like it was a joke.
"Look, grandmother, you think this is funny because you are accustomed to them, but I don't like them. They frighten me. Actually, they make me sick! You wouldn't laugh if she'd bitten me, would you?"
She asked me to take some refreshment out to my grandfather, and I never expected to meet another snake. As I was walking along the rough road, there was another long snake lying on a branch of a big oak tree. I was very frightened! What could I do? I couldn't possibly get to where grandfather was. I started to run towards the farm but granddad must have spotted me.
"Ida, come here, now!"
"No! No!" I answered, "There's a big snake on the branch of that tree."
"What, that one?" he said.
"Yes."

"Don't be silly, girl. That snake isn't even poisonous!"
"You are all mad! You are all mad! I'm not coming here any more!"
I left my grandfather's refreshment on the ground and turned back
to go and play with my cousins.

Sometimes we found ourselves getting into all sorts of mischief
including death-defying games such as swinging from tree to tree
along wires to cross the river. My cousin and I used to climb the
tall fruit trees and hide from my mother. They were the happiest of
times.

One day I was in a field with my father, pulling potatoes. It was a
very hot day and after a while we stopped and sat down under a fig
tree for a bit of shade. We had a cold drink and then my father
started humming a tune. It sounded lovely.
"What's that, dad?" I asked.
"Well, it's a song that someone wrote during the Abyssinian war.
It's called *Little Black Face* (*Faccetta Nera*). I won't sing you the
whole song because it's a long one, but I'll sing you the chorus."
And he started singing.

Faccetta nera	Little black face
Bella abbissina	Lovely Abyssinia
Aspetta e spera	Wait and hope
Che gia' lora si avvicina	The time grows near
E quand saremo	And when we are
Vicino a Te	Near to you
Noi ti daremo	We will give you
Un'altro Duce	Another leader
Un'altro e Re	Another King.

"Was her face dirty?" I asked. My father laughed.
"The people of Abyssinia have got dark skins, they are black. Let
me tell you a story. If your teacher ever asks you for a history
essay, it will come in useful. Mussolini, our Duce, is a clever man.
At first he was good to the people and, although he was a Fascist
and went around beating up people who were Socialists and those
who refused to join his party, he did many good things to help the
workers. He instituted the Cassa Malattia (The National Health)
whereby employers had to pay their employees sick pay. Also,
although he practically militarized the young, both boys and girls
were sent each year on holidays to the mountains or the seaside
for free. Mussolini wanted a strong nation, so he promised every

family a thousand lire for each boy born. The Lazio region is a plain, an area of many miles which, because it was so low lying, was just a swamp. He had the swamp drained and two towns were built on it: Littoria and Pontinia. Mussolini was also a very ambitious man. In 1938 things were not going well in Italy. Employment was low. At least a hundred of thousand workers were without work and that meant they had no money to feed their families. People emigrated from many villages and towns, some to France, some to Germany, many to America. To stop all that, Mussolini sent big shots into the towns and villages to make speeches. They talked about Abyssinia as a marvellous country where millions of people could find work. They could build roads, schools, houses, theatres, all sorts of things. They talked about the Abyssinians as savages living in caves. Anyway, after that they declared war on them and sent thousands of soldiers to fight them. As you know, I was one of them. Abyssinia became an Italian colony. You may not understand it all now but in the future, when your teacher asks you for a composition about Italian history, you will know all about it."

My father was right. I didn't understand everything he told me at that time, but a few years later I found out that those men had been telling lies and the Abyssinians were not savages but nice people.

Time went on and brought some changes. My teacher, who usually wore colourful blouses, came to school wearing a black one. We all looked at her and she must have noticed, because she smiled.
"Vi piace la mia blousa?" she said (Do you like my blouse?) "È l'emblema del Fascist." (It is the sign of the Fascists).
Then she went on about Mussolini and what he had done for the country. At the end of her speech I realised that we girls had been incorporated into the Fascist gang. We were now "figlie della lupa" (daughters of the Roman she-wolf). I didn't understand what it meant at that time. Every Saturday we had to parade in the square and do gymnastic exercises.

One thing I remember was, when I was six years old, my mother made me a little black costume. It had two pockets in front and a round collar buttoned at the back with a blue ribbon tied in a bow at the front. This was to show which class we were in.

When I was seven years old I was in the first class. Our lovely young teacher, the nice one who owned the castle, wasn't there any more, for some unknown reason. The new teacher was a man. He wasn't very kind to us but he was a very good teacher. He was a very hard person and the children were terrified of him, but for some reason he was very kind to me. When the children needed to be excused for personal reasons, he didn't allow it, and for that reason they used have accidents and wet themselves. One day I was sitting with another girl on the school bench. Her name was Delia and she was very frightened of him and wouldn't ask anything. I realised I was wet and couldn't understand why; so I asked her,

"Delia, have you had an accident?"

"Yes, I have." she said.

 "I'm sorry." I said.

 "I'm frightened when we get up and leave the school, the other children they will make fun of us."

 "Don't worry," I said, "We'll run."   In fact that is exactly what happened: we ran out as fast as we could.

He also was very cruel to his own children and when his daughter was disrespectful he took her to the front of the class and hit her and pulled her hair. I was good friends with her and felt very sorry for her.

He was also a good Fascist. One day he came in wearing a black shirt.

"There'll be no lessons today." he said, "Cerarca (a Fascist big shot) will come and talk to you." We were quite happy: no lessons! But our enthusiasm disappeared when the man arrived. He was rather small and was wearing a black uniform with a lot of medals hanging on the front. As he came in, he gave the Roman salute.

"Viva il Duce!" he shouted, raising his arm straight above his head in a Roman-style greeting. Well, we all stood up and did the same. Then he started talking and went on for a long time, boasting about our beloved Duce who would guide us to victory and prosperity, who loved us all, and so on. We were all getting tired and wanted to sit down. One or two tried but a shout from the teacher made them stand up again. I didn't understand much of what the man said.

The only thing I did understand was what the young teacher had told us before: that we were daughters of the Roman she-wolf.

Nothing else changed. We still had to march every Saturday in the village square, parade, do exercises and sing Fascist songs. We didn't have a bad time in the village square, apart from having to listen to endless speeches about Fascism and the beloved Duce. We learned a lot of gymnastics and sang Fascist songs.

Giovinezza! Giovinezza!	Youth! Youth!
Primavera di bellezza	Spring of beauty
Nella gioia	In joy
E nella speranza	And in hope
Il tuo canto	You sing
Squilla eva	Ring and go
E per Benito Mussolini	For Benito Mussolini
Eia eia alala	Eia eia alala.

We had to march like little soldiers, one, two, one, two, but one Saturday I had had enough of it. When the teacher put us in marching order, he put me in front of two big boys and I began to panic because I thought I wasn't going to be able to keep ahead of them and they would trample me down. So I moved out of the way and let the march go on past. The teacher stopped the march and tried to put me back again, but I would not have it. I began to scream and scream and the teacher was very embarrassed, not knowing what to do. Everyone standing there watching the march laughed. That day things didn't go his way; he had no choice but to send for my mother to come and fetch me.

As I've said, I didn't understand much of this business but few years later I found out the reasons behind it all. Mussolini was a man obsessed with legend and history, and in particular everything to do with ancient Rome. A legend said that a she-wolf brought up Romulus and Remus, the little boy twins who were supposed to be the founders of Rome. The 'fascio' (the bundle of twigs cut with an axe) in the middle of the Fascist's symbol was also a Roman symbol. The legions that had conquered many nations marched carrying the 'fascio' at the front. 'L'unione e la forza' was the Fascist's motto ('United we will be strong'). All of this Mussolini had taken from the ancient Romans.

In the First World War Mussolini had been only a corporal, but he was a clever man. He was also a good speaker. He had that magnetism that pulls people. In 1922 he joined the Socialist Party but when he realised that it was going nowhere, he founded his own, Il Fascismo. In 1923, just before the election, some of the deputation were beaten up by the *Camice Nere* (the Fascist 'Black Shirts') and then resigned, so and he and the Fascists won the election.

Mussolini gained power, but the King was against him. He went to Rome with a thousand of his men and asked for a meeting with the King. When he was in his presence he said,
"Maesta' vi porto una nuova Italia, un'Italia Fascista. (Your Majesty, I bring you a new Italy, a Fascist Italy)." When the king didn't say anything, he added,
"And with me are a thousand men: they are the Black Shirts." The King got scared and made him prime minister. Thus Mussolini took power. Maybe it was that thirst for power that prompted him to ally with Hitler.

Anyway, as I said earlier, we were daughters of the she-wolf and Mussolini had thought of something else for the boys. They, too, had to parade in the square and also had to carry rifles, taller than themselves, and perform exercises with them. They were called 'Ballilla' after a historical character. For many years Italy had been under Austrian domination. Then one day in 1888 something happened to change all that. It began in Milan. Austrian soldiers were forcing some local men to pull cannons up a steep hill. Suddenly a young boy picked up a stone, threw it and killed an Austrian officer. All the men turned on the soldiers and captured them, then moved the cannons around to face the troops. That sparked a flame and all over the country men fought the Austrians and in few days Italy was free. That boy was called Ballilla.

CHAPTER TWO – A PAINFUL TIME

Apart from playing in the fields with the girls, nothing special happened but one day I saw people walking about all scared. I asked a woman what was going on.

"We are at war." she said. I didn't know what it meant but quite soon I found out. I saw mothers crying and saying goodbye to their sons, young women giving their last kisses to their boyfriends and husbands. "May the Lord bless you and keep you safe." were their last words and then they left. I was told they would go to a foreign country to face the cannons, bombs, machine guns and mortars. I didn't know what those things were, but knew they must be terrible.

Time passed and the war went on. Now all the young men had disappeared. In the fields and the farms one could see only women and old men working. They had cultivated and ploughed the fields to produce everything that could be sold or kept for the winter months. More and more women went around with red eyes, puffed from crying. Each one had lost a loved one: a fiancé or husband or son or brother. A letter had arrived: "Your son died a hero", "Your husband is on the missing list."

The war was going badly. After early victories, there were only defeats. I heard my uncle and my father talking.

"Mussolini should have not declared war." they said, "We weren't prepared for it, we didn't have enough weapons or enough armoured cars or enough petrol." Some of the soldiers had antiquated rifles from the previous war. Of course, you had to be careful of what you said or the Fascists might call you a "Defeatist" and you would be arrested.

Quite soon men in Fascist uniforms came to the villages. They were arrogant and behaved as if the villages belonged to them. One day they went to a farm and took away a fat pig and few chickens. Everyone was scared of them.

All the villas had tall iron railings.

"The country is in need of iron for constructing cannons." one of them said. They loaded everything onto a lorry and took it all away. They even took the railings from the monuments to the First World War in the village squares. A few days later they came again and went round all the houses. This time they asked all the married women to give them their gold wedding rings and gave them shiny rings instead.

In the villages we were all right with regard to food but in the cities people were almost starving. More and more people came to try and buy food from us. At first, granddad was happy to oblige but later he had to stop selling or we would have starved. Bad times were coming.

Over time more and more men, some as young as nineteen, received orders or joined up voluntarily. Some were already in the army, some were in their forties and some even in their fifties. All the villages looked nearly deserted, and still the Fascists came and made speeches, almost forcing men to volunteer. A young man, who had been exempted from military service because of illness, was beaten up and almost killed. 'Inboscato' one of the Fascists called him. At home I asked my father what that word meant.
"An inboscato," he said, "is a man who pretends to be sick to avoid military service. In short, it means you are coward (pauroso) or have no guts." I felt very sorry for that young man, as it was not his fault that he was ill.

Bad news came. Germany and Japan had been fighting against China, Russia, and England. France had been overrun by the Germans and now was out of the war. Up until that time, the Americans had stayed neutral but the Japanese had bombed and partly destroyed their fleet in a place called Pearl Harbour, and so they entered the war and became our enemy. I heard my uncle saying to my father,
"America is a big continent, much bigger than Europe. They've got everything: coal, petrol, iron and money. They can combine millions of dollars with plenty of weapons."

I understood most of what he said because at school I had been doing geography and, although I was very young, I knew that a time of suffering, a very bad time would come for all of us. What I'm going to tell in the next few chapters is something of what happened or what I heard from others and added to my diary several years later. I want you to get an insight into what was happening and how things were at that time. I also did some research to get the facts right. These episodes are a part of Italian history and really happened.

I was eight years old in 1943, a year of surprises, a year when so many things one thought would never happen, did happen, a year of changes, and a painful year for everyone. The war was going badly for us. In the terrible Russian winter, many thousands of soldiers, who were not equipped with warm clothing, had died in the icy snow. In Africa also many had died in the hot desert or had been taken prisoner by the British. Of the army of which we were so proud, only a few divisions remained, some in Yugoslavia, some in Greece, others in Albania. If the enemy invaded our country, we would have no soldiers to defend us.

There was talk of treason, too. Someone said one of the Deputation to the Parliament in Rome had been arrested and put in gaol. Someone else said that all the barrels sent to our troops in Africa, which were supposed to contain oil and petrol, were filled with water; the contents had been sold and the money sent to a Swiss bank account. Another said that a wounded soldier, back from the front, had talked about how the soldiers were unable to shoot the rifles, machine guns and cannons because the wrong ammunition had been sent. The country was in chaos, food was very scarce and the shops had no clothing to sell. Terrible news was circulating.

June 1943, Sicily: for a long time the British had been bombing the island, causing terrible destruction. Now they had landed their troops and, with practically no fighting, had overcome the defence garrison and occupied the island. People were getting tired of the Duce and his Fascist followers. Now the enemy was on our doorstep. Soon the country would be invaded. Already, in towns and villages, some of the arrogant, nasty Fascists had been beaten up. People were giving back what they received from them.

The middle of June was very hot. I watched the 'planes flying over the village. Lately, more and more 'planes were coming to bomb our cities: Milano, Firenze, Bologna, Napoli. More cities were being bombed and more residential areas, theatres and railway stations were being destroyed. Rome was still safe because of the Vatican and the Pope. It had been declared an Open City. Now, people in the towns and villages began demonstrating, carrying placards which said 'Down with Mussolini! We want peace! Down with the Fascists!' and other such slogans. At first, the Fascists came in with truncheons, beat them up and dispersed them, but soon the crowds came back in their thousands and could not be stopped. The trouble went on and our King, Vittorio Emanuele Terzo di Savoia, was too scared to do anything. Some of the Deputation voted against Mussolini. They were arrested but the Carabinieri freed them. Something had to give. At the next meeting of Parliament, the entire Deputation voted against Mussolini, but then could do nothing because it was surrounded by Fascists.

On 25th July General Badoglio invited Mussolini to meet the King, who wanted to sort things out and come to an agreement with him. Mussolini went into the meeting without his escort of Fascist guards. There was no Deputation present, just Badoglio and some generals. After they sat down, Badoglio, who had been made Prime Minister by the King, said to Mussolini,
"The King is very displeased with you. His Majesty has never been happy about your alliance with Hitler. That was a mistake. If you want to carry on being head of the government, you must abandon him, declare an armistice and get our country out of this war."
Mussolini looked at them with hatred in his eyes.
"No," he said, "I am the Duce. I will not." Badoglio put his hands on the Duce's shoulders and said,
"I arrest you in the name of the King." and he made a sign to the Carabinieri, who had been waiting, and they took him away. Badoglio went back to the King.
"Well, did he accept?" asked the King. Badoglio shook his head in denial.
"I arrested him." Now, together, they worked out the details: Badoglio contacted the Allies and made an arrangement for a meeting and when his request had been accepted he would sign the armistice and Italy would be out of the war.

All this was not made known to the Italian people for some time. They watched the Fascists going round with their tails between their legs but did not understand why. Then the news began to circulate.
"Mussolini has been arrested! He is confined under guard on a mountain in the Abruzzi. The king will punish him!" Yet no-one knew what would happen next. Everywhere people were confused. For quite a few weeks nothing happened. 'Planes kept flying over to bomb our cities and life went on as usual. Then, towards the end of August, Italian soldiers arrived from Sicily. They

had been taken prisoner but the Allies had let them go. Then the 'planes stopped flying over and the bombing stopped. What was happening?

Something else had the people puzzled: more and more German soldiers were entering the country through the Brenner Pass.
"Let them through," said the soldiers who were guarding the pass, "let them through. After all, they were our Allies!"

What I will tell you now refers to a specific day, but it was also the beginning of a painful and terrible time, a time that will never be forgotten by us Italians.   No-one knew for certain how many Germans there were in Italy. They had all left the towns and were converging on a place in the Trentino region. They seemed to be waiting for something - and then it happened. Taking advantage of the capture of the British General, Badoglio promised to release him if he helped to open negotiations with the Allies, which he did. Badoglio thanked him for their success in obtaining good terms for Italy. On 3rd September, he signed the armistice, which came into force on 8th September. On same day, the British and Americans troops landed at Reggio Calabria. When the day came, the news of the signing of the armistice was broadcast by the radio: "The war was over in Italy." Or was it?

What everyone had predicted happened. Allied troops landed in Salerno the following day, 9th September. By that time, we were no longer the enemy.   'What about the Germans?' you might ask. Hitler's spies had told him what was going to happen and he was ready. The soldiers guarding the Brenner Pass, who had been abandoned by their officers who had put on civilian clothes and disappeared, were left without orders and didn't know what to do. They threw away their weapons and started for home. The three divisions of German troops that Hitler had kept ready on the other side of the border, stormed through. They were joined by the other troops from Trentino and together they started the invasion of Italy. In three days they occupied all the major cities including Rome. History at times plays funny games with people and with nations. The Germans were our allies, now they were our enemies; the British and Americans were once our enemies and now they would be our liberators!

From that time on the Germans were very nasty to us. We Italians had betrayed them and they said we would all be punished.

September was the month for news, mostly bad. From Albania, from Greece, from Yugoslavia, our soldiers came back. They had thrown away their weapons and were coming home. But they didn't get very far. German soldiers stopped them, loaded them in cattle trucks and made them build fortifications. Some mountain troops tried to oppose them, fighting in the Alps for a few months, but it was no good. Many were killed or captured and those that survived retreated into the mountains.

News came about the King and Badoglio. They had managed to escape and were now in England or Spain. Then came news about Mussolini: a German officer called Skorzeni had been sent by Hitler to free Mussolini and, with group of soldiers, he parachuted onto the roof of the hotel where he was held. They soon overcame the guards and Mussolini was a free man. He was taken back to Rome. With the King gone, he was now in charge. Later, surrounded by his Fascist hierarchy, he instituted a Republic. He called it the Slo' Republic and proclaimed himself President.

CHAPTER THREE – MUSSOLINI LOSES THE WAR IN ITALY

Mussolini didn't know at the time, but it turned out later that he commanded nothing. He was just a puppet being pulled by the strings in Hitler's hands. Soon people found out what the Germans had meant when they said we would be punished. They started taking anyone they found on the streets and forcing them, both men and women, to work in armaments factories. Some of the young women were kept for their pleasure. They entered houses and stole anything of value and anyone who complained was loaded into a truck and sent to Germany to build fortifications. They went around the countryside and stole horses, pigs, cattle, anything they could lay they hands on from the farms. People were terrified and stayed inside their houses.

Now the Allies had started flying over the cities again to bomb places where the Germans were, as well as factories, railway stations and bridges to stop the Germans moving their troops. The 'planes flew over the cities two or three times a day and people went into bomb shelters for safety. The Germans saw that they could take advantage of the 'planes coming over to capture more men. They used a trick, starting the alarm sirens when there were no 'planes in sight. As they heard men and women run into the shelters, not knowing that it was a false alarm, they went there and took the people away to armaments factories to work under guard, or sent them to Germany. That trick didn't last very long because, when the sirens sounded, people stopped going to the shelters.

I have written about what happened all over Italy. Now I will tell you what happened to my family in our village. One day I was with my father in the forest when I saw a man running towards us. He was shouting, but we couldn't understand what he was saying. As he got nearer, we heard the words,
"The Germans, the Germans!"
"I do not understand that silly man, Mussolini," my father said, "letting all these Germans occupy our country."

Our village was invaded by Germans. At first they did nothing. They just walked around looking at the place. Then they put up large tents and started cutting down trees. My father was very angry.
"Those trees were my living!" he said, but he couldn't do anything

to stop them. The Germans went on cutting them down until a very large area was cleared and they moved cannons in, facing the direction that the Allied troops might come from. Then they went around the countryside and took animals from all the farms. The farmers complained but it was no use, they took no notice.

One day something nasty happened to my father. He was in the woods and had almost finished cutting down a tree when he saw a man coming towards him. He had a thick stick on his shoulder and his face looked familiar. At the same time he saw German soldiers coming up the hillside. The man must have seen them as well, because he started to run. He almost reached the wood when he stumbled on something and fell and one of the soldiers was on him. The man stood up and tried to hit the German with his stick but the others arrived. They hit the man with the butts of their rifles and the man fell to the ground. Suddenly, my father remembered. He knew the man. It was Pasquale. He had just arrived back from Abyssinia.

The Germans had made a new law that if any Italian tried to harm a German, he would be shot immediately. My father approached the Germans and tried to talk and defend Pasquale, but the soldiers didn't understand and turned nasty. Then, when my father became insistent, they hit him and took him and Pasquale away into a big tent where there was a German officer who could speak a bit of Italian. My father tried again to speak on Pasquale's behalf, but the Germans were adamant. The man had tried to kill a German soldier, all Italy was betrayed, he was an enemy and my father, by trying to help him, was an enemy as well.

They took them both into a field and made them dig two large holes, one for each of them. Then they shot Pasquale and his body fell into one of the holes. Another young man, who worked for my father, saw it all. Luckily the Germans didn't see him. He ran back to our family in the village and told them what had happened. The Festa family was in pandemonium! In the meantime, my father was trembling, awaiting his fate. But the Germans must have changed their mind about him. He had helped them cut down trees many times. So they hit him several times and left him unconscious, but they spared his life.

After that, for a few weeks nothing happened. Many soldiers left the villages and went to Monte Lungo and Monte Cassino. We were told that they would build defences in those mountains. They even dug holes under Cassino Abbey, not caring about the Benedictine monks there. Many Italian men worked there on the fortifications. The Germans had taken their sisters, wives, even their mothers and if they didn't work they had been told they would be shot. The men had to dig holes in the mountains where cannon and machine guns would be placed. At the Abbey, the Benedictine monks knew they would have a very bad time.

The men who stayed in the village were happy when there were only just a few Germans and they could get on with their work, repairing roofs and walls and laying stones on the road. The sudden arrival of about a hundred German soldiers took them by surprise. They left some to guard the men and the others went around the other villages and into the countryside to pick up anyone they could find. Some of those who were working in the fields tried to escape, but the Germans had been clever. They had approached on two sides and they caught everyone.

By 23rd September my father was slowly getting better and recovering from his ordeal. When the Germans arrived, he was in bed having a rest. The soldiers smashed down the door with their rifles and told my father to get dressed. They took him away, along with Augusto Pescarino and his son, Lorenzo, who were our friends and also relations, and Signor Maddalena, my future husband's father. That evening the bells of our church rang 'al martello' (when the bells toll slowly) and all the women and children went to church to pray. In all, forty three men were taken. The villagers thought they would be sent to the mountains to build fortifications. Instead, they were all sent to Germany.

The days after that seemed longer than ever. My mother kept crying and the house felt empty without my father. By the middle of October, Germans were taking men to send to Germany throughout the Italian peninsula, but finding very few. Nearly all the able-bodied men, even young boys, had gone to the mountains. They were very angry because they were being made to help the Fascists. Mussolini was now helping Hitler, not only against the Allies, but also against his own people.

CHAPTER FOUR – DESTRUCTION AND HOPE

Something got everyone wondering. It began with the Alpine troops. Many of the German and Fascist outposts were raided. No-one knew who it was that took their weapons, ammunition and food. Slowly they found out. Many escaped soldiers had been hiding, along with elderly men and boys as young as sixteen or seventeen. They had no alternative except being sent to Germany. All over Italy, men and young boys had gone into the mountains to organise themselves with arms stolen from the Germans and the Fascists. At first they were called 'Patriots', later they changed their name to 'Partisans'. Many of them of them had come from Yugoslavia, having learned the ways of Tito's Partisans.

For a while they went on with their raids. Then they started blowing up bridges and railway lines to stop the Germans running their trains and, on instructions from the Allied commanders, they committed other acts of sabotage. Then Hitler put a stop to all that. He sent the SS to discourage them – an army of men without scruples or pity. In Russia, they had killed thousands of people and destroyed entire villages.

Mussolini didn't want to lag behind and put together his own group, if not worse than the SS, at least as bad. It was made up mostly of men who had been taken out of various gaols. The Black Brigade was so-called because they dressed all in black. On their caps they wore a death's head. Their task was to fight and destroy the Partisans. "They'll soon get rid of them." it was said. Later, people said, "I don't think they are a menace, just an annoyance!" Mussolini didn't want to look bad in Hitler's eyes.

In our village people were very upset. It was the middle of October when many families left their houses and were forced to go into hiding because it was no longer safe to stay. There were only a few people left, women and old men. Some young ones, who managed to hide in the woods, came to the village for food or clothing, then returned to the caves. No-one was doing any work and the fields were full of weeds. There were just a few Germans left and they didn't bother us because we were such a small remnant of the once numerous population.

One day they started roaming the countryside, digging holes and

then covering them up. The people in the caves were baffled. An old man, who had been in the First World War, said,
"They are laying mines." Then he explained what a mine would do. "If you touch it or tread on it, it will blow you to pieces." After that, everyone was afraid, even to live in the caves.

Most people had started taking refuge in the caves soon after the Germans took the men away. For the people that remained, there was a period of quiet and everyone was thinking about the coming winter. How were they going to find food? How were they going to feed their children? Their only hope lay with the Allies but, after beating the Germans on the Salerno beaches, they had been stopped and were still a long way away

One day something terrible happened, so terrible that it left the people in terror. It was 1st November. Some German soldiers, wearing different uniforms with armbands carrying the swastika with two Zs on top, were going to Cave. They went first to the village of Orchi and shot fifteen people, threw incendiaries into all the houses and destroyed the village. After that they went to Cave and killed a man who was standing in front of the church. They went around all the villages picking up men and causing more destruction. The men they managed to take were mostly elderly, but they did catch a young boy of sixteen, Antonio Pescarino. He was hiding in a wood at Pitiano and had come to the village to see if he could find something to eat. His father, Augusto, and his brother, Lorenzo, had already been captured by the Germans. They took Antonio along with an old man called Domenico and his son-in-law, who had both been ill, and another young boy of fifteen. They herded them like sheep and forced them to walk all the way to the village of Faeta, and there they beat them up, forced them to dig a large hole and shot them with machine guns, leaving the bodies uncovered. Then, back they came. Everybody was terrorized but they couldn't leave the bodies uncovered, so men went to Faeta and buried them.

"Why did the Germans do such a terrible thing?" everyone was asking. There were rumours that a man had killed a German. Someone had been seen carrying the body of a German soldier but nobody knew anything. Time passed and the questions remained unanswered. Who was the man? Why did he kill the German? People grew very angry.
"If I find out who it is," a man said. "I'll kill him!"

"You are right," said another, "he deserves to be killed."

"Look at the damage he has caused." a woman said, with tears in her eyes, "Because of him, my beloved husband is dead."

Then a man came from Cave. Everyone knew him. For many years he used to come to our village to buy milk almost every week. He knew the answer. He told this story:

"I went to Orchi to buy milk. Just outside the village Rocca Pietro had a little farm. He was a good man who wouldn't hurt a fly. He did very little on the farm because had been wounded in the First World War and could hardly walk. He had three cows, but one of them was special. She gave lots of milk that was very sweet and creamy. Everyone in Cave wanted that milk. Pietro never went to the village. The children made fun of him because he was lame. They shouted and threw stones at him. Anyway, that day I'd almost reached the farm when I saw some Germans coming. I drew my cart into some trees and hid behind them and I saw what happened. Pietro was in the stable feeding the cows. The Germans arrived. There were six of them. They entered the stable and took this cow out. Pietro came out with his pitchfork in his hands. He put it down and tried to plead with them, but they laughed. Pietro must have been desperate. They were taking his cow! He kneeled down and again pleaded, gesticulating with his arms. Again the Germans laughed and one of them hit his shoulder with the butt of his rifle and knocked him down. Pietro stood up, picked up the pitchfork and stuck it in his stomach. Coldly, one of them shot him. Then they picked up their companion and, pushing the cow, went away with his body. I couldn't leave him lying there, so I dug a hole and buried him, and that is how it happened."

"Poor man," said the woman whose husband had been killed, "forgive him."

"There is a limit to what a man can bear!" said the other man, and everyone agreed with them. No-one hated Pietro or blamed him for what they had lost.

CHAPTER FIVE – THE MEANING OF WAR

It was cold. Winter had come early and the pale sun was trying to give warmth. I was in the fields with my mother, planting out the cabbages that we had grown indoors, when I heard a terrific noise in the sky. I shaded my eyes with my hand and looked up. Just above me was a 'plane. It was very low and kept going around in circles. It seemed to be in some kind of trouble. Then there was more noise. The German soldiers on the hillside had opened fire with their machine guns. I saw several shiny things coming off the 'plane. Then there was an explosion in the village and I saw smoke and flames coming from the houses. I heard the sound of glass breaking and the air displacement was so strong that it nearly knocked the chicken house down. We only had two chickens left, but they looked all right.

For a few moments I stood there not understanding what had happened. Then I grew scared. I stopped a woman.
"Where are you going? What has happened?"
"They'll kill us all! They've destroyed the houses!" she replied, "We must go to the caves otherwise we'll all be dead."

For a few minutes my mother stood there not knowing what to do. Then she shook her head a few times.
"Let's go home and get a few blankets and a couple loaves of bread."
"Where will we go, mamma?" I asked.
"We'll go and shelter in the caves as well."

The caves, like the castle, the villas and some ruins that an archaeologist had attributed to the Romans, were part of the history of our village. An old man said that for many years the caves used to be mined for various materials. One of them was used for the construction of water pipes, another yielded a shiny, brightly coloured crystal used for making brooches and chains. Most of the soil in the area is very sandy and people at that time used it to build houses. In fact, the villages were built because of the caves in the first place. In olden times, when groups of people roamed the countryside looking for suitable places to settle, they chose to build their houses near the caves.

The cave we went to had several sections, some big and some

small. Some had doors made of solid timber and some had iron gates, but our cave's doors were made of bundles of small branches so as not to attract any attention. When my mother and I arrived, quite a few people were already there. My Uncle Joseph and aunt and their seven children were there, as well as Pasqualino and his wife and seven children, (they were friends of my family) and several other women and children. At first everyone looked confused, but slowly began to calm down. My uncle said,

"We do not know how long we will all have to stay here. We must organise ourselves."

"You are right, Joseph, tell us what to do."

"For a start, we need some straw, and then we'll see."

I could see my uncle taking charge: the bully taking charge again, just like grandfather, I thought.

Not too far from us were farms with haystacks. There was no-one around so we took great bundles of straw back to the cave and after a while everyone had a bed of straw to rest on. Some sat on the ground making comments.

"Not only are the Germans trying to kill us but the Allies seem to want do the same." Pasqualino said. "What a world we live in!"

"That pilot only thought of his own life. He didn't care about all of us." my uncle butted in. "If that 'plane had been flown differently, the Germans would not have shot it down and caused a disaster for all of us. It's not only the bombs, but also the aeroplane that caused this disaster."

"You are right, I never thought of that," Pasqualino replied, "but in a week or two the Allies will be nearer, we hope."

A lady said, "I've lost my house, anyway."

"Me, too." another woman's voice added.

"And me." from several voices. It appeared that seven houses had been destroyed and others had been badly damaged. Very few had suffered no damage at all.

A few days went by. All the women had brought some food but, with so many mouths to feed, it was getting short. My mother stood up and moved towards the entrance of the cave.

"I'll go to the village to get some food." she said.

"But the Germans will be very angry, they won't let you pass." my uncle said.

"But I must try, otherwise what are we going to we eat?" she said, and off she went.

She was away for quite a while and I was getting worried. What if the Germans beat her up? My uncle must have realised I was worried. He came up to me and stroked my face.

"Don't worry, little one," he said, "your mother is a clever woman. Nothing will happen to her." His words calmed me down.

I heard someone coming, stood up and ran to the entrance. It was my mother. She carried a large basket on her head. My uncle had also come out.

"Help me, Joseph," she asked him, "it's heavy." My uncle took the basket off her head. There were two big round loaves of bread that she must have baked and it was also full of grapes. My uncle kept talking and I was looking at him. He was a clever man.

"How old is he?" I asked my mother.

"Forty two." she said. I didn't really know him, but could see that everyone was taken with him. He seemed to have a sort of power over people. He wasn't very tall but he had a powerful body.

I took my eyes off my uncle and looked at my mother. At one time she was always cheerful, but ever since the Germans had taken my father away she had changed. Many times I had seen her with eyes red from crying, but she was very proud and I never saw her in tears. I looked at her hair that had once been beautiful, brown and long. I believe she was my uncle's age.

"Why didn't grandfather come with us, mamma?" I asked her.

"Well, my girl," she replied, "your grandfather is as stubborn as a mule. You can take him to the well but you can't make him drink. He is such a stubborn man that if you tell him to do something, rest assured he will do something else." My mother had been talking in a loud voice and everyone heard her and had a good laugh.

"Just like my poor husband!" an old woman said.

One day I heard my aunt Nicolina say,

"That woman takes such chances for all of us. It is very dangerous. One of these days we may not see her again."

That sent me quite out of my mind and I ran out of the cave and towards the village. Uncle ran after me but he wasn't able to catch me. I reached the big house where grandfather was. It was shattered. There was glass all over the floor and somehow I managed to cut my foot. I ran upstairs and heard my grandfather swearing, using the most terrible words any man could say to another human being:

"Hay mortacci tuoi, tu puzzi di merda, se tu porti via qualche cosa di qui' io ti taglio la testa!"(You smell of shit! You take anything out of here and I will cut your head off!). He had an axe in his hand, but the German soldier had a gun pointed at him. I could see that the young soldier was very frightened. He was very young and only obeying orders. Small as I was, I understood that my granddad was in terrible danger. I shouted,
"Granddad, look, I've cut my foot!" He was distracted from the situation, put the axe on the table and attended to my foot. Right then more soldiers arrived and took all the furniture they wanted. I asked granddad,
"Per piacere nonno viene con noi nelle grotte." (Please, granddad, come with us to the cave). He said,
"No, bambina, tu vai. Io devo stare qui' per la casa, e per tua madre," (No, child, you go back. I must stay here to look after your mother and the house).

Mother baked some bread and made sure granddad was all right. I went back to the cave. We were all very upset. Mother shared the bread amongst everyone but it wasn't very much because there were so many of us. I took my piece of bread and went outside the cave. There were a few German soldiers there who came towards me and one of them took my bread away. I screamed and screamed. He must have told me to be quiet, but I wouldn't and he pointed a gun at me. Then he must have felt sorry because he went away and came back with a piece of brown bread. I took it but didn't eat it because we had been told only to eat things given to us by our own people, in case they were poisoned.

With nothing to do we were getting bored. I had a very special doll but I couldn't play with her because there were so many other children and it would have created friction. Mother told me to put it away in box and hide it in a corner, but they found it. So my cousin Alfredo said,
"I have an idea! Why don't we dig a hole and put it in and bury it, and when it's time to go home we will dig it up and everything will be all right?"

One day we were picking up little pebbles and throwing them in the stream, but after a while we got tired of the game and I went to sit on my own. I don't know why but my father's face came before my eyes. Poor daddy, I thought. What will he be doing? Will he have enough food to eat or will the Germans starve him? I did miss him and the way he used to look at me with his beautiful hazel eyes. I really loved him.

The cave we were in was called the Seven Fountains and I wondered about the name.

"Uncle Joseph," I asked my uncle, "why is this cave called Seven Fountains when I can't see seven but just one spring of water coming through the rock?" My uncle laughed.

"It is not the cave but the whole area that is called the Seven Fountains. What else do you want to know?"

"Tell me why the Germans haven't sent you to Germany, like dad?" I said.

"Because I was more cunning than your dad was." and that was all he said! One morning I woke up and my uncle wasn't there.

"Where is uncle, mummy?" I asked. She shrugged her shoulders and opened her hands wide to signify 'Who knows?' and I had to be content with that. I waited all day but he didn't come back. Maybe the Germans had caught him, I thought. But then, I thought, no-one is too clever for them! Days went past and there was no sign of him. A few times I went out with mother and helped her bake bread and pick grapes. With no-one to pick them, those grapes had grown as sweet as sugar and I couldn't stop eating them.

"Don't eat too many, Ida." mother warned me, but I didn't listen and later I regretted it. My stomach was like a stormy sea!

A noise woke me up. It was a continuous noise. What was happening?

"Those are cannons." said the old man, "The battle has begun."

My cousin and I went out of the cave. Looking up we saw fire and smoke from the village.

"This time," my cousin said, "they'll destroy the village." Everyone started to pray but the noise continued.

"Oh, my God!" a woman cried, "Why do the Germans bombard us and destroy our villages?"

"It is not the Germans, Signora Carla," said the old man who knew what war meant, "Sono gli Allegation (It is the Allies). The front is far away, at least fifty kilometres, and they cannot shoot from below to above. Some shells are falling on our villages. They don't do it on purpose."

"I understand what you say," she said, "but anyhow we are the ones that have to pay the price. If a bomb or a shell falls on the entrance to this cave, we shall all be buried alive."

"My dear lady, in war those who really suffer are the people who are innocent." the old man said. The noise went on. We could hardly talk to each other; it kept us awake. From time to time it stopped and mother went out to get a few things. Once she brought back some cotton wool and stuffed it in our ears so we had a bit of peace. How long were we in that cave? Time passed. One day followed another in endless succession and the word 'time' lost its meaning.

Then one day there was silence and, after all that noise, I could almost hear it. Then another noise came, the noise of running engines. It seemed to be coming from the National Road.

"The Germans are going!" the old man said, laughing, "They are going!" Was the ordeal over? When it got dark cautiously us kids went out. There was no-one around. In the distance, in the light of a burning fire, we could see a lot of smoke. What would we find when we went back to the village? Was anything still standing? We all stood there, stunned. Was it all over, then? Then we saw the soldiers, about twenty of them, coming towards us. They were talking among themselves.

"Maledetti tetedeschi!" (Cursed Germans! They are still here!) Vincenzino, one of my cousins, swore. He was fifteen and quite clever.

"They are not Germans. They are English. Look at them, they have different uniforms. Are they Americans?" another asked.

"Hai sentito? Uno ha detto 'yes'! (Did you hear? One of them said 'yes'!) They are English!"

It was then that I saw a round, very shiny object still partly buried in ground. I bent down to pick it up when a shout stopped me cold. A soldier wearing his army uniform was shouting furiously. I couldn't understand what he was saying but I moved away. He came and gently started digging around the object and, after he uncovered the wires, he cut them with a pair of cutters.

"Had you picked it up or just touched it," he said, "it would have blown you to smithereens." He was laughing but looked relieved. He took my arm and shook it.

"Never touch those things," he shouted, "they are death itself."

I just stood there confused and a bit of scared. What had I done? What was he saying?

"You must not touch those things," a voice beside me said, "Sono la morte. (They are death.)" His Italian was bad but I understood.

"Grazie, Signore." I said to the man who had saved my life. He mumbled something that I couldn't understand and patted my shoulder.

"Ha detto che lui ha una bambina come te. (I also have a child like you.)"

"Are you Italian?"

"No, my father was." And that was my first meeting with the liberators. We said goodbye to the English soldiers and slowly mother and I started walking up the hill.

When at last we reached our village, Catailli, the sight sickened me. There was no longer a village. The destruction was almost complete. Everywhere I could see ruins, walls standing but all broken where a house once stood. When we reached the square it was even worse. There was no trace of the two old palaces. The old church, the church where I was baptized, was practically gone. From a cross still stuck on the one of the walls, Christ looked at us, sadly.

"Quarda, Ida, (Look, Ida)," mother said to me, "Anche Gesu' e addolorato. (Jesus is very sad.)" Mother was crying. I was young but I could understand how she felt. I, too, felt broken up like the walls.

"Andiamo a casa, mamma. (Let's go home, mummy.)" I took hold of her hand.

"A casa? Ci sara' angora la nostra casa. (Home? If it is our home.)" she said. I didn't know what to say. Leaving all the sadness behind, we started to walk. Mother was still crying and kept her head down. When we were about halfway a man came towards us. It was uncle.

"Quarda, mamma, c'è lo zio. (Look, mother, it's uncle.)" I cried out. She lifted her head up and smiled.

"Where you been all this time, Joseph?" she asked when he reached us. "We were very worried about you. We thought the Germans had taken you." He laughed.

"It's a long story, Angelina. Let's go home and I'll tell you."

"A casa? (To the house?)" she said with surprise in her voice.

"Yes, to the house. It's still there, in a very poor condition but still there." All the glass in the windows was broken and the roof showed light through broken tiles. There were quite a few holes in the walls but all in all, compared to the ones we had seen in the other villages, it was not too bad.

My uncle and I started to clear some of the rubbish that had accumulated during the bombardment and then I swept the house until it was almost habitable, apart from the windows. Mother lit the stove and was cooking something. Uncle and I went down to my father's workroom to look for some glass. We had a stroke of luck. In the corner we found some plate glass and went outside to try to replace some of the broken panes. He couldn't find any putty so had to fix them with nails and later look for a shop in the area that might be open. I was still sweeping when mother called, "Il pranzo e. (Lunch is ready.)" I washed my hands and sat at the table. Mother brought lunch. She had found a couple of eggs and some spinach at the back of our garden and with that had made a large omelette. Uncle came and we started to eat. We were halfway through the meal when my mother asked,
"Now, Joseph, tell me what happened to you? Come on, tell us!"

"That day when I left the cave, I was desperate to go to the village to see if it was at all possible to buy some tobacco. I soon realised what had happened in the village. I saw a group of Germans coming down from the hills. They did not see where I came from, otherwise I would have put you lot in danger. I decided to stay away from the cave. But they saw me and ran after me and tried to take me. I started to run towards the woods. I knew it had been raining so the stream would be full and not easy to cross. It was just as I thought. They continued to follow me, but they were on the other side of the stream. They pointed a rifle at me and asked me to stop there. I hid behind a tree so they couldn't shoot me. Then I threw a big stone into the stream so they thought I had run through the water. After little while, they went off and I found a hole in a tree and went inside it. But when I tried to get out, I couldn't - I was stuck."
"How did you manage to get out?"
"I heard different voices speaking in a different language," he said, "and I knew they weren't German. I began to shout and the English came and helped me out, and that's the end of the story."

My mother had a good laugh. I pretended to be cross because she was laughing at my poor uncle's misadventure, but inside I was laughing as well.

After doing his best to put the windows straight, my uncle left and mother and I went around the house to check the extent of the damage. All the photos and pictures on the walls were broken.

Mother let out a shout of joy when she found the picture of St Barbara. It was all covered in dust, but otherwise intact. We took all the broken ones off the walls and, after a little cry, mother put them outside to be burnt. Our lovely furniture, except those pieces which the Germans had taken away, was all in splinters but inside our clothes, although covered in dust, were all right. Mother lit a fire and heated some water, took them out and gave them a good wash and hung them out to dry. Slowly the house was getting straight.

It was then I remembered the chickens. Were they all right? I went to look. Yes, they were happily pecking away at the food my mother had given them. I knew that when she visited from the cave she had been feeding them. I looked inside the nest and found two lovely eggs. Those would be nice for supper. The coop looked all right. Uncle must have mended it. I was just about to go indoors when I hear a great commotion. Quite a few people were walking up the hillside towards Bellmonte villa.
"Dove state andando? (Where are you going?)" I asked a woman.
"Andiamo alla villa Bellmonte. (We're going to the villa Bellmonte)" she replied, "Le bombe l'anno distrutta, e la gente è rimasta intrapolata dentro. (The bombs have destroyed it and there are people trapped inside.)" I saw my uncle carrying a big pickaxe and others were carrying spades and shovels. A few women were crying. I knew that the owner of the villa was not there, but the caretaker and all the servants were. My uncle waved to me.
"I'll come and see you later." he shouted as he went past. I waved back then I picked up the eggs and was just about to go inside when I heard a loud noise.
"Dov'è la villa? (Where is the villa?)" the soldiers driving the car shouted.
"La su' sulla collina. (Up there on the hill)" I shouted back, pointing. Then I went inside and told mother.
"Che Dio li protegga. (God protect them!)" she cried, making the sign of the cross.

It was midday. Mother had baked some nice bread and made an omelette with the eggs and spinach. After the bad food we had eaten in the cave, I really enjoyed the warm, crusty bread and the omelette was delicious. After doing the washing up, mother and I went outside to see what was happening. People had come back down from the hillside.
"Li, havete trovati? (Did you find them?)" mother asked, "Are they

safe?"

"Not yet," a woman answered, "they must have taken refuge in the cellar."

"Poor people! Let us hope they are safe." mother said. We went back in and started cleaning the house. We were both very thirsty but ever since the Germans took the cows away there was no milk to be found in the village. Also, we had no coffee. Mother went down to the cellar and came up holding a bottle.

"I was keeping this for Christmas," she said, "but we shall drink it now to give thanks for returning home. Get the corkscrew." I got the corkscrew out of the drawer and a pair of glasses. She opened the bottle and filled one glass and poured a tiny drop in the other.

"So little!" I complained. She laughed.

"Children must only drink wine with water. Drink that as it is and then drink water afterwards." I did what she said. The wine was sweet but also very strong. She poured a bit more in my glass and filled it with water. It was still nice.

After all the work, we were having a rest when the noise started again. The British are coming back in their car, I thought. We went outside. It wasn't only the soldiers, everyone else was coming back. There were five bodies in the vehicle and many people were carrying others.

"All dead." a woman said, "They were in the cellar but they didn't have any air. Fourteen, all dead." Mother was left without words.

"I've opened a bottle of red wine, Joseph," she said after she had regained her composure, "come and have a drink and invite the English soldiers, too." My uncle made a gesture to the soldiers to come inside and they stopped their car and three of them came in and sat down.

"Thanks to them, we found the bodies," my uncle said, "without their machinery we would never have been able to find them. There was a terrific amount of rubble." One of the soldiers spoke Italian.

"Noi presto and are e Americani venire. (We will soon have to leave and then the Americans will arrive.)" They said 'thanks' for the drink and went away.

"All dead," mother said, letting out a big sigh, "and that beautiful villa, it was more beautiful than the others."

"Dear Angelina, you are right," my uncle said, "but war is not safe for anybody. At least they will have a Christian burial, their names will be carved on their graves and people will be able to pray at them." I looked at my uncle with surprise. He cared for those people and I had thought he didn't care much about people. What he had seen must have shocked and moved him.

It was now the beginning of December and Christmas was drawing near. The English had gone and a couple of weeks later we were at peace. I was looking in the hen coop for some eggs when I saw some soldiers coming towards the house. The English are back, I thought, and then I looked more carefully. They had different uniforms and different caps. Are they American? I came out and waited for them. They were all young and good looking.

"Siete Americani? (Are you American?)" I asked one of them.

"Yes, we are."

"Il mio nome è Marco mio padre era Italiano, voi una cioccolata? (My name is Marco, my father was Italian, would you like a chocolate?)" one of them said, handing me something in shiny paper.

"Si grazie, Marco. (Yes please, Marco.)"

"Here, have some chewing gum."

"What is it?"

"You put it in your mouth and chew." Marco said. It was then I noticed all the soldiers were chewing continually.

"Can I give my mother some of the chocolate?"

"Yes, go to your mother, but we want to talk to your father." The mention of my daddy brought tears to my eyes. Marco noticed something was wrong.

"Why are you crying?"

"The Germans took my daddy away to Germany." Marco told his companions what I said and everyone made a fuss of me. Instead of one chocolate, now I had seven plus seven chewing gums. I went and gave half the chocolate to my mother and unwrapped one. It was delicious. My mother saw my red eyes and asked me what was wrong, so I told her what Marco had said about father.

"Well he's not here, but someone must talk to them." Right then, Uncle Joseph came in with my two cousins, Mario and Alfredo. I was very excited to share the chocolate with them. Uncle and mother went to see Marco and his companions.

CHAPTER SIX – THE ALLIES COME TO LIVE WITH US

They were gone about ten minutes. Marco explained to my uncle that the Germans had moved out of our village, but they were not very far away. In fact, they were in Mignano di Monte Lungo about fifteen kilometres away. He asked uncle if they could stay in our house and install a telephone there and reassured him that my mother and I would be quite safe with them there.

"We will have some guests." she told me, "Marco and his friends are coming to stay with us." And so at last, for the first time since my father had been taken away, we had company. Marco and his three companions, Luke, Alex and David, came to live with us. They were all young, except David who was about thirty, and good looking.

From that day on our lives changed. Although they were out all day surveying the area, they were in every night and after supper they played games. Whenever any of them was losing, David in particular, they shouted funny words. I picked up a couple of these words and one day I said them to Marco. At first he laughed, but then turned kind of cross.

"You should never say those words again." he said, "Quested sono parolacce hai capito? (Those words are very bad ones and you must not repeat them, do you understand?)"

"Yes, Marco." I answered.

On 6th December the telephone didn't stop ringing. I picked it up and the voice at the other end was swearing at me. I assumed the person was asking me to put the telephone down and because I didn't understand, he became very angry and distressed. The German army had dug themselves deep in the mountains of Monte Lungo, Cassino and Camino. We were told that there had been many battles there but the Germans still hung on. Many thousands of young men died there on both sides under artillery fire.

On the morning of 8th December, the Allied infantry was involved in another big assault and among the dead there were also many Italians, youngsters and former soldiers who had escaped deportation, sought refuge in the mountains and later joined the Allies. It was said that after the battle it rained and the water running down the mountain was red with the blood that had been spilt. The US troops captured Mignano Di Monte Lungo, leaving San Pietro exposed. The Germans launched a strong attack to mask their withdrawal and most of the poor people of that village died. The few that were left lost everything; not even one house was left standing; the village was completely destroyed. All these men had fought and sacrificed their lives for their ideal: to be free from the Nazis and from a regime and a dictator who had brought ruin to the nation and caused so much suffering to its people. As Churchill said, 'They will be remembered.' After the war, a cemetery was built and a monument erected to their memory at the bottom of the mountain, with all their names on it. Every year on 8th December a big ceremony is held there, with full military honours.

Then Marco explained why we children must not touch the telephone and why the soldier had said those bad words to me. He made me promise never to repeat them again, so I promised. I never understood what those bad words meant until I went to England.

As I said, our lives changed. Before, mother and I and all the villagers struggled to live on what we had, but now we had plenty. They brought white bread, which we had never seen before, tins of tuna, beef and salmon, sugar and coffee and many other things. Mother used to do the washing, cooking and others chores. During the time they were with us, they repaired the house and made sure our back garden was free from mines. They even ploughed it so mother was able to plant new vegetables. Mother said to me,
"Manna has been sent from Heaven!" or, as the English would say, 'a blessing in disguise'.

Mother wasn't very old and was always full of energy. She was very tidy and clean and nothing was too much for her. Marco tried to teach me English and his friends Italian. It was December and Christmas was knocking at the door. One day I was in the chicken house when I heard someone calling my name. I came out and saw Marco and Alex.
"Voi venire con noi? (Do you want came with us?)" Marco said. I saw Alex was carrying an axe so I guessed where we would go.
"Si lo vengo. (Yes, I'll come.)" I said and all three of us, with Alex in front, Marco and I following, started walking towards the woods. I knew we would cut a young pine for a Christmas tree. Alex had a

kind of pan with a long handle and was sweeping the ground with a circular motion. I was just going to ask Marco about it when I remembered that day at the caves when the English soldier saved my life. He had the same tool and was doing the same thing. Alex was looking for mines. We kept going. Suddenly, he stopped and made a sign with his arm and we stopped as well. I watched him digging the soil with a long knife then cutting something. He lifted a round object and threw it in the stream nearby, where it exploded. He said that it wouldn't hurt anybody anymore. He said, "Be careful, there may be more." and we kept walking. On one side, under a burnt out tree, was a big bunch of winter flowers. I tugged my hand to get free to pick them for mother, but Marco held onto me tightly.

"Don't be silly," he said, "you heard Alex." I realised then that I, too, could get hurt like the old man in the village who put his foot on something and lost his leg. He was so badly wounded that by the time the doctor saw him he had lost so much blood the doctor couldn't save him.

Now we entered a wood in the area called Marzecane, on the far left, near Canzirri. The farmhouse in Patieno was where my grandfather on my mother's side lived. After they cut down most of the trees to use the wood for making fortifications, the Germans had thrown incendiary grenades to burn down the rest. These woods had been one of my father's businesses before they took him to Germany. The war had broken my grandfather's heart. He loved his farm and now with no fruit trees, no cows, no livestock whatever and no wood he felt his life was finished. He had tried to save his animals but it was no use. He hid them in caves and camouflaged the entrance with tree branches but the cows would moo and the sheep would baa, so consequently the Germans had a good laugh.

In the Marzecane forest, the tall trees had all gone but there were some young ones coming up. Marco and Alex found one big enough, cut it down and we started on our way back. When we got home, mother was waiting for me.

"Where've you been?" Then she saw the two Americans and stopped. She didn't look well and I could tell that she had been crying.

"Cos'è successo, mamma? (What ever is the matter?)" I asked. "È morto mio padre, tuo nonno. (My father - that is, your granddad - is dead.)" she said. He had had a heart attack. I didn't know what to say. Bloody Germans, I thought, using one of the swear words I had promised Marco never to say again. I looked at my mother again. She got ready to go to the masseria (the farm).

"I must go to him. Your grandmother and your Uncle Charley need me." she said and she was off.

Mother was away for about three days and I carried on doing the cooking. Unfortunately there was only one thing that I knew how to make and that was 'La carne in humidor', a kind of stew. By the way they looked at me I could tell our guests were beginning to get fed up with it.

When mother reappeared, she looked very unhappy. She burst into tears and had a good cry. After a while she was all right. She wiped her eyes and said,

"Your granddad's wish was to be buried on his farm land." With the church in ruins, the priest found it very difficult to get there, so it was impossible to give him a Christian burial.

"Mother, what about a coffin?" I asked.

"Well, dear, it's not very easy to find a carpenter, so your Uncle Carluccio had made one. I expect it will be all right for the time being until we can give him a proper Christian burial." Marco was outside doing something and I went out and told him what mother had said.

"Tell her not to worry," he said in Italian, "we've got an army chaplain who would do it. I'll tell him."

On the day of the funeral, an American chaplain came to our house. He didn't look like a priest, but he was. A few people from the farms nearby, my Uncle Joseph and aunt Nicolina all made a kind of procession. We went to the masseria (the farm). When we got there, everything was ready. My granddad lay in a coffin made of wooden planks. In a field not very far from the farm the neighbours had dug a grave. They picked up the coffin and after a few words from the chaplain my granddad was laid to rest. My mother and Uncle Carluccio and his family had a little cry and we all returned home. Granddad had had his wish.

It was Christmas Eve. The boys, with exception of Marco, had gone out. I suppose they couldn't stand mother's mood any longer. She had been crying all day. She had cooked supper and then sat in the corner of the fireplace feeling miserable. I was certain they would find somewhere to enjoy themselves. In the corner stood the little Christmas tree adorned with coloured ribbons and little candles burning. There were no presents under it. With our recent loss, no-one was in the mood to celebrate. Marco was like a son to my mother. He tried to cheer her up but had little success. I wasn't feeling very cheerful myself. Although my granddad had always been very moody and almost unapproachable ever since the Germans had destroyed his farm, I did love him and missed him. Now I was getting moody myself!

"This won't do, Ida." I said to myself. Marco said,

"Cheer up or Christmas will become another funeral!" Almost like an answer to my thoughts, from the direction of the village square, came the sound of a song. I listened to it for a few seconds then went outside, compelled by it. I had never heard it before.

"Silent night - notte silent." a voice beside me said. Marco had also come out. A moment later mother also joined us.

"Cos'e è quella canzone?" I asked, "È bellissima. Come si chiama? (What is that song? It is beautiful. What is it called?)"

"It is 'Silent Night', and there is a beautiful and very moving story about it."

"Go on, Marco, tell me the story." I pleaded. The last note of the song died away and then a little while later started again. The singer has been asked for an encore, I thought. Still we stood there and listened to it again and although I didn't understand the words, which were English, I enjoyed it.

"Tell the story, Marco." I asked after it ended.

"Andiamo dentro e faccio il coffee. (Let's go inside and I'll make coffee.)" mother said, "It is a little cold out here." Only then I realised that I was frozen! We went inside and in a few minutes mother brought coffee.

"Well, here goes." Marco said, and started to tell the story. Although I have written it in English, he spoke in Italian so mother could understand.

"My father told me this story. He was there when it happened. It was wintertime in 1917 and Christmas Day came. The war had been going on for well over two years and the dead on both sides could not be counted. It was somewhere in France. The shooting was incessant on both sides of the trenches. Then, first from the Austrian side and then from the Allied side, it stopped. All the soldiers laid down their rifles and the machine guns and the cannon stopped. The silence was uncanny. Then in the Austrian trenches someone started to sing. Like tonight, the voice was so powerful and, although the words were Austrian, because of the melody and the singer everyone listened enchanted, dreaming of their family, their wives, children, mothers, sweethearts. Then somebody came out the trenches and walked towards the other side, soon followed by others. The other side did the same and they met halfway. No longer enemies, they embraced each other and exchanged gifts. The song had done that, and it became part of history."

"Chi la scritta quella canzona.e la sua musica? (Who wrote the song and the music?)" mother asked.

"No-one knows." Marco replied, "Maybe the artist got killed. No-one knows." And because of the song and its story that Christmas was an unforgettable one for me.

Christmas was over and the battle continued between the Allies and the Germans. The children looked forward to 6th January, Epiphany, when the old witch, unlike Father Christmas who gives presents to everybody, only gives presents to the good children; the ones who are not so good get coal and ashes. We all put socks out behind our beds hoping for a nice surprise. In those days the children usually expected an orange, nuts and dried figs. But this year nobody expected anything.

I woke up. The room was very cold and my hands and face were frozen. I didn't have a watch but I could tell it was very early, about six o'clock. I rubbed my hands together to warm them up, got out of bed and peeped outside. All I could see was white. The snow seemed quite deep. Then the sun came shining through the window. The snow won't last long, I thought, the sun will melt it away. I was a bit warmer when I'd got dressed and then I remembered today was the day of the *bafana*, the old witch. For a minute I stopped and wondered if I would get a present. Without much hope, just out of curiosity, I went to look behind my bed and saw a parcel. It was quite big. For a while I just stood there looking at it, afraid it would disappear. With trembling fingers I untied the ribbons and let out a little cry of joy. Then I grew very excited! I shouted,

"Mamma, mamma, come and see what the old witch has brought me!" The label said 'To Ida from Marco, Alex and David'. It was a pair of sandals, but I was surprised to see that one was different from the other.

"Oh, no! They don't match." Marco and his friends were hiding behind the door to see my reaction. I heard a voice which made me jump.

"Do you like your present? (Ti piace il tuo regale?)" said Marco. I picked up the sandals to show him.

"Sono realmente belle ma nosi accompagnano. (They are really lovely but they don't match.)" I said. Marco laughed.

"Shochina! Sono due paia differente, le abbiamo cosi'tu puoi scgliere quelle che ti piacie di piu. (Silly girl! We got two from different pairs so you could choose the ones you like best.)" Marco was right, I'd been silly. People don't make such stupid mistakes!

"Grazie, Marco." I said, "You have been very kind, all of you." Then I pointed out the ones I wanted, the ones with gold stripes, and he wrapped them up and went away. About half an hour later, he was back and handed me another parcel.

"Tieni adesso si accompagnano. (Here you are. Now they match.)" I felt a bit mortified as I should have known. However, I soon regained my cheerfulness and put them on and went to the kitchen to show mamma. Marco had seen that I had grown of out of my shoes so they all went to buy me a pair.

"Look, mamma, what they have given me!"

"They are beautiful and you're a very lucky girl." The sandals fitted me perfectly. I went out to see to the chickens. My feet were cold before but now they felt nice and warm because I wore the wool socks which my grandmother knitted for me.

I had just finished feeding the chickens when I heard a terrific noise. I went outside to look. The whole of the sky was full of 'planes. I'd seen quite a few before but never so many. They were flying in the direction of Cassino town. A little while later came the rumbling of explosions.

"Poor people!" I thought, "The 'planes will drop lots of bombs. Of course they will aim at the fortress and the fortifications, but many will fall on the town and Cassino Abbey." I'd heard people say that in the Abbey, where the Benedictine monks lived, there were many masterpieces by the best and most famous Italian painters and sculptors. They would be destroyed and it would be a great loss not only for Italy but for the whole world of art. As I was having this thought I saw Marco coming back. I decided to ask him, he would know.

"Marco," I said, "Will all those 'planes drop their bombs on the mountains and around the Abbey where the Germans are dug in like rats?"

"They will cause a lot of damage to the buildings, but the masterpieces will be safe. I heard a rumour that the Pope has been in touch with our commander, General Mark Clark, and asked for time. It seems that the German generals are involved as well. The whole art world is involved and will help. Only when the masterpieces are safe in the Vatican will the Abbey be destroyed."

I'd never heard Marco make such a long speech before and by the way he talked I realised that he, too, cared about those masterpieces.

CHAPTER SEVEN – THE BATTLE OF MONTE CASSINO

One day I had a shock. Marco and his friends were leaving.
"Angelina," he said to my mother, "we have enjoyed staying with
you. Ida has been like a little daughter to me and you've been like
a mother. I'll write when I return to the States ….if I'm still alive."
And they left for the front line. I knew that he could not stay forever
but I was very upset and cried all day. I had lost a dear friend. He
had so done much for me.

A few days later more soldiers arrived. They were French and with
them came some very strange men. They were very dark and on
their heads they wore something funny. Someone told me that the
things were called 'turbans' and they had to wear them because of
their religion. The men were Moroccans and because of their
religion they were called 'Mussulmen'. I was very puzzled. There
were other strange men with them who were black as coal. Now I
had heard about *Faccetta Nera* (Black Face) but until then I'd no
idea what these men looked like. Fortunately none of them came
to our house. They stayed a week or so and then left for the front
line. I was told that there had been a lot of fighting but still the
Germans were hanging on.

Monte Cassino 15th February 1944

Monte Cassino 15th February 1944
Some of the facts and episodes, which I'm going to tell in the
following pages, are not part of my life. I've entered them because
is happened in my childhood. They are also a part of the Italian
history.

In February the Allies were all round Monte Cassino. There were
many savegeli attacks and expected them to keep progress all the
way to Rome, but once again German troops had stopped them,
spited of their lost on both sides the bombarded day after day, and
there died in the thousands. The Allies didn't know the Germans
had dug tunnels underneath Monte Cassino with spy-holes, so
they could attack the Allies without being seen.

The war brought an even greater impact to the town and
surrounding district. In one night and one day one hundred and
forty-two B-17s, B-25s and B-26s blasted it. The Allies thought the
enemy was actually in the monastery on Monte Cassino. They
knew it would be very controversial to destroy the monastery but

they thought it was the only way to beat the enemy, who was fighting for every yard of ground. So it became impossible for them to save the monastery. The American and British commanders were anxious to relieve the Allied division which was being attacked at Anzio.

The civilians from the Monte Cassino district went into hiding in the monastery because they thought it was the only place that would never be bombarded. On 15th February the Americans and British bombed the historic buildings of the beloved monastery without let up until it was completely destroyed. Even then bombs continued to fall. But the enemy paratroops were holding fast and soon they faced the Allies around embattled Cassino. The town and all the surrounding area were completely destroyed.

Lt General Sir Bernard Freyberg and his newly-formed New Zealand Corps had the task of assaulting the heights. He had asked for the bombing of the monastery on the grounds that the German artillery was using it as an observation post. But the Americans didn't like the idea of bombing. The decision was only taken when General Sir Henry Maitland Wilson, the Supreme Allied Commander in the Mediterranean, flew over the monastery and thought he saw radio aerials. But he was wrong: the Germans weren't occupying the monastery. In fact, they had previously helped the monks to remove all the paintings, fine art, books and historical manuscripts to transport them to the neutral Vatican City for safe keeping.

The plains surrounding the town of Cassino were easily observed from the monastery and had been deliberately flooded by the Germans (on 15th December 1943). Poor people, poor children of Cassino! Poor soldiers! They died in thousands and lost everything. It came became a burial grand of many Nationality, and still there now include Monte Lungo. In meanwhile our zone which was the borough of Conca Campania, Mignano of Monte Lungo and many more places left with only women and children, and only few men.
Some the Allies came through our villages, but some wasn't very nice, and could not be trusted, but the war kept on and on.
 The American gave warning of the bombing by dropping leaflets round Monte Cassino and the monastery on 13th February 1944, but the Germans told the monks that the Allies wouldn't be so able

to commit such act, that is a hoax. The Monks decided to take shelter in the deep cellars with other civil refugees.

On 15th February the Allied 'planes kept on and on over the monastery and spectacular fireworks illuminated the sky. The troops in the valleys and on the plains couldn't believe what they were watching. There were so many bombs they rocked the hilltop. Flames everywhere lit up the sky. The aircraft delivered their lethal cargo leaving clouds of smoke. It was impossible to take it all in.

To help the situation the Fifth Army dropped three hundred and fourteen heavy and medium shells into the rubble. The Allies were flabbergasted, but it pleased the Germans, who said,
"Poor idiots! We never believed they would do that!"

After the aerial bombardment, the New Zealand Corps and the Fourth Indian Division began their assault on the night of 15th February but were repulsed by German paratroopers. This tragedy was even worse: about six hundred people died in a few minutes and there were many casualties. The attacks continued on 15th, 16th, 18th and 20th March but all attempts to take Monte Cassino failed. Then there was a six-week interval before General Alexander regrouped and reinforced for more attempts, which started on 11th May.

The offensive was launched along a twenty-mile front running from east of Casino to the sea. The British pushed over the Rapid River very quickly but the Germans managed to contain them. On the coast, the Americans broke through the line but were held at Santa Maria Infante, a few miles to the northwest. The French, a few miles east of the Americans, crossed the Garigliano River and were able to cut off German communications. Kesselring, the commander of the German forces in the south of Italy, realised his position was lost and ordered a withdrawal on 17th May. On 18th finally after a battle that lasted seven days the polish overtook over the Germany army and 860 Polish soldiers died and near three thousands, were wounded in that terrible battle.

But General Mark Clark, commanding the American troops on the front at Cassino, made a terrible mistake. He left gaps open on both Highways 6 and 7. The Germans stormed through and 35,000 of them escaped capture and joined Kesselring's Army. It was said later that this mistake meant that the war in Italy dragged on.

However, the way to Rome was now open for the Allies and on 4th June the Eternal City was at last liberated. But the Germans were not yet defeated. They still occupied parts of central Italy and all the north. Mussolini was still in power and Allied 'planes still dropped bombs on our cities. They were meant for the Germans but they also killed civilians and destroyed buildings.

With the liberation of Rome and the defeat of the German Army everyone was expecting that the Allies would keep up their advance but a surprise awaited them. In same month, June 1944, they withdrew most of their troops from Italy for the Normandy landings. Only enough soldiers were left to keep the Germans in check and the war came to a standstill.

The Germans were now in complete charge except in the mountains where the Partisans had grown stronger and stronger, with the help of the BBC, the British radio broadcaster which kept them in touch with events. They had received automatic weapons (including the famously useful Sten gun), ammunition, dynamite and many other things. Now they were well-equipped. They attacked German and Italian Fascist outposts, killing soldiers and taking everything they could find, then destroying the buildings. They laid mines on the railways to stop trains taking goods out of the country, and they destroyed bridges.

In spite of that, the Germans, with typical Teutonic mentality, regarded them as just an annoyance. A few well-armed men would get rid of them! So they sent a couple of hundred men and waited for the outcome. They had a surprise. The soldiers encountered a well-armed and well-organised enemy. After a few hours they were beaten. Quite a few were left on the ground and the survivors came back with their tails between their legs! Still the commander didn't give in and sent a very strong contingent back again, including the Fascist Black Brigade.

This time they went into the mountains and found no-one! Where had all the Partisans gone? Someone must have warned them! Germans are a strong and intelligent race but they can also be very naïve. They were the occupiers of the country so they thought they were also the master! With the advent of Nazism, brainwashed by Hitler's speeches and propaganda, they believed themselves to be the Master Race. Other races and peoples were considered by them to be inferior, though very cunning; they could show smiles of welcome and hide a knife up their sleeves. What the Nazis didn't understand was that now they were hated by everyone, even children, women and old men. All the world was against them. So it was obvious to everyone that they were going to lose.

Now the bridges and the depots were blown up. 'Planes came over and bombed their headquarters and their stores. The pilots seemed to know exactly where they were! The game of cat and mouse had begun. And so the months went past. As they had done in Russia, Poland and elsewhere, the SS, the Gestapo and Mussolini's Black Brigade started their reign of terror. People were arrested and tortured. Entire villages were looted and burnt to the ground. Many innocents were killed. And still bridges were blown up, 'planes kept on bombing and the Partisans kept attacking. Yet they refused to accept that their power was running out.

In Germany the end of the Third Reich was drawing near with some generals even attempting to kill Hitler! The winter had gone and spring 1945 was well advanced when Allied troops returned to Italy for the last offensive. All the Partisans came down from the mountains to join them. The Allied 'planes dropped leaflets on Parma asking the soldiers to surrender. Hardly a shot was fired. When the first tank arrived there, all the soldiers threw down their weapons and surrendered. The war in Italy ended on 29th April when the surrender was signed by General von Vietinghoff and this became effective on 2nd May.

People came out from the cellars where they had been hiding and danced in the squares. They embraced and kissed each other. After years of suffering and anguish, they began to believe that they were free.

Then came the news that nearly all the Black Brigade, who had tried to run away to Switzerland, had been captured. Mussolini, who had tried to escape by train wearing a soldier's uniform, had been recognised and arrested by Communist Partisans. They had kept him confined in a cellar for a few days and then shot him. His body and those of his lover, La Petacci, and of a Fascist official who was with him, had been hung upside down in the square of a little village near Milan, Piazza Loreto, for everyone to see and despise! And that was the way the infamous Duce ended his life.

The celebrations lasted several days. There were banquets, fireworks and dancing. Then came the days of reckoning when informers and collaborators were beaten up and arrested. Women who had been with the Germans were taken to barbers' shops and had their hair shorn with razors close to the skull and were made to parade in the streets to show their shame. Now the Partisans joied the Americans searching for war criminals to arrest them. The Carabinieri were the only force keeping order. Slowly things began to calm down. Men began to look for jobs, repair their houses and look after their families.

CHAPTER EIGHT – THE PRISONERS OF WAR RETURN

A couple months passed. People were just beginning to forget about the war when something happened to remind them of it. Men came back from Germany. They were in very bad condition, thin and pale. Some were covered in bruises, others had lost all their teeth, a few could hardly stand. "Lasciatemi stare! (Let me be!)" they would say when they were asked about Germany.

Uncle Augusto Pescarino had been killed in Germany but his son, Lorenzo, managed to get back home and what a shock it was when he found out that his young brother, Tony, had been shot by the Germans behind Faeta.

Mother and I hoped and waited for father's return, but nothing happened. Months went past and we began to lose hope.
"Mi Domenico e morto! (My Dominic is dead!)" mother kept crying. I refused to accept it. Deep in my heart something told me that my father was still alive. Time went on but there were no signs of father anywhere.

My granddad Festa was very ill. He was very old. He told grandmother that his only wish was to know if his son was alive. Two days later my uncle received a letter from my father. My uncle told granddad that my father was alive so my granddad died happily. He had his wish!

Soon my daddy would come home, and so we waited but the days and the months went past and no-one came. It was now the end of August and my cousin and I were looking forward to going back school. It was 5th September when I was in the chicken house feeding the birds. I stood and looked at the cabbages. Soon they would be ready to eat. In the corner of my eye I saw someone approaching. He looked like some of the men that came from the towns to ask for food. His trousers were full of holes and I could see the tips of his toes sticking out of his shoes. He had long hair and a long beard and he was very thin. I looked at him more carefully and my heart beat faster. I started to run…
"Daddy, daddy!" I cried out. He bent down and picked me up in his arms. My daddy was home at last!

He told my uncle that he had walked from Germany to our village after the war was over. Occasionally he managed to hang on to the back of a train. All the time he was on the road he lived off dandelions.

After he had a good bath my mother gave him a haircut and shave and he put on his clothes and began to look human again. Then he asked,
"Angelina, what has happened to our family? And what has happened to our business?" Ah! Here we go, my mother thought.
"Look, Dominic," she said, "the story is too long for me to tell you now and you are not well enough to take it all in, so try to have some food and rest. You will soon get to know what happened here." He went to sleep in a nice, clean bed for the first time since 16th September 1943.

Then my mother told him we had lost both grandfathers and many people he knew weren't with us any more because the Germans had shot them, and all the rest he could see for himself. He also found out from my uncle how we lost all our businesses. He was very sad, and said,
"I heard on the radio in Germany about the great battles of Cassino and Monte Lungo but this is worse than I could imagine." In fact it was more than he could take in.
.

On 15th October the school opened again and we began to learn what we could in the poor amenities available to our teacher. My uncle and my father began to think about how they could start their business again. The future was very bleak but they had no choice but to start to pick up where they had left off and do the best they could with very few men.

Nobody knew how but Lorenzo Pescarino had managed to get hold of some kind of explosive and, without telling my father, he thought he could use it to bring the trees down instead of cutting them. He told my cousin, Natalino, to stay well away while he did it. My cousin protested,
"Lorenzo, I don't know why but that is not the way my uncle wants us to do this. It is very dangerous." Lorenzo said,
"Don't be silly, I know what I'm doing. I've been in Germany and I saw how it's done there many times." He insisted he knew what to do. He made a hole near the tree and put in the explosive with a long fuse which he lit, then ran away and waited. When it didn't explode he went back to look, but while he was looking the device

exploded in his face. He was taken to hospital and was left completely blind. My parents were very upset and it made their business even more difficult.

As time went by people tried their best to forget the horrors of the war and yet from time to time it came back to haunt us. People couldn't easily forget the millions of Jews who died in German concentrations camps, nor the uncounted numbers in Hiroshima and Nagasaki in Japan who were pulverized by the explosion of the atom bombs.

Even in our village the war kept coming back. In spite of all the efforts on the part of the American soldiers to clear the mines laid by the Germans, many still lay buried in the fields and woods. Some were found and defused, others caused death and destruction. The tribulation continued for us. A boy of fourteen who was working with my father was one of the first casualties. He was cutting down the stump of a tree when there was a terrific explosion. My father ran to the spot to see if he could help but when he got there, there was no trace of the boy - just a few shreds hanging from the trees. The boy must have stepped on a mine. My father and uncle were very upset by what had happened and there were several more cases. One of my father's workers lost his left foot. A couple boys were very lucky: they had been throwing stones at a tree and must have hit a mine. There was an explosion but the boys got away with just a few cut and bruises. It seemed as if it would never stop, tragedy after tragedy, as time went by.

In 1946 another tragedy struck which left the villages paralysed. A group of five boys, all brothers, were out playing in a small wood in Conca. As they were climbing, they were throwing stones everywhere. A worker who was cutting down a tree tried his best to warn them.
"Stop throwing stones! It's very dangerous!" he said but they didn't take any notice of him and went on with their game. Suddenly there was an explosion followed by others. Several mines must have blown up together. Of the five boys very little was left. Later a few people came and picked up all the bits they could find, put them in a coffin and took it to the church. After the priest had performed the rituals for the dead, it was taken to the local cemetery and buried. All the people in the village and even some from other villages attended the ceremony. Then we all saw the

parents of the boys and tried to give them a little comfort in their grief. Later many masses were celebrated in their memory and a stone with all their names on was erected on their grave. I went many times to this grave and every time someone had laid fresh flowers on it. The village people did not forget them.

Just a few months after, there was another similar incident. One of these boys was my second cousin, Americo. There were many more; it seemed as if the tragedies would never stop.

Life was very harsh and whatever we tried to do we couldn't make much progress. At the same time, my mother was getting very depressed because of the lifestyle we were leading and I became unhappy because of her misery. One day I went to school and the teacher told me to stand up. He said,
"Ida, I love my mother very much. I want you to learn this poem for tomorrow. It is very special to me and will be for all of you, too."
When I went home my mother wasn't at all happy. She had a lot on her mind and I couldn't get any sense out of her. I was very annoyed. When I looked at my homework I realised that the poem I had to learn was all about mothers. I was not in the mood to learn it so I looked in another book and found another poem which I thought would make everyone at school laugh.

> Adesso vi racconto un fattarello
> Dun tale deve essere un grandissimo Porcello
> Ha un tipo secco e allampanato..
> E per scherzo frullo viene chiamato.
>
> È sempre ozioso la' tutto il giorno
> È girando di sera e' mattina dieci ne
> È penza e venti ne conbina
> Questo Annoia e quest infastisce
> Ma di fare scherzi mai la finisce.
>
> Ieri L'altro Su' aut bus mi trovay
> Il bruttissimo tipo ritrovai.
> Quano senti un colpo al vetro
> Che stava alzato li dietro.
>
> Grido' furioso il conducent.
> Se tu non sai stare in modo fra la gente,
> Se tu non sai che signfica l'educazione

Va pure in mezzo hai porci sodicione.

Chi si pernette di dirmi maiale?
Cosa dunque ho fatto di male?
Leggete sull sportello,
È vietatato ha sputare sul pavimento

Now I will tell you a little story
About someone who must be the biggest pig of all.
He is a crude and loud sort,
Playing silly jokes, as ignorant as a pig.

He plays the idiot all day long
Wandering around from morning till evening,
Counting up the amount of trouble he sets out to do,
Annoying and irritating everyone.
He never stops playing jokes.
The day before yesterday, when getting on a bus,
I met this awful man again. He spat on the bus
window.

"Get off, you back there!" the bus driver shouted,
"If you don't know how to behave among people,
"If you don't know what education is for,
"Go and live with the dirty pigs where you belong!"

"Who gave you permission to call me a pig?
"What I have done that's pig-like?"
"Look behind you, look at what is written on that sign:.
" Spitting on the floor is prohibited."

Well, all the class burst into laughter but the teacher wasn't amused!
"Ida, you have disobeyed me! For this you will be severely punished." he said. "First you will have ten rough blows to your hands and then you will have to kneel for two hours on a granite floor for detention." I stood up and said,
"But, sir, you can give me twenty very heavy blows if you want to, but you can't keep me here for two hours because I've got to go home and cook my parents' dinner. They won't be very pleased with you when they come home and they haven't got any dinner!" and before he could answer I said, "What about if I make a deal with you and I read the poem you asked me to learn and apologise

58

to the class?"
"All right, I agree." he said. The class was terrified because they
didn't know if I was going to be able to do what I said. I started:

Mia Madre
Non sempre la belta' cancella
O lo sfiorar le lagrime e ghi affanni
Mi madre ha sessanta anni

Piu' la quardo e piu mi senbra bella.
Non ha un squardo.. un accento..
Un sorriso.. un atto che non mi tocca dolcende I cuore

Ha!.. se fossi pittore non chiederey
Ha Raffaello Urbino il pennello divino.
Ma Vorrei ritrarla quando io mi inchino
E le bacio la sua treccia bianca…

Oh! quando è in ferma è stanca
Nascone il suo dolore sotto A' un sorriso
Ma Vorrei poter cambiare la mia vita
Vedere me vecchia è lei ringiovenita.

My Mother!
The years don't ever change
The beauty of my mother.
Brushing away the tears
And the breathless sighs.

My mother is sixty. The more
I look, the more beautiful she seems.
Every one of her words, smiles,
Actions touches my heart sweetly.

Ah! if I was a painter
I would portray me kneeling at her feet
And kissing her white plaited hair
When she is sick and tired
She hides her pain under her smile.

I wouldn't ask Raphael of Urbino
Of the divine brush to paint her,
But I would rather see me

Old and her young again.

All the children were relieved. The teacher came up to me and said,
"Well done!" and gave me a sweet. That evening I heard him telling my mother about it all and they both had a good laugh. That pleased me more than anything as I hadn't seen my mother laugh for a long time.

One day the teacher set us a composition all about the history of our village. There were about twenty of us, both boys and girls.
"Many of you have been through bad times. Some of you have lost dear relatives. Our beautiful villages have been destroyed. It is up to you to make people see how they once were and you can do this by learning about our ancestors, our customs, our dialect. This will be our first lesson. Books have been written about all this but if you cannot find one, ask the old people. They will know. I, too, will tell you what I know. When you have gathered all the information you can, write an essay. It is not only for the school, but also for our neighbours and for the future so that our village histories will not be forgotten. When you have written them, they will all be gathered together in one book."

The lesson ended and I went home by myself and talked to an old person I met. I managed to gather lots of useful information but could not get anything positive with the regard to our ancestors. Some people said they came from Czechoslovakia, some said from Greece, some said from Turkey. I did not know what to believe. I thought if grandfather from the farm had been alive he might have known, but he wasn't. Yet I knew about something important: the caves! I went home and asked mother if she could give me any information.
"I don't know where our ancestors came from but I think your grandfather had a little booklet about our customs." she said. She went into the bedroom and came back with a little book.
"Keep it, you'll find it useful." I sat down and started to read. It was all there! I got hold of a sheet of paper and started to write:

Ida Festa: A short essay on the history, tradition and customs of the villages and inhabitants of Conca della Campania and environs.

Nothing much is known about our ancestors. However, they must have been good navigators, nomads or gypsies, probably

Sidicini or Osci or Struchi. We can assume that they probably came from Czechoslovakia. What we can be certain of is why they stopped in our valley and built the villages. The reason was the caves. For many years now the caves, probably of volcanic origin, have been quarried for their rocks. Tufo is one sort, used mostly in the construction of water pipes. Another is called Lapillo, a crystal of various colours used for making rings, brooches and necklaces. There are others but these two are the most important.

The population of Cave and Catailli was and still is very religious. For instance, before putting the dough in oven to bake bread, the housewives would always give it the benediction. The bread was considered sacred, like the host. Before starting anything, people would always pray. The church bells were rung every morning at six to remind people to thank God for the day to come and for the day that had passed. For many it was almost a superstition.

In olden times, there were no water pipes in villages and the women, young and old, all dressed in black with colourful scarves covering their heads and black aprons, used fetch water from the spring. (This style of dress is still worn nowadays but only by the old women.) They carried containers made of terracotta and an old lady had to give her blessing to the water before they could fill their containers. That superstition still persists.

There are many religious fêtes in the villages, in particular for the Assumption, for Cave's patron, Saint Bartholomew, for Catailli's patron saint and many more. Another typical fête was Carnival, known as the Feast of Freedom because everyone wore masks and pulled each other's legs, knowing that they would not be recognised! At the end of Carnival a puppet made of hay and straw and covered in fabric was burnt. Everyone pretended to cry and the women pretended to pull their hair out. It was a lot fun. That was followed by Quaresima, a puppet looking like an old lady dressed in black that signified penance. It was hung from a rope between two houses for everyone to see.

The name of my village, Catailli, comes from the Latin for 'cave' and the ruins on the hillside indicate that the Romans might have lived here, or maybe spent holidays here.

There were beautiful, old villas around the hillsides but our best feature was the pastoral church, now partly destroyed. After research was done it was found to have been built in 1573 and is now considered a monument of national importance.

I can't find anything more about our villages, but I have found out about the region in which we are situated: Conca della

Campania. It lies between Mignano di Monte Lungo and Rocca Monfina. Mignano di Monte Lungo is down below us and is all flat. We are about three hundred and fifty metres above sea level and Rocca Monfina above us is about one thousand metres above sea level approximately

From the top of the terrace of Signor Maddalena's house you can see the national road that goes straight to Rome, called Casilina. Along there my granddad and grandmother lived in a place called Patieno.

Mignano di Monte Lungo, Presenzano Mignano and joins the river Volturno. There is proof that the district had been occupied by Etruscans. There was a date found in a place called Starza to the southwest of the Town Hall. It is a kind of cemetery built as a single grave in which they found terracotta coins and a terracotta lamp.

In the caves in the mountain of Cesima are fragments of millstones used for crushing wheat and pressing olives to make oil. It is thought that the people of that time commonly used these materials for this purpose. The tradition would have been established by the soldiers of Silla after the Roman conquest of the Campania in the century before Christ.

The only thing we really know for certain is that the name 'Mignano' has a Roman origin.

At one time all the houses in this area belonged to someone whose name ended '-ius'. In Roman times it must have been a very important region and had its own ruler. You can find out more about the history of Mignano and the other villages from books.

I gave my essay to the teacher and she was quite impressed. "You could become a writer."
"I found all this out from a book about the history of Mignano di Monte Lungo." I explained, surprised by what the teacher said.

One Sunday and we went to church as usual. As I'd nothing much else to do, I then went to Conca. I went to the corner of the main square to see what was still standing. Nearly all the buildings had been restored except the big palace of Duke Bartoly and the lovely church which had been badly damaged. Seeing the church made me very sad as it had been a beautiful building that had stood proudly welcoming people to prayer, giving comfort to the faithful and peace to their souls through the centuries. Now it stood forlorn, half destroyed.

My cousin Mario and I sat near a lovely open fire and father came in. If he was in good humour we would ask for a story and he would always tell us one. He knew many children's stories but what we liked to hear about most was when he was in Abyssinia.

"One day," he said, "the commander asked me and few other soldiers to go deep into the forest to see if there were any people that needed help. We didn't find any people but we did find many different sorts of wild animals: big snakes so enormous they were wound round tree trunks and could eat you up in minute, big elephants, tigers and many more. They were beautiful to see but also very frightening and very dangerous. In one part of the forest there were a lot of monkeys with their babies. We were fascinated by them. We all thought it would be a good idea to catch a couple of the little ones and take them with us back to the camp to keep as pets, and when we had finished our military service we would be able to bring them home to Italy. We were all excited at the thought that one day we would see the reactions of our children as they came face to face with real monkeys and not just ones in books. My companions and I were overjoyed to think about what pleasure this would bring. But we were in for a big surprise: the old monkeys gathered all around, armed with stones! They made sure we wouldn't go anywhere with their babies. They attacked us from every corner of the forest. There were so many of them it was impossible to get away. We were defeated! The only way to escape was to let the baby monkeys go and hope that the adults would forgive us and let us return to our camp. In fact that is what happened. When the adult monkeys realised their young were free, they dropped their stones and went back to their usual activities and we returned empty-handed - but with a beautiful story to tell our children about life in a forest in a country far away from Italy!"

We thought it was very funny that soldiers with guns were defeated by monkeys with stones. We wanted to hear more stories about the jungle but my father was not in the mood.
"Children," he said, "that is enough for now. I'm tired and I want be left alone!"

The 6th January is the day of Epiphany and the custom in Italy and other countries, as I've said before, is that an old witch flies around on a broomstick visiting children's houses. If they've been good she will fill their socks with oranges and dried figs, and if they've not been so good they get ashes and coal. The old witch brought both to my cousin and me. 1947 was a very cold year and the snow on the ground was much deeper than other years. The school was in the next village, Cave. Halfway there we thought: if the witch thinks we are not so good, we might just as well not be good, so let's make a snowman instead of going to school! We peeled our oranges and ate them and tore the peel into tiny pieces, the size of very small buttons, and with them we wrote on the snowman:

> The old witch is very rich
> Flying around on a broomstick
> Telling boys and girls
> To be good and not to be crazy.
> But if we are impertinent,
> The old witch will take us away
> To the villages of Epiphany.

We were very cold! We said to each other,
"Let's go the olive press. We'll be able to warm ourselves there."
It was a very big room with the olive press in the middle. Inside it were two large, round stones with a rod passing through the centre, the middle of which was attached to a rope. The rope was attached to the horses which walked round and round, pulling the rope and making the big round stones grind the olives until the juice came out into a big container. The olive stones would get pressed again and used for the fire. There was the most beautiful fire in there and we didn't take long to warm up. Nobody took any notice of us and we stayed there, amused by watching the horses at work. The teacher had notified our parents and a search party was sent to look for us – but all they found was the snowman. We got home before they did.

January1948: Mother now began to be much better. One evening after supper, father and I were sitting in front of the fire. Mother had gone out to see some friends and I was thinking about doing some knitting when father started to talk. He told me about a woman who had saved his life. When he was taken to her house, he was very weak from the beating he had received from the Germans. A long journey in a cattle truck with nearly a hundred men packed as tight as sardines with no food or water had made his condition worse. When he had left the train in Germany he could not stand up. The soldiers had tried to make him walk by pushing and kicking him, but when they realised that he couldn't, they just left him to die. He was very cold and he must have must passed out. Water splashed on his face revived him. Then he saw the woman. She helped him to get up and slowly, with her help, they reached a house. There she lit a fire and warmed some broth. After he had drunk it, she put him to bed. Slowly his wounds healed up. One day, when she went out, the Nazis came.

After that he didn't want to say anything else and I didn't ask him. I was young but I understood that the terrible experience he suffered must have been too much to bear and father wanted to forget it. Poor daddy!

So far I've talked of everyone else, but what about me, you may ask. Well, I would have liked to have had more schooling to achieve my dream of becoming a writer. I kept writing down anything that came into my head for my diary, and time will tell! For the time being I stayed in the village and helped my mother. Later, maybe, I would go to a big town or even to Rome and try to get some kind of education and make a better future for myself. However, things were much brighter now.

Yet from time to time I cannot help thinking about the days following the end of the war. It was like waking from a bad dream and finding that the reality was even worse than the dream! Whenever I think about those days a shiver runs down my spine. Hard as I try, I still can't forget them.

In most of the villages, nearly all the houses were destroyed or very badly damaged and with no men to repair them, most of the women and children had to live in poor conditions. Of the beautiful villas, whose owners had given work to quite a few families, only one or two were still habitable. Of the owners there was no trace. After much debating with the Conca authorities, permission was finally granted for the villas to be occupied by families who had lost their homes. Starvation threatened everyone.

My husband's family had many relatives in America who helped, especially Francesca, my mother-in-law Stella's sister. It was only with their help that they managed to survive with the many young children they had. Other people were helped by the Red Cross but it was not enough. The initiative came from the young men and women who went away to the nearest towns to work in shops and factories. Soon they were able to send money to their starving relatives and things began to get better. In our home, though, things remained bad for a long time. Father was still in a bad away. Poor man, he had suffered a lot. It took a long time for him to get back on his feet but, thanks to Uncle Guiseppe and his children, the business was just able to provide us with enough m-oney to stay alive.

CHAPTER NINE – AND NOW I'M GROWN

Time has flown and the year is 1950. The war is now a thing of the past. People will think it was a bad dream, an incubus that disappears when one awakes. All over the country, thanks to the help given by the Allies, the work of reconstruction has almost ended. Soon the last vestiges of the war will disappear and everyone will forget and start to heal and, in time, the wounds will become less and less painful.

In our village there have been big improvements. Houses have been repaired, the fields are now yielding lots of produce, shops have opened up in all the villages, and work to repair our beautiful church has just begun. In our home, too, things have started to run smoothly.

Father is now all right and seems to have forgotten his terrible ordeal. A year ago, he bought an entire mountain with Uncle Giuseppe, whose sons are cutting down trees, selling the timber and producing charcoal. They have quite a few good workers now, mostly Gypsies from Romania and Poland. Others are ploughing the fields and sowing crops.

Mother is better now, much happier and I'm now grown up. I know that men and women bring children into the world, but I still don't have a clue as to how it's done! I only know that when my cousin Alfredo and I were about six years old we went to Sunday school and the teacher asked us,
"Who is our creator?" Alfredo said,
"Mummy and Daddy in bed." I gave him a shove and said,
"Don't be silly, God is our creator!"

When the war came, everything stopped but by October 1945, Alfredo and I had started to go to Sunday school, had Confirmation and our first Holy Communion. In all our villages at that time there wasn't anything else except work and church. Every Sunday we went to church in the morning and Sunday school in afternoon and evening. The church put on many functions and all the young people took part. We became the youth wing of Catholic Action and we all gathered every so often to see what we could do to help others less fortunate than ourselves.

We had a lot of dogs as my father had a great fondness for them. I also had a cat. Sometimes I got very cross with my father because, if any of the dogs were ill, he would immediately call out the vet, but when my poor cat wasn't well he didn't take any notice! One day my cat started bleeding from her tail and I was very upset, holding on to her while mother said,
"Put that cat down, you will catch her disease!"

One day I went in bathroom and realised I'd started bleeding. I was very frightened but couldn't tell my mother because she would have been angry with me, after she had warned me so often about the cat. I grew very miserable. My cousin Marietta noticed there was something bothering me and asked what was wrong, but I wouldn't say and she got cross.
"Ida, I don't understand what sin you have committed but, whatever it is, why don't you go and confess it and then you will feel better?" I pulled myself together and went to the church and told the priest that I was miserable because I had disobeyed my mother and because of that I'd caught the cat's disease. He asked me what was wrong with the cat and I told him. He said,
"Go to your mother or to your cousin Marietta and tell one of them just what you have told me now." I went to my cousin and told her what the priest has told me to do. She was flabbergasted.
"Oh, no! My goodness, you didn't tell that to the priest, did you?"
"Yes, I did."
"Now you are a young woman."
"And what I was before?"
"You were a girl. Now you must not let any boy touch you otherwise you will have a baby." I was so naïve and asked my friend what this was all about but she didn't know any more than I did. Marietta told my mother and they laughed. Mother said,
"Ida, it is time for you to learn few things." Then she told me about my condition and, as they say in England, all about the birds and the bees. After she finished, I just stood there and didn't know whether to laugh or cry. It then dawned on me that I was no longer a girl. Now I understood what my cousin Marietta meant when she told me I was a young woman.

CHAPTER TEN – MY FIRST JOB

"Well, Ida, now that you are grown up, what do you intend to do?" mother asked me.

"I don't know, mother. I'd like to go to a big city and be employed in a boutique." I replied.

"Pero' devi imparare qualche cosa d'altro. (That is fine but before you do, you need to learn a few things.)" Mother went on, "Now you are a young woman but you were born in a small village and before you go to the city you need to learn how to behave with different people. First, because of the war you didn't have as much education as we would have liked you to. The war made it impossible for us to be able to do more for you, so you lost that chance. In the city you may get the chance to find a good education. You will meet people from different classes there and you'll have to learn how to behave with them. When you are sixteen and you have learnt all those things, then you can go to the city."

"Cosa lo faro' in tutto questo tempo, mamma? (What am I going to do for all that time, mother?)" I'd never heard mother talk about this before!

"Tua zia Lauretta ha detto che ti che ti insegnara' a come produrre il tessuto. Lo sai che ha un telaio ed è molto brava a farlo. Nello stesso tempo ti insegnera' le buone maniere. (Your aunt Lauretta is willing to teach you how to make cloth. At the same time you will learn good manners.)" And so it was decided for me: I would learn how to make cloth. I wasn't very keen on the idea but mother knew best. Besides, what else could a fifteen year old with no experience of life do in big city like Rome? So, on rolled 1950 and 1951!

I liked aunt Lauretta. She had been a nun for many years but, because of her blind sister and her mother's poor health, she had asked to be released from her vows to look after them and had obtained a special dispensation from the Pope. She had a kind of workshop in the basement of her house and was well known for her cloth which was sold in many shops in many cities. I had nothing to lose and lots to gain from being taught by her So, I put on my best dress and went to see her in workshop. When she saw me she stopped working.

"Have you come to see how the cloth is made?"

"Mother sent me. She said you would be willing to teach me."

"Do you want to do what I do?"

"To tell you the truth, I would really like to look after sick people. I would like to be a nurse. Mother said you could teach me good manners."

"Maybe you don't know this but when I was a nun my order helped the sick and the needy. I will teach you but there is one thing you must do in return. From now on it will be your duty to keep the church clean and change the flowers when they have withered. Is that all right?"

"Yes, aunt Lauretta, I will do as you say. Many thanks." I went home and said to mother,

"It is all sorted out. Like you said, she will teach me many things but," I added, not very happily, "I will have to clean the church." Mother didn't seem to notice my mood; we had supper and I went to bed.

That night I lay awake for a long time, thinking. I was too excited. It was early days yet, but now I knew what I wanted to do with my life. My future was beginning to show itself in the desire to look after the sick. Then I thought about aunt Lauretta. She was older than my mother and, although she had left the convent and was free to do what she wanted, she had never married. Once I'd heard my father talking about her. She had gone into the convent when her fiancée had been killed in the First World War. Would I do the same and go into a convent? I had a little laugh to myself. Not likely! I will look after the sick but I'll also get married and have children, and with that thought in my mind I smiled and went to sleep.

I woke up next morning and after saying my prayers I still felt excited. I got dressed, had breakfast, did my chores and started to walk to church. I didn't know but another marvellous surprise awaited me. Aunt Lauretta had told me that we would start work in a week's time, but I wanted to start my work in the church straight away. The floor was not too bad; I soon finished sweeping it. All the flowers were withered but someone had brought fresh ones. I threw the old ones in the dustbin, changed the water in all the vases and put the fresh ones in. They looked very nice. I went to the sacristy to see if everything was in order and there I saw the manifestoes. There were several of them all ready to be displayed outside. I picked one up and started to read. I very nearly cried out loud for joy!

'The Pope', it said, 'has declared the year 1950 to be a Holy year, a special year for all Catholic people. In all the cities and villages of Italy there will be great celebrations. In Rome, the Pope will officiate publicly and give benedictions at Pentecost, 29th May.'

Underneath there was a note from our parish priest offering a free journey to Rome for the young people and a few adults. Anyone wishing to go should write his or her name at the bottom of one of the manifestoes. A journey to Rome! I nearly passed out. Another dream had come true! I had to go home and tell mother. I wrote my name and address at the bottom of the sheet and was away like a shot. On my way home I met one of my cousins together with another girl.
"Ho una notizia meravigliosa da darvi, ragazze! (I have marvellous news for you, girls!)"
"Cosa Fai ti sposi? (What's that? Are you going to get married?)" one of them joked.
"I'm not joking, girls. We are going to Rome! Go inside the sacristy and put down your name down on the sheet that's on the top of desk. I've done it already. Our parish priest has organised a journey. We are going on the 29th!"

I left the girls and rushed on home. I was over the moon! "I'm going to Rome, I'm going to Rome!" I was singing Then I started to run and ran all the way home I arrived puffing away like a pair of bellows. As usual mother was in kitchen preparing lunch.
"Why are you puffing like that?" she asked.
"Because I've been running" I replied.
"Che bisogno c'è da correre. Non brucia mica la casa? (What need is there to run? The house is not on fire.)" I went straight to the point.
"Mamma, ho bisogno di un vestito nuovo. (Mother, I need a new dress.)" She looked at me in funny way.
"Ida, Ida! Lo so che ormai sei una signorina. Ma hai tante bluse e gone. Un vestito nuovo si compra solo in occasion speciale. (Ida, Ida! You have plenty of blouses and skirts. We can only buy a new dress for a very special occasion.)" Now I had her! I told her about the journey and when I'd finished she just looked at me and said,
"You can't go to Rome wearing a skirt. We haven't got much money, but we will find enough for a dress for you. Tomorrow we'll go to Rocca Monfina and buy one. Now, let me be because your father will be home shortly and lunch must be ready." Mother

always said this. Even when my father was in Germany, she still said, "My husband and I ...." She was a remarkable woman and loved my father very much.

And so the following day, after I'd fed the chickens and mother had tidied the kitchen, we went to Rocca Monfina. It was a big village and it seemed as if the war done very little damage to it. There were quite a few shops. Mother knew where to go so we walked straight in. I looked at several dresses but the one I liked the most was made of special silk. It was pale pink and all pleated in front. I tried it on and it fitted me like a glove. Mother made a face when she heard the price but then she shrugged her shoulders and smiled. I knew then that the dress was mine. I was admiring myself in the mirror when a young man came in. He was quite good looking. He looked at me and smiled and that made my day.

At last, the day of the big adventure dawned. It was very early in the morning, just about five o' clock, when we had to leave, all of us very excited and a little uncertain. How well will I cope? I had a good wash and put on the dress.
"Ciao, mamma!" I shouted. She came out of the kitchen and kissed me on the cheek.
"Fai la brava, Ida." she said. I smiled to myself; of course I'll be good. I kissed her back and left.

Everyone was assembled in the church square. All my cousins were there and three of my friends: Clorinda, Anna and Maria. I knew all the boys and looked for the one I liked but he wasn't there. Maybe he had not been told or he didn't want to come. All together there were twenty of us plus three grown ups who I supposed would be our chaperones: the parish sister, my aunt Nicolina and aunt Lauretta.

It was a Sunday when as a rule there was no transport available but our priest had made arrangements and a big bus was waiting. It would take us to Mignano Di Monte Lungo to catch the train coming from Napoli. It was now just a few minutes to six and the train arrived. So far I'd only seen trains in pictures. This was quite a long one, fifteen carriages or more. They all looked alike, the same shape and colour, like little huts with lots of windows. It arrived making a lot of noise and then screeching, iron on iron, it stopped and its engine at the front let out a burst of steam and smoke. A man in a kind of uniform made sure that everyone got on board then blew his whistle. Puffing away like an old man with asthma, and still blowing steam, the train started to move. Slowly it increased speed and looking through the window one had the impression that all the trees on both sides of the line were following the train. Nearly everyone had taken a seat but some of us girls stood by the window looking out.

We went through many villages and made short stops in a few towns. At about nine o'clock we arrived at the station terminus. We alighted and outside a bus was waiting, La Circolare Rossa. We all got on and the bus drove off. It was like living in a fairy tale, one of those fables that my father used to tell me when I was small. For all of us who had never been outside our little village it was fantastic. These were marvellous experiences. The bus stopped at Piazza Risorgimento and from there we walked along Via S. Amerinziana and arrived at Piazza S. Pietro and the Vatican. We all felt like little children who had just been given their first toy.

We were all very young, not in age but in experience, and we had never dreamed of seeing those shops full of everything, those brightly lit windows, those palaces, restaurants - so many beautiful things! The enormous square of S. Pietro with so many columns and all those people filling it! We waited. The Pope came out of the Vatican window and made a long speech and gave everyone the Benediction 'Urbis et orbi' (For all the peoples of the world).

After the ceremony we all went to eat in a restaurant and then visited the Cappella Sistine where all the best Italian sculptors and painters, like Michelangelo, Rafaello, Giotto, Canova and many more, have left their masterpieces which the whole world envies. We were all over the moon.

Then we went to see the Coliseum, that beautiful edifice, over two thousand years old, which reminds us of our ancestors, the Romans. What else can I say? It was an experience that us youngsters would remember all our lives. After all that, we went back to the station and returned home.

A few weeks had gone past but the memory of that journey was still very much on my mind. The experience of Rome had made me think about quite a few things. I had looked at the Roman girls. They seemed to be so sure of themselves! I knew that one day I would go to the city; that was the place where my future lay.

However, like a fledging that's eager to leave the nest and launch itself into the great, wide sky but has to wait until it learns to fly, so I, too, had to gain experience and learning. Judging by what aunt Lauretta had said I would have to wait until the right occasion presented itself. Knowing how resourceful she was, I had a feeling that the right occasion might present itself sooner than mother might expect. So for the time being, I was quite happy to work with aunt Lauretta and acquire as much experience and learning as I could. Rome would still be waiting and keep a place open for me.

CHAPTER ELEVEN – THE BIRD LEAVES THE NEST

Weeks had gone by and one day aunt Lauretta and I had to do a special job. I got up early, dressed and after breakfast went to see to the chickens. There were three eggs in the nest. I picked them up, went back indoors and got ready to go leave.
"Io vado, mamma. (I'm going, mother.)" I shouted.
"Val bene, Ida, no c'è bisogno di gridare. Non sono sorda! (All right, Ida. There is no need to shout. I'm not deaf!)" mother said. She didn't seem to be in a good mood.

I was not going to the church so I went straight to my aunt's house. I knocked and she opened the door and we went down to the basement. That was where she worked. It was quite a large room. Against one of the walls was a big loom with lots of wooden spindles. I counted twenty-four and on the floor twenty-four containers and lots of balls of thread, some cotton, some wool and some silk. There were also four pedals and a large comb. There were other things and, although I tried to visualize how the weaving was done, I was quite lost.

My aunt started to talk and I missed a few words. The balls of thread used depended on what one was going to produce: cotton, wool or silk. At first I found it very difficult but eventually I began to produce good work, and before long I could make cloth of all kinds. My aunt was very pleased with the results and I thanked her for teaching me how to weave.
"Ida, now it's about time I taught you how to take someone's temperature, how to give an injection, how to treat wounds, and other things to do with first aid."

At home I was learning geography, maths and history from the books she had given me. Slowly I was giving myself an education, and enjoying it. There is a special word for that in Italian, 'autodidatta', self-taught! Like the fledging has to do before leaving the nest, I, too, had to learn how to fly. Let my wings be strong enough to take me to Rome! Roma! Every night I dreamt of that city.

Time passed. I went on with my two jobs, working with my aunt and keeping the church clean. We didn't work all the time, so I'd time left to get on with my studies. I became quite good at cloth making and my aunt was pleased with me. Did I want to become a weaver? Not likely! I wanted more from life than that. I was having those thoughts as I cleaned church, when I saw my aunt coming in. She had news for me. We went back to the house and she told me what she had in the back of her mind.

A lady had written to her who was the daughter of Count Pallavicini, the owner of the one villa that had escaped destruction. She had a little daughter about two months old. The lady had had a lot of trouble with the delivery and was poorly and could not stand the heat in Rome. She would be arriving shortly and asked my aunt to find a young woman to look after the baby girl.
"Idovina a chi ho raccomandato?   (Guess who I have recommended to her?)" my aunt said. I was surprised. Surely not me! My aunt seemed to read my thoughts.
"Si tu. Ho raccomandato a te. Non si sa mai, se tu ti comporti bene puo' anche darsi che quando la contessina ritorna a Roma, ti porti con lei. (Yes, I've recommended you. If you behave nicely it could even happen that she takes you with her when she returns to Rome.)"
"Oh zia adesso mi fai sognare! (Oh aunty! Now you're giving me fantasies!)"
"Don't go too fast. I only said 'maybe'. But I know her well and I'm certain she will ask me for advice. Tell me, Ida, what do you want to do with your life?"
"What I would like is to have more education so I could become a doctor. At the moment I can't even become a nurse. I need to take exams but because of the war I have had no chance to. But I'm still hoping that one day I will become a nurse and be able to look after people."
"With good will and strength of character, one can achieve anything. I used to work as a nurse and I will teach you. I'll also give you books and you can study. Are you happy about that?"
"Oh, aunty, you will make my dreams come true! Thank you."
"There is something else. The countess will pay you and you can save the money and use it when you need it."

On my way home I nearly got run over by a horse and cart that was coming down the road.
"Hai la testa nelle nuvole?" the driver shouted at me. He was right, I was on Cloud Nine!

When I got home I told mother everything. At first she was not very happy, but then she must have changed her mind.

"All right, Ida, if you want be a nurse, I wish you good luck!"

A week went past and nothing happened. I was getting frantic. Would the young countess accept me? I was still hoping, but hope was beginning to fade. Yet I should have had more faith in my aunty.

It was 15th June. After I had done my chores at home, I went to the church and did the cleaning and changed the flowers, and then on to aunty. At that time she was teaching me how to look after a baby. She had got hold of a big doll and showed me how to pick it up without hurting it, how to change nappies, how to give it a bath and many other things. But I still didn't know when the lady would arrive or if, when she came, I would be suitable for her. But I thought that whatever I learned would be useful for the future, so I did my best.

"Today she will teach me something different about first aid." I thought and went in. She looked happy and smiling. Lying on the dining table was a dummy.

"Let's pretend this is a man who has been fished out of the water half drowned. To bring him back to life, first we have to press and relieve his chest several times. Then we have to open his mouth and breathe in several times to help his lungs expand. If he is still alive, he should throw up all the water he has swallowed. By the way, Ida, the young countess is coming on 18th June and you are to look after the baby." I just stood there petrified, lost for words. I wanted say 'thank you' but I couldn't. Aunty looked at me and laughed.

"Well, are you happy?"

"Yes, aunty, I'm really happy."

I couldn't wait for those days to pass. I went on doing things as if I was in a dream. Mother noticed it.

"Ida, smettila di sognare, quello che verra', verra'. (Ida, stop dreaming. What will come, will come.)"

"Yes, mamma." I said, but deep inside I was all at sixes and sevens.

Finally the day came. I was in my aunty's house when I heard a noise outside. My aunty rushed downstairs and I looked out of the window. A big car had stopped in front of the house. A driver in uniform wearing a cap opened the door and a woman carrying a baby alighted and my aunty opened the front door for her. She entered the house and came up. She was quite pretty but very thin. The baby also looked very small. The lady looked at me and smiled.

"Questa è sua nipote? (Is this your niece?)" she asked.

"Si, chiama Ida. (Yes, her name is Ida.)" my aunty replied.

"Piacere di conoscerti, Ida. (Pleased to meet you, Ida.)" she said. I made a little bow and she laughed.

"Chiamimi Gabriella. (Call me Gabriella.)" she said and that was it. I'd been accepted and now I was some sort of governess.

"Ida, your aunty has told me that you like children and I'm quite sure that you will look after my little Renata very carefully. Maybe you know that I suffered a lot during her delivery. I've not got much milk but your aunty has found me a woman who has agreed to give hers to Renata. Now I must go. I'll see you all tomorrow, all right?" she said, extending her hand and then she left. I left the house and went home. My mind was like a windmill. Mother looked at me.

"There is no need for me to ask you how it went, I can read it in your face! When do you start?" she said.

"Tomorrow, mamma."

"Let me give you some advice: little ones are very fragile and it's very easy to hurt them." She sounded very concerned.

"Thank you, mother, for your advice. Don't worry, Aunty Lauretta has taught me a lot. We have practised many times with a big doll and I think I've learned how to do things, but I'll be very careful."

"Good girl. I've always known that you are wise. Get on with your career and may God look after you." mother said. Her words brought tears to my eyes. I put my arms around her and gave her a good cuddle. Now I was sure that the only thing she wanted for me was to get on with my life. What she had said up till now was just from the usual apprehension a mother has for her daughter.

"Thank you, mother, for your kind words. I love you so much."

"Oh Ida, Ida! Now you're making me cry!"

The day flew past and the following morning I got up early, had a nice bath, went to feed the chickens, had another wash and then put on my best dress, the one I wore on my trip to Rome. After breakfast I was ready. The Villa Pine wasn't too far from my house. It was halfway between Cave and Catailli. When I got there I could see why it had that name. Pine trees surrounded it. One was especially huge. It must have been at least a hundred years old. Around the villa was a large garden. The big, iron gate that the Fascists had dismantled and taken away had been replaced. It stood open. I went through it and was now surrounded by flowers, roses in particular, of different colours and each one more beautiful than the last. It was a marvellous sight.

I arrived at a beautiful, carved portal with an old bell-pull. I pulled the chain and there was a sound like church bells. The door opened and a woman let me in. She was the wife of Pietro, the caretaker who looked after the villa in the owner's absence. I knew her well; I had often seen her and spoken to her in church on Sundays. She was the mother of one of my girlfriends, Giovanna, who was a nice girl but mad about boys. I could see her happily married with lots of kids. Good luck to her. Maybe I'll be like that one day … but not yet.

"How are you?" I asked, as she let me in.

"Well, thank you, and your mother?" she replied

"She is well, thank you." I went upstairs. Gabriella was sitting in an armchair doing some embroidery. She put the work down and stood up.

"Benvenuta, Ida. Vieni ti porto nella camera di Renata. (Welcome, Ida. I'll take you to Renata's bedroom.)" I followed her.

It was a small room but very nice. All over the walls were pictures of animals and there must have been at least twenty dolls of all sizes. When I first I saw her, Renata had been all wrapped up but now she was lying in her little cot I could see how small she was. Gabriella leant down and kissed her, then stood up.

"I'm going back to my embroidery. If you need me for anything, ring the bell. Later on Mrs Filomena will come to give her her milk. Do you know her?" Gabriella asked.

"Yes, she is my godmother. Mrs Gabriella, don't worry. I love children and I will be very careful with your little Renata."

The young countess left and I looked at the little one. She was sound asleep. I got my book out and went on reading about first aid. Then, from the corner of my eye, I saw Renata shuffle in her cot and then she started to cry. I looked at her and began to panic. I'll have to pick her up! It is one thing to do it with a doll but here was the real thing. I had to do it. I bent down, put one hand under her little head and the other under her bottom. I lifted her body to one side and the smell told me why she had started to cry: she needed to be changed.

"There you go, Ida," I said to myself, "you can do it." I got hold of the nappies.

"Ora cambiamo i pannollini e tu sarai bella e pulita. Che ne penzi mia piccola. (Now we will change your nappies and you will be all nice and clean. What do you think, little one?)" I said to the baby, as if she understood my words.

The door opened silently and Gabriella stood there looking. I lifted the little dress up, undid the pins and removed the dirty nappy, cleaned her little bottom with wet cotton wool, dried her properly and put some cream on so she would not have any sores, just like my aunty had taught me. Then I fixed the clean nappy with the pins, picked her up and put her back in the cot. I stroked her face and she took hold of my finger.

"Now you are nice and clean. Go to sleep. Later we will have a little bath, my beautiful baby."

All this time Gabriella had been standing in the doorway.

"Well done, Ida. Now I know Renata is in good hands. But tell me, why do you keep on talking to her? Do you think she understands you?" she said.

"I think so, madam. My mother and my aunty have both told me how important it is to talk to young children. They understand that you love them, they are not scared and don't feel lonely."

My godmother had arrived and didn't seem surprised to see me. After greeting each other, she started feeding Renata.

"While Filomena feeds my little one, come with me, Ida." I looked at her with surprise but followed her as she took me to her bedroom and opened the wardrobe. Inside were several dresses, almost new, some large ones and some smaller.

"These frocks are much too large for me. Maybe they'll fit you. Try one on." I looked at her. She was about my height but much thinner. I took my dress off and tried on one of the larger ones. It fitted me like a glove.

"Non sola la misura. Ma ti sta' anche bene. Sembra che è fatto per te. (Not only is it the right size for you, but it suits you nicely)" she said. I stood there a bit confused. Gabriella laughed.

"I can't wear them any more so, if you want them, they are yours." she said with a smile. What could I say? I had only one dress and suddenly now I had four!

"Non ho parole come ringraziarla, Signora Gabriella. È molto gentile. (I cannot find the words to thank you, Mrs Gabriella. It is very kind of you.)"

"Don't even think about it. But from today on you must call me Gabriella. I'll tell Maria to put them in a case so you can take them home. All right?" I couldn't say anything. I just stood there with tears in my eyes.

CHAPTER TWELVE – THE BIRD HAS FLOWN

I didn't have a watch so didn't know what time it was. Renata was still sleeping and I was getting a little bored. Maria came in.
"La signora mi ha detto di chiederti se c'è di particolare che non puoi mangiare. E cosa ti piace. (Madam has asked me to ask you if there is anything in particular that you cannot eat and also what you like best)" she said. I was more and more surprised by Gabriella's thoughtfulness. I thought for a while and then said, "No. Thank her for her kind thought and tell her that I can eat anything and I have no special preferences. I always eat what I have on my plate."

Maria went back and I started preparing what I needed for Renata's bath. The little bathing bowl stood in the corner. I picked it up together with a large china jug and went to the bathroom. I gave the bowl a good wash, filled it up with hot water and took it back to the bedroom. Then I went back and filled the jug with cold water. There were two tables and I rested the bowl on one and put a soft towel on the other. Then I waited for the little one to wake up. When she opened her eyes, I bent down to the cot and talked to her.
"Ora bambina mia ci facciamo un bel bagnetto! (Now, my girl, we will have a nice bath!)" She looked at me and moved her little arms as if she understood. I put some cold water in the bowl and tested it with my elbow. Just right! I bent down and gave her my little finger. She got hold of it and tried to pull it towards her mouth.
"Birricchina! Questo non è da mangiare. (Little rascal! This isn't something to eat.)"

I lifted her out of the cot and rested her little body on the towel. I removed the little dress and the nappy. She was very small.
"Vedrai come ti piace. (You will like it.)" I said and gently put her in the water. She did like it and made a little noise and moved her legs. I left her in the water for a while, gave her a good wash and then took her out, dried her little body, dusted her with some baby talcum powder, put on a clean nappy and put her back in her cot. Another hurdle jumped, and I'd done it with flying colours!
"Ti è piaciuto, Renata? (Did you like it, Renata?)" I asked her. She moved her little arms and legs and made little noises. Yes, she had liked it. I could see her eyes beginning to close.

The door opened and Maria came in.

"Il designate è pronto. Io guardo la bambina. (Lunch is ready. I'll look after the little one.)" she said. Suddenly I felt famished. I stood up and went to the dining room where Gabriella was already sitting at the table on which stood a big bowl of pasta *al sugo*. After the pasta, Pietro brought in *cotolette di vitello* - veal cutlets - and salad. It was a nice lunch. I thought I deserved it.

"Se vuoi Ida, puoi rimanere qui' a dormire. (If you wish, Ida, you can sleep here)" Gabriella said. I thought about it.

"Si, mi piacere, Gabriella, (Yes, I would like to, Gabriella,)" I said, "but first I must ask my mother."

"You are right. If your parents are happy, I would like to have you here." she said and we left it at that. I said goodbye to her, picked up the case with the dresses in and left.

At home I showed the frocks to my mother.

"Look, mother, at what Gabriella has given me as a present. They were too large for her," I said.

"La contessina è molto brava con te. Come è andato il primo giorno? (The young countess is very good to you. How did your first day go?)" mother asked me.

"Very well, mother. I changed the nappies first and later on I gave her a bath. The little one was very happy."

"All of a sudden you have become a child expert, Ida! You will go very far!" she said, laughing.

"There is one thing, mother. Gabriella has asked me to sleep at the villa. What do you think?" She looked at me in a funny way then she smiled.

"Non mi dispiace. È arrivata il momento che tu cominci a vivere la tua vita. (I don't mind. The time has come for you to live your own life.)" I was grateful for those words.

"Ti voglio bene, mamma, e verro atrovarvidi quando in quando. (I love you, mamma, and I will come to see you and dad every so often.)" So it was decided and from that day on I stayed at the villa.

Renata was as good as gold and every night she slept soundly. During the day I took her out in her pram into the garden and around the countryside. She always enjoyed it. Once, a little bird, a robin, landed on the top of the pram. Renata's eyes sparkled with excitement and she tried to touch it. Of course, the bird flew away and she had a little cry. I was getting more and more attached to her. She was such a lovely girl! She had a better colour and her little face was filling out. Gabriella's health had improved and I could see that she had put on weight. We had established a routine and the only breaks were when I went to see my parents and to the church to do some cleaning and change the flowers. After all aunt Lauretta had done for me, I wanted to show my gratitude.

On one visit I saw father. He looked well. Soon, he told me, he and Uncle Joseph with his helpers would start cutting down the trees on the mountain they had bought. If I go to Rome, I will miss them terribly, I thought, but that's life.

And so the dreaded day came. Gabriella called me in. I knew what she would tell me! She had made something for my mother, a little table centrepiece decorated with flowers and leaves. It was beautiful.
"Questo è per tua madre. (This is for your mother.)" she said. Then came the crunch, the words I was dreading. She made me sit down.
"A fine di settimana noi andiamo a Roma! (At the end of the week we'll go to Rome.)" I was shattered. She realised that and smiled.
"Would you like to come with us, just for a short while? I would not want to be an obstacle to your career. Your aunt has told me all about your dream." Again I was stunned, but this time for joy.
"Oh yes, thank you. I have grown so attached to you and Renata that the thought of not seeing you both anymore … "
"Well then, everything is sorted. You must ask permission from your father and mother." I couldn't say any more. I went back to Renata's bedroom. She was awake and when she saw me she made that little noise. I picked her up, gave her a big kiss and she got hold of my hair.
"I'm coming with you to Rome!" At the end of the week, Gabriella had said. Today is Thursday; two days to go. I must go home and sort things out.

My mother and father looked pleased when I told them and wished me good luck. Mother was very pleased with her present and straightaway she put it on the dining table. I had to go and see my aunt Nicolina and Uncle Guiseppe and all my cousins, but first, Aunty Lauretta.

She was very pleased to see me.
"So, you are going to Rome!" She had a little laugh. "I knew it

from the start but I didn't want to spoil the surprise!"

"Naughty aunty!" I gave her a big cuddle.

"Write to me sometime and tell me how you get on." I promised I would and thanked her again and gave her a big kiss. Then I went to see the tribe. It was nearly midday and they were all there, all eight of them with my Aunty Nicolina and Uncle Joseph. I kept it short, gave each of them a big cuddle and went back home.

The last evening at home was time for advice: Do write to us! Don't make us worry! I promised and went to bed for my final night.

The following morning I got up early. I had a nice bath, breakfasted and went to say goodbye to the chickens. Mother and father were up. Gabriella had said that I would be picked up, so we waited. I heard the noise of a car and went out. The same car with the same driver was waiting. Father brought out my things and put them in the boot. I gave a big hugs and kisses to my parents, got into the car and we were away off to the villa.

Gabriella was there and Renata in Maria's arms. As I took hold of my little treasure, they got into the car and we all drove off.

"Rome, Rome!" my heart sang, "Here I come!" The bird had flown the nest and the great blue sky was waiting.

After travelling through various villages, Andrea got onto the motorway and the journey began in earnest. It would take us about an hour and a half to get to Rome, Andrea had said. The seats were very comfortable but there was no baby seat so I held Renata in my arms. At first she was asleep and I gazed out of the window. I could see the last vestiges of the war still showing its ugly face: many fallen trees that no-one had bothered to clear, dead stumps with roots pointing to the sky, huge holes that no-one had filled in. As we got nearer to the battlegrounds the sights were even worse: scattered farmhouses lay destroyed and abandoned; what once were happy communities, luxuriant fields and thick woods were now a silent desert. All the farm animals had been taken away by the Germans; all the farmers had gone to the cities to work in factories. It was a very painful sight. I looked at Gabriella and from her expression I could tell that she felt the same as me.

I had to stop looking. In my arms Renata had woken up and was showing signs of distress. I told Gabriella and she told Andrea to pull in to the next lay-by. In a short time he stopped the car. I had all I needed with me: nappies, talcum powder, a thermos filled with warm water, a towel and a little bowl. It was a bit cramped on the seat but I managed. I laid Renata on the seat and removed her dirty nappy, washed and dried her little bottom. A sprinkle of powder, a clean nappy and it was done. I sat there with the dirty nappy in my hand. Gabriella made a sign with her hand pointing to the window and I threw the nappy outside. Gabriella laughed, then gave me a big smile.

"Brava, Ida, stay dinventanto una esperta. (Well done, Ida, you're becoming a real expert.)" Her words made me feel proud of myself.

There were no more stops after that and Andrea drove fast until we reached the city. There, because of the traffic, we had to crawl but eventually we arrived in Corso Trieste. Andrea pulled into what looked like an alleyway. As we drove in, I realised it was a cul de sac, flanked on both sides by tall iron railings with a gate at the centre   As we got near I could see it was no ordinary gate and I couldn't find the words to describe it. It was made of wrought iron made to look like leaves, flowers and rosebuds. It was beautiful. The villa looked beautiful, too: two little columns supporting an ornate porch, all in marble. As I was admiring it, some people came out. A young woman came up to me and took Renata from my arms.

" Poverina, deve essere affamata. (Poor little thing, you must be starving)" she said and rushed inside. I stood there a bit confused still feeling the warmth of the little body.

"Marta è la balia di Renata. Come Filomena, anche lei ha perso un bambino ma non ha potuto venire all villa con noi perché ha due bambini piccolli da accudire. (Marta is Renata's wetnurse. Filomena couldn't come with us to the villa because she has two little ones to look after.)" Gabriella said. I was relieved. We all went in. I wanted to look at the gate and the villa a bit longer but there would be ample time for that.

We went upstairs and Gabriella took me to my room.

"Questa è la tua camera, Ida. (This is your room, Ida.)" she said and left. It was quite a nice room with a chest (como'), a small wardrobe (armadio), a bed which looked very comfortable and a small piece of furniture with little drawers and a large mirror. On the top of this were a brush and several combs. There were also two chairs. At home I had to comb my hair standing in front of the mirror of the wardrobe. Now I could do it sitting down.

There was a knock on the door.
"Entrate! (Come in!)" A young man came in with my case.
"Grazie."
"Io sono Michele il giardiniere. (I'm Michael the gardener.)" the young man said.
"Grazie, Michele. Io mi chiamo Ida. (Thank you, Michael. My name is Ida.)" I said.

I opened my case and put my away my things, then sat in front of the mirror and combed my hair. I saw some drops on the window; it had just started to rain. I had left my zoccoletti at home and only had a light pair of shoes with me. I have some money, I thought, so must go out and buy some better ones or a pair of boots. Again there was a knock.
"Entrate!"
This time it was Gabriella. In her hands she had a pair of boots. They looked new.
"Fuori piove. E ho pensato che tu hai bisogno di questi. Mi vanno un po' stretti e non li ho mai messi. Provali. (It is raining and I thought you could do with these. They are a little tight for me and I've never worn them. Try them on.)" she said, putting the boots on the floor. I knew it was just an excuse but I could not offend her by refusing. She was so kind! I tried them on and they fitted perfectly.

"Mille grazie, Gabriella. Tu sei un tesoro. Adesso devo andare a vedere il mio tesoruccio. (A thousand thanks, Gabriella. You are a treasure. Now I have to go and see my little treasure.)" Together we went to Renata's room. Gabriella opened the door very slowly. Renata was fast asleep in her little cot.
"Dorme come un angioletto! (She sleeps like an angel!)" I said. Gabriella looked at me.
"Tu le vuoi realmente bene, è vero? (You really love her, don't you.?)" she asked.
"Yes, I'm really attached to her and when I leave I will miss her but, if you don't mind, I will come to see her every so often."
"Puoi venire quando vuoi, Ida. Sarai ben venuta. Adesso vieni con me che ti faccio visitare la casa. (You can come anytime you want and you'll be welcome. Now come with me and I will show you around.)"

I followed her like a child with a new toy. I was discovering things that I had never seen before. She took me all around the place. One question was burning on my lips: as yet I had seen no sign of her husband or her parents. Where were they?

Gabriella must have been a mind reader because she said, "Giacomo mio marito è un avvocato ma è anche amministratore di dverse ditte con mio padre. Al momento sono andati in America per affair è mia madre è andata con loro. Il mio nome da donna sposata è Gherardi ma, siccome mio padre è un conte, tutti mi chiamano Contessina Pallavicini. (Giacomo, my husband, is a lawyer and also an administrator for several firms. He works with my father and they have both gone to the United States on business. My mother has gone with them. My married name is Gerard, but because my father is a count, everyone calls me Contessina Pallavicini.)"

The mystery was solved. We carried on going around the place. On all the walls were beautiful pictures and ornaments.
"Di sopra ci sono dieci camere da letto. Ma quelle no sono importante. A questo piano c'è il tinello dove io faccio il ricamo. (Upstairs there are ten bedrooms but they're not important. This is where I do my embroidery.)" We were in a large room with a very big table and chairs. On top of the table was a large porcelain ornament with little angels supporting a bow. It was beautiful. Gabriella saw me looking at it.
"Quello è un capodimonte. È molto anticoe di valore. (That is Capodimonte. It is an antique piece, very valuable.)" There were ornaments and pictures everywhere.
"Questo è il salotto. (This is the sitting room.)" I could see she was getting a bit tired and I was right.
"Un altro giorno ti faro' vedere la sal di ricivimento e la libreria. Ora andiamo vedere se Renata è sveglia. Ti dispiace? (Another day I will show you the reception room. Now let us go and see if Renata has woken up. Are you disappointed?)"

She was right. Renata was awake and in need of attention. After that time in the car, I had become quite an expert and in no time Renata was cleaned up and back in her cot. This time I picked up the dirty nappy and went to flush it down the loo. I had a little laugh to myself thinking what I had done in that lay-by.

When I came back from the bathroom I had a look outside. It was still raining so I picked up my book and read until Maria, the housekeeper, called me to go to lunch.

It was Sunday. I opened the window slightly and in came a festive sound of bells, some very gentle, others more powerful. Sunday and hundreds of thousands of people will be going to church and I, too, would like I to go, but I'd only been to Rome once so how would I find my way around such a big city? I'd just seen to Renata and she was lying in her cot kicking her legs happily. At home I always went to church on Sunday! Well, there was not much I could do.

While I was having those thoughts, the door opened and Gabriella came in. She was all dressed up.
"Io vado in chiesa, vuoi venire? (I'm going to church, would you like to come?)" she asked me. My saviour! She must have guessed what I was thinking.
"Yes, I would like to come, but what about Renata?" I said.
"Soon Marta will come to feed her and in the meantime Giovanna can look after her. Let's go!"

Giovanna was the house-keeper and Gabriella had everything sorted out. I bent down and gave Renata a big kiss and Gabriella did the same. Then we left the room and went downstairs. Andrew the driver was waiting in the yard. We both got in the car, Andrew started the engine and we were off. There was a lot of traffic but the young man seemed to know his way about. After many twists and turns, we arrived in a very big square, St Peter's Square, and there was the cathedral. Andrew stopped the car. He would come and pick us up when Mass had ended, he said and left. We crossed the square and went into the church.

We only just got in because the place was packed with people. There must have been at least a thousand of them. Anyway, we squeezed in and I could admire the beautiful church. It was illuminated by hundreds of chandeliers. Like the Sistine Chapel, the ceiling was covered with paintings, these ones by Raffaello and other famous Italian painters. Everywhere was rich with marble statues and pictures of saints. It was a monument of art. I thought to myself that, as I began to know the city better, I would return to visit it again.

All through the long Mass, officiated by a bishop, we had to stand up, pressed in by bodies, but at last it ended and we got out. I saw the car parked in a corner of the square and pointed it out to Gabriella. We went over and Andrew held the door open for us. We got in and he drove away. Gabriella looked tired but she was smiling. For me it had been quite an experience!

The traffic was the same as before but Andrew took us straight back to the villa and we got out.
"Do you mind, Gabriella, if I stay out for a while? I would like to look at the gate."
"Stai fuori fin che vuoi, Io penzo che Marta stia dando il latte a Renata. Io vado du. (Stay out as long as you want. I think that Marta is feeding Renata. I'm going upstairs.)"

It was indeed a beautiful gate. I touched one of the roses with my fingers and it was like touching a real flower. It was painted black. If the roses had been painted pink and the leaves green, I thought, one would think that they were real roses and leaves. Only a real artist could have created such perfection! I could see that the railings surrounding the garden looked new and I couldn't help wondering why the Fascists had removed the railings and not this gate. Maybe Gabriella would tell me.

I went back in and up the stairs. Gabriella was on the landing.
"Marta is feeding Renata. Come with me and I'll show you the rest of the house."
I followed her as we went through the rooms I already had seen and then we came to a new room. It was huge and in the middle was a massive table, solid walnut with carvings all over it. I couldn't say exactly how big it was but I counted twelve chairs on each side, all walnut, all carved. It was a beautiful sight. There were many antique stands, also carved, and on each one stood a vase. They all looked old and beautiful. The four walls were covered with pictures.
"This is the reception room. At one time they used to do a lot of entertaining here." she said.
"A reception with a difference!" I thought.

We left this room and went to another which had just a few small tables and chairs, also carved. The walls were covered with bookshelves all round to a height of about two metres and above them were pictures of women in crinolines and men in armour, uniforms and peculiar clothing. I realised I was looking at history.

"Those are our ancestors." Gabriella said, pointing at the pictures. She went to one of the shelves and pulled out a book.

"You said you wanted learn about medicine. This book is from the fifteenth century. Here, you can read about the way medicine and surgery was practised in those days." she said and gave me the book. I thanked her and we left the room. She went back to her embroidery and I to my little treasure.

She was fast asleep and I opened the book and began to read. While I was reading, the door opened slightly and Giovanna came in.

"Ida, you have been here in Rome for a few days, how do you like it?"

"Oh, I like it very much. It has been one of my dreams. It is so big, so many shops and churches and so many people! I never heard so many bells ringing! This morning Gabriella took me to church in St Peter's and I was amazed to see such beautiful paintings. I learnt about these things at school but now I've seen them with my own eyes. I saw a beautiful marble sculpture by Michaelangelo and the art of the great Italian painters like Rafaello and Giotto and many others."

"You have only just started on Rome!" Giovanna said, "Wait until you have been here longer ..."

While we were talking, Marta came to say farewell.

"Goodbye, Ida, goodbye, Giovanna. I have to go to see what my two little rascals have been up to."

"Oh! I knew you had children. How old are they and who looks after them while you are here?" I asked.

"I have a boy and a little girl and I have just lost a third one. I'm so sad. He would have been such a lovely little lad if he had lived." Then she paused and said, "My mother looks after them when I come here to feed Renata. It's difficult because I live a bit far away but I need the money. Do you have any relations here in Rome?"

"Oh, yes," I said, "I've been told that my Aunty Catharine and Uncle John and their three children live not very far from here."

"Where do they live?" Marta asked.

"Well, I have the address but I haven't the faintest idea where it is. As you know, I've only been in Rome for few days and it will take me a long time to find my way around, don't you agree?"

"Oh, no, I don't think so. It won't take you long. It seems to me you're a very quick lass. Anyway, where does your aunty live?"

"Wait a minute, Marta, and I'll go to my room and get the address for you to see."

A minute later I came back and Marta and Giovanna were laughing about how Renata was beginning to get interested in her surroundings.

"Here it is, Marta."

"Oh, my goodness me, I know this lady! We don't live very far from one another. I see her nearly every time she goes to Corso Vittorio Emmanuele to do her shopping. What a funny coincidence! Wait till I tell her, she will be surprised. I live at No. 16 via Fanfulla Da Lody and she lives at No. 18. Well, well, I'm amazed!" Giovanna said,

"Which borough is this place in?"

"It's in Prenestina, just behind Porto Maggiore, not very far from the Termini station. In fact, John, the husband, works in the Termini station for the Grotti Celoni."

"And what is that?" Giovanna asked.

"It's a transport service which goes from Termini station to the outskirts of Rome. It's for the industrial workers, it's a very busy line."

I wondered what Aunty Catharine and Uncle John would say when they heard this news. I expect they would be very cross with my parents for not letting them know I was in Rome.

"Marta, I'm very much obliged to you for being so kind as to tell me where my aunty lives. Please tell her when you see her that I will come to see her and her family when it's convenient for her, if Gabriella gives me the permission, of course" I said.

"Oh, I'm quite sure it won't be any problem. As you know, Gabriella is a very kind lady and she will be only too pleased for you to be able to see your relations. Ida, tell me how many children they have. I've only seen a little boy."

"Oh, she has three. You don't see much of the two older ones because they are at school most of the time." I said.

"How old are they?"Americo is about four. I would very much like to give you some money for Aunty Catharine, if that's possible, so she could buy something for the children."

"Oh, yes, Ida, I'd be more than happy to do that for you. I'm sure she will appreciate it. But now I must go. What will my mother and the children say? I have been here much longer than usual. Dear me, I must go now. 'Bye, Ida, goodbye, Giovanna. I'll be back soon to feed Renata." Marta said and off she went.

I held Renata in my arms and played with her. She was a beautiful baby and I was getting very attached to her. Then I thought, one day I'll have to leave her, and that made me very sad and I was miserable.

As usual on Monday everybody was busy doing what needed to be done in a big house. Gabriella did her embroidery, I stayed with Renata and all the staff got on with their routines. Gabriella noticed I was very anxious and said,
"Ida, you look as if you are upset."
"Gabriella, I'm very fond of Renata and you and it's the thought that I will have to leave you all behind that is hurting me. I know that I will have to come to terms with these things in life but it's not easy."
"Oh, Ida, Ida!" she said, "You can stay here as long as you like. But it will be sad for the three of us. I know about your ambition to become a nurse and to work with people in hospitals. I have a lot of connections and if you need any help I will be here for you. But let's not think about that today. That's for another time. Let's go out and enjoy ourselves."

On Tuesday 4th October Gabriella took me to the church of St Agnes, which is in the borough of St Amenziana, not very far from Corso Trieste. The church of St Agnes was built on top of the catacombs where her remains and those of other Christians are still, for the world to see. I was very moved to see what happened to these poor people. It made one think what evil people there were at the time of Emperor Nero. History tells us he and thousands and thousands of others enjoyed watching big, ferocious animals, which were kept in cages in the Coliseum with nothing to eat, attack the poor Christians that were thrown to them. It made me very sad.

"Gabriella, today I found out that Marta doesn't live very far from my aunty. In fact, she lives just two doors away – what a coincidence! She knows my aunty and I took the liberty of sending her a message asking her when it might be possible to visit her and her family. Now I'm waiting for a reply and then I will kindly ask your permission to visit her."
"I didn't know you had an aunty here in Rome, Ida! That pleases me very much."
"Well, Gabriella, I'm so happy to be here in Rome that I forgot to tell you, but now I've come to my senses and thought I'd better do my duty and visit her and her family. I haven't seen the children

since last year when they came to the village." I said.

"Of course you can go any time you like. My chauffeur will take you whenever you like."

"I would like that very much. Thank you, Gabriella."

"I will tell Andrew to leave you there and come to fetch you later, if you like."

"That would be splendid, Gabriella. Again, thank you very much."

Next day Marta came and said,

"Ida, I have good news for you. I've been to see your aunty and she was very surprised to learn that you are in Rome. She didn't know anything about you being here but she said she would be more than pleased to see you whenever it's convenient for the countess. And she also said that your uncle from Catailli will be visiting his son, Natalino, who is in Rome doing military service, and he will be able to pay a visit as well. So there will be a nice family reunion on Sunday the sixth."

"Thank you, Marta, for being so kind." Then I went to see Gabriella in her embroidery room and I told her what Marta had just told me and she said,

"Oh, this is good news for you."

CHAPTER THIRTEEN – MY FUTURE IN ROME

Sunday morning 6th October and I was very excited and at the same time very frightened, not knowing what my future in Rome would hold. I went downstairs and said goodbye to everybody.

"I'll see you all later." Andrew was there with the car ready to go. I jumped in and away we went.

As Andrew was driving, he tried to be a good guide and every time we passed a statue or a monument he explained the meaning of it. He would tell me the history of each place. Then he asked,

"Ida, why do you want to leave the countess?"

"I don't want to leave but I only came for a very short time." I said, "Gabriella only came to the village because she wasn't well and while she was there she needed a young girl to look after Renata and a wet-nurse to feed her. But here she has Giovanna to look after her and Marta as a wet-nurse, and I knew that. She brought me to Rome because she knew I didn't like the village and also to help me to fulfil my ambition to become a nurse. She thought I would stand a better chance here in Rome but we didn't know that you can't become a nurse before you are twenty-one and I'm only sixteen. The other obstacle is that no young girl can enter the profession unless she is a nun, and I have no intention of becoming one. So I hope to get a job and save money to be able to get more education and learn about medicine."

"So you want be a doctor!" Andrew said.

"Yes! But I need to study a lot. Also, at the moment it's not common for women to become doctors, but who knows? Maybe the time will come when you don't need to be a nun to become nurse, and you don't need to be a man to become a doctor. I have to rethink what my future will be. Right now I need to get a job to be able to support myself and, as I said, to save money for later."

"But Renata will miss you, Ida," he said, "and we all know Gabriella is very fond of you, as are the rest of the staff, including me."

"But I will come back to see you all," I said, "as soon I've settled down in a job I like."

"We've reached the borough of Prenestina and soon we'll be at your aunt's."

"Thank you, Andrew." Five minutes later we were at her door.

"Goodbye, Andrew. I shall miss you. I will see you later."

"Do you really mean that?"

"Of course, I shall miss all of you but I will see you again, Andrew."

I waved to him and knocked at Aunty Catharine's door. She opened it and we hugged one another.

"Where are the children, aunty?"

"I sent the big ones to the market in Corso Vittorio to buy fresh vegetables and fruit. They'll soon be back," she said, "and little Americo is playing with the boy next door. Now, Ida, tell me all about your countess and how you liked it there."

"Well, aunty, the countess brought me to Rome. I can stay with her until I find a job and then I will be free to leave. She is very kind to me and she told me she will be there for me when I need her."

The children came home from the market and Americo returned from playing with his friend next door. When they saw me they ran to me and I hugged all three of them. At about ten o'clock my uncle arrived and aunty said to him,

"Joseph, I have a surprise for you." He said,

"I think I know what this surprise is."

"And what is it?"

"My niece is here in Rome with the countess for a little while."

"But today she is with us." And then she called me and said,

"Ida, come and see who is here." I ran to him, put my arms around him and gave him a big hug, and said,

"Oh, uncle, it is nice to see you! How is everyone at home? How is my mamma and dad?"

"Everybody is fine. Your mamma and dad are missing you, as all of us do. Anyway, are you all right? Can you come home with me today?"

"No, I'm still staying with the countess and when I finish there I will find another job here in Rome."

"Well, we'll see about that!" Then aunty called Elena and said,

"Elena, take Ida with you and go to the butcher and buy a kilo of his best meat. As Uncle Joseph is here, I will make a nice stew. Ida, will you make sure the butcher gives Elena what I ask for: nothing but the best?"

"Yes, aunty, we will make sure the butcher does that."

So Elena took me along via Casilina. I thought, this is the very road that, if I travelled on for a couple more hours, would pass near Patieno where my grandmother's farm was, and that made me feel nostalgic for the times before the war. My cousin and I had such happy times as little children. Now I'm at the other end of via Casilina.

Along this road there was a convent and I saw some nuns dressed all in white. They were looking after some poor, frail old ladies. I thought, one day I will be able to do that. Elena said,
"Ida, can you wait here for a minute or two? I want to say 'hello' to my teacher. She is a nurse and a teacher. When she's not teaching, like today, she looks after old people."

Elena only took a few minutes and was soon with me again. Then finally we found the butcher's shop and went in. Elena said,
"Good morning, signor Mario. My mother would like a kilo of the best stewing meat you have." The butcher said,
"Ah, let me see now, I have a lovely piece of horse meat here. It will make a beautiful stew. I know your mother would like it." Elena said,
"If you say so!"
"Why horse meat?" I asked.
"There is nothing else, miss." the butcher said.
"Why is there nothing else? We've never eaten horse meat before." I said.
"Well, you will eat it now, because I haven't got anything else! Let me tell you, young lady, that we have had a war and the Germans took all the livestock from the farms for their own use, to feed their army and their people in Germany. Our poor farmers were left with nothing. When they finally left, only horses and some sheep remained. That's why we only have horse meat and lamb, but not very much lamb. There won't be anything else until the farmers re-establish themselves. Now, do you understand, my little lady?"
"I understand and I remember the war very well. My grandfather had a farm and died from a heart attack because he couldn't bear to see his farm without his beloved animals."
"I'm sorry, young lady. So, you know what the war meant."
"Yes, I know what the war meant. It's the reason I'm here in Rome. I couldn't stand the misery the war left behind in my village any longer." Then Elena and I said,
"Good bye, signor Mario."
"Goodbye, girls. Elena tell your mother I'm sending her the best meat I have. All the best to your family."

We returned home and aunty was ready to cook the dinner. In no time it was ready. Uncle Joseph, Uncle John, Bruno, Elena, Americo, Natalino and I sat at the table. Aunty arrived with a beautiful dish of *pasta asciutta* and after that we had the meat made *al ragu'* with a salad bought from the market in Corso

Vittorio, then fresh fruit bought from there, too. Uncle Joseph couldn't stop praising Aunty Catharine for such a wonderful meal. He said what good meat it was and then,

"I know we have had a terrible war but nobody will make me eat horse meat!" I said,

"Uncle, what do you think you have been eating today?"

"I didn't eat horse meat, did I? Oh! No, no!"

"Yes, uncle, you have and you enjoyed it, didn't you?" I said

"Well, I did enjoy it very much. From today on I will have to change my mind and eat horse meat." Aunty Catharine was very cross with me but everybody else had a good laugh.

After dinner it was time for him to go back to Termini Station to return to the village. He turned to me and said,

"Ida, are you coming back home with me now?"

"Oh, no, uncle. I'm staying with the countess."

"When do you think you will come back home to your mother and father?"

"I don't want to go back to the village."

"Have you thought for a moment what you will do here in Rome?"

"Yes. I will find a job."

"Do your mother and father know about this?"

"I told my parents about my intentions and with a bit of persuasion they agreed with me. I promised I would look after myself and they would always be proud of me. I would never do anything they didn't want me to. They said they trusted me and they know I wouldn't do anything to upset them. I've been brought up to believe in God and to try to keep the Ten Commandments and in that way I will never shame our family name or myself. One day I will work in hospitals and look after people less fortunate than me."

My uncle lost patience with me and said,

"You will come home soon, my dear girl!" Then he left. Aunty Catharine said,

"Ida, what was all that about with your uncle?"

"You always said to me: don't worry, Ida, if you don't want to stay in the village, you don't have to; I will try to find you a job in Rome. And here I am, aunty, and I'd be very grateful to you and Uncle John if you would have me here with you. I will promise you both to do my best. It would give me the opportunity to find a job and be able to support myself and pay you for my keep until I'm old enough to go to work in a hospital and help people in need, give them love and support as well as medical care."

Aunty Catharine laughed.

"Oh dear, dear Ida! You live in a fantasy world! Will you stop dreaming? Let me tell you that this is a dream you can't achieve. For a start, you are much too young. You need much more education, a lot of training and a lot of financial support which you don't have. But I'll see what I can do to help you find a respectable job which you can manage to keep."

There was a knock at the door. It was Andrew, come to fetch me back to the villa. I said,
"Goodbye, Uncle John." I gave a big hug to the children. Then aunty said,
"Ida, don't worry. I'll see what I can do for you." Then she kissed me and we said goodbye.
"Thank you, aunty. I know you will do whatever you can for me and I appreciate it very much. Again, thank you."

I got in the car with Andrew and off we went.
"Have you had a good time with your aunty's family today?" he asked.
"Yes, I have, but I couldn't stop worrying about Renata and I missed Gabriella and all the staff, including you, Andrew."
"I tell you, Ida, Renata and Gabriella will miss you very much, too, but I hope we will still see each other."
"Oh yes, I'm sure we will, without any doubt. When I come back to see Renata and Gabriella, I will make sure I see all the staff including you."

We reached the villa. Marta was feeding Renata and Gabriella heard I was back and looked pleased.
"Oh, Ida, you are back. How is your aunty and her family?"
"They are all very well," I said, "thank you for asking, Gabriella. My aunty said she would help me to find a job."
"I'm sure she will do her best, but remember I'm here, too, and if you need any references I can give them."

Marta knew I had been to see my aunty and she came to enquire how everything went. I told her,
"Marta, everything went all right, thanks for asking and thanks also for what you have done for me."
"I'm very pleased for you, Ida."

A few days later Marta gave me another message given to her by my aunty. It said:

'Ida, I was reading the newspaper and just by chance I looked in the advertising pages and read that the textile factory is looking for young girls to work there. They have special apprenticeships for girls who want to learn how to make cloth. I thought how appropriate this would be for you. But you must go to an interview, so you will need to ask permission from the contessina as soon as possible.
Lots of love, Aunty Catharine.'

After I'd looked after Renata and made sure she was all right, I went to see Gabriella and let her read the message my aunty had sent. Gabriella said,
"Oh, Ida, this is not right for you! This is what you ran away from. I always understood that you only wanted do medicine."
"Yes, Gabriella, you are right but I can't go to work in a hospital until I'm twenty-one and I'm only sixteen. When I'm twenty-one, I'll need financial support to achieve my ambition, which I don't have, but if I take this job I'll be able to pay for my education. But I don't know if I'll get the job. Will you give me permission to go for an interview?"
"Just tell me when you want to go and I'll tell Andrew to drive you there. I'll also give you a letter to give to the manager. You can telephone your aunt and arrange the appointment."
"Gabriella, you are so kind to me. People like us don't have telephones but I'll send a message to my aunt through Marta."
"After the interview, Andrew will bring you back here. Is that all right?"
"Thank you, Gabriella, you are a treasure. I don't know what I would do without your help. Thank you very much."

Marta took the message back to aunty for her to arrange the interview with the manager of the textile factory. It was called La Mila. The appointment was made for Monday 26th October. Andrew had got the car ready to take me there. In the morning I looked after Renata until it was time for Marta to feed her. Giovanna came into Renata's room and said,
"Ida, the car is ready when you are."
"Thanks, Giovanna. Tell Andrew I will be there in a few minutes. First I have to finish looking after Renata." But Andrew came up and said,
"You'd better do it quickly otherwise you will be late." I said goodbye to Gabriella and she kissed me, gave me a letter to give to the manager and wished me luck. I went downstairs and there

was Andrew waiting for me. I got in the car and off we went.

While he was driving he said,
"Ida, do you have to go?"
"Andrew, I only came to work for Gabriella for a little while because she wasn't well and came to the village to have some rest. While she was there she needed someone to look after Renata and a wet-nurse to feed her. But here she has Marta as a wet-nurse and Giovanna to look after her."
"Well, I'm very sad that you're going and so is Gabriella. We all know she likes you very much, as well all do."
"But I will come back to visit Renata and Gabriella and everyone. I look forward to it."
"If you say so." he said.
"Time has flown, Andrew, I think we are in Fanfulla da Lodi. Look, there's aunty waiting for me with the address and directions to the factory – it's outside Rome."

Andrew stopped the car right in front of her. She said,
"Here you are, this is the address and the directions. You must go, otherwise you'll be late. It takes about twenty minutes from here by car. The place is Tore Nova and the factory is called La Mila, it's written on the building. You can't miss it. John does that line with the Grotti Celoni goodness knows how many times a day. There's nothing to be afraid of. Good luck!"

About twenty minutes later we arrived and I was surprised to see such a big place. At the front the factory was pleasant looking. On it was written 'La Mila'. I was quite impressed. Andrew stopped the car at the corner of the yard and made a sign for me to get out.
"I'll come back in about half an hour." he said, "Best of luck, Ida." I was a bit puzzled and for a few moments I just sat there.
"Why have you stopped here, Andrew?" I asked him. He just looked at me.
"Ida," he said, "you are going to apply for a job. What would the manager think if he saw you getting out of a Bentley car with a driver in uniform?" It took me a little time before I understood what he meant.
"I'm sorry, Andrew. You are right." I got out of the car and walked towards my future.

A woman was walking towards me.
"Excuse me," I asked, "where do I go for the interview?" She

pointed to a door inside the hall with a glass panel. I knocked on it. "Come in!" a voice said, so I went in. It was quite a large office and sitting behind a desk was a man. He was about forty with a kind face. I stood there uncertain what to do. He must have realised because he pointed to a chair.

"Take a seat." he said, "What I can do for you?" I sat down and felt much more comfortable.

"My name is Ida Festa and I have an appointment for an interview." He looked at some papers on the desk.

"Oh yes. Your aunt made the arrangement. Let me ask you a few questions. How old are you?"

"I'm sixteen. I have a reference." I said and gave him the letter. He opened the envelope and read it.

"Your present employer states that you have done this job before. Also that she thinks highly of you."

"Yes, my aunt in my village has a loom and I worked with her for several months. It was a handloom. I've been told that here the weaving is done by machine. I don't know much about machines but I'm a quick learner." I was beginning to gain confidence. He looked at me and smiled.

"I'm sure you are." he said. "You are very young, Miss Festa, but I admire your spirit and I'm willing to give you a chance. It will be just a trial run of two months, after that we'll see. Satisfied?" I was over the moon. It had been easy!

"Thank you, sir. I will do my best." He just laughed.

"I'm certain you will! By the way, judging by your accent, you are not a Roman girl. Where do you come from?"

"I come from a little village called Catailli di Conca, very near Mignano di Monte Lungo and about twenty kilometres from Cassino in the Campania Region. The war destroyed most of the villages and I had to get away. That is why I came to Rome."

"Tell me, Miss Festa, I know the war made it very difficult to go to school, but did you manage to get some kind of education?"

"Sir, I've been to school but I would have liked much more education. Just after the war it was impossible for us girls to go above elementary level. I have a certificate in the fifth level from primary school."

"What subjects you did enjoy most?"

"I enjoyed school very much. I liked mathematics, history, Italian and many more subjects. I'm only sorry I couldn't have done more."

"I'm very sorry about what happened at Cassino. We also had something like it in Anzio. Now, because you have experience in cloth-making, as I said before, I will offer you ten thousand lire a month, just for two months. If you qualify, and I'm sure you will, it will go up to fifteen thousand. Will you accept that?"

"Yes, sir, I very much appreciate it."

"Don't call me 'sir'! I'm not the count, you know. My name is Ruggiero. Now, I'll take you around the factory and introduce you to many of the people who work here. I'm sure you will like it here and you will make lots of friends. I hope you will be very happy with us. If you have any problems, please come and tell me and I'll do my best to see you're all right."

The place was massive and there were about one hundred cloth frames just like the loom aunty had, except hers was manual and these were all electric machines. I had never seen so many young girls working together like that before and I was very frightened just by looking at them, never mind working there with them. And what about these electric machines? Would I be able to manage them? But then I thought this is no time to panic. I must take courage and get on. It was not time to be scared otherwise Catailli awaited me, and that was the one thing I didn't want. As these thoughts were in my mind, walking around the place with the manager and trying very hard to smile at everybody, inside I was scared out of my wits!

"Is there anything more you would like to know?" he said.

"No thank you, sir. I will learn as I go along." I said.

"There you are, young lady, now you've seen the place and I'm sure it frightened you, but you'll soon get know the job and the people and I hope you'll be very happy here."

"I'm sure I will."

"And now, when do you think you'll be able to start work?"

"Well, signor Ruggiero, I have to give the countess two weeks notice before I can come here and work for this firm. I want to thank you very much for giving me this chance. I will try my very best."

"I'm happy for you to start the week after next which will be Monday 9th November. Come at eight in the morning and report to this office, please. Goodbye, Miss Festa. I'll see you in two weeks time starting on Monday. Take care."

"I will be here." We shook hands and I said,

"Goodbye. I'll see you soon."

Andrew was in the car waiting for me at the end of the yard. I felt like singing. He saw me smiling and he knew I'd got the job. As I got near he got out and opened the door.

"Here you are, miss." he said, jokingly.

"Thank you kindly, sir." I said, making a bow. I got into the car and we drove off.

"Everything all right, Ida?" he asked.

"Yes, I got the job!" I replied.

The traffic was very heavy and I had butterflies inside. I was very frightened! He drove through the streets and squares of Rome without saying a word. We reached the villa in Corso Trieste and I looked at it and thought soon I would have to leave Renata and Gabriella, the one who looked after me and made me feel like a princess. And then? What would happen to me among all those factory girls? It made me feel sick, so sick I would not have minded going back to Catailli to my mum and dad to feel the security of my home. For the first time I missed my cousins, my Aunty Nicolina, Aunty Lauretta, the two grandmothers and all the cousins at the farm. A great fear came over me. I wanted to cry and I began to shake like a leaf. I lost all my courage and no longer harboured the fantasy of practising medicine or anything else. I asked myself, 'Who am I?' I felt like a little, unloved child lost in big, big world. I was very, very melancholic and felt as if I'd been dropped in deep hole.

I got out of the car and rushed upstairs to see my little one. Marta was still there. I picked her up and held her close to me and said, "Oh, Renata, I love you so, and I've got to leave you. You will grow up and you might hear my name but it won't mean anything to you. But I will never forget you. You'll stay in my heart forever."

I realised Renata needed attention so I laid her on the bed and changed her nappies and put her in the cot. Marta walked in.

"How did it go?" Marta asked. I was tired of repeating the same thing so I lifted my hand with the big thumb up.

"Good, well done! I'm off now. Ciao." and she went. I bent over the cot.

"Now we'll have a nice bath!" I said to Renata. I went to the bathroom, got everything ready and went back to the bedroom. I'd only just started washing her when Gabriella came in.

"Well, how did it go?" she asked, "Oh, Ida, you have been crying."

"Oh, Gabriella! I got the job but now I know I'm not so strong and I don't have the courage I thought I had. I'm really, really frightened, Gabriella. It's true but it can't be helped. I knew I came here only for a short period of time and I do understand that you brought me to Rome but you didn't really need me here but, because you are a kind, loving lady, you thought it would be good for me to see what life is like away from the village. You let me stay in your mother's room and she will be coming home soon with your father and husband and it will be difficult to explain to them what I do here."

"Oh, Ida, it's not as bad as that!" she said.

"Well, Gabriella, I have been here for nearly two months and I've seen and heard all around me the goodness of your heart. I have no words to thank you enough, you've been so kind to me. But now it's time for me to understand that I have to work and be responsible for my future."

The weeks passed very quickly and Gabriella arranged with Andrew to take me to my aunty's house on 6th November. It was a horrible day and didn't stop raining all night. They say that in Rome it doesn't rain by the drop but by the bucketload. Renata was upset, as if she understood my position. Gabriella said,

"Ida, maybe one reason I like you so much is because I never had a sister, the same as you. We understand one another because we both missed having a sister to share all our thoughts with." We both cried.

"The Mila manager said he would like me to start work there on Monday 8th November," I said, "is that all right with you?"

"Yes, of course, but I will arrange with Andrew to drive you to your aunty's on the 6th so you will have time to settle down. I'm glad you understood my predicament. Remember that I will always be here for you when you need me."

"Oh Gabriella," I said, "I will miss you and Renata!" We hugged one another and I held Renata very close to me for a minute or two. Then I ran out of Renata's room with a lump in my throat so big it was difficult to breathe!

This coming Saturday I will leave Gabriella for good, go to my aunty and a chapter of my life will come to an end. What will the next chapter bring? I know I will miss Gabriella and Renata a lot.

The day came that I left Gabriella and Renata for good and my next chapter opened. I should have been happy but the thought of leaving them make me very sad. Well, as they say, life must go on. I would come to see them from time to time but now I would try not think about them but think about my future. At nine o' clock I was called and Andrew came to take me to aunty's. I only had one case but the night before Gabriella had given me another one. Everything was packed. I gave the last caress to Renata and her little hand took hold of my finger. I was still stroking her face when Gabriella came in.

"Andrew is waiting." she said, "Are you ready?" Tears came to my eyes. She came towards me and put I put my arms around her. "Come back and see me some time." she said. Maria came in and took one of my cases.

"You know I will, Gabriella, I won't forget you. You have done so much for me." I said. She gave me an envelope.

"I've spoken to the Mother Superior who is expecting you at the nursing home. Take care, Ida."

I couldn't take any more. I gave a big kiss to Renata, a last cuddle to Gabriella, picked up the suitcase, rushed downstairs, ran to the car, got in and we left.

At this time of the morning there was a lot of traffic but eventually we got through town. Then, to my surprise, Andrew stopped the car.

"Why have you stopped, Andrew?" I asked him.

"Before you disappear for good, Ida." he said, "I'd like to talk to you." I took a good look at him. He was quite good looking!

"What about?"

"I would like to take you out dancing or to the cinema." he said, "Would you like that?"

"Well, Andrew, I can't dance!"

"I'm not a good dancer myself," he laughed, "in fact, I'm taking dancing lessons. I tell you what: why don't you come with me? We can both learn. Would you like that?" I thought about it for a while.

"You know, Andrew," I said, "I think I would like that!" Then I thought, I've not even arrived at my aunty's house and I've already agreed to go out with a man. I'm only sixteen and aunty and uncle are responsible for my wellbeing; they wouldn't ever permit such a thing! What will they think of me?

"Andrew," I said, "my aunty has only seen you a couple of times so she doesn't know you yet. Let's be friends for a while before we go dancing together."

"Whatever you suggest." he said.

"If you really like me, come and visit me at aunty's house so they can get to know you and maybe then they'll allow me to come out with you." I said.

"Yes, you are right, Ida, that was silly of me. I never thought about your position. Now I fully understand what you mean. You know what? I'll write to you and we can take from it there." He started the car and drove on to aunty's.

We both got out of the car and Andrew picked up the cases and walked with me to the door.
"There you are, Ida." Aunty came to the door and said,
"Welcome home, Ida. Ask the young man in for a espresso coffee."
"Oh," I said, "Andrew, aunty is inviting you in for a cup of espresso."
"Thank you, I would really appreciate that." he said, picking up the suitcases and coming in. Aunty was in the kitchen busy at the stove.
"Ida, ask the young man to sit down." she said, pointing to a chair near the table. When the coffee was ready aunty served it in beautiful little porcelain cups with special coffee biscuits. Then she said to him,
"How long you have been working with the countess?"
"A couple of years."
"The countess has a beautiful villa in the village, the only one that wasn't destroyed by the war. They often came and spent long holidays there. Ida was very lucky to be with the countess. She is a very kind lady." aunty said.
"I've been there and agree with you, it is beautiful. All the family are very nice people."
"It will be difficult for Ida to go to work in the factory with all those girls. She is very young and inexperienced to be with a lot of people she's never seen before."
"Signora Catharine I'm taking dancing lessons. Would you give permission for Ida to come to have some dancing lessons with me?" She was shocked and for a moment she didn't know what say. Then she said,
"Why not? As long as Elena can go with you both."
"That would be fine." Andrew said, "I must go now otherwise the countess will want to know where I am. Thank you for the coffee and for looking after Ida. I know the countess is very worried about her. Ida, I'll pick up you and Elena tomorrow night at seven p.m. Signora Catharine, thank you again and don't worry about the girls. I will look after them."
"You'd better!" she said. We walked back to the car and before he got inside, he turned and waved. Then he drove off.

Elena came in and said,

"Mummy, I saw a beautiful car near our house. Is daddy going to buy it?"

"Oh," she said, "if your father wins the lottery! But you can go in that car tomorrow with Ida to have a dancing lesson. What do you think about that?" aunty said.

"Oh mummy, that would be just wonderful!" Elena said. I was also very happy about Elena coming with us as it made me feel more secure. Aunty said,

"Ida, come with me and I'll show you to your room." Once again I picked up my cases and followed her.

The room was rather small and almost bare. There was a chair and a small wardrobe with several drawers.

"Put your things away and then come to the kitchen and I'll make you another cup of coffee, if you like." aunty said and left. I opened the cases, sorted everything out and put it all away. In a corner hanging on the wall was a small mirror. I looked at myself.

"Not bad, Ida." I mumbled and then I tried the bed. It was nice and soft. "I should be all right here." I said to myself. I left the room and went back to the kitchen.

"Everything sorted out?" aunty asked, "Here is your coffee, just made." Two coffees in a very short time, I thought to myself, I do hope I will manage to get some sleep tonight!

"Yes, aunty, thank you. Everything is in place." I sat down and tried the coffee. It was not too strong.

"Well, Ida, from now on you'll be with us. I will wash your things and do the cleaning. I would like to treat you as a guest but times are hard. However, until you are qualified and get full wages, you need only pay six thousand lire per month. Are you happy with that?"

"Yes, aunty, thank you. I'm more than satisfied." I got up and went to my room. I'd forgotten about the envelope. It wasn't sealed. Inside were two sheets of paper and twenty thousand lire! I was rich! Together with my own money, I now had fifty thousand lire! One note was for the Mother Superior, the other was from Gabriella and read:

> 'This is your salary for the month plus extra for you to buy the things you need. Come and see us some time!
> Love, Gabriella.'

As I've said many times, she was a real treasure. I will never forget her. I could feel my eyes growing wet and I put the other note back in the envelope and sealed it. Tomorrow I would go to see the Mother Superior. Why does everybody like me? I'm nothing special!

I was just combing my hair when Elena came in.
"Would you like come with me, Ida?" she said, "I'm going to the shop."
"Yes, Elena, I will come with you," I said, "but another time, knock, all right?"
"Sorry, Ida." she said, "Another time I will." I put my coat on and on the way out I shouted,
"I'm going to the shop with Elena, aunty." Without waiting for an answer we went out.

Elena seemed to know her way around the city. It was not too hot but the sun was shining. We stopped at a bar and I bought two ice-creams and that made Elena very happy. The streets were full of people, mostly young men and women who probably worked in offices and were out for lunch. I kept stopping and looking at the shop windows. There were so many beautiful things, things I had never seen before! One day, I thought, when I have plenty of money, I will buy beautiful dresses, comfortable shoes, warm coats…. I shook myself. Stop dreaming, Ida! You're going to be a factory worker with a miserable ten thousand lire per month! Then I reproached myself. Stop complaining: you have a place to live and a job to go to, what more do you want from life? A few months back I thought it would never happen, but it had!

"Ida, there is the shop." a voice said. I'd forgotten about Elena. The shop she was going into was a grocer's. She bought potatoes and vegetables. Then we turned back. At the bar I bought two more ice-creams and this time we sat down to eat them. When it was time to go home, I took the bag from Teresa and we went back.
"Where have you been?" aunty said, "You have been away for a long time." Then she saw a bit of ice-cream on Telena's top lip and laughed.
"Who paid for it?" she asked.
"Ida paid for it, mum. We had two." Elena said.
"Rolling in money, are you?" and again she laughed.
Elena laid the table and I went to my room to read a bit of my

Elena

"Lunch is ready." Both Natalino and my uncle were working so we were on our own. Aunty had cooked spaghetti *al sugo e frittata di spinach* (pasta with tomato sauce and spinach omelette). I enjoyed the meal. Later I did the washing up and then went back to my room. What am I going to do this afternoon? I thought. Then it came to me. There was something I wanted, something I had dreamed of for a long time. Now I could afford it. A little watch! I will go out and buy one. Elena must know where to buy one. I opened the door and there she was.

"Are you coming with me for a stroll, Elena?" I asked her.

"Oh yes," she said, "where are we going?"

"I want to buy a watch. I'm sure you know where I can get one."

"Yes, I know somewhere not too far away."

"Right. Let's go then."

We got on our way. Once more I noticed how well Elena knew her way around the streets. She stopped and pointed.

"There it is." There in front of me were hundreds of watches, little ones, big ones, some silver and some in gold. I bet they are expensive, I said to myself. Well, let's go in and see. We went in.

"What can I do for you two little ladies?" the man behind the counter asked.

"I want to buy a watch." He put his hands under the counter and took out several to show us. They were beautiful. I picked one.

"How much is this one?" I asked.

"Ten thousand lire." he said. Then he saw the look on my face. He put his hands under the counter again and came up with different watches.

"These are stainless steel." he said, "They are only three thousand."

"That's more like it. I'll have this one." I pointed my finger at one and he tried it on my wrist. It fitted perfectly. He took it off and put it in a box and gave it to me.

"It is a twenty-four hour watch. Remember to wind it up every night." I paid and we went out. It was nearly two o'clock, time to go home.

When we got home and I was going to my room, I heard Teresa say,

"We ate another ice-cream and Ida bought herself a watch." I smiled to myself. Now auntie will realise I'm no longer a little girl!

Uncle John and Natalino had come home.

"Have you settled in all right, Ida?" uncle asked.

"Yes, uncle, thank you." I answered. We sat down and had supper. Later I did the washing up.

"Elena and I are going out tonight. Andrew is coming to take us to a dancing lesson."

"Mum, which dress shall I wear?" said Elena.

"Put on your new one," auntie said, "the one with the pink flowers. With your blonde hair and brown eyes, you will look just beautiful, as always."

"Mum, can I have some money so I can take the dancing lesson as well?" said Elena "I don't want just to be Ida's chaperone."

"I'm afraid I can't give you any money." aunty said, "Your father doesn't get paid before the end of the month."

"Aunty," I said, "I will pay for Elena's dancing lesson."

"Thank you, Ida." Elena said and put her arms round my neck and gave me a big kiss.

"Andrew seems a nice lad," aunty said, "but do be careful, you two."

"We will, aunty. We are just good friends and I'm too young for anything more." She smiled and left. I left my room and the bell rang. I rushed to the door. Andrew was there, all done up and looking very nice. He looked at me and whistled.

"Let's go." he said. We got in the car and drove off.

Andrew drove for about twenty minutes and then stopped. We were in a square and right in front I could see a church. Almost opposite was a low building. I could hear music and realised that it came from that low building. We got out of the car, went in the building and up a flight of stairs. On the landing was a desk where Andrew stopped, said a few words to the young lady behind it and we all went into a large room. On the floor about twenty couples and some children about the same age as Elena were moving around, following the instructions shouted by a lady. The children seemed to be following the instructions better than the grown-ups. On one side there were tables and chairs and we sat down. He told the lady that we were partners for that evening.

"If you and Elena like what you see," Andrew said, "you can book some lessons. Five lessons cost three thousand lire. What do you two want to drink?" He took me by surprise. It was the first time that a man had offered me a drink! What I should say? I thought for few seconds then I remembered that Gabriella had bought me a drink which I liked.

"I'll have a fruit juice, please, Andrew." I said. He turned to Elena and said,

"What about you, little flower?"

"The same as Ida, please, Andrew." He went to the bar and came back with three drinks on a tray.

"Would you like to have a try?" he said, pointing to the dance floor. Try? I thought why not? I got up and we joined the other couples. Andrew put his arms around my waist and I tried my best to follow the lady's instructions and the rhythm of the music. At first our feet got in each other's way. It was mostly my fault. But slowly we managed to do it right. I looked for Elena and was surprised to see she was enjoying herself with another child.

Now we were actually dancing!

"You are a natural dancer! It won't take long for you to learn." Andrew whispered in my ear.

"Go on!" I said, smiling. The music stopped and we went back to our table and the drinks. I'd enjoyed myself!

"What was that dance?" I asked.

"A waltz. Did you like it?" he said.

"Yes, I did. I think I will book some lessons." We had a few more dances and then it was time to go home. On our way out Elena said,

"Ida, stop at the desk. We want to book some lessons for both of us."

"Yes, we want to learn." Then we got into the car and Andrew drove us home.

"Bye, Ida, bye, Elena. I'll pick you both up next Saturday." He bent over and kissed me on the cheek. He left, and for few minutes we just stood there. Then my hand went to my cheek and I touched it gently.

Aunty had given us the key. We opened the door and went in.

"We must go straight to bed," I said to Elena and gave her a kiss. A few minutes later we were in bed. That Saturday night I could not get to sleep. I looked at my watch. Eleven o'clock. I'd been in bed for over an hour! In my room at Gabriella's I just touched the sheets and fell asleep. What was wrong with me? Again my hand went to my cheek. I felt confused. My mind was in turmoil. It was my first kiss from a man, but it was not just the kiss. It was some thing else. When Andrew had put his arms around my waist, I felt a peculiar but pleasant sensation. Then, during the dance when our bodies touched, the sensation increased all over my body!

What was it? Tomorrow I'd ask aunty, she would tell me.

On Sunday morning I woke up and looked at my watch. Eight o'clock. I had slept after all! I jumped out of bed, got dressed and went to the kitchen. Aunty was already busy at the stove. I sat at the table, had some breakfast and told her all about it. She laughed.
"Ida," she said, "you are a young woman. What you felt is a very normal thing. Your blood and your body reacted to the physical nearness of a man. How do you think I had my children? When God sent Adam and Eve out of Eden, He told them to go forth and multiply. He had given them something for that and what God gave them, we have inherited. That something is pleasure. It has partly to do with having children. When you find the right man, you will find out."

It was still a bit confusing but I was beginning to understand. This had to be what the big girls in the village had called 'sex'. But I was very young and I had ample time to find out. There were more important things to do.
"How do I get to the nursing home?" I asked aunty.
"Walk to the top of the road, turn right and right again and you will get there." she said. So I went back to my room, picked up the letter and was on my way.

It looked more like a hospital than a nursing home. It was a very large place and behind the counter was a nun.
"Excuse me, sister," I said, "I would like to see the Mother Superior. I have a letter to show her." She pushed a bell and a few seconds later a young nun arrived.
"Take this young lady to the Mother Superior."
"Please follow me." the young nun said and I followed her. We went all the way upstairs and she knocked on a door.
"Come in." a voice said and we went in.
"This young lady has asked to see you, Madre." the nun said. It was a small room and sitting behind a big desk was another nun. She gave me a sign to sit down. I gave her the letter. She opened the envelope and read it, then smiled.
"Ah, Gabriella." she said, "She has done a lot for us! So, you want to learn about nursing?"
"Yes please, Madre. I wanted to be a doctor but because of the war I could not get any education. I'd like to look after sick people."

"Are you working at the moment?" she said.

"I'm starting a job tomorrow in a factory." I said.

"And if I said 'yes', when could you come?" she said.

"I could come Saturdays and Sundays. I live just up the road. It is only a short walk."

"Well, my girl, I like you and I say 'yes'. Come and learn here. You can have meals with us. All right?" she said.

"Yes!" I almost shouted, "Thank you with all my heart, Madre. Goodbye."

"Goodbye, Ida. We'll see you next Saturday." she said. I left her office and made my way back home.

When I got to my room a thought came to me. I still didn't know how to get to the factory. I decided to ask my uncle or aunty. I went into the kitchen but uncle was nowhere around so I asked aunty.

"Well," she said, "at the top of our alleyway, turn right. After about a hundred metres there is a bus stop. Take the number five. It will have Termini Station written on it. When you get there, ask one of the security guards, there's always one there, for the Grotti Celoni. I'm quite sure he will take you there or he will tell you how to get there. Your uncle drives the bus to the Mila."

"Thank you, aunty," I said, "that's another thing sorted out." I went back to my room and picked up my book. I looked at the watch. It was past twelve, time for lunch. I put down my book and went to the dining room. They were all there. I sat myself down and we had lunch.

"Catharine said about you getting to the Mila." my uncle said, "Don't worry, I will talk to the security man and he'll look out for you."

"Thank you, Uncle John, that's very kind of you."

"Well, you are family."

"What are you doing this afternoon, Ida?" my cousin Natalino asked.

"Nothing special really. Why?"

"There is a good film on at the Odeon. It's *Quo Vadis*. I thought that maybe we could go to and see it." I was very surprised. I knew what films were but I'd never seen one.

"Yes, I...."

"It's a story set in ancient Roman times after Jesus was crucified. It's about the persecution of the Christians. I've been told that it is a masterpiece. It starts at three, so we should leave the house at two to get good seats." It was all settled and I went back to my room to study a bit and wait for his call.

A knock came. I was ready. We went out and began to walk. It was quite a long walk but at last we stopped at a bus stop and shortly after the bus arrived. We got on it.
"Two for St Agnese." Natalino said and before he had a chance to get his wallet out, I paid for the tickets. We sat down. St Agnese reminded me of something. Then I remembered that about three weeks ago Gabriella had come into my room.
"Today," she said, "I want to show you something nice and very old. Get yourself ready. Maria will look after Renata."

"Natalino," I said, "I never saw so many beautiful pictures. There were lovely glass candelabra. The whole church was a picture. We stayed there for a little while and she took me to see the catacomb where the first Mass was celebrated. In those days they lit torches. During the tourist season there are better lights, but at this time of year, Gabriella said, not many people visit."
"It was very nice of Gabriella to take you there." Natalino said, "From what I've been told, she is a nice lady."
"She is a very special lady." I said.
"I agree, she is one of the best." he said.

The bus stopped in the square and there was the church. It was the same one. I thought of Renata and missed them all. I looked at my watch. Nearly three o'clock. My little girl is having her bath now, I said to myself. Well, that is life. We got off the bus and walked a little way, went inside the cinema to the ticket hatch behind which sat a woman.
"Two tickets, please, for front row seats." Natalino said. She gave them to me and he paid. We then gave them to a man at the door. Natalino seemed to know all about this, but for me it was a new experience. He took off his jacket and put down the seat.
"Make yourself comfortable." he said. I took a look around. There weren't many people. In front of me was what looked like a very large white sheet. That must be the screen, I thought. Natalino gave me a little bag.
"What is it?" I asked.
"Open it and see." he said. I opened the bag. Inside was what in the village we called *granturco*, but this was blown up.
"Popcorn. It comes from America." Natalino said, "Try it!" I did and it was delicious! The lights went out and the big sheet lit up. The film began.

It was a beautiful story, just like Natalino had said. As it spooled on I saw the Coliseum and the catacombs as they looked in olden days. It was an experience I would never forget. When it ended, we left and walked back to the square, caught the bus and went home.

"Thank you, Natalino." I said, "This was a marvellous thing to have done for me." He just smiled. It was nearly supper time so I went to my room to change my clothes, then went back to the dining room and sat down with the others. We had supper then Natalino and I played cards for a while. My uncle stood up.

"Good night to you all." he said, "I'm off to bed." I looked to my watch. It was only nine o'clock!

"He has to get up at five." aunty said. Natalino got up, too.

"I'm off as well. Good night." And he was off.

"How was the film?" aunty asked.

"It was marvellous, aunty." She was taking the dishes away and I realised that she wasn't really interested. I got up and did the washing up.

"Good night, aunty. I'm going to bed."

"Good luck with your job, Ida." she said.

I lay in bed thinking about the film. Then I remembered aunty's words. The job! I'd forgotten about the next day when I would start my new job. All of a sudden I was scared. There will be a lot of strange girls. Will they accept me or make fun of me? For the second time I missed the security of my home, of my mother and father, of my Aunty Lauretta and my cousins. Once again I felt like a lost child and the thought of the unknown made me shake like a leaf. I put my head under the sheets to hide and shed a few tears. Gradually I began to calm myself down. I was a grown up girl. I could cope with anything. I would show them!

On Monday morning I woke up early and felt great. I'd regained confidence and now I was ready for anything. I got dressed, went to the kitchen for some breakfast and said goodbye to aunty. Just as she'd said, the bus stop was just a short way up the road. I waited for a number five bus to arrive and jumped on it.

"Termini." I said to the driver. He gave me a ticket and off we went. The journey took about twenty minutes. When I got off, I saw a man in uniform.

"Excuse me, could you please take me to where Mr John is? I'm his niece."

"John told me you would be coming. Follow me." he said. He was very nice. I followed him and there was my uncle, who had seen me coming.

"Ida, you are just in time." he said, "Will you please jump on that one?" He pointed to one of the Grotti Celoni. "I'm the driver and I'll take you right there."

"Thank you, Uncle Ezio." After a few minutes we left.

The Grotti Celoni was full of women, mostly young, some middle aged. They must have come from all over the city. There was an empty seat and I sat in it beside a woman who looked about forty. She had a nice face.

"Pardon me," she said, "are you going to the Mila?"

"Yes." I said, "It is my first day and I'm scared. I've never worked in a factory before."

"Nothing to be scared about." she said, "Have you done this job before?"

"Yes, with my aunty. But the weaving was done by hand." She laughed.

"Well, it's much easier with a machine! You'll soon learn. Tell me, you are not from Rome. Where do you come from?"

"From Catailli, a little village about twenty kilometres from Cassino."

"Ah, Cassino! That's the place where they fought all those battles." Her voice had changed. "My brother died there." she almost whispered. She still feels the pain, I thought. She cleared her throat.

"I'm so sorry about your brother." She didn't say anything.

"Tell me," she said after a while, "have you been working in Rome?"

"Yes, I've been looking after a little girl for a countess..." She put her hand on my mouth and I couldn't finish the words. It scared me. For a moment I wanted to run away, but I controlled myself. I remembered that there was no other way but to continue to do this. It would only be temporary until I saved enough money to do what I really want to do. She removed her hand.

"There are many nice girls that work in the factory, but there are also many nasty ones. They'll pick on you and make your life here miserable, first because you are a newcomer and second because you are nice girl. But don't worry. I'll look after you. By the way, my name is Giuliana and I'm a chargehand."

"Thank you, Giuliana." I said, "I'm very grateful for your kind words."

The Grotti Celoni had arrived and my uncle saw that I'd already made a friend.

"Goodbye, uncle." I said, "I'll see you tonight." He gave me a smile and I followed everyone getting off. I stayed close to Giuliana.

"Go to see the Personnel Manager." she said, "He'll take you around the factory and I'll see you inside." She left. I went to the office and knocked at the door.

"Come in." a voice said and I entered. The man I had met at the interview smiled at me.

"Good morning, sir." I said.

"Good morning to you, Miss Festa." he replied, "I'll be with you in a minute." He sorted out a few papers on his desk and got up. "Come with me and I'll take you in."

We left his office and went into the factory building. There were more than fifty women there. I noticed that some of the young ones were walking back and forth carrying rolls of cotton. Maybe, I thought, they were learning the job. I saw Giuliana and she waved. All this time the manager was just looking at me. A woman of about thirty was coming towards us.

"Anna," he said when she reached us, "Miss Festa has just joined us. Her name's Ida. I'll leave her in your hands." He nodded his head in salute and left.

"Well, Ida," Anna said, "What do you think?" She made a gesture with her arm towards the workers.

"Very impressive." I said, "I've only worked on a little handloom before!"

"You'll soon get used to the machine." Anna said, "You'll probably find it easier than doing it by hand!" Giuliana was coming towards us. Anna saw her.
"I must go now. Giuliana is one of our chargehands and will tell you what to do. I hope you'll be happy here." Then she left.

At last the week was over. Giuliana asked me if I wanted to work on the following Saturday for overtime but I said no, thank you, as I had a previous appointment. I went out to the Grotti Celoni and home.
"Well," aunty asked me, "are you happy with your work? I think you might have found out by now." For a time I did not know what say.
"I suppose it is all right. What's for dinner? I'm famished!" I said.
After a while I went to my room, sat down and thought about it. I had mixed feelings. The work was all right but a bit boring, much too repetitive. In the morning we started at half past seven. We all went down to another floor where there was a store with all kinds of material for weaving cotton, silk, hemp and linen. There were also large baths. A chargehand told us what to use for the day. We washed all the raw material and hung it up to dry. There was a pump blowing hot air and when the material was dry we took it upstairs. We had nothing to do with the machines. Men worked on them, one man per machine. Each frame had thee shuttles and we fed raw material into them. It was converted into thread and rolled up. Every machine had a meter and we had to watch it. If at any time the meter reached 70, we had to shout to the man in charge to stop his machine, unload the sheet, roll it up and take it down to the store. One of the chargehands would come with us, make an entry on a label, stick it on the roll and that was it.

I had made a few friends among the girls. I liked one in particular very much, Angelina. But there was one who didn't like me. Her name was Carla. Every time we worked together she would call me names, push me or sometimes pull my hair or knock the material out of my hands. I got tired of it, but she was a big girl and I was a bit afraid of her. I should have reported her but Angelina advised me not to. I would have been considered a snitch by the other girls.
"Just ignore her." she said, so I did nothing. Anyway, I had

something nice to look forward to. Tomorrow night I was going dancing with Andrew and on Sunday I was going to the nursing home. To hell with Carla! I hate her! I picked up my book and immersed myself in it.

There was a knock at the door. It was Elena
"Supper is ready." she said. I put my book down and followed her.
"Thank you, Elena" We went into the dining room and sat at the table. They were all there, uncle and Natalino included. We ate minestrone soup and omelettes with salad. After the meal it was time for me to get ready. Andrew would be arriving soon. I went to my room, put on my best dress and looked in the mirror. I heard the bell and rushed to the door. Andrew looked at me and whistled.
"Go on, you!" I joked. We got in the car and left.

The evening was over. It had been nice. We were now in tune and enjoyed ourselves. On the door step, Andrew tried to kiss me on the mouth but I turned my face so the kiss landed on my cheek.
"I like you, Andrew," I said, "but I'm too young to get involved. Let's be friends." He didn't say anything, just smiled and went on his way. In my room I thought about him. He is nice and kind and good looking. I shook myself.
"You've got plenty of time, Ida, plenty of life lies ahead." I said to myself. I got undressed and into bed. I had no trouble sleeping now. I had a lot to look forward to. Besides, I would not stay at the Mila for ever.

Another day dawned. I had a good wash, combed my hair then went back to the bedroom and put on one of the dresses Gabriella had given to me. I had a look in the mirror and said to myself,
"You look all right, Ida. This brings out the best in you." I went to the dining room where all the family were waiting for breakfast. I sat at the table and Elena looked at me in admiration.
"Look at Ida, mother! Doesn't she look nice?" Aunty brought my plate and looked me all over.
"That is a nice dress." she said, "Where did your mother buy it?"
"She didn't buy it. Gabriella gave it to me." I ate my breakfast and was ready to go. "I won't be home for lunch or supper, aunty." I said and left.

After a short walk I was there. The same nun greeted me.
"Good morning, Miss Festa." she said.

"Good morning, sister." I replied, "Please call me Ida."

"I'm Sister Elena." she said and together we went upstairs to a very large room with about twenty beds. There were only women in there and they all looked quite old. Some were lying in bed, others were sitting on chairs. Sister Elena introduced me.

"This young lady is Ida." she said, "Today she will look after you. If you need anything, just ask her."

"Welcome, Ida." they said, almost in one voice, "Nice to meet you."

"There are other people in private rooms as well." sister said, "Come with me and we'll go to see them." So I followed her.

There were ten small rooms and in each one was a man or a woman. Once again, Sister Elena introduced me and they greeted me. I was very, very pleased.

"There's not much you can do for them at moment," she said, "but later on you will look after these people as well. You are a clever girl and you will learn. I'm sure you will do your best. Now we'll go back to the main room. Lunch is at twelve o'clock. Come with me and I'll show you where the refectory is." I followed her as she showed me around and then I went back to the main room.

"Do what you can for these ladies," she said, "and if there's something that you can't cope with, call the one of the sisters." She showed me the bell and left.

For a while I didn't know what to do. I sat and waited.

"Ida!" a voice called, "Can you get me some water?" I looked and saw in one of the beds an old lady moving her hand. I got up, went to her, picked up an empty jug and went to the bathroom to fill it. When I returned I filled up her glass.

"Thank you, Ida." she said with a smile. After that I had no peace. There were about twenty women in the room and every one of them wanted something. I enjoyed doing it. When I looked at my watch it was coming on for twelve o'clock, so I got up.

"See you, ladies." I went to the refectory for lunch.

I thought I would find only nuns but to my surprise there were quite a few young girls there. As I went in, one of them who was about my age looked at me. She was quite pretty with long, fair hair.

"My name is Carolina," she said, "but you can call me Lina." That was nice, I thought. I extended my hand.

"Pleased to meet you, Lina. My name is very short: Ida." I said. She shook my hand with a firm grip.

"My pleasure, Ida. Tell me, where do you come from?"

"I come from a little village in the Campania region. Tell me, Lina, do you want become a nurse?" She laughed.

"Oh no," she said, "I want to become a doctor. I'm studying. I come here in my spare time to get some practice." Her words made me sad. She must have realised because she put her hand on my shoulder.

"What's wrong, Ida?" she asked. I tried to calm myself.

"Nothing, Lina." I said, "You see, since I was a little girl I've dreamed that I would become a doctor. The war in my village decided differently. Because of it, I could not get a proper education and now I have realised that it's too late. But I'll be happy to become a nurse." Her hand tightened on my shoulder.

"It's never too late." she said, "Where there's a will …..! However, a nurse is as good as a doctor. Doctors could do nothing without nurses."

"I agree with you, Lina, but I'm famished! I'll go and get us some lunch." I said and stood up and went to the counter. Sister Elena was dishing out the food.

"Everything all right, Ida?" she asked.

"Fine, sister, thank you." I picked up the full dishes and went back to the table. We were too busy eating to do any more talking.

"See you tonight." Lina said.

"Yes." I said, "I'll see you, Lina."

Once again I was very busy, only little things but they kept me going from one bed to another so the time went past quickly. I'd just sat down when a shout made me jump.

"The butcher is here!" shouted the lady who had wanted the water earlier. I looked at the door. My new friend Lina was just coming in with a large tray in her hands. The old lady smiled and made a sign with her finger, like stabbing. At first, I was confused but then I understood. Lina would give injections to some of the ladies. She started on her round. At each bed she looked at the forms and then selected something from the tray. I could tell that all the ladies loved her. She was very quick at her work and was soon at the last bed.

"Ida, come here." she said. I was surprised but went to her. She showed me the syringe.

"Have you ever given an injection, Ida?" she asked me.

"No, I haven't." I said

"Well, this lady needs two injections. I'll give her one and you watch." She bent down and inserted the needle.

"You try. Push the needle gently for about two centimetres, then push the plunger slowly until it's empty." I was scared but I tried it. The old lady didn't even flinch. I was over the moon. I had given my first injection! The old lady looked at me and smiled.

"You know, Ida, you have got a very light hand." she said, and that moved me so much I could have cried! After that it was just routine: straighten a pillow here, help a lady to sit, adjust a bed. One of the ladies had made a mess with her food so I had to clean her and change the sheets.

From Luisa, a frail old lady, I learned a few things. The nursing home was run by the Vatican and only the people in private rooms paid. One of the nuns was a doctor and two nuns were full-time nurses. There were about fifteen young girls like Lina doing voluntary work. The nuns hoped that one day they would be able to join the Benedictine order. When we left, others would come in to do the night shift.

It was all quiet. I looked at my watch: nearly seven. It was time for supper.

"Good night, ladies," I said, "be good!" They all laughed.

"Good night Ida." I went to the refectory and sat down at one of the tables. A few minutes later Lina came in and went straight to the counter. Then she put her plate on my table and sat down.

"How did it go?" she asked.

"Well, just routine. And you?"

"A few more injections to the private patients." she said, "Nothing special. Where do you live, Ida?"

"Not very far from here, five minutes walk." I finished my meal and stood up.

"I'm off. Bye, Lina."

"Bye, Ida. See you tomorrow." For a few seconds I didn't say anything.

"Well," I said, "I can't come tomorrow. You see, Lina, I'm working in a factory." She looked at me a bit surprised.

"Ida, Ida," she said, squeezing my shoulder, "there is nothing wrong in working at a factory. Not everyone can afford to do sweet nothing. See you next Sunday." I could have kissed her.

"See you next Sunday, Lina." I was on my way out when she called me. I stopped and turned around.

"Are you working on Saturday, Ida?" she asked.

"No, I finish working on Friday night. Why?"

"Well, my family came from Viterbo only few months back and I don't know anyone in Rome yet. I thought that we might go out somewhere together. You are a likeable girl and we get on nicely together. What do you say? I've got a little car." she said.

"I like you as well and, like you, I don't know anybody. I live at Fanfulla da Lodi, number eighteen." She smiled.

"Good, I'll pick you up at two on Saturday afternoon. Take care."

I woke up suddenly and took a quick look at my watch. It was late. I dressed in the bathroom, splashed some water on my face and went for breakfast. I must buy myself an alarm clock! While I was eating Natalino came in. Shall I ask him? Yes.

"Natalino, I need a favour." I said.

"Anything for my lovely cousin!" he said. I knew he was joking but I didn't have time.

"I need a small alarm clock. Can you buy me one? Not too expensive. I'm always late in the mornings." He looked at me and smiled.

"Yes, cousin, I will." he said.

Thank God the week was over. I was in my room reading a book. Soon Elena would come and call me for supper. It was a funny week! For the first three days Carla had never left me alone. She messed about with my shuttles and once she had kicked me.

"Go back to your cows and your pigs." she had said, spitefully, giving me a push, "We don't want you here." Angelina had tried to make her stop but Carla had turned on her quite nastily and kept on bothering me. Then the chargehand, who must have seen Carla's behaviour, came over and sent her to work on the machine at the other end. I was quite relieved. Now I would have a bit of peace. It was Friday afternoon. In a few hours the week would be over. Suddenly I saw Carla leaving her machine and coming towards me. Oh, not again! I thought. She came and gave me a push that nearly knocked me over.

"Stop that!" I heard somebody shout. Carla stopped. I looked up. It was Giuliana, looking very angry.

"Leave her alone!" she almost shouted, "Just because you were born in Trastevere and Ida was born in a mountain village, you think yourself superior. She is better than you. You have left your machine without permission. If you do it again and keep bothering her, you may get the sack." Carla looked at me in a nasty way but went back to her machine.

"Thank you very much, Giuliana." I said. She smiled.

"She will leave you alone now." she said and caressed my face.

I left the factory and when I got home, another surprise: Marta had brought me a letter. I opened it. It was from Andrew. He was very sorry but he was unable to pick me up on Saturday. The count and Gabriella's husband and mother were back from America and he had to drive the count to Milan on business. Did I have to say goodbye to dancing? Teresa and I still had three lessons to go. I decided to ask Natalino to take us there, or, better still, tomorrow I would see Lina and I could ask her.

I went to my bedroom to change and there on wardrobe shelf was a little clock. Natalino had left a note with instructions. He was a good lad. I changed. After supper I played cards with Elena then it was time for bed. Lately I had had trouble getting to sleep, but tonight I would sleep like a log. I had too much to look forward to. I wound up both my watch and the clock and closed my eyes.

In the morning I felt marvellous. After breakfast I would go to the shops with Elena and then do a bit of studying. I was looking forward to the afternoon when Lina had said she would take me on a drive around Rome. It was ten o'clock. Soon Natalino would come home. He worked on a shift from ten to ten. The note said that he'd paid three thousand lire for the clock, so I got the money ready for him.
"Here is your money, Natalino. Thank you again."
"Don't mention it." he said.
"Are you coming, Ida ?" Elena asked
"Yes, Elena. I'm coming." and off we went to the shops.

On the way back I carried the bag. It was quite heavy and it was a long walk. No ice cream today, the weather was quite cold. I put the bag in the kitchen, went to my room, combed my hair and then lunch was ready. They were all there, including Uncle John, who also worked shifts. We had our lunch and then I told him about Carla.
"Someone should teach her a lesson." he said.
"Well, uncle, I'm sure that it will be all right now. She is well away from me and she has got be careful or she'll get the sack."
"All the same, it is not right." my aunty said. After lunch I went to my room to get ready and looked at my watch. Just gone half past one. I took my time then I heard the doorbell. I gave a last stroke to my hair and went to the door. To my surprise I saw Natalino there talking to Lina. The two of them were so engrossed they hardly noticed me. I gave a little cough and they turned round.

"Ciao!" Lina said, "Are you ready?" She took her eyes off Natalino and looked at me.

"Where are we going?" I asked

"Around and about."

"Before we go, Lina, I have a favour to ask. Tonight Elena and I are supposed go to our dancing lesson but unfortunately the person who takes us is not available." Lina didn't let me finish.

"Of course I'll take you both" she said.

"I'd like to come to as well." Natalino said. She looked at him and smiled.

"With pleasure" she said. So it was all sorted out. I smiled to myself. My plan had worked! We got into the little car and left.

"I don't know anything about Rome." I said as we drove through the city, "I've seen the Coliseum, the Sistine Chapel, the Catacombs and St Agnese's church and that's the lot." Lina drove into a little alleyway and stopped the car. She got a little book out of her bag and looked through it.

"I will take you to the Palatino." she said, "It's near the River Tiber. In my opinion the best of the ancient Roman masterpieces are there. The Romans were fantastic builders and what remains gives a good idea of their civilisation." We went through many streets full of people strolling along. Then she stopped in a large area where lots of cars were parked, got out, went to the slot machine nearby, put some coins in and stuck the ticket on the car window.

"Let's go." she said. We walked for a bit then suddenly before my eyes were beautiful squares filled with buildings, fountains and beautiful columns. Many were just ruins, but still showed the skill of the builders and artists.

"That is the Quirinale, the place where the senators used to make the law." Lina said, "And this complex is the Foro Romano. There's more. There is the Arch of Massimo Severio." It was a marvellous sight but I couldn't quite take it all in. Also I was getting a bit tired of all those ruins. Lina have must understood the way I felt because she said,

"You have seen Rome as it was. Now I'll take you to see the modern Rome."

We left and drove back to the city. As we were travelling along one street, I thought I recognised it.

"Lina, can you stop a minute?" I said to my companion. She stopped the car.

"What's wrong?" she asked.

"There's nothing wrong. I just want to check something. I won't be long." I got out of the car and walked around. I was right. It was where Gabriella lived. I got back in the car.

"Lina, I need to ask you another favour!"

"Yes, Ida, what is it?" she said.

"This is where Countess Gabriella lives. When I lived in my village, I looked after a baby who is the grand-daughter of Count Pallavicini. When his daughter, Gabriella, who is the mother of this little girl, came back to Rome, she brought me with her. I'm very attached to her and the little baby. I would like to see them." I said. Once again, Lina didn't let me finish.

"Of course, Ida, I'll take you. Was that the house you went to check?" Lina was a real friend, I thought. I had been very lucky to meet her.

"Yes, Lina," I said, "that was her address."

"Well, you tell me when you want to go and I will be here for you." Lina said. I had to make contact with Gabriella first to make sure she would be in. Lina started the car and we were on our way once again. She drove to a large square and stopped the car. I reconised it as St Agnese.

"Is this the place where we are going tonight?" I asked.

"That's enough for today. Let's go home." she said. We got back into the car and half an hour later arrived at my aunty's house.

"Would you come in for a drink, Lina?" But she wanted go.

"What time does it start tonight?" she asked.

"At half past seven." I said.

"Right. I'll pick the three of you up at seven o'clock." she said and left. I said goodbye to her, went inside and straight to my room. What a day we had had!

As usual, aunty was busy preparing supper.

"Aunty," I said, "what number does Marta live at?"

"Forty-three." she said, "Why are you asking?"

"Well, I would like see Gabriella and I want to ask if she can take a message to her."

"She lives just around the corner. Why don't you go to see her now?" she said.

"Good idea, aunty. I'll go and write a note. Aunty, have you any writing paper and an envelope?"

"You'll find some in the top drawer of the sideboard in the dining room."

"Thank you, aunty." I went to the dining room, found the paper and wrote the message. It was a short one. I just asked Gabriella to tell me when it was convenient for me to visit her. I sealed the envelope, walked to number forty-three and gave Marta the message.

"Would you please give this to Gabriella?" I said.

"Of course I will." she said. "How are you getting on at the Mila?"

"Quite well, but I'm looking for something better!"

"The best of luck." she said and patted my shoulder. I said goodbye and went back home. Later we had supper, then I went to my room to get ready. I'd just put on my best dress when there was a knock on door.

"Come in." I said. It was Natalino. He was all done up and looked very nice.

"What is her name?" he asked, "And where did you meet her?" I couldn't help laughing.

"Her name is Carolina, but you can call her Lina. I met her at the nursing home. She is studying to be a doctor. Her family come from Viterbo and I don't know how old she is." I said.

"Thank you, Ida, she is very nice." Natalino said and left the room.

We were in the lounge waiting when the bell went. Natalino stood up and ran to the door like a shot. I smiled to myself. Natalino had fallen in love. I wonder what it feels like, I thought as I went to the car. Lina lifted up the front seat for me and Elena to sit in the back. My cousin sat in the front and we drove off. They were so intent on talking and looking at each other that she nearly knocked over a man who was crossing the street. After that she concentrated on driving and we got there in one piece! We left the car and went upstairs. At the desk we had to leave our names, then we went inside and sat at a table.

The music started. No-one picked me up for the first dance so I got myself a drink, sat down and watched the others. At first their feet were getting in each other's way, but slowly they seemed to get the rhythm of the music and got in tune with each other. Elena and the boy she met the week before were dancing beautifully.

"I wish aunty and uncle were here," I said to myself, "I'm quite sure they would be very proud of their little daughter." While these thoughts were in my mind, a young man came to my table. I looked at him and he was smiling.

"Would you like to dance the next one with me?" he said.

"Yes, thank you." He was quite good looking but not in a feminine way. I stood up and surprised myself. I realised I could dance quite well and enjoyed myself.

The last dance was a competition for the young ones of Elena and Luigi's age. Lina, Natalino, myself and the young man sat at a table and enjoyed watching the young ones' competition. To our great surprise Elena and Luigi won the competition. We were all over the moon. Elena, since I bought my watch, kept asking aunty if she could have one, too, but aunty couldn't afford it. It was time to go home. The young man who danced with me was called George.
"Ida, see you next Saturday." He said and that was all.

Next morning I had somewhere to go. After breakfast I put on a nice dress and walked to the nursing home. As I went in, Sister Elena stopped me.
"Good morning, Ida." she said with a smile, "I'll come up with you to the main room. By the way, will you be with us for Christmas?"
"Well, sister, I haven't seen my parents for three months. I expect they'll want me to be home for the festivities at Christmas." I said.
"Oh, I understand. Your parents will want their children home for such an occasion. As you are just learning here, you can go home anytime you like. It is all right with us."

As we went in, an old lady shouted,
"Here comes the other butcher!" Sister looked at me.
"What does she mean?" she asked.
"It is a joke." I said, "She calls Lina 'the butcher' because she gives injections. Since I gave an injection, I'm 'the butcher' too."
"Oh yes, Lina told me about it. That is why I came with you. She is very busy in the private rooms so I thought you could give the injections to these ladies. There are only seven that need them." she said.
"I'll be happy to, sister, if you think I'm capable." I said.
"Right," sister said, "I'll come with you and you show me." Together we went into the large room.
"Here comes the other butcher!" the old lady shouted and all the others had a good laugh. Sister Elena showed me a large tray.
"Here are all the medicines which are needed." she said, "On each bed there is a chart. Look at it and choose the right medicine. Then take the liquid up into the syringe." As she was talking we were walking around. She stopped by one bed, looked at the chart and picked up a phial.
"Here you are, Ida. Have a try." she said, handing me a syringe

and the phial. I knew how to do it from what my aunt Lauretta had taught me in the village. I rubbed the phial with the little file and then cracked the top off. I inserted the needle and sucked in the liquid. The old lady was ready. I was about to give her the injection when a shout stopped me. I stood there confused.

"You have to push the air out of the syringe," Sister Elena said, "otherwise it is very dangerous." She took the syringe from my hands, pushed the plunger gently and let a few drops spill out.

"Now you can give the injection." she said, giving it back to me. No-one had ever told me that before. Now I gave the old lady her injection and she didn't flinch.

"Lina was right," sister said, "you have got a light hand. From now on this will be your job." She patted my shoulder and left.

I went on with the injections and had just finished when Lina came in.

"How are you doing?" she said.

"Quite well. I've done them all. I like doing it and I think I'm not too bad. What do you say, ladies?" I asked loudly.

"You have hands as light as a feather." one lady said.

"Yes, yes!" the others shouted. It was all in good fun.

"You have been a great help, Ida." Lina said, "I couldn't have coped with this room as well as the private rooms. Now I'll have a bit of a rest."

"It's for me to thank you," I said, "now I am learning nursing!" She laughed.

"You know, Ida, I like your cousin. How old is he?"

"Twenty-one, I think. And you, Lina?"

"I'm eighteen but I think I'm still too young. Nowadays boys want sex and I'm not that type of girl. To me, sex comes after the wedding. What do you think?"

"To tell you the truth, I will never, ever do anything like that. I come from a very strict background. If I did anything like that, my family would disown me. Besides, I'm a very firm believer in God and that is one of the commandments I will keep."

"By the way, when do you want to go and visit your former employer?" she asked.

"I've sent her a message and when I get the answer, I'll let you know."

"I must go now. See you at supper. You know I'm working on Saturday morning." she said and left the room. After that it was just the usual routine.

On Monday morning the postman came quite early and I received a letter from my parents. I didn't have time to read it so I took it with me to the Mila. I thought I would read it in my lunch hour. As usual it was another boring morning with Carla making fun of me. At lunch, Angelina had already got a table for both of us.

"Thank you, Angelina. I've had a rotten morning but there is one consolation: I received a letter from my parents. I do hope it's good news."

"While you read your letter, I'll go to the counter and get us some food." Angelina said. The letter was from my dad and he said,

'Dear Ida, your mother and I are looking forward to seeing you. It is three months you have been away from us and we have missed you very much. We don't want anything else for Christmas except for you to be here with us. Since the day you left, this house hasn't been the same. Please come home! As soon you receive this letter, do send an answer and give us good news.

All our love from Mum and Dad.'

This letter brought tears to my eyes. Angelina came with a tray full of food and said, "Ida, why you are crying? Whatever is the matter? Is your family all right?"

"Yes, I'm all right but my parents are asking me to go home for Christmas. I can do that. On the notice board it says that the factory will be closed from the 23rd to the 8th of January. I enjoy Rome very much. It is only Carla that makes me unhappy. But the thought that I haven't got to stay here forever makes it easier for me. I do thank you for your love and support, Angelina." I said.

Lunch was over and we had to return to our machines. I'd just inserted a new spool. It would be a long time before the meter reached 70 so I had plenty of time to think. I must write to my mother and father and Aunty Lauretta. I had missed them, too, but I'd been too busy thinking about my future. I needed to realise that my future was in God's hands. Tonight I would write to them and promise to be with them for Christmas, and then my conscience would be clear.

And so the day was over and at last it was time to go home. I caught the Grotti Celoni and went home. After supper I went to the lounge and wrote two long letters, one to my parents and one to Aunty Lauretta.

'Dear mother and father, today I received your letter and it pleased me to know you are both in good health. I have enjoyed my stay in Rome very much indeed. Aunty Catharine and Uncle John, the children and cousin Natalino are all very nice to me, but there is no place like home and this is even more so at Christmas time. Natalino and I will leave early on Thursday the 23rd and we should arrive in Mignano Di Monte Lungo about 11a.m. Anyway it will be before lunchtime. Can you meet us at the station, as we shall have lots of luggage? In some of my earlier letters I told you about the two jobs I have here in Rome. The Mila will be closed from the 23rd and the nursing home never closes but Mother Superior said I can leave when it is convenient for me to travel, which I think is very nice of her. In the nursing home I have met a very dear friend, Lina. She is studying to be a doctor and is a very trusted friend. Even Natalino likes her very much. Mum and Dad, I think this Christmas will be magic!

I saw some Christmas trees in a market in Corso Vittorio Emanuele. It was wonderful to see it early in the morning when all the housewives were buying vegetables and whatever they needed for their families. The trees looked very pretty but no one of them will meaning more to me like the one the American soldiers made for me when they were in our house and we sang 'Silent Night'. That was a beautiful moment which will remainder in my minder for the rest of my life .I hope every year to see snow on top of the mountain of Cesima.

I will ask Lina if she can take me to the best shopping centre in Rome to buy presents for you both and for all my cousins. A football for Mario and Alfredo, a nice shirt for VVincenzo, and many more things for the rest of the family. Mum and Dad you both must wait until I come home! For Aunty Lauretta and Aunty Nicolina. It will be a surprise. I can't say how much I want to see you all again. Will Uncle Giuseppe and Aunty Nicolina come to the station as well? Natalino is also very excited at the thought of his family being there to greet him. The 23rd of December can't come soon enough for both of us!

Love and good wishes from your daughter, Ida.'

Three more days had passed when I got home one evening and found the note that Marta had brought. It was short but made me very happy. She would be home all afternoon on Saturday, Gabriella said, and both she and Renata were looking forward to seeing me. On Saturday morning I walked to the nursing home and left a note for Lina. That morning I put on my best dress and spent some time in front the mirror.

"You'll do!" I said to myself, picked up my book and waited. About two o'clock Lina came and picked me up. I couldn't wait to see my little treasure. At this time of the day there was hardly any traffic, so we got there in a very short time.

"When do you want me to pick you up?" Lina asked. I wasn't quite sure.

"Make it two hours, Lina." I said, "If I leave before, I'll wait at the top of the street." I got out of the car and walked the short way to the gate. I stopped for a while to admire its beauty, then I pushed the bell. A couple of minutes later Maria, the housekeeper, came. She gave me a big smile.

"Nice to see you, Ida. How are you?" she said.

"Very well, Maria, thank you. And you? Is the contessina in?"

"I can't complain. Yes, she is waiting for you. You look nice." I just smiled. Maria came up with me to the landing. A lady came out from one of the rooms. She stopped and looked at me.

"You must be Ida." she said, "I'm Gabriella's mother. Thank you for looking after her and Renata when they needed you most. You did a good job." she said. I was a bit embarrassed.

"Thank you, countess, for your kind words. Renata is a lovely girl." I said.

"That's all right. Let's go and see her." and together we entered Renata's room.

She was lying in her cot. I bent down and she smiled as she had done many times before. She stretched out her little arms for me to pick her up. I did and her little hands caressed my face. I kissed her and held her tight. She had grown quite a bit and was a beautiful girl. How much I had missed her little face!

Gabriella came in. I put Renata down and Gabriella embraced me.

"You look very nice, Ida." she said, "Let's go to the lounge for a drink and you can tell me all about what you've been doing." We went and sat down in the comfortable armchairs and a little later Maria came in carrying a large tray which she put on the table. On it were cups and saucers and a plate with pieces of what looked like jam tart. She poured the coffee, cut the tart and served it on the plates. We drank the coffee. The tart was delicious.

"Now, Ida, tell me everything." Gabriella said. I told her about the

Mila and she got worried when I talked about Carla.

"You should leave that place and find something better." she said.

"I don't intend to stay there long." I said, "Thanks to you, I've been accepted at the nursing home and I'm learning a lot. It is my intention to find work in a hospital as a nurse and take a certificate." She seemed quite impressed.

"Let me know when you do that."

"Thank you, Gabriella. You have been very kind to me. I don't know why!"

"Because I like you and you deserve it." We sat talking until it was time for me to go. I went back to Renata's room, gave her a cuddle and a big kiss and put her back in a cot.

"Come see and see us again." Gabriella said.

"I will, Gabriella, I will." I felt tears in my eyes. She embraced me and I left. At the top of the alley I could see the little car. My thoughts went back to Renata and Gabriella and once again I longed to stay with them and see the child grow her first tooth and take her first step. Then I said to myself,

"Go on, Ida, they don't need you. You must look in a different direction for your future. They've done their best for you and they'll be there if you need them." I made my way to the little car and got in.

"Ida, you look very sad. How's the little girl?" Lina asked. I burst into tears.

"Oh Lina, Renata is as beautiful as ever. She's growing so fast! But I'm very sad not being able to look after her and I do miss her immensely."

"You must look to the future, Ida. You want to be a nurse, don't you?"

"Yes, I do want to be a nurse but I don't like working in the factory. Some of the girls are nice but some of them can be very nasty and truly I never liked cloth-making anyway. It's very boring."

"Let's forget about Renata and Gabriella. Where do you want to go this afternoon?"

"I received a letter from my parents. They wrote that I must come home for Christmas, so what I need to do is go and look around the shops and get some ideas for presents for them and the rest of the family."

"Lovely. Now let's go and have a look at the shops." Lina said, "We'll look for a place to park my little car." Not very far from Via National we found a car park. Lina spoke to the man in charge and gave him some change. He smiled and said,

"Don't worry, miss, I'll look after your car." We walked to the shops and came to a very big street. The sign said Via Barberini. On both sides were shops full of clothes, shoes and jewellery the like of which I'd never seen before, and many other nice things.

"Lina, I never even knew there were such beautiful things. It's all making my head spin!" I said.

"Ida, come here and look in this window and tell me what you see."

"Well, I see many beautiful wedding dresses."

"They are beautiful dresses. Can you see yourself in one of them one day, walking down the aisle with a handsome young man?"

"All that talk makes me laugh. I'm only sixteen and I haven't the faintest idea what it's all about. Anyway, what about you? I can see you as a beautiful young bride one day, with all the glamour in the world!" I said. Lina laughed. We walked and walked and eventually reached Via Frattini and Via Condotti. I was tired and could see that Lina, too, had had enough.

"Let's stop somewhere and have a rest." Lina said and I agreed. The first bar we found, we went in and sat down. Lina ordered two black coffees and buns and we rested our tired legs.

"Have you had enough, Ida," she said, "or do you want to see more shops?"

"I have had enough for today, thank you, Lina. Let's go home." We got back to the car and half an hour later we arrived at aunty's house. I said,

"Lina, I'm sure aunty would like you to come in for a drink."

"Not today, Ida. I want go home. I'm very tired. Tell your aunty I'll be happy to come in another day. See you tomorrow." She left and I went in the house. Aunty and Natalino were having coffee. Natalino said,

"Ida, where have you been all day?"

"I visited Gabriella and after that Lina took me to a beautiful part of Rome to see the beautiful shops."

"Why didn't you invite her in?" he said.

"She said she was very tired and she wanted to go home,"

"What about the dance tonight?" he said.

"She didn't say anything about tonight, and she was very tired. I expect she's got to catch up with her studies. Anyway, you and I have got more important things to do." I said.

"Like what?" I didn't answer his question at first, then I said,

"Well, I received a letter from my parents and they said we must go home for Christmas. We must buy presents for our family. There are so many of them, if we buy all the presents we need to, it will be difficult to pack them in the little luggage we have."

"So we not only have to buy presents, we've also got to buy luggage to pack them all in!"

"Mother and father said they will be waiting at Mignano station on Christmas Eve to welcome us."

"Oh isn't that nice? I expect it won't just be aunty and uncle but also a good part of my family, too."

"We will look forward to it."

"I'm looking forward to sitting near the beautiful fire and eating Christmas Panettone"

"So am I. I'm thinking about all that home cooking our beloved beloved would do it.

We be able to worship in our beautiful church and all the carol singing. Mother always so fussy about the cleanliness of the house. Natalino, think! Your brothers will be gathering wood for the fire, and they'll be looking for a big Christmas tree in the forest with my father. It will be like it always used to be before the war. Grandmother told us that time of the year was just beautiful with all the festivities. I'm really looking forward to Christmas day."

"I was looking forward to going to the dance tonight with Lina even more than to Christmas in the village!" Natalino said.

"But when we come back from the village, we can go to more dancing lessons!" Elena came in and said,

"I'm very excited about the dance tonight. I might win another competition."

"I'm sorry, Elena but we can't go tonight. But when we come back from the village after Christmas things might change." I said.

On Sunday I walked to the nursing home and as I entered I met Sister Elena.

"Good morning, Sister Elena."

"Good morning, Ida. You know your routine and if anything bothers you, you know where I am." she said. Not long after that Lina came in.

"Ida, I'm very sorry about last night but I just couldn't manage it. I was too tired and besides, as I told you before, I like your cousin but I'm much too young to start a relationship. Also I have to concentrate on my studies." she said.

"Don't worry, Lina, I fully understood. We are going on holiday soon for Christmas. But I shall miss you; you are such nice girl. There are not many people like you or Gabriella." I said.

"What a coincidence! My family and I are also going away for Christmas. When we meet again, we'll have a lot to tell each other!"

The day went very quickly. The old ladies kept telling us stories of their lives and times, some of which were very entertaining.

Monday came round again, another boring day, I said to myself. Carla will be full of mischief, as always. But the thought that I would soon be on my way to the village to stay with my mother and father kept me from letting Carla worry me. Angelina, as always, was very kind and very thoughtful.

"Ida, today you look much more relaxed." she said.

"Well, Angelina, quite soon this factory will be closed for Christmas and my cousin and I will go home for a holiday."

"That's very nice for you. Merry Christmas and happy New Year to you both, you deserve it."

"The bad news is that I'll have to come back here." I said.

"Oh, Ida, it's not as bad as all that. I know that Carla has been behaving badly towards you, but she is a very silly girl and you shouldn't take any notice of her. She will soon stop this nonsense, you'll see. But I'm so glad you're getting a holiday. I know you're looking forward to it and when you get back everything will be all right."

"I do hope so, Angelina."

My cousin and I took a day off and went shopping all day long to where Lina had taken me a few days before. Natalino said,

"I've been in Rome longer than you have and I never knew about these posh places. How come you know more than I do?"

"I know about Via Barberini, Via Frattini and Via Condotti because Lina brought me here. As you can see, this is a shopping centre for people with a lot of money, but today we'll pretend to be rich and we'll spend a lot of our savings." I said. We bought more presents than we could possibly pack in our cases. I also bought a present for Gabriella and a toy for Renata and a nice blouse for Lina and many more presents for my aunty, uncle and the three children. My post office savings took a good knock!

The holidays began. Natalino said,

"Well, no more work now until after Christmas. It's nice to think the holidays have started. This time on Friday the twenty-third we shall leave Rome for the village."

"I shall pack my luggage," I said, "and if it is anything like my usual packing, I shall be trying to get too many things into too small a space!"

"My dear cousin, you need to buy another suitcase; you have much more than you can possible carry in that one."

"What time we will leave Termini station?" I asked.

"09:05 a.m. As you said, Ida, my family will also be waiting at Mignano Station to welcome us." Aunty and uncle said,

"We want to come and see you off. So Bruno, Elena and little Americo

"But, aunty and uncle, do you realise what a big effort it will be to carry all that luggage to the station? We don't expect you to drag the poor children out of their beds as well." Uncle said to aunty,

"They are right; we can't all go to the station. That will be ridiculous. You all stay at home. I will come to the station with you. Aunty and the children can say goodbye here." Natalino said,

"That is better, Uncle."

"Natalino, I feel very excited at the thought we shall soon be home with all the family." I said, "I'm thinking about how excited the young ones will be, gathering the wood for the fire and waiting for Father Christmas to bring all their toys."

We left Termini station at five minutes past nine from platform seventeen, direct to Cassino and Mignano di Monte Lungo. After travelling for two hours we reached our destination. All the Festa family were there waiting for us. It was the most wonderful moment, embracing my parents and the rest of the family. When we reached our village, it all seemed different. Somehow those horrible feelings that the village wasn't there any more all went away. I appreciated the love of my parents and the rest of the family, aunty, uncle and all the cousins I had always loved and respected, young and old alike. All my girlfriends from the village seemed so different. I was glad to be with them. It was wonderful to be there and see my beloved church that I felt my duty to keep clean. It was just beautiful to be able to go and worship God and Jesus and to sing Christmas carols again. Of course, 'Silent Night' still had special meaning to me, as well as this one:

Oh come, let us adore Him,

Oh come, let adore Him,
Oh come, let adore Him Christ the Lord!

For two weeks we were in heaven but the thought of going back to Rome and returning to work in that factory almost scared me. What a comfort for me it was to know that Lina and the old ladies would be there waiting for me to help them. I enjoyed that job and for the time being I would have to put up with Carla.

Epiphany was the last day of our holiday. Natalino and I left our beloved family and made our way to Rome. Aunty Catharine and the children were pleased to see us back, especially Elena. I expect the only thing in her mind was the dancing lessons. The eighth of January was our first day back at the work. The thought of Carla made me feel sick but I tried not to let her worry me. Inside I felt unhappy about the fact I had been there well over three months and yet she still felt hostile towards me.

I noticed that Carla was always there before anybody else and for some reason my machine would not function properly. The electrician couldn't understand what was wrong or why the same trouble occurred time and again. For health and safety reasons he thought it best to teach us how to turn off the mains, how to manage if the machine went wrong and, if there was an emergency, how to run away from it quickly.

A week passed without any incident. I was happy with the rest of my work and my beloved Angelina was always beside me during the break. I had a reasonable week but I was glad when it was over and I could go back to the nursing home and meet my lovely ladies and the precious Lina. I was very excited. I had so much to tell her about the village and the wonderful holiday I'd had.

On Saturday Elena kept on and on about the dance. I said,
"Elena tomorrow I will see Lina and be able to arrange something definite about it." I knew jolly well that Lina wouldn't take us. She'd told me very clearly that she was too young to get involved with my cousin. The only hope was Andrew.

At last Sunday morning arrived. I walked to the nursing home, went in and Sister Elena was waiting for me. As soon as she saw me her face lit up.
"Ida, welcome back! All the ladies have missed you; they've been

asking when you would be back. Anyway, have you had a nice Christmas holiday?" she asked.

"Oh yes, sister, it was wonderful. But now I'm back here in the nursing home, I very much appreciate your love and support." I went upstairs to the big room and they all welcomed me back. Five minutes later Lina arrived. It was a great joy to see each other again. She said,

"We've got a lot to catch up on. Tell me, when do you want to see your countess again?"

"Lina, it's very cold and before I go to see her, I need to go shopping to buy myself a decent overcoat. The one I have now is a bit tatty." I didn't finish speaking before she said,

"Right, I know the shop for you. It's in Via National. I think they have got just what you need. I'll take you there next Saturday."

"Lina, you are an angel. I don't know how to thank you for your kindness."

It was the end of January and it was colder than ever but the Roman girls tried to show off, Lollobrigida-style. It was much too cold to wear the spring fashions but that didn't seem to bother them. I would put on the dress Gabriella gave me during the summer, which looked much better than any other dress, but I badly needed a nice, fashionable overcoat. Now I began to see the fruit of my work in my post office account and I could afford to do what everybody else was doing and more. I was looking forward to Lina taking me to Via National. Every day seemed a year but at last Saturday arrived. In the morning I was excited. I'd done the usual chores like every other morning and impatiently waited for Lina to arrive. At two o'clock I jumped in her little car and off we went.

We left Fanfulla da Lodi and went through Port Maggiore and Piazza Della Republic into Via National. There were very many shops but one was special. It had special clothes, mostly for petite ladies. It was expensive but I didn't mind. For once I wanted show the Roman girls that, even if I was from a village, I could look just as good as anybody else. I tried on more than one. At last I found just what I wanted. It was a beautiful camel one, very fashionable and fitted me just perfectly. Lina also liked it very much. She said,

"Ida, you do look elegant!"

"Thank you for helping me. I do appreciate it very much."

"Now, Ida, where do you want to go?" Lina said.

"I'll leave it to you, Lina."

"I thought we could go to the hillsides. There are seven of them surrounding the city and they all have names. We'll start with Caelilan." We left the city and went to a hill surrounded by woods. It was beautiful. The trees had lost all their leaves and the ground looked cold and bare but the place hadn't lost its magic. There were birds I hadn't seen before. We strolled along and there was a little bar where we had a drink. We sat down and Lina ordered two Coca-Colas.

"It comes from America," she said, "and is all the rage. You'll like it." Then she offered me something. I recognised it and my mind went into turmoil. It was chewing gum! Suddenly I was a little girl again.

"Have one of these." Marco had said; Marco, David, and Alex, the three American soldiers who had stayed at our house.

"What is matter, Ida? Are you all right? You're not well!" I heard her voice but my mind had gone back many years. Then I told Lina all about the bombardments, the caves, about my father being sent to Germany, about the Americans.

"The Germans killed a lot of our village men, including my cousin Tony. He was only fifteen years old. They killed him because he took a piece of bread. Another soldier put a gun to my head for the same reason. You know, Lina," I ended, "I nearly got blown up by a mine!" And I told her of the British soldiers who had saved my life. She was listening and her face showed her concern.

"You have had a bad time, Ida." she said, "I would have gone mad with fright." It was time to go. I'd enjoyed the trip.

"Can we come again?" I asked her.

"Yes, if you like. I'll pick you up at seven." she said and left. I was surprised, after what she told me about my cousin. I thought she wouldn't take us to the dancing lessons any more but I had got it wrong. What she really meant was that she didn't want to start anything serious because she was too young and she had her studies to think about. Above all, she was brought up properly by good, Christian parents and I had a great respect for that.

"Elena you may be able to win another competition this evening!" Elena was over the moon. Once again we went to the dance hall. I looked around and there was George. The music started. Teresa found her young friend. Lina and Natalino got up to dance but George stayed sitting down. Then, when I thought that he had forgotten me, he stood up and came to our table.

"Remember me?" he asked jokingly. I got up and we joined the others on the dance floor. After that we danced together all evening and until it was time to go home. Teresa was very disappointed because she didn't win the competition.

For a while Carla kept her distance from me. I thought at last I could relax and get on with my job. A couple of months passed. It was the end of April. The spring was very beautiful, flowers everywhere and the warm sunshine made me feel very special when I wore one the dresses Gabriella gave to me. And of course I had money in the post office. I was content because I had begun to see the fruits of my labours.

One Monday morning, when I got inside the big room at the Mila, I saw Carla at my machine. She had a knife in her hand and she was doing something to the electric wire. Suddenly she let out a shout. I realised what was happening. I turned the mains off. When I went near her she was on the floor shaking. I realised she had passed out and I could see that she couldn't breathe. I didn't panic. I undid her dress, like I had done to the dummy at my Aunty Lauretta's. I pressed her chest, put my mouth on hers and blew air inside her lungs.
"Tell someone to call an ambulance!" I shouted. Carla was still unconscious but I could see she was breathing and had stopped shaking. Not long after that an ambulance came and she was taken to St John's Hospital. I stood there shaking. It had been quite an ordeal. I thought Carla would die. All the girls and chargehands stood around me. Anna came to thank me, then the manager, Signor Ruggiero, arrived.
"Well done, Miss Festa." he said, "You can expect a bonus this month in your wages."
"You should have seen her." a girl said, "She pressed Carla's chest like they do in hospital and then she gave her the kiss of life."

Carla remained in hospital for two weeks. During that time an investigation was made. The electrician came and looked at the wiring and said,
"She must be mad. She was trying to cut the wire with a knife. She electrocuted herself. The speedy action from the other girl saved her life." After a month Carla came back and she nearly got the sack. But she did come to apologise for being so silly and thank me for what I had done for her.

One day Uncle Joseph came to Rome to pay us a visit. He'd been told about the incident in the factory and he was very concerned for my wellbeing, working in such an environment.

"Ida, how long do you think you will be able to stay in this job?" he said.

"Well, uncle, I'll stay in this factory as long as it takes me to save enough money to pay for a better education. I'm already working at the nursing home one day a week for experience and you can rest assured that in time I will achieve what I've always wanted."

"Oh, Ida, you live in a fantasy world. Stop dreaming!"

"She wants to be a doctor now, don't you, Ida?" aunty said, "She's met a girl at the nursing home who is studying to be a doctor. What Ida doesn't understand is that her friend is in a better situation financially."

"Yes, aunty, I would like to do just that but I know it is impossible in my situation. But I don't intend to be a factory worker all my life. The time will come when I'll be in a better position than I am now. You'll see."

I became very popular at the factory. Giuliana said,

"I knew you were something special when I met you on the Grotti Celoni the first day you came to work here. You know what, Ida? That girl tried to electrocute you."

"It had never occurred to me but I have a good God who protects me." I said.

A few more weeks passed and, thanks to Lina, I went to see Gabriella a few times and went out with her. I was beginning to know the city quite well. Also, thanks to her advice and the work I was doing, I was learning a lot. Everything should have been great but it wasn't. Lately I was waking up in the morning and my eyes were hurting. At first it wasn't too bad but gradually it got worse. One morning I woke up and couldn't open my eyelids. What it is wrong with me? I went into the bathroom and splashed some water on them. Slowly I managed to open them. It was Saturday and I went to the nursing home. I asked Lina to look at them.

"They are very red." she said, "You'd better see the doctor."

At the end of Sunday I went home and thought about it. On Monday my eyes were a bit better. I was worried but hoped they would get better without any fuss.

The factory had received a contract from abroad and two weeks before we had started working with mohair, a type of wool from Angora goats. It broke easily, producing a lot of dust. I was sure that was when the trouble with my eyes started. I was learning a lot about how blankets and jumpers and all kind things were made. Anna said to us all,

"Girls, I'm sorry, this contract is going on for six months." We were all flabbergasted because we had realised the health problem. Because of my eyes I took Lina's advice and arranged to see the firm's doctor. He came to see me and said,

"Miss Festa, you have a terrible allergy and it could well be the dust from the wool which is affecting your eyes. I will take a sample then I can tell you for sure, but you'll have to wait for it to go to the laboratory. After a couple of days I'll be able to tell you exactly what it is."

A week later he said,

"My dear girl, the result has arrived. It is the dust from the wool that's caused this allergy to your eyes. I'm afraid you can't work here any longer if you want to get better. You'll have to look for another job." So then I thought, now what will I do?

"Oh no! I like this job now Carla doesn't bother me anymore." I said, "This can't be true, it can't be true!" The doctor gave me a certificate with the clear statement:

> 'If Miss Festa continues working with this material she may lose her sight.'

He put the note in an envelope and gave it to me to give to the manager. I went back into the big room and spotted Giuliana. I gave her the envelope. I was just about to start the machine when I saw Carla. She came straight towards me. Here comes trouble, I thought but I was wrong: she looked very weak.

"I want to thank you for what you did," she said, "and apologise for the trouble I caused you. I've been told that I could have died." I just put my arms around her.

"Forget it, Carla." I said, "That is the past. Besides, I may have to leave the Mila."

By that time all the girls had surrounded us.

"Leave the Mila, why?" Angelina asked, "We all like you." I told them all about my trouble. I began to get very agitated and in a moment of desperation I walked out of the factory, very distressed. I took the Grotti Celoni back to Termini station and, instead of going home to aunty's, I took the 61 bus around Via National to the Coliseum, through Piazza Venezia, over the Castle of St Angelo bridge, through Borgo Pio and into Piazza St Peter. I walked about a hundred metres into the church to pray for my predicament.

While I was there my eyes were hurting badly. I was desperate. My life, that up till then had been going so well, was all in ruins! What would I do without a job in a city still strange to me? I thought of mother and started to cry. Then a voice startled me.
"Why are you crying, young lady?" I turned and saw a priest beside me so, between tears, I told him about my troubles.
"So you see, Reverend, my family lives in Catailli, near Cassino and I live with my aunty but I have to pay for my keep. What am I going to do without a job? I wanted become a nurse and in my spare time I've been looking after old people at the Retreat. But now I'll have to leave everything."
"That is interesting." the priest said, "You're nursing at the Retreat? The nuns in the Vatican also do nursing. They nurse not only in Rome but also in other towns. Have you ever thought of becoming a nun?" That took me by surprise and I didn't say anything.
"Well," he said, "you can decide that when the time comes! Would you like to come to the Vatican to help the nuns there? That would also help with your education." I couldn't believe what I was hearing. I said,
"What about the money?"
"Don't worry about the money. You will be paid ten thousand lire a month and everything will be provided for you."
"What about references?"
"The references must come from your village and from a person who knows you well in Rome but not a relative. And if the references are good I'll have a word with the Mother Superior. I'm almost sure she will have you, but she is in charge and it will be up to her. Tell me more about the Retreat you work for in your spare time. I tell you, my child, if everything goes well, you will have been recommended by God!"

Well, I thought, who could be a better referee than Gabriella? She had been very upset when I told her I was going to work in the textile factory. I remember she said,
"Oh no, Ida, you can't do that. If I remember right, that it is the very thing you ran away from. Remember what I told you before: when you need me, I'll always be here for you."

In addition I gave the names of the priest in my village and the Mother Superior from the Retreat. I stayed a little longer, said more prayers and then left. Outside I looked at his card. 'Archdeacon Pietro Casteletti' it said. I didn't know what an Archdeacon was but I would ask aunty. I waited for the bus to take me home. I felt over the moon. I thought God is good, He never lets me down, He is the Provider. I was so distracted that I nearly got on the wrong bus. I laughed and an old lady looked at me in surprise. She must have thought I was going off my rocker but I didn't care. I knew for sure Jesus was with me. I saw a number 61 for Termini and jumped on it. In less than half an hour I was at the station where I waited for a number 58 which took me to Fanfulla Da Lodi and at last I was home.

It was time for lunch. Uncle and Natalino were there and during the meal I told them about my adventure. They all had a good laugh.
"You live in a fantasy world, Ida." my uncle said, "It is about time you accepted life as it is and stopped dreaming. By tonight that priest will have forgotten all about you."
"He was not a priest, uncle." I said, "I don't know what he was, but he was not a priest." Then I gave his card to aunty and all three of them looked at it.

By 26th May my eyes were much better and I thought I would go to the Mila to pick up my wages. When I got there I looked for Anna. She was one of the chargehands and I found her in one of the offices but she didn't have the wage packets.
"Go to Signor Ruggiero's office." she said, "He wants to talk to you." I went to the office where I first had my interview and knocked on the door.
"Come in," a voice said, so I did. "Ah, Miss Festa," he said when he saw me, "how are your eyes?"
"Getting better, sir, but…" He didn't let me finish.
"Yes, I know, I've read the doctor's note. Does that mean you're leaving us? We'll be sorry to lose you. You are a good worker and a nice girl. Here is your wage packet. The extra is for what you did for that girl, Carla. I wish you luck and take care!"

Three days went past and there was no news. Uncle and Natalino were smiling at me as if to say, "I told you so!" Two weeks and still no news. I refused to believe it. Deep inside I was quite sure God was at work and sooner or later something would happen. Without anybody knowing, I packed my two cases.

One Sunday the Mother Superior called me into her office.

"Ida, here, I have a letter from the Vatican asking me all about you. Tell me how you ever managed to become involved with such a place?"

"I don't know, Mother. I was in a very difficult situation and I called upon God and He answered my prayer."

"Indeed He did. You're only sixteen and I have been told by Sister Elena that you know how to look after old people and, if I understood her right, you would like to become a nurse. In the Vatican you will be able to study to become one. We all like you and we are sorry you won't be here for long but we wish you well. I give you my blessing. By the way, the Vatican tells us that they will send someone to pick you up. Take care and 'bye for now." she said.

Now I was in a dilemma. Why was it that every time I met somebody special, after a while I lost them? It happened with Gabriella and Renata: they were very dear to me and now I didn't see them as much as I would like to. And now Lina. She was such a nice girl and she had been good to me. If I went to the Vatican it would mean I wouldn't be able to see her much any more. I must have a talk with her, I said to myself, and explain the situation. I know she will be very sad and so am I. When I get to the Vatican I'll try to speak to the Mother Superior and see what can be done to visit Gabriella and Renata and see if it will be at all possible from time to time to go out with Lina.

I went upstairs to the private rooms where Lina was working, with tears in my eyes. Lina noticed immediately that I was upset.

"Ida, what is wrong?" she said.

"Oh, Lina! I have got a job in Vatican City but I don't know if we'll be able to see each other any longer." I could see she was very upset. Then she said,

"You can go to work in the Vatican but that doesn't mean you'll have to join a closed order of nuns. Of course we'll be able to see each other, not as often as we would like but we will, you'll see."

On 2nd June 1952 about ten o'clock on a beautiful morning I could sense that everything was going to be all right. The chauffeur knocked at 18 Fanfulla Da Lodi and asked for Miss Festa. My aunty was flabbergasted and said,

"May I ask who you are?"

"I've been sent here by the Vatican. Here are the papers for you to

see. I've come here to take Miss Festa to the Vatican City." I can't describe my aunty's face. I said,
"Goodbye, aunty." and kissed her, "I will come to see you as often I can. Please tell Uncle John cousin Natalino and the children that I will come and visit as soon as possible.

CHAPTER SEVENTEEN – I LEAVE FOR THE VATICAN

I left for my new life in the Vatican. As I got into the car I felt as if I was going to a different planet. When we reach St Peter's Square the chauffeur drove to the left of the cathedral. There are two big arches and on both sides were Swiss guards. About five metres away was the Vatican Army. He drove on and before long stopped in a big square. He opened the door and I got out in front of a beautiful palace. There was a large door where he rung a bell. A nun dressed all in white came to the door. The chauffeur said,
"Miss Festa for Mother Superior." He saluted me. "Take care." he said and left.

The nun took me to a large waiting room with a big table and many chairs. She pointed to one of them, told me to wait there and left. I began to be very anxious. For a minute I wondered what I was letting myself in for, then a feeling of wellbeing came over me and I began to calm down.

The little nun came back again and said,
"Miss Festa, please come to meet Mother Superior. She is ready to meet you." We went through a long corridor until we reached a door. The nun knocked and a small voice said,
"Come in, please." It was a small room and behind a large desk was a very old nun. She said,
"Please sit in that chair." At first she did not appear at all friendly. She looked over her glasses and smiled.
"Tell me, Ida," she said, "how old are you and what have you been doing at the nursing home?"
"I'm sixteen and I have been looking after the old ladies and giving injections."
"You look older than your age. So you already know about nursing?"
"Yes, Mother, but I have only had a very little education."
"Well, you appear to me to have had more than the other girls here." she said, "Ida, I like you and I'm sure you will do well here. I welcome you among us. Now Sister Caterina will show you around the place and then to your room."
"Thank you, Mother. I'm very grateful to you all and I will do my best."
"And we will do our best to teach and train you to achieve the best while you are in our care. We will help you to become a good

Christian and to work with pride in everything you do." Sister Caterina said,
"I will show you around and let you meet the other girls. I'm sure you'll like them and they will like you when you get to know each other."

She took me to a sitting room where there was about a dozen young girls talking amongst themselves. The sitting room was very large with a marble floor and many, many armchairs. Lots of watercolours hung on the marble walls alongside interesting oil paintings by Italian artists like Giotto. There was a very nice piano on one side of the room where the girls and the nuns sang beautifully. The dining room was very big and pleasant with two large, dark oak tables with twelve chairs on each side and there were two big sideboards with a couple of lamps. The floor and the walls were again all marble. Then there was a library, covered in books from floor to ceiling. Every section had its own light so it was easy to locate the books.
"Why is this room so dark?" I asked.
"The room must be kept dark to protect the books from the light in order to keep them in good condition."

Off the long corridor were many bedrooms with beautiful bathrooms and lavatories. Then she took me into a bedroom and said,
"My dear girl, this is your room."
"Oh thank you, Sister Caterina. This is a good size." In the room was a comfortable bed, a wardrobe, a chest of drawers and a small table with a chair.
"We do have central heating in the winter and in the summer there is air conditioning, which you will find very comfortable."
"Thank you. I'd like to thank Mother Superior for having me here." Sister Caterina smiled. She took me to the kitchen. Again it was enormous with a big table, two electric cookers, two gas ones and many larders.

The first day I was there all the girls and the nuns got up about six, washed and tidied their rooms and then went to church. Everyone was responsible for their own personal hygiene. When we came out of church we had a breakfast of one or two rolls of bread and butter, jam or marmalade, milk and coffee. Some of the girls smiled and some didn't appear very friendly. Inside I had butterflies. I hoped I wouldn't have the same problem I had in the factory. But I soon realised my fear was unfounded. The girls at the Vatican had more education and much more respect for each other and there was no way would I find myself in the position I was in at the Mila.

At about eight o'clock we went to the library to get the programme for the day. The nuns took us everywhere and taught all of us in the same way. They emphasised how to make the best of ourselves. I soon started to make friends. There was one very special one, tall and slim with light brown hair and very dark eyes. She kept smiling at me and I smiled back. She came up to me and said,
"Are you new here?"
"Yes, I am."
"Pleased to meet you. My name is Eugenia. What is your name?"
"My name is Ida. How do you do?"
"Well, Ida, I think you and I will be good friends."
"I'm sure we will."

The first day I was there Sister Caterina took me to I Derizione Sanitario. It was the equivalent of a casualty ward staffed by nuns with a couple of doctors on duty, but nobody came in there for help. Sister said it was just as well as they didn't want to frighten me on my first day.

We got back to the convent at about two and had a lunch of *pasta al ragu'* followed by a small piece of meat with salad and afterwards a piece of fruit. After that we were free to do what we liked, though we couldn't go out anywhere. I didn't know what to make of such a beautiful place. Eugenia said,
"Ida, in the first week everything seems strange to you, but after a few days you will settle in." Sister Caterina said,
"Ida, in the Piazza del Giurament there is a special library for people who want to know more about the Vatican. Ask Eugenia to take you there."
"Eugenia, where is Piazza del Giurament?" I asked her.
"I'll take you there."

It was a very hot afternoon, comfortable inside the palace but when we stepped outside it was like walking into a fireball. Eugenia said,
"We are in the Piazza Belvedere. You see that palace there? It's the Pope's residence, they call it 'Apostolic'. One side of it faces St Peter's and one side faces out here. That building there is the

post office, the one on left is the Roman Observatory and they have them all over Italy. Next to the Observatory is the office of the Vatican newspaper. The funny looking building is called Annona. It's the shopping centre for the people who live in the Vatican."

"Can we buy clothes there?"

"No, Ida." she said, "It only sells meat and vegetables, mostly from Castelgandolfo, the Pope's summer residence which has a big farm and supplies nearly all the Vatican's needs. The rest of the food we eat is delivered by the Vatican Store and is very cheap but we don't pay anything. Next to that is the Piazza del Giurament. It's a very large square named after a big celebration held every year for the new Swiss guards. They promise to be faithful to the Pope and the Vatican. Since the early 16th century the Swiss guards have protected the person of the Pope and they still wear the same uniform, probably designed by Michelangelo. On the right side of this square is the Vatican Library with a beautiful garden surrounded by trees. The library is run by the monks and underneath it are the archives where all the Vatican's history is kept." I found all this very interesting and said to myself,

"If it's allowed, I will spend a lot time in there."

"Ida, it's time to go back to the convent for supper," said Eugenia, "and later all the girls and the nuns will meet in room number 6 for a special conference with the Pope."

We went back and not long after we were sitting in the big dining room for supper. For starters we had chicken soup, then a slice of beef cooked *alla pizzaiola* with vegetables and then a piece fruit, all of which I liked very much. Soon after supper we prepared to meet the Pope, who at that time was Pious XII. Room number 6 was a very large, elegant room where the Pope received many people and conducted many ceremonies.

Life here was very active but I enjoyed every minute of it. Two days a week we would go to Gemelli Hospital where Vatican residents went if they needed to. It had always been my dream and now I saw first-hand what a hospital was really like and what the work involved. There were many sad stories. I liked the children's ward especially. Eugenia also enjoyed hospital work. Sister Caterina said,

"Ida, I've been told that you want to take nursing seriously. Here is your chance to get to know more about general hospital work." I was over the moon.

At that time there were about twenty patients in the children's ward and some of them were very poorly. Samantha had Cystic Fibrosis and was made a lot of fuss of by her parents. They appeared to be very well off and whatever she needed was provided.

Next to Samantha's bed was another little girl. She was very slim but had a big swollen tummy and her body was very yellow all over, so she looked jaundiced. She was very poorly, a sweet child but no fuss was made of her as she lay all alone in that little bed. She had beautiful eyes and a big smile on her little face but had nobody to love her. I was told by the sister in charge that she came from a very wealthy family. Occasionally her mother came to visit her and would sit near her bed without saying a word to her, just concentrating on the book she had brought. She wouldn't stay longer than half an hour, hardly spoke and then left without even turning back and waving to her poor little child. When the sister in charge finished telling me about her, I was overcome with anguish. Poor little girl! I grew very fond of her and would sit beside her bed trying my best to help. But there was very little I could do for Belinda apart from tender loving care.

She was seven years old and a very clever and sensitive girl. On one occasion when I sat with her she said,
"Ida, my mother came to visit me today and I could see how ashamed she was of me."
"Oh, Belinda, what do you mean?" With tears in her eyes she said,
"My parents are ashamed of me."
"But why?" I asked.
"Maybe because I'm not as beautiful as my sister and since I can remember I've always been unwell. You see, my parents are very high ranking and so our house is full of people from high society. They do a lot of entertaining. My sister is healthy and beautiful and they are very proud of her. She is presented to the guests on every occasion, but I was always kept hidden away and you can see why. Look at me. Don't I look ugly?"
 "Look, Belinda, this is impossible. Every parent is very proud of their children, however many they have and whatever they look like. To them, they are all beautiful. If your parents didn't let the guests see you, it was only because you weren't well and they tried to protect you. And if your mother doesn't say anything to you it's because she is so very sad to see you unwell." I tried very hard to encourage her but I understood what Belinda said and felt. I wasn't surprised at how she felt as I saw with my own eyes the

coolness of her mother towards her. I bent down, embraced her, gave her a big kiss and said,

"Belinda, you are a beautiful and intelligent child. You will get better and everything will change, you'll see. I'm a nobody with no status but I have a lot love to give you and I promise I'll always be your friend."

It was time to go back to the Vatican. On the way I couldn't stop tears coming to my eyes. Eugenia came towards me and said,

"Ida, what's happened?"

"Why?"

"Because you look very upset." she said.

"Eugenia, I don't understand how the world can be so cruel. Did you see that poor little child, Belinda? She is always by herself, poor little mite." Then a big convulsion came over me and I couldn't stop crying. Eugenia said,

"Please, please, Ida, stop crying. This isn't the way. You must not get upset like this. It is not good for you."

"I'm sorry, Eugenia. I can't help it."

"Please tell me what happened in hospital today."

"Eugenia, it's a long story and I can't tell you now. I will tell you when we're back in the Vatican." Now I realised how hard it is to look after children like Belinda without getting emotionally involved.

It was two o'clock and we all went into the dining room for our meal but I didn't feel hungry. I wanted to go to my room and try to calm down. Eugenia didn't know what to do with me. She went to Sister Caterina and said,

"Ida is very upset and doesn't want to come to the dining room for a meal." Sister Caterina came to my bedroom and said,

"Ida, what is wrong with you?"

"Oh, sister," I said, "today I have seen a very sad situation: a poor little girl so ill and so unloved. I find it very difficult to come to terms with her predicament. I promised I would never leave her and would stay near her, no matter what."

"I will have a word with Mother Superior and see what we can do for this little girl. But now go and wash your face and join Eugenia and the girls in the dining room for your lunch."

After lunch Mother Superior sent for me and said,

"Ida, I've heard about the little girl. We will help the best we can but there is a limit to what we can do. She still has a mother and father, even if they don't do much for her. What about if I give permission for you to visit her every day? The hospital provides everything she needs, but if you think she requires anything else we can try to get it for her. Is that all right?"

"Thank you, Mother, for your understanding."

The next day Mother Superior came into lunch and said,

"Tomorrow afternoon at four there is a meeting in the lounge. I want every one of you to be present." The next day we were all in the lounge waiting for her to arrive. She entered, clapped her hands and said,

"From next week we will have a different programme. You will divide into small groups. Sister Teresa and Sister Caterina are in charge. I don't want any nonsense. You will obey them and do whatever they ask. This is necessary for your training so that in the future, whatever situation you find yourself in, you will be able to cope." Then she left.

Sister Caterina was in charge of Eugenia, Delia, Nicolina and me. Sister Teresa was in charge of the other group. The two sisters would put up a notice on the board with the programme of jobs we would do during the week. In the first week on Monday and Tuesday Delia and I had to help the nuns to look after the very young children in the kindergarten. Delia was a nice young girl, full of fun. She wasn't very tall, had blond hair and brown eyes, and was well educated. Looking after the little children was fun and we both enjoyed it very much. On Wednesday Eugenia and I went to Gemelli Hospital to help the nuns there. I always went to the children's ward so I could sit with Belinda all afternoon, if she needed me.

About two weeks later I had a shock. I was by Belinda's bed when she said,

"Ida, tomorrow I'm going to the operating theatre. Please don't get upset if you don't find me back here. I will be with Jesus. I want you to be happy for me."

"Belinda, please don't talk like that. You will be fine! When I come tomorrow you'll be here and eventually you'll getter better. Do you understand?"

"If it pleases you to believe that, so be it." After two hours it was time for me to go home and I bent down, embraced her very tightly, kissed her and said,

"God bless you. I'll see you tomorrow and I will pray for you tonight."

When I went in the next day I walked into the ward and looked for her little body in her bed but she wasn't there; the bed was empty. Belinda had gone to Jesus just as she'd said. I was very sad but understood that she knew where she was going. Now she wasn't suffering any more, but it wasn't easy for me to accept that it was better for her.

We continued to go to Gemelli Hospital but I always felt an emptiness inside me because Belinda wasn't there any more. The thought that she had no pain made it easier to bear and to get on with my work. Sister Caterina would take Delia, Nicolina, Eugenia and me where she needed help, mostly to private families to teach us to cook.

I had been there six months and was beginning to know the place better. As I said, one way you entered the Vatican was from the main road, Via Della Conciliation, near the Tiber and St Angelo's Castle. The other way was by Piazza Risorgimento on a road called St Amerinziana. The number 61 bus would go through the square and stop just behind the big columns in St Peter's Square. There are two entrances to the Vatican, one on the far left of the basilica, where I first came in, by the two big arches guarded by Swiss guards and the Vatican police. No car can enter unless it has a Vatican registration or a special permit. That road takes you all around the city to the other entrance at Via Porta Angelica in the Piazza Risorgimento. The Porta Angelica entrance is guarded by the Italian police, the Carabinieri. To the right is a church, named after St Anne, mother of Mary the mother of Jesus, where ordinary people can worship. On the left there is a post for the Swiss guards and a few metres further on there in a checkpoint manned by the Vatican police. It is impossible to enter without permission.

The Apostolic Palace of the Pope has one side facing St Peter's Square, where the Pope gives the benediction every Sunday. The other side faces Piazza Belvedere and the palace where we lived. In Piazza Belvedere were I Derizione Sanitario, the post office, the fruit and vegetable market, the butchers, the newspaper office and the Roman Observatory. Next to it is Piazza del Giurament with the archives and the Vatican Library and about fifty metres beyond that is the Vatican garden. There are all sorts of buildings there, some more beautiful than others.

At that time there were about two thousand people resident in the Vatican, most of them people of the church like priests and nuns, bishops and cardinals, and not many private families, only very privileged ones like the Rossis and a few others. The Vatican has a very tall wall around it which cuts it off absolutely from Rome. It is completely independent from Italy and every other country in the world. It is a country in its own right. But Italy and the Vatican have maintained extremely friendly relations. The Pope has full legislative, executive and judiciary powers in the Vatican.

Time passed and now we were thinking about what the nuns could teach us. To become a nurse at that time you had to be twenty-one and, above all, be a nun. But I had not had that call from God yet. After a year, Mother Superior called me and said,
"Ida, today Lady Rossi asked me if I had any special girl who would be able to cook for a family of six people and I noticed you like cooking very much, so I recommended you. I think you will be the right person for the job. They had one lady there for a long time but now she's left. Now, would you like to do that?"
"Yes, Mother Superior, it will be a challenge for me." It was spring 1953 and I was eighteen years old but very naïve about the world.
"I will call Lady Rossi and she will interview you in the library."

Two days later I met her. She was very sweet lady, petite with blonde hair and blue eyes. She was wearing a beautiful pleated blue dress with a real pearl necklace around her neck. She was about sixty years old and appeared to be very nice. I couldn't stop admiring her beauty. I felt quite comfortable in her presence and learned that she also liked me, so I went to cook for her family of six.

There was Lord Carmine who was about seventy years old, not very tall and carrying a lot of weight. He had very thin, white hair and, like his sister, blue eyes. Looking at him I guessed he was a very powerful gentleman who wouldn't let anybody get in his way. His brother, Lord Beniamino, was about sixty-five years old, the father of three grown-up children. He was astonishingly good-looking with grey hair and brown eyes and very tall. When you were in his presence you knew he was in command. At the same time he was very kind, placid and understanding and loved his children very much. He had lost his wife when their children were very young. Lady Giovanna had been much younger than him. I was told she was beautiful inside and out. There were pictures of her everywhere in his house and at his office. I'd been told that she loved to cook for the family herself. Although she'd died, in Lord Beniamino's eyes she was still there beside him. On top of his bedside cabinet was a gold casket in which he kept his wife's hair and it had a glass top so he could always admire it. He was much loved by his children, his brother and sister, and was well respected by the Vatican residents. One of his staff was called Giuseppina. She was one of his housekeepers at a house the family owned in a village. When she came to Rome from the village, she used to say to him,

"Lord Beniamino, you look like a king." We all laughed at the way she said it. It amused him and everybody around him.

His eldest son was Lord Giannfranco who had graduated in law. He looked exactly like his father and as the first son was due to inherit the title and the position of his uncle, Lord Carmine, but he wouldn't benefit until Lord Carmine died. The late Pope Paul XI made him editor of *The People* newspaper. Like all his family, he was very nice.

The second son of Lord Beniamino was Giulio. He was twenty-four years old and a graduate engineer and architect. In wartime, Lady Giovanna was very ill and she couldn't supervise what was going on. The milk for the Vatican came from Castelgandolfo, the Pope's summer residence, and it wasn't pasteurised therefore it needed to be boiled for at least four minutes before it could be given to the children. Because that wasn't done, Guilio caught a disease (Fever Mortises) the effect of which was to make him grow very, very tall. So he was a very tall young gentleman, very good looking and full of fun. One day I was in his office and noticed he was drawing a beautiful English cottage. I looked and said,

"Giulio, one day I will have a house just like that."

"Ida, don't make me laugh! Tell me how on earth you can even think of it. It would cost a lot of money. Dream if you want to, but it would be better if you faced reality and concentrated on the things you can achieve, not on the things you can't."

"I know it's a dream, but sometimes dreams can come true."

"Well, Ida, as you wish, but don't count on it."

The third son was Roberto. He was very handsome and studying philosophy at Rome University. His father didn't like it, but he did. The father wanted his third son to be like his brothers, but no, he wanted to be a professor of philosophy and I believe he was very successful in doing this. I thought he was a nice fellow, just like his brothers. They were and still are the very best people I ever met, a marvellous family.

After the morning routines, I would go to the library, get the menu for the day and the money to buy all the ingredients, then shop and cook the food. The Vatican had its own market in Piazza Belvedere. Lord Carmine was single and had a dog, Dick. After two o'clock there was nothing for me to do and I thought it would be nice to take the dog for a walk in the garden.
"Lord Carmine, can I take your dog for a walk in the garden, please?"
"Yes, Ida, of course," he said, "anytime you get bored, please do so. I think Dick will be rather pleased, don't you?"
"I will look after him, sir."
"I think he will look after you, too."

The first day I took the dog for a walk we went to the Vatican garden. I left Piazza Belvedere and in the next square a ceremony was taking place for the new enrolment of Swiss guards. It was held once a year and the Vatican invited honourable guests to witness the guards swear allegiance to the Pope and the people of the Vatican. I went through the gallery and then through the gates to the Vatican garden. As I entered the sight took my breath away. The garden was just beautiful! There were plants I'd never seen before, all in flower. There were thousands of species of all colours. It is difficult to describe such a picture.

There were many interesting and beautiful buildings that I never knew the use of until I went to the library and read all about them. I found it all very interesting. As you enter the garden on the right is the small house of Pious IV which housed the Vatican Museum. On the left was the Vatican Radio and Television building and next to it the beautiful Palace of Justice. Not very far from that was the large Houses of Parliament and there were many more. There were waterfalls large and small. One of the largest and most beautiful was called Eagle Fountain. It must have been fifty metres high. The water dropped into a big basin. In the middle of the garden there was a grotto just like the one in Lourdes in France. The Pope would go there every day from two to four. The gates were closed so he wouldn't be disturbed.

The Rossi family was and still is very aristocratic. I found a picture of them with King Vittorio Emanuele and Queen Elena of Savoy in their drawing room.

It was very hot, as always in August. The dog couldn't bear the heat so I took him to the garden for walks. As soon as he saw the water he'd jump into a fountain. He enjoyed swimming and once he was in the water he wouldn't come out. I got scared in case he might drown. Quite a few times I got very concerned when I lost sight of him then, when he finally reappeared, what a relief it was!

One day I was strolling along on the left side of the garden when I heard voices speaking in a foreign language. I walked along a wide path and there in front of me were beautiful gates like those at Gabriella's villa in Corso Trieste but much, much bigger. They were double gates, very tall, oval and if they were both open you could get a double decker bus through. There were a lot of people standing on the other side of them, admiring the beautiful garden. I asked the gardener,
"Signor Giovanni, who are those people looking at us and making all that silly noise?"
"Miss Festa," he said, "those are foreign tourists. They come from all over the world to visit the Sistine Chapel. Through those gates they get a glimpse of our beautiful garden."

There were two big columns where the gateposts were. To the left on our side of the gates was a long wall, near to which grew what looked to me like giant oranges. But they weren't oranges, nor were they lemons. Curiosity got the better of me and I picked one and peeled it. I couldn't make sense of it. The inside appeared to be cotton wool! I broke open another and another until I'd made a lovely mess on the pavement. The gardener must have called the duty guard who came rushing to me and said,
"Miss Festa, whatever do you think you are doing to these poor fruits?"
"They're not fruits. They're cotton wool." I said.
"Whatever they are, they are not for you to vandalise. Now let's clean up this mess you've made"
"What kind of fruit are they, then?" The gardener came and explained.
"These plants came from Israel as a present to the Pope."
"I'm sorry to have vandalised your fruits." The gardener laughed and said,
"Don't do it again, will you? Next time you want to know anything,

just ask one of us gardeners and we'll tell you."
"Thank you. I promise not to do it again."

A month later a lot of work started in the garden. They were putting pipes under the ground. Once I was playing with the dog and stumbled on a valve that hadn't been installed properly. It was September and still very hot. That day there were a lot people in the garden and the Vatican Army was doing some kind of training. The water rose from the ground like inverted rain. Before they knew it the poor guards were completely soaked. So was I, Dick the dog and everybody else. The only consolation was that in no time everybody dried out again. Soon everyone had heard about what had happened in the garden and had a good laugh. They said,
"Ida, you've done it again!"

CHAPTER EIGHTEEN – LIFE IN VATICAN CITY

At that time there was no television, so in the winter months we'd sit and talk about what we'd done in our earlier lives, bad or good. Giulio, Lord Rossi's second son, told us all a story:

"When I was about fourteen I had done very well at school and passed my exams with good marks so my father was pleased with me. He gave me a present of a toy cowboy gun. In summer we always went to the mountains for our holiday to a place call Bracciano That year I took my cowboy gun. Not very far from where we stayed was a place where nuns and girls lived. It was protected by barbed wire and there was just one little gate through which the nuns and girls could go in and out. I liked one of the girls there but she didn't like me. She called me 'Long Legs'. I was quite annoyed with her and wanted to take revenge. There was no running water where they lived so the girls had to go to a well with buckets on their heads. I waited outside the barbed wire and asked Teresa where Angelina's room was. She said,
"When you come in the entrance, there is a corridor to the right and her room is number eight." I thanked her. I think she said number eight because that was the Mother Superior's room and she wanted to cause a surprise, which is exactly what happened. That evening I waited until all the lights were out. When I thought the time was right, I took my gun and went through the little gate. It was very hot and all the windows and doors had been left open. I went in the front entrance and down the corridor, counting the numbers. When I reached number eight, the door was already open and I fired three times and ran away. Because I was in such a hurry, instead of finding the little gate, I jumped over the barbed wire and ran back to my room without anybody seeing me. Mother Superior and all the nuns started screaming,
"We've been shot, we've been shot by an intruder!" The police were called. Everybody had heard the noise but there were no signs of gun shot. Mother Superior claimed it was a divine miracle, "I have been shot but I'm all right!" All the papers reported it as well as Vatican Radio. Bells were rung and all the churches celebrated the good news at Mass. Pope Pious XII announced a holiday. One week later my family and I were back home in the Vatican again. I was in agony, limping very badly. When my family asked why, I said I had fallen from a tree while we were on holiday.

Father said I ought to go to I Derizione Sanitario and see what they could do. The doctor said,
"Lord Giulio, whatever have you done here? I'd better give you an injection against tetanus then you can tell me how you did this injury to your leg. Those wounds look as if they are a week old." I made up all kinds of stories but he knew I was telling him pork pies. But I could never tell anybody the truth. I think the doctor knew I had damaged myself on barbed wire. Now, ten years later, I make my confession!"

One day I was in the library with Lord Beniamino to discuss the menu for the day and after he'd gone I looked for a cookery book. After a while I found one of the late countess's cookery books. I was over the moon. I didn't tell anybody but kept the book well guarded. I began to cook like she did, using this book which was mostly full of recipes she had written. She must have been a wonderful cook. Now, the Lords didn't understand how it was that I could cook the same recipes as the late countess. They were all full of praise for me, but at the same time mystified. I heard them discussing it among themselves.

It was December 1953 and those who could afford it were busy with Christmas shopping. Others were in Via S Amerianziana, not very far from the Vatican gates, waiting for the church to give them something to help them survive. The Vatican was preparing a big feast for the very poor people of Rome. Of course, they couldn't help everybody but they did their best, along with all the parish churches in the city. Each church had a Nativity with a crib where little baby Jesus lay in a manger. They were beautifully made, very lifelike and there were competitions between the churches. They say that in Rome there are more churches than houses. The nuns took us around to visit the Nativities. I thought the Vatican one in St Peter's Square was one of the best. It had a big Christmas tree and everything looked so beautiful.

There was much festivity all around us, but I had only one thing on my mind: the Christmas dinner I had to cook for this special family. I'd spent a few sleepless nights in my room studying the countess's book. What kind of food had they had when she was alive? What could I suggest to him the next morning when we met in the library to discuss the menu for Christmas day, without letting him know that I already had an idea? I had found out more or less what kind of food they used to eat on Christmas day and wrote it down, pretending that it was my idea. Two weeks before Christmas, Lord Rossi said,

"Now, Christmas is coming and we must discuss the menu for that day."

"Yes, sir, I haven't got an idea," I said, "but my aunty would always do a starter of chicken liver pate on special crusty bread with grated truffle over the top, or melon with Parma ham. Next, *tortellini alla Bolognese*, which is small packets of pasta stuffed with pork, ham, parmesan and a little nutmeg with Bolognese sauce. Next, stuffed and roasted guinea fowl and a whole piglet spit-roasted with the all the trimmings. Next, *panettone ripieno* or *tiramisu* with bread from Siena or bread *certoso* from Bologna. These are the kinds of sweets we have at Christmastime." The Lord said,

"This is very funny. My dear wife would have done this kind of menu with the help of the lady we had here. But how can you manage all that by yourself? We'd better ask one of the nuns to come and help you."

"Oh no, sir, I easily manage by myself." I said.

"That would be too much to ask of such a young lady."

"Oh no, I will manage easily, you'll see, sir. Everything will be all right."

Three days before Christmas I was all prepared. I had everything in place. I had bought all that I needed for the big day and the day before I prepared it all. On Christmas Eve I made nice eel soup, which is an Italian tradition.

Christmas Eve was a time of mystery and magic. I felt so happy and relaxed. I'd never felt that way before. After we'd been to church, we went to bed. In the morning I couldn't open the door of my bedroom, it was so heavy. When at last I managed to push it open, I found a big sack full of presents. I never knew such beautiful things! I loved every one of them. There was also an envelope and when I opened it I couldn't believe what I saw. There was a letter from the Pope who had sent a present to my parents with one hundred thousand lire and wished them a Merry Christmas! At that time, one hundred thousand lire was a lot of money. I was very happy.

CHAPTER NINETEEN – THE CHRISTMAS DINNER

Christmas 1953. After I looked at all my presents it was time to go to morning Mass. Soon after that I began to cook the Christmas meal for the first time. It was a success, everything worked out just as I had planned and the Rossis were very pleased with how it went. The meal started with toast cut into triangles with chicken liver pate and grated truffle. This was followed by *cappelletti alla Romana* (egg pasta filled with meat and cheese and seasoned with fresh herbs and nutmeg with tomato sauce). The third course was guinea fowl roasted in honey. Fourth was fillet of beef with mayonnaise and salad. Fifth was *panettone ripieno, panforte di Siena, pane certoso di Bologna* and *zuppa Inglese* (English trifle).

For the New Year's meal, the starter was salami with olives and anchovies followed by *tortellini all'Italiana*, then roast turkey with all the trimmings, and *zampone* with *lenticchie tacchino con castagne* and *panforte di Verona* and *frutta secca*.

Christmas festivities continued until 6th January, Epiphany. Epiphany is when the three kings arrived from the Orient to pay homage to the baby Jesus, the saviour of the world. As I said before, Italian children believed in an old witch who visited those boys and girls who hung a stocking behind their bed. If the witch thought they had been good, their received a present in their stocking; if not, they got ashes and coal.

When Christmas was over, for a while life returned to how it normally was in winter. We all looked forward to the springtime. In Italy we have four seasons. By March we began to feel spring in the air and I could return to my beloved walks in the garden with the dog. The 21st March is St Benedict's day when the swallows fill the sky with music. It was magic; everything was beautiful. It was a joy to see the tourists again, visiting the Sistine Chapel and admiring the perfume of our beautiful flower garden through the big gates.

Lord Beniamino said,
"Tomorrow is Good Wednesday and we must prepare the menu for Easter day. I'm sure you already know what we like."
"Yes, I have an idea." I said.

Lady Mary was such a nice person. She did a lot of voluntary work and knew about my ambition to work in a hospital and become a nurse when I was old enough. Near Easter time she said,

"Ida, would you like to visit the hospital with me?"

"Yes, please, I would like that very much." I was overjoyed to be able to visit the hospital I had heard so much about: the St John Lateran.

"Tomorrow," she said, "I will take you to Piazza S Giovanni in Rome." That was how the Vatican people would speak about Rome. For them it was and still is another city in another country.

On Easter Thursday afternoon the driver of the Bentley car took us to the hospital. We got out and she told him to come back in two hours. We went into the hospital and she talked to various people and asked the doctor which patients needed most help and what she could do for them. The doctor gave her a list of people needing help.

"I will do my best to meet their needs." she said, "Ida, sit in the corridor." I went into the corridor and sat on one of the benches. I watched her walk away from me. As usual, curiosity got the better of me and I followed her. She went into a room and closed the door. I looked through the keyhole and was astonished at what I saw. She was washing somebody's feet. When she came out I said,

"Lady Mary, why on earth were you washing an old man's feet?"

"Well, Ida, it's Easter time when Jesus washed his disciples' feet and He gave us an example of how to be humble. It doesn't matter who I am. I'm not different from anybody else. People like me came into this world just the same as everybody else did. We have had privileges but that doesn't make me any better than anybody else in the eyes of the Lord."

"I don't understand you. If God gave you these privileges and made you be born into a very rich family, surely you have been chosen by Him."

"Oh, Ida, you are a child in many ways! I don't expect you to understand everything that I'm trying to tell you but I let me explain in a simple way: I'm a Lady, so what? The title doesn't make any difference to the soul inside my body. It's what is inside you, your soul, that counts. All the rest is nothing. It's just earthly things which in the end don't mean anything at all. We came with nothing and we will go with nothing. Do you understand me now?"

"I don't know. I suppose so."

"Oh, Ida! I am what I am. You are just eighteen and you have your life in front of you, but make sure you live life according to God's will."

"I think you have been privileged to come onto this earth with all the amenities you need. You can do anything you like because of who you are."

"You only see the earthly things and not what I'm trying to explain. All right, you can make cloth, you can look after children, and now you've proved that you can look after yourself and you can cook for six people. There are many things that you can do that I can't. I could say that you've been privileged because of what you are able to do. But what is important is to believe in God, as we've been taught by the church. It is important to be a good Christian and to do whatever you can to help others. 'God so loved the world that He gave His only son ... and whosoever believes in Him shall be given the right to be called son of God and shall never perish but shall have eternal life.' That is what we must do and that is what I've been trying to tell you this morning. Now do you understand?"

"Sort of." By the end of this discussion we had reached the Vatican and I thought,

"Well, I've had my lecture and I asked for it! I'd better be quiet in future."

At Easter we went to church at six in the morning, so I had five hours to cook the meal. Starters was chicken soup, then *tagliatelle alla Bolognese* followed by a whole young lamb with garlic and fresh rosemary, potatoes roasted in the meat juice and fresh peas. I'd baked a beautiful Easter cake full of fresh cream. Finally there was coffee. It was a big success. The Rossis liked it very much and gave me a generous tip which pleased me very much.

That July was very hot and as usual I took the dog for walks in the garden. While the dog enjoyed himself, I ate pinenuts. Cardinal Rancalli, who later became Pope John, said,

"Bambina, fermati di mangiare quelli pini, non allungo avrai un forte mal di pangia. (Child, stop eating these pinenuts or in no time you will have a very bad stomach ache.)" I went home and did have stomach ache. I said to a nun,

"That cardinal must be a witch."

"Don't talk about the cardinal like that." said the nun, "He is a very good man, actually, one of the best."

"Well, he said I would have stomach ache and now I have."

"You don't need to be a witch to know that. Anybody could tell you that if you eat that kind of stuff you will have stomach ache. It serves you right. You should eat proper food but you will eat things that don't do you any good."

One day when the Rossis were having dinner, Lord Carmine was eating chicken with fresh lettuce that had come that day from Castelgandolfo, the Pope's summer residence. One of his nephews had put a plastic worm on his lettuce. The old man knew it wasn't real but, so as not to embarrass the person who had served him, he stood up, took his plate and threw it out of the window. After dinner was cleared up, the nun on duty at I Derizione Sanitario reported that they couldn't understand why a Swiss guard came in with a bad injury to his head. He'd needed quite a few stitches and when they'd asked him how it had happened, he said that he didn't know. Later the nun found out: it was so hot that the guard had taken his helmet off for a minute, which was against the rules so he could have been punished. But it was just at that moment that he passed under Lord Rossi's window. He couldn't make a complaint because he shouldn't have taken off his helmet!

Eugenia, one of my best friends, also worked for an aristocratic family. She telephoned just before two o'clock one afternoon and said,
"Ida, it's very hot today so why don't all us girls meet in the garden for a picnic this afternoon? I'll telephone around to see who wants to come."
"Whatever will the nuns say?" I said.
"Why should they say anything? We won't do anything wrong. What we do in our own time is nothing to do with anybody, as long we don't break any rules."
"All right, Eugenia, where shall we meet?"
"You come here to me and then we'll go together and meet the other girls in the garden near the Eagle Fountain."
"But how can I come to you when I don't know where you are?"
"Don't worry. I'll tell you where to come. Go through the archives and through the gallery. When you reach the gate to the garden, go left. After a few metres turn right and you'll see a door. Go in that door and you'll find a corridor. If it's dark, you'll find a light switch along the wall. When you come to a door, ring the bell and I'll be there." I arranged with all the other girls to meet in garden, prepared everything we would need and took it all to the meeting place. The gardener was there and I said,

"We're having a picnic. Would you mind looking after the basket until we're all here?"

"No, Miss Festa," he said, "but I'll pray that none of you come back so I can call the other gardeners and we'll be able to eat your feast!"

"No chance!" I said, "We'll all be back!" I went back to the garden gate and did what Eugenia had said but in the corridor I didn't find a light switch. Instead I felt some kind of flesh near my legs. I screamed and screamed and all the lights went on. I can't describe the horror when I realised that I was in the dormitory of the Swiss guards. They all jumped up and none of them had any clothes on! Of course, it was a very, very hot day and after wearing that funny uniform they must have been glad to be able to take all their clothes off. It was just as much of a shock for them as it was for me. Somehow I got out but I was so shocked I just wandered around until Eugenia found me.

"Ida, whatever is the matter with you?"

"Let's meet the others and I'll tell you what happened. It's not funny." I said.

"I don't know what happened, so how can I say if it's funny?" she said. We both started to walk towards the garden gate without saying a word. At last we reached the Eagle Fountain and all the girls were there waiting for us. They all said,

"Whatever is matter with you, Ida?" I didn't know what to say but I pulled myself together and eventually told the story. They were all sorry for me but it didn't take long before all the residents of the Vatican got to know. They all had a good laugh and didn't forget for a long time, much to my embarrassment.

Every year we had a month's holiday in August to be with our families, which I enjoyed very much. I also enjoyed reading poetry. Every time I came back from holiday Lord Beniamino said,

"Ida, what songs or poetry did you learn in your village?"

"I didn't learn a new song, but I did learn a new poem." I said.

"May I hear this new poem?"

"Oh, yes." I replied. After I recited the poem, he looked very shocked and said,

"In which book did you find this poem?"

"Not in any book, sir. I found it on your own son's desk." He looked more cross than ever and said,

"You mustn't recite this poem to anybody. It is not a proper poem and you must not repeat it, do you understand? I will have a word or two with my son." I have never understood to this day what it was all about. I only know that when I saw Lord Giannfranco he told me off for going to his desk and reading what I was not supposed to and he called me a naïve little child. I protested, saying,

"I'm not a child."

"And what do you think you are?"

"I'm grown up now. I'm nineteen years old."

"You may be nineteen but you still don't know anything otherwise you would understand what that poem meant. You had no right to look on my desk." I said to myself, "I'd better be quiet." and went away. I made sure I kept out of his sight for a while until everything cooled down.

Lady Mary heard all about it and must have felt sorry for me because she said,

"Ida, tomorrow after five I would like to take you to Rome with me to do some shopping. Come to meet me near Lord Carmine's office and I'll be there. If not, I'll be inside talking to Mother Superior." Lord Rossi's special office was opposite the entrance to the Pope's apartments on the right of the square. I said,

"Thank you, Lady Mary. I very much appreciate you being so kind."

"Ida, you know I like going shopping and it's nice if you can come with me. We'll go to a coffee bar and have a nice espresso together." I was very excited about being taken to a coffee bar. This is lovely, I thought.

Next day as soon as I finished work I got ready to go shopping. I went to the place she said she'd be but instead of going right I went left. I was fascinated by all the beautiful rooms, one after another, and lost myself wandering around as if in a fairytale. Before I knew it I was in the Pope's bedroom! Mother Superior was there and said,

"Ida! What do you think you are doing in here?"

"Who is that old man in bed?"

"He is the Holy Father." She took me out of the room and said,

"How on earth did you find yourself inside here?"

"I was looking for Lady Mary." I said, "She told me she'd be in one the rooms near the Lord Carmine's office."

"But that's not here. It's on the opposite side. Wait here while I ask a guard to take you to her." I said to myself,

"Oh no! I've done it again!" The guard laughed and said,

"Well, miss, not many people have seen the Pope in bed, but you have!" At last I met Lady Mary and she said,

"Don't tell me you got lost again."

"Yes, I did and I ended up going into the Pope's bedroom. Luckily Mother Superior was there and rescued me and got the guard to bring me to you." I said.

"Not again! Well, not many of us have seen His Holiness in bed, but you have. I expect he was asleep but if he'd been awake he would have had a laugh."

"Lady Mary, I was so frightened when Mother Superior told me where I was that I lost my senses."

"Poor Ida, you have had quite a few shocks today."

"I think I have!" We went shopping and Lady Mary bought me a lovely dress. We went to a bar and had espressos which I thought were just fabulous.

Then tragedy struck and I became unwell and unable to work any more. For no reason at all, my legs became very painful and the doctor diagnosed deep vein thrombosis. I needed a lot of rest and decided to go back to live with my parents for while until I got better. I was given some work to do while I was in the village. I tried my very best but with little success.

While I was there I fell in love with a boy from the village but both his parents and mine didn't like the idea. I returned to the Vatican and he went to work in Switzerland. We corresponded for nearly a year but both of us felt it was no use. We decided there was nothing between us to make it worthwhile continuing to write.

On 2nd February, Rome woke up under a thick blanket of snow. The Vatican looked picturesque. A few of us young people in the Vatican went into Piazza Belvedere. We couldn't contain ourselves and began to bombard each other with snowballs. We had a lot of fun. But the snow kept on and on and we all got fed up with it. In April the snow was still coming down and by that time we had all had enough of it.

Now I was coming of age. I had always dreamed of being twenty-one and now renewed my ambition in my mind. The administration at the Vatican had given me money to get better from my illness and some extra to help my parents because my father wasn't well. I had no intention of staying as a cook or looking after children. My intention as always was to work in a hospital. But at last I began to realise what my Aunty Carmel had told me: I was a dreamer. In

Italy at that time only nuns could be trained as nurses and all that I had learned in hospital and by looking after children was no use to me if I didn't want to become a nun. I wanted to help people without becoming a nun. A lot of pressure was put on me to become to be one. They said,

"Nuns look after children, nuns can work in hospitals. You can study and become whatever you want to be, but you must become a nun." I knew I didn't have the calling for that vocation. I wanted to be a good Christian, have a family and help others less fortunate than me.

I sought advice from Lord Rossi and told him I was prepared to go abroad, learn languages, come back to Italy and teach children languages. Lady Mary didn't like the idea of me leaving the Vatican at all but I knew that sooner or later there wouldn't be a job for me unless I did what they wanted me to and I wasn't prepared to do that. Lord Rossi said,

"Now, Ida, I will give you a reference letter to help you wherever you want to go. Make sure it's with you all the time. I will give you a contact in London at a convent in North Hampstead where you will be able to stay. They will help you with whatever you need there. They'll help you to find a college to learn English. But you mustn't say anything. You'll need to go back to your village to get a passport."

"Thank you, sir, I very much appreciate your help. I'll keep in contact with your family."

On Thursday 1st August 1956 I was supposed to leave the Vatican City to go to my village for two months holiday. It would give me the chance to apply for a passport so I could go abroad. When it was time to go back to the Vatican, I would go to London and nobody could do anything about it.

I received a letter from the young man I had corresponded with. He wrote:

> 'Dear Ida, I would like to know which day you're leaving the Vatican to go back to the village.'

I wrote back and said:

> 'I'm going back to the village on 1st August for two months holiday.'

He wrote back and said:

'Good, I will wait for you at Rome Termini Station so we can travel together and discuss our future together.'

After I read that I thought,
"Oh no, what will my family say when they see us arrive together? The gossiping will never stop and it will be an embarrassment to my family and to the Vatican. Even if we do nothing wrong, just travel together, that will be enough to set a lot of tongues wagging." I went to Lord Rossi and said,
"Sir, can you change my holiday so that instead of leaving on 1st August, I leave on Wednesday 31st July?"
"Ida, what is wrong?" he asked.
"Nothing, sir, but I can't go on the first. I must go a day before. I can't tell you the reason because it is much too personal."
"All right, Ida. I trust you. If you can't tell me, as a father I understand that you must have a reason. I will make sure you leave on 31st July."

So Wednesday 31st July came and I went for two months holiday as I had always done each year. When I returned I would make my decision. I wouldn't let the nuns know about my plan, but Lord Rossi would know all about it because he would help me to achieve it. I said 'goodbye' to everybody including my special friend, Eugenia. The chauffeur took me in the Bentley car to Termini Station. He said,
"Goodbye, Miss Festa. I will be here when you come back."
"Goodbye, Vincenzo." I caught the train from platform 17 direct to Cassino. At Cassino station one of my family would meet me and take me home.

The next day the brother of my ex-boyfriend arrived but he didn't have his brother with him. His mother asked,
"Annold, where is your brother?"
"I left him at Rome Termini Station," he said, "waiting for Ida to arrive from the Vatican so they could travel together."
"But Ida arrived yesterday." his mother said. He arrived a day later. He and his family weren't very pleased with me but I didn't mind. My reputation was much more important than they thought.

CHAPTER TWENTY – PREPARING MY PASSPORT

A couple of weeks later I received a contract from London saying I could work and study there as long as I liked. In Italy, August is holiday time for everybody and it is impossible to make any applications then because no offices are open.

One day at the beginning of September I started to walk from Catailli to Conca Campania. On the way I met the mother of my husband-to-be. She was very friendly towards me and wouldn't stop talking. I knew that my family and her family had always been friends but I didn't know that her son had any feelings for me. I didn't have any thoughts about him. After I managed to get away from her, I wondered what it was all about. What she'd said didn't make any sense to me.

When I reached Conca I went to the Register Office for my birth certificate. When I came out I met the owner of the castle. At the beginning of my story I mentioned that his sister had taught me for a little while before the war and then she had left. The war had brought everything to a standstill. After it finished, the few men that were left tried their best to help us. Don Ricardo, the owner of the castle, was one of them. He was present at my last exam. He said,
"You missed three years of school yet you passed your exam with very high marks and now you're reaping the benefit. You are only in the position you are in today because you made an effort in everything you did. God has blessed you."
"I didn't think much of my education," I told him, "but I had no choice. There wasn't anything else to be done at that time. Soon I'm leaving the Vatican to go to London to study English. When I come back, with help from the Vatican, I hope to be able to teach English to little children."
"Ah! I know you will be a success. You've always been a good scholar. Tell me, Ida, where are you going now?"
"I'm applying for a passport. I've already got my birth certificate so now I'm going to the police for them to confirm that I was not in any trouble while I lived here."
"But it's much too far to walk."
"I don't intend to walk. I will wait for a courier to take me there."
"But that won't be for a long time."
"Well, I'll just have to wait." I said.

"Wait a minute. In my castle we have a private school. One of the teachers lives near there. He'll finish his lecture in a few minutes. I'll ask him to take you there and bring you back." He went back into the castle and a few minutes later he came out with a young man.

"This is the young lady I told you about." he said to him, "Will you take her and when she's finished bring her back, please?"

"Yes I will, Don Ricardo." The teacher opened the car door for me, shut it, went to the other side and jumped in. I waved to Don Ricardo and the young man drove away. About fifteen minutes later we arrived.

"Will you stop here, please?"

"I have to go to the next village so we'll drive there first and stop here on the way back. That way you'll have more time to do what you want." I began to wonder about this man. I said to myself,

"This man is not what Don Ricardo thinks he is." He began to drive along what appeared to be a very deserted road. Then he said,

"You are in my hands now and I can do what I please with you." I looked at him and said,

"If you touch me with one finger I will open the door of your car and kill myself." I began to put my hand on the door handle.

"Have you forgotten who asked you to take me to the police station? Think what will happen to you if you do me any harm. You just think!" And he said,

"I was only joking. I just wanted to see what kind of girl you are."

"You were not joking. You would have taken advantage of me if you thought you could get away with it. You are a bad man, that's what you are. Turn the car around right now and take me straight to the police station, where I was supposed to go in the first place. You'll find out who I am there, for a start. Then, when we get back to Conca, I'll tell Don Ricardo what kind of man he employs in his private school."

"Oh don't do that, please! Honestly, I was only joking." he said.

"I don't care if you joked with me. I don't think for a moment you are a man who can be trusted with anybody."

"Miss Festa, if you tell Don Ricardo I will lose my job. I will be a finished man. Please don't do that to me, I beseech you, don't!" Now he was driving back to where we should have gone in the first place. When we arrived there he said again,

"Please don't do that to me. If you say anything I will be a finished man. I really didn't mean it."

"So you keep saying. I don't know what you mean. I only know what you said to me. I told you before, you are a bad man. You

176

just can't be trusted."

We went into the police station and I said,
"Good afternoon. May I speak with the Chief Inspector, please?"
"Who may I say wants him?" the policeman asked.
"Tell him I'm the niece of Giuseppe Festa." The Chief Inspector came out and said,
"Good afternoon, Miss Festa. How is your uncle?"
"He's well, thank you."
"What can I do for you today?"
"Sir, I have permission to go to England to learn English and I need a document from this office to be able to get my passport."
"That will take a little while. Will you please make yourself comfortable, you and your friend?" After a few minutes the papers I needed were ready and he said,
"There you are, Signorina, and tell your uncle I will see him tomorrow at the bar for a cup of coffee and a chat."
"Yes, sir, I will tell him. Thank you and goodbye." We went back to the car. The man drew a long sigh of relief and said,
"Thank you very much."

When we reached Conca he said,
"Can I take you home, please? And can we meet again?"
"You have the cheek to ask me out after all you have said? Never in my life do I want to meet a man like you again." and with that I opened the door of the car and ran into the house as fast as I could.

After a few weeks I had finalised the details of my passport and began to prepare myself to leave Italy, unbeknown to the nuns in the Vatican. I wouldn't go back there any more.

Before I left I wanted to change the picture of St Barbara and replace it with one of the Vatican, so I waited for my mother go out, otherwise she would never have let me do this. The picture of St Barbara was very dear to my mother but to me it was a reminder of very sad times in our lives. The picture of the Vatican was something very dear to me. I'd met good people like the Rossis there and I wanted to change the bad memories for good ones. At last my mother went out. I bolted the front the door and went into the room where the picture was. As I looked at it, it appeared as if St Barbara wanted to say something to me. I said to myself,
"Don't be silly, Ida, it's just a picture." I shook my head, took the

picture off the wall and put it gently on my bed because I didn't want to break the glass. If my mother saw what I was doing she would have gone mad, and if I'd broken the glass it would have been even worse. For a few minutes I thought how awful it was of me to do this, knowing how she loved the picture. Then I said to myself,

"Go on, Ida, do it quickly and make a good job of it. When she realises what's happened it'll be too late to tell me off because I won't be in this country any longer. I'll be on my way to England." But I still had a funny sensation. Behind the picture were thick pads so I took a razor from my father's cabinet and cut all around the frame. I took a deep breath. What was this? I was trembling as I saw big notes of what looked like paper money with five figures written on them. I was confused and shocked. I didn't know what to do with that amount of old money. I knew it was the kind that was no longer in circulation. Mussolini's face looked out from the notes. I was frightened. I thought if I told my mother she might have a heart attack and if I told my father he might be very cross with my mother, after all the hardship we'd suffered after the war. I wasn't sure what would come of it.

When my father had come back from Germany, he always used to ask my mother,

"Angelina, what happened to all the money we had?"

"Some of it was stolen," she said, "and the rest was taken by mice to make nests for their young ones." I remembered that happening but she must have forgotten that most of the money was kept for safety behind this picture. Now here it all was, good for nothing! She had always kept that picture well guarded but, what with the worry of the war, she must have forgotten about it. I expect it amounted to their life savings.

I thought I would seek advice before saying anything about it. I took all the money and put it in a bag, sealed the picture of St Barbara and put the Vatican picture back in my case. I went to County Hall in Conca to see Lorenzo De Felicia who was a good friend of the family and very trustworthy. It was the last day of September and still warm. I reached Conca all hot and bothered and went into Uncle Lorenzo's office (that's what my cousin and I usually called him).

"Uncle Lorenzo, may I have a private word with you, please?"

"Yes of course," he said, "I'm having my break in half an hour so I'll be with you soon. For the time being, sit there," he pointed to a bench in the corner of the waiting room, "until I'm ready for you." So I waited for a half an hour and then he came and said,

"Here I am, young lady. Shall we go home and have a nice cup of coffee?"

"Yes please, Uncle Lorenzo." We arrived at his house, which was only a few yards from his office, and he said,

"Now, tell me what is bothering you."

"I don't know how to begin. In few days I will leave the Vatican to go to England to learn English. Before I go I thought I would change a picture of St. Barbara for one of the Vatican and, as I did so, look what I discovered!"

"Oh my goodness me! What is that? All your father's savings? You know that this money has no value. These notes were taken out of circulation fourteen years ago. You'd better not tell your father otherwise there will be trouble. And you'd better not tell your mother otherwise the shock might kill her."

"So what can we do with all this money?"

"Nothing. We'll have to dispose of it."

"How do we do that?"

"We'll have to burn it."

"Surely not!"

"I know it'll be difficult for you to watch but, my dear, these notes are worthless and they'll only make trouble for your family. Before I do it, you must promise me you'll never, ever say anything to anybody about it." I began to cry and said,

"I promise to you that I will never, ever say anything to anybody ever."

"I know it hurts you and it hurts me, too, to do such a thing when I think of all the work your family did to make this money and all your hardships after the war. To think, all the time this money was behind the picture! If she had remembered before it went out of circulation, things could have changed. You would have had a different life altogether."

As I said, the weather was still hot so there was no fire laid. He put the notes in the grate, struck a match and they went up in flames.

"I was never able to study to achieve my ambition. Instead it's been very difficult for me and still is to this day." I said, "I'm still no better off than when I first began to dream about a life full of success." I went home very upset. My parents thought it was because I was sorry to be leaving Italy. They said,

"Ida, if you don't want go, don't go! Stay here with us. We only have you."

"I must go and get on with my life." I said, "There is no other way."

I was very angry that the money had been wasted. Why was my mother such a silly woman? How could she have forgotten all that money behind the picture? Now I understood why the picture was so important to her. Yet if it meant so much, why, oh why didn't she remember?

October 11th couldn't come soon enough. I wanted to leave this country and never come back. I told myself I'd better say goodbye to all my cousins and aunties and friends before they realised why I looked so angry. I went around, said goodbye and gave big kisses to my parents. As I got near the coach, I saw the mother of my husband-to-be again
"Goodbye, Ida." she said, "I hope you'll write soon. Aldo is very concerned about you going to a foreign country all by yourself."
"You tell him not to worry. I will enjoy travelling abroad. It will be a new adventure for me." She looked at me and wondered why I was so eager to leave Italy. In my heart I thought it would be good to be out of this country for a little while. I realised I was blaming my mother for everything.

The coach began to move, taking me to Mignano di Monte Lungo station. From Mignano I took the train at seven in the morning for Rome. At ten I left Rome for London. I reached London on October 13th at eight in the evening. It was all ready dark and I went to the hotel that Lord Rossi had booked for me.

CHAPTER TWENTY-ONE – THE BEGINNING OF A NEW LIFE IN LONDON

The evening was very dark and damp. I entered the hotel which seemed very large. I went into the reception area, registered and the porter took my case upstairs to my room. I gave him a tip and said in Italian,
"Grazie mille. (A thousand thanks.)" I refreshed myself, changed my dress and went downstairs for supper.

The dining room was very big with a Persian carpet on the floor. There were lots of tables with white tablecloths all set for supper. Many people were already eating. Some tables had four chairs and some had only two. There was a very long sideboard, a couple of red lampshades that gave a nice colour to the room, and a big fireplace with a beautiful coal fire that made it feel very warm and comfortable. I sat all by myself and couldn't understand anything that was said. I didn't like the food but ate it anyway. Then I followed the other people into the lounge.

This was a huge room about seventy five feet long and forty feet wide. There was thick carpet on the floor, lots of watercolours on the walls and some large, interesting oil paintings a bit like those in the Vatican but not by Italian artists, though they were just as good. There were lots of people relaxing, chatting and smoking cigarettes. I thought they all seemed very nice.

Next morning, 14th October, I woke up, opened the window and smoke came in the room. I couldn't see anything outside. It looked as if London was on fire! I thought I'd better not get in the lift as it might be dangerous, so I ran downstairs to see what was going on. I found everybody sitting down and nobody worried about anything. I shouted in Italian,
"Fuoco, fuoco fuori c'è fuoco! (Fire, fire, outside there is a fire! London is on fire!)" but nobody understood. They all looked at me, wondering what the matter was, not understanding what this foreign girl was saying. The receptionist knew I was Italian so she called the Italian Embassy and asked them to speak to me. An Italian said,
"Signorina Festa, what is the matter?" I said,
"There is a fire here but nobody is taking any notice." They said,
"Oh dear, no! This is fog, not a fire."

"But I've never seen it like that in Italy before."

"But this is London and not Rome," he said, "In London there is always plenty of fog, and I can assure you that there's nothing to worry about. London is a big city with millions of houses and each one has five or six fireplaces and they are all in use now! This is the beginning of your stay in London and there are many other things which you will get know in time! London is what it is." And with that he said goodbye.

It was time for me to take a taxi and go to the convent in North Hampstead. There was a sister there who could speak a little Italian. She welcomed me,
"I'm Sister Mary and I speak a little Italian. I will try to help you as much as I can. Now, this is your room and later on there will be a nice English dinner for you."

My room was a good size with a comfortable bed, a bedside cabinet with a light, a chest of drawers, a wardrobe and a nice armchair. After a day or two Sister Mary said,
"My dear, I've been told you have come to England to learn English. I will arrange for private lessons in Golders Green College, which is not very far from here, but you must catch the bus. There is a stop just a few yards from here and the bus will take you right to the front of the College for Foreign Students. There also is an underground station, just one stop away." At that time of year, by 5 p.m. London was very dark. It was also damp and so foggy and smoky that it could almost choke you. There wasn't much light; it was very dim and horrible. I was scared and my fear was made worse because I couldn't speak or understand a single word of English.

After three or four lessons I had a very frightening and terrible experience. As I came down the stairs outside the College there was a car with the door open. A man tried to pull me into the car. I struggled and managed to get away from him but in doing so I lost my first year book, which was essential for my English lessons. But the man still followed me. I thought if I crossed the road to the traffic lights I would lose him because he'd have turn the car around, which wouldn't be easy. But at that time there weren't many other cars about and he did turn around and followed me. I realised he was trying to get me again. There was a bus at the bus stop and I jumped on. The bus conductor asked me where I wanted go, but I wasn't interested in a ticket. I was watching the car to see if he was still following me. I was very frightened. I knew I was in great danger but I couldn't tell the bus conductor what the trouble was and he kept insisting on the ticket.

I spotted Golders Green underground station and jumped off the bus while it was still going, went into the underground and managed to lose him. When I reached the convent I said,
"Sister Mary, I will not be going to the College any more because I'm rather scared of the dark. I had a very frightening experience tonight. In Rome we weren't ever allowed to go out after eight p.m., and I don't want go out in the dark even if I am twenty-one."
She said,
"My dear, you are right. London is very dark and dangerous for young foreign girls like yourself. I will telephone the College and see if it is possible to take daytime lessons."

Sister Mary telephoned the College and enquired if it was at all possible for lessons for the foreign students to be in the daytime.
She told the people at the College what happened and said,
"These poor student girls do not know London and it's not right for them to be out in the dark and it's not safe for them. They can't speak English therefore I'm very concerned for their safety."

I realised I wasn't the only foreign girl in that place. There were other foreign girls lodging there, not Italian but from many other countries. The College told Sister Mary that daytime lessons were impossible because there weren't enough girls. Then I decided to take a job as domestic and learn the hard way.

Sister Mary called a taxi to take me 79 Rowland Drive in Golders Green. I paid the taxi and said,
"Thank you very much." Those where the first words I learned. It was a detached four-bed room house called 'Shalom'. It was about one mile from the High Street. There was a big garden all around it. I went in the gate and walked down the path to the front door. There was a smooth lawn in front of the house with a bed of roses in it. A gentleman opened the door and said,
"Good evening, Miss Festa. We've been expecting you." I just nodded my head and he let me in. It was a beautiful house: there was a hall, a dining room, a very long sitting room, one big window facing the front garden, and French doors looking onto the back garden. There was a kitchen with a larder, a breakfast room, a garage and large garden at the back of the house.

They had only one boy of ten years old. His name was Mark and he was very nice. The lady was tall and good-looking with blonde hair and the gentleman was nice. I liked the family very much. I didn't have any idea how an English family lived, their customs, their diet or how they cleaned their house. They didn't tell me anything but just assumed I knew it all. If they had bothered to get an interpreter, I could have served them better.

I couldn't possibly know what they had for breakfast. They had bacon and eggs and toast and marmalade and three or four cups of tea. Sometimes they had fish or other things. On the continent we had a roll with jam and a cup of coffee.

This lady expected me to put a cloth round my head and to scrub the front door steps. I never thought I'd have to scrub front door steps! I had to set the table and cook and serve a big breakfast. After they'd finished, I cleared the table and did the washing up. The gentleman went to his office, the lady would take the boy to school and then I expect she went to work in an office or a shop. I didn't see anybody again until the evening. After they left, I would go upstairs and make the beds, dust, clean with the electric machine, come downstairs, clean the stove and fill it up with coke so that we had plenty of hot water all day. Then I took the ashes from the sitting room fire and relaid it with paper and sticks so it was ready to be lit when they came back in the evening. They only needed to put a match to it.

Monday was washing day, Tuesday was ironing day, Wednesday was baking day and so on. I didn't finish work until ten o'clock in the evening, six days a week. One day a week I worked until two o'clock and then had the rest of the day off. I couldn't learn any English because I didn't see anybody all day long. In the evening they came in about seven o'clock, had their meal and then they would sit and read, have a chat together by themselves, discuss the business of the day and after that they would go to the sitting room and have coffee.

Once I was told off because I used butter to make roast potatoes instead of margarine. I didn't understand anything about English cooking, so I just did what I did in my own country. We always cooked with olive oil but, because I didn't have that, I used butter instead of margarine.

I'd been there four months when something happened that was very upsetting. The lady of the house had a parrot and, before she went to the office, she would clean out the cage and feed him. Once when doing this the bird flapped his wings, the cage fell down and the glass broke. She then cut hardboard, fixed it all round and went away without telling me anything. I know I couldn't understand the language but she could have shown me; it wouldn't have been difficult. After all, she soon made me understand when she didn't like something I had done. Now I know what had happened: the bird had made a hole in the hardboard. But I didn't know then and I opened the window to clean it and the bird flew out of the window, and that was the end of the parrot. I can't put it into words: when the lady came home, she went ballistic.

I couldn't take any more. With that I packed my case and off I went to Hampstead and I told them what had happened. Sister Mary said,
"My dear, I have news for you. Just today a gentleman has been here and asking if there was any chance at all of getting a girl with a good knowledge of Italian. He wants his son to learn the language. He was a prisoner of war in Italy and the Italians not only never put him in prison, but they looked after him so well that he says if he hadn't had a family in England, he would have liked one in Italy. He hopes that when he retires he will go back there with his family to live."

Sister Mary was very happy because she knew the situation in the previous house and that I would never be able to learn any English there, and that that was the reason I came to England. So she told this gentleman that I could not do the housework if I was to teach the boy Italian and give proper attention to his needs.

Next day I went to meet Mr and Mrs Green and little John in a beautiful detached house called 'The Evergreens'. It was in Hendon, not very far from Golders Green, NW11. The house had four bedrooms, a sitting room, dining room, a big hall with a breakfast room, a kitchen, two bathrooms, a garage and large gardens at the front and back. They had a daily helper for five days a week. My wage was five pounds a week, which at that time was a lot of money. Mr and Mrs Green had various shops in Oxford Street. I was left caring for John and the house along with their daily helper. John spoke English and I spoke Italian so he helped me and I helped him.

Every morning at seven o'clock I would go into his bedroom and say,
"Buon giorno John," and he would say,
"No, Miss, it's 'Good morning'." Then I would get him up, take him to the bathroom, wash him and teach him how to brush his teeth. Then I would ask him what he wanted for breakfast in the morning. He would say,
"Oh no, Miss, not 'in the morning' but 'this morning'."

When he didn't understand me he would go upstairs and throw all his toys out of the window into the garden down below. I said,
"Oh no! Tu lai hai buttati dalla finestra e tu li raccoglierai. (You've thrown them out the window so now you will pick them up and take them back upstairs)" he said,
"But I don't understand you, Miss."

Mr Green's father and mother lived in St George's Drive near Victoria station and he took us there for the day. At about 1 p.m. his grandmother said John could go to the park if he wanted to see the ducks. His grandfather said,
"I'll drop you both there and then you can come back by yourselves." He took us to Kensington Gardens. I looked at the road and thought it was quite easy to get back - I thought! It was a beautiful day, there was a little wind that moved the leaves on the trees and that made you feeling the spring air, for a while I thought I was In the Vatican garden again as I strolled around the park with little John. The fresh air and the beauty of the flowers made me feel so happy and great satisfaction to have a little boy with me, for whom I was responsible.

There were big and small trees everywhere just bursting into leaf, beds of spring flowers everywhere so beautiful that made me feeling so happy to be there. People of all ages in very walking along the paths but also across the grass that would never be allowed to happen in the Vatican.

We passed many beautiful places, but what John liked best of all was the pool in which ducks were swimming. Many children played happily with their parents, and some had dogs with them. I realised John also liked the animals very much because he wanted to play with them.
I wished I could speak English and explain to him, that he could also have a pet if his parents permitted. There was also a statue of

Peter Pan in bronze, but John was not interested, but what he liked best of all was the boats in the water. He was getting very excited about the all these things, but I couldn't understand him. I saw people playing cricket and wondered what these grown-up men were doing. I didn't understand the game and thought they were rather silly.

The time was getting on, and John became restless, but where is the way that brigs us home? Then I understood how difficult was to be in country with different language. I didn't understand and great fear came over me. John realised I was in a panic and he started to cry. I held his hand tight and hurriedly turned down one path, to the right and then left, with the hope one of them would take us home. Instead we found ourselves in Hyde Park. I was confused and quite frightened more than ever. I wanted take John to his grandmother, but more and more I felt I was incapable of finding the way which I once thought was easy to remember.

I ran around, left and right, and asked several people the way of St George's Drive, but I was horrified when I release no body understood me. We walk and walk until we came to a very large place. There where so many people of all nationality, my only hope was to meet some body who might spoke my language and would be able to help me to find the way home. But no instead I saw a man standing on platform speaking about politics, I thought! Some of the people just walking along and dint take any notice what the man was saying others asking questions and making silly gesture, some of them laughing to the poor old man. I felt sorry for him, but I also saw groups of people were singing, with all their hart, he must be a preacher of the Gospel, because I knew the tune of the songs they were singing.

   Later on John's father told me that was the famous Speaker's Corner in Hyde Park.   Mr. Green said, "Perhaps there is nowhere else in the world a place like this," and I quite agreed with him.

I was very tired and more and I wanted anything else in the world just take that little boy home. At last we found the park gate at Marble Arch, but this was more frightening than ever. There were tall buses I had never seen before and all kind of cars yellow, blue and green. There long endless queues of buses everywhere; it didn't matter where I looked there were masses of people hurrying along while we stood wander how on earth we will be able to go home. By that time I was very upset. Poor little John wanted go home and his grandmother was waiting for him. I was sure she'd have made tea for him and was wondering what had happened to us, where we were and how much longer we would be. I thought about it all and got more frightened.

We crossed the road and I spotted a policeman. At last I had hoped he would understand me, I said In Italian, "Per piacere Signore mi può dire dove è la strada che va a St. Giorgio Drive?" (Please, Sir, can you tell me the road goes to St. George's Drive?) But again with great horror he didn't understood a word I said, I then released it was no use I was lost, and I needed help, and I was in difficulty. For a moment I close my eyes and I prayed to God to help me to take John safe to his grandmother, when I felt a tap on my shoulder. I opened my eyes and I see a very tall young man very elegant wearing a suit that we call in Italy the Prince of Wales suit.
He said in Italian, "Lei è Italiana? (Are you an Italian?)"
I said, "Yes I'm Italian, and I'm lost, I need to take this little boy home to where is grandmother is. But I don't remember the way, and nobody understands me when I ask people where St George's Drive is!"
"Don't worry Miss I'm English, but I have studied Italian and I can help you."
I shouted, "Oh, thank you Sir." I then realised God had answered my prayer.
I told him he was the kindest man in world and I thanked God for him. He said he also was a Christian and God knew I needed help. And not long after that we were home at last!

Now Easter was upon us. Julie came home from boarding school. I didn't know who she was. As far as I knew, Mr. and Mrs. Green had only one son, little John. I didn't know anything about the daughter they had in boarding school. I could not understand why Julie put the bread I bought in the dustbin. I was so naïve about everything and had a lot to learn. Easter is for Christian people, but Jews call it Passover and at that time they can't eat any bread with yeast in it, according the law that God gave to Moses:

> 'The children of Israel murmured against Moses; and Aaron in the wilderness said unto them," Would to God we had died by the hand of the Lord in the land of Egypt when we saw the fleshpots and when we did eat bread to the full; for ye have brought us forth into this wilderness with hunger." Then the

Lord said unto Moses, "Behold, I will rain bread from heaven for you and the people shall go out and gather a certain ration every day, that I may prove them whether they walk in the law or not."

That is why the bread the Jews eat must have no yeast.

This girl, Julie, liked to enjoy herself. She met all her friends and had parties in the house every night. They were pyjama parties. I was so naïve and didn't know about the way of life in England or anywhere else. I just saw this girl causing havoc in the house and creating a mess everywhere.

Once I decided to take little John to a children's film and when we came back there was mess everywhere, teenagers playing in pyjamas, partying in all the bedrooms, including mine! I was furious. I couldn't understand whatever the matter was with these children, because I'd never played like this. I didn't know this was the kind of thing children did when their parents were away. I just couldn't understand and I was very annoyed. Julie came home from the boarding school, her parents were out of the country on business trips.

On Monday morning the daily helper came in, very upset. She told Julie off and the girl said the house belonged to her and she didn't need to come back any more; and so that was the end of the daily helper. When her parents came back and found we hadn't got the daily helper any more, they had to decide what to do. It was almost impossible to get help for the house. Mr Green took a day off. He spoke to me in Italian and asked if it was possible for me to take John to the nursery nearby for nine o'clock then go home and do some housework, prepare dinner for John and at one o'clock go back to the nursery and bring the little boy home. Now Julie was going back to the boarding school, I thought it wouldn't be so difficult to run the house and look after the little boy. But it was a big house and a big responsibility to look after the child as well.

I had started to speak English. Life was very full but I enjoyed the challenge. Sometimes John would make me very cross, but also sometimes very happy and sometimes I couldn't do anything but laugh.

One day, before she went out to her business, his mother said,

"Ida, I've bought a nice piece of fish for you and John and I'd like you to cook it in milk and butter. I've put it in the refrigerator. There are plenty of vegetables. Is that all right?"
"Thanks." I said, "I'm sure John will like the fish very much." Before I went to the nursery I got everything ready so that when I came back I only had to mash the potatoes with milk and butter, cook the carrots and cabbage, and make a rice pudding.

I usually sat with him, but this time I had so many jobs to do that I thought he would be all right on his own. A little while later he said in Italian,
"Signorina, posso lasciare il tavolo per piacere? (Please, Miss, may I leave the table?)"
"Have you finished?" I asked.
"Si, grazie. (Yes, thank you very much.)" Ah, what a shock! The table was a complete mess. He had only eaten the mashed potatoes and the rice pudding and put all the fish and the vegetables under the tablecloth. Well, I just had to laugh, without letting him see me. I made it look as if I was very cross and said,
"John, look at the mess you have made. Why did you put the fish under the tablecloth?"
"I didn't like the fish and the vegetables." he said, "I only liked the mashed potatoes."

I grew very fond of the boy. After all, he was always with me and it was through him that I began to speak English. He also learned to speak Italian well. When we had had the daily helper, I had more time for little John but now I didn't find it so easy.

One day I had a terrible fright. John asked me if we could play hide and seek. I said,
"Yes, you go and hide and I'll count up to fifty and come looking for you." But I had so much to do the fact that John had gone and hidden somewhere went completely out of my head. When I remembered, an hour later, I went completely mad. I searched the house but the little boy was nowhere to be found I was desperate. I didn't know what to do and finally summoned up my last bit of courage and went next door in the hope that he was there, playing with the children. No, he wasn't there, so I went to the house on the other side. No, he wasn't there either. I no longer knew what to do. I went into the garden, very upset. As I sat on the garden chair, on a pile of cushions, there was a loud scream which made me jump up. It was John who had fallen asleep while he was

waiting for me to find him! I can't describe the relief.

It was a lot of responsibility to look after such a big house and such an active child, but I loved him very much and I enjoyed the challenge and was grateful for the opportunity. I liked the people I worked for. I still think they were the best people I worked for. Mr Green wasn't at home very often but he was a gentleman. When he was at home, he played the guitar and sang Italian and English songs. The food was the best English sort but we Italians always think we can do better! That was forty-six years ago and now I think the English can cook as well as anybody else.

I liked the way they looked after one another in their own community. I was told that when any of their children got married, they all got together to buy what they needed to give them a good start in life. If a family couldn't pay their bills, the community would always pay for them. I think that is wonderful.

Life was grand. Of course, like everybody else at the time, they had their problems, but they were well-supported by the community. I didn't see the lady of the house very much because she wasn't there most of the time. When she was there, she was very pleasant. She was very pretty and once asked me if she looked like Gina Lollobrigida. I said she was even prettier than Lollobrigida which made her very pleased and next time I saw her she brought me a dress from one of the many shops she had in Oxford Street.

As they say, all good things come to an end. One thing I learned was never to talk about politics or religion with the people I worked for. They paid a good wage and I would leave it like that. Mrs Green wasn't often at home but one week she was and she started a conversation with me about Passover. She said,
"The Roman soldiers were very bad for my country."
"How do you know?" I said, "You weren't there. And, after all, the Romans civilized your country."
"My country was much more civilized than yours." she said, "Rome didn't even exist in Abraham's time. We didn't need Julius Caesar to make us pay taxes to support the Roman people." And then she began to talk about Pontius Pilate and said,
"He wasn't much good for anything." I know I shouldn't have taken any notice. At that time the war was still very fresh in people's minds and all the things that so-called Christians like Hitler had

done to the poor Jewish people in Germany.   But I said,
"Ah! You Jews were the very people who killed Jesus."
"We didn't kill him." she said, "the Romans did."
"The Jews said, 'Away with him!' and crucified him." I said.   Then I
thought I'd better be quiet.   I needed a new permit to work in this
country and to continue to learn English.

I went to the convent to say goodbye to Sister Mary, because she
would soon be transferred to a different country.   I would lose the
security that I'd had until then.
"Sister Mary", I said, "I've had a conversation with Mrs Green in
which I think I wasn't very nice."   Then I told her what had
happened.   She said,
"Now you have learned to speak English quite well, don't you think
your next permit could be for working in the hospital so that one
day you might succeed in becoming what you want to be?"
"What do I want to be?"
"My dear, you like that little boy so much you've even forgotten
your dream!"
"What was my dream?"
"Don't you want be a nurse?"
"Yes, but what about John?"
"Don't worry, my dear.   He has very rich parents and they'll soon
have someone else to look after him.   They might have to employ
another daily helper, too.   They won't find it easy to get someone to
clean their house and teach their child like you have done.   It is
about time they understood that there are not so many girls as silly
as you have been, willing to do two jobs and get paid for one.   I will
make a telephone call today to the matron of Edgware Hospital to
make an appointment for you very soon."

After a few minutes the appointment was made.
"Next Wednesday at two o'clock go to Edgware Hospital.   It is not
very far from here.   I know you will find it easily, now you've been
in this country nearly a year." I said,
"Thank you very much.   I don't know how I will ever manage when
you aren't here for me any more."
"You will manage.   I will ask God to look after you.   Remember he
will never let you down.   Pray always and trust in Him, OK?"

So I went to the house and by chance Mr Green was there.
"Mr Green", I said, "I need time off on Wednesday 2nd October,
please."

"It will be very difficult, but I'll see what I can do, Ida." he said. October 2nd came and I went to my interview with the Matron of the Edgware General Hospital. She said,

"Where do you come from and how long you have been in England?"

"I'm twenty-two and I've been in England nearly a year."

"Why do you want work in a hospital?"

"Since I can remember, I have always wanted work in a hospital and look after people less fortunate than I am, not only to give them medical care but also tender, loving care. Unfortunately in my country only nuns are allowed to look after sick people. Here, I have a letter from the Vatican City written in Italian and English."

"We'll be very pleased to have you here to work with us." she said.

So then I had a big dilemma. I didn't mind leaving Mr and Mrs Green and the lovely house, but I did mind leaving the little boy John, very much. But I summoned all my courage and gave notice to Mr. and Mrs. Green.

A new job and a new life. Now I started work in a hospital as a nursing assistant and my life was so different it seemed like another world. It was such a big place with so many people from all walks of life. It was a different environment but I knew I would enjoy it. After all, I wanted to be a nurse whatever the cost. I had left Italy in order to achieve my dream of being able to look after people. This was what I wanted in life. But I couldn't get the little boy John out of my mind. After few days I couldn't stand it any longer and I went back to see him on my first day off.

I took some sweets and planned to stay with him for while, or possibly take him to a children's film at the local cinema, if the parents allowed me. I went to the nursery and waited until the children came out. They all came out but John was nowhere to be seen. I went inside and asked for John. I said,

"Where is John Green, please?" The lady in charge of the nursery recognised me and asked me into her office. I went in and she said,

"Please, Miss, do sit down," pointing to a chair, "I have something to tell you." I knew from her look that something had happened but I could never, ever have been prepared for what that teacher had to say. She took a deep breath and said,

"Little John is dead." I couldn't understand and said,

"I don't understand what you're saying. Will you please explain to me what those words mean?" She took a newspaper and showed me a picture of a little boy who had been hit by a car. There was a little body lying on the ground and a policewoman was covering it with a cloth. For a moment I couldn't take it in, then I screamed and said,

"No, no, not John! It can't be. Please tell me that little body is not John." I burst into tears and the teacher tried to comfort me but it was no use. I was completely inconsolable. She called a taxi and I asked the driver to take me to the convent in North Hampstead.

When Sister Mary saw me she ran up to me and said,
"Ida, what has happened to you?" I couldn't speak. She took me to the rest room, sat me on a chair and gave me a glass of water. Then she said again,
"Now, tell me what has happened." I looked at her and said,
"John Green, the little boy I looked after, is dead."
"Oh no! My dear, how did it happen?" I gave her the newspaper and she read it and gave a loud scream,
"Oh no, no!" The other nuns heard the scream and came in wanting to know what was going on. She composed herself and said,
"I'm very sorry, very sorry, my dear, for you and the poor, poor parents and the sister of that poor little boy. If it is any consolation to you, God has saved you from this terrible, terrible tragedy."
"How has God saved me? Please tell me."
"The paper says that you had left and Mr and Mrs Green had employed a German girl. She was taking him to the school, she held his hand but he pulled himself away and ran into the middle of the road. The poor girl tried to catch him but it was no use. The boy just ran in front of a car and the driver could do nothing about it. Now you see, my dear, if you had been there, how could you ever live with such a tragedy? It happened, you have been spared, but that poor, poor French girl, I feel very sorry for her as well."

A few days later I went to the house, but the curtains were drawn and I didn't have the courage to knock at their door, so I returned to the nurses' home and tried very hard to put it behind me and do my best at the nursing job.

I made a few friends there. One of them became a very good friend. She was the daughter of people at the Swiss Embassy and was in London to study English. Like me, she wanted to look after

sick people. We had to work very hard. At that time, the matron and sisters ran the hospital and it was very well managed. The wards there were very clean, the patients were well looked after, everything was sterilised by us under the supervision of a sister in charge. We started at seven thirty in the morning and had half an hour at ten o'clock for a cup of coffee or tea and a cigarette. The day room was so full smoke it was difficult to see one another! One nurse offered me a cigarette and I said,
"I don't smoke."
"My dear, this is the way to be sociable," she said, "to enjoy a cigarette after lunch with the other nurses." I said,
"I don't understand, I've never smoked before and I don't think I want to start now. I don't wish to acquire that kind of habit."
"Let me explain. If you want to be sociable, you buy a packet of Senior Service and you offer them around. We all do it. That is how life is here." So I did it and nearly choked myself! I just wasn't able to smoke.

One nurse called Jacqueline said,
"Ida, I want you to meet my parents and all my brothers and sisters." She took me to a very small flat. There was a very large family in that little space. I met them all and after a while she said,
"Now I'll take you to buy something to eat." She took me to a nearby shop where there were lots of boys with motorbikes dressed in funny suits. They appeared to be her friends and they chatted together and she said,
"I've brought my Italian friend to give her a treat." She bought two big packs of what looked like scrunched up newspaper and said,
"Tonight, you and I will have a good, tasty supper. This is fish and chips. Open the paper and put salt and vinegar on it and then eat it. It's traditional English food and this is one of the best." I opened the newspaper and it was a very tasty meal. I'd never had it before. We didn't need a table but we ate and walked along the road and both enjoyed it very much.

I began to make many friends. One was from Switzerland and another from Spain. I thought life was beautiful. I also had a family friend who wrote to me from Italy very regularly. Bruna was the daughter of people at the Swiss Embassy. She spoke four languages: Italian, French, German and English. Pilar Isle was Spanish, and Jacqueline was English. I thought nothing could possibly go wrong ever again and I took it for granted that everything would remain the same.

One day matron called me into her office and said,

"Miss Festa, I see you have made friends with the Swiss nurse, Bruna Rossa. She is in London to study English. What about you, would you like to go to college with her and learn English? Then you will both be able to train to be SRNs." I said,

"Yes, I would like that very much."

"Well, I'll arrange for you to go to college with your friend."

Bruna was a lovely girl, very well educated and, as I said before, she spoke four languages. Also, she was a good nurse. She had everything going for her and she was a lot of fun to be with. She was full of life. We went to the college twice a week and after three months of going there we both entered the nursing school at the hospital.

There were students and nursing assistants, staff nurses, sisters, matron, porters and cleaners. There were two shifts: one from seven thirty in the morning to five in the afternoon, with a half hour coffee break and one hour for lunch; and the other from seven thirty in the morning until two in the afternoon, with a three hour break and then again from five to eight in the evening. There was also a night shift from eight in the evening to eight in the morning, with a break in between. Other hospitals had different shifts, but they were more or less the same throughout the country.

When we began training, we spent three months at the nursing school working from eight to five, Monday to Friday. After that, we were sent onto the wards for three months. Each ward was run by a different sister in charge, and she would make a report about our progress and hand it to the nursing school head teacher. At that time, Edgware General Hospital was the main one, and there were two others: Hendon Isolation and Colindale Geriatric. It would take three full years to complete our training.

Hendon Isolation Hospital was situated in beautiful part of Hendon Central. In the spring, the garden was full of flowers and it was a nice atmosphere. It all seemed just beautiful to me.

My Spanish friend, Pilar, was much older than me. She was a very nice person and she thought she had to look after me because I was young and naïve about the world around me.

At Christmas in 1957 there were so many parties! I didn't

understand because I had never experienced anything like it in my life before. There was a big party in the nurses' home and one at the college that Bruna and I were invited to. I said to my friend Pilar,

"I won't go for various reasons: one, I have a correspondence with an Italian boy who is a friend of my family. He lives in the same village as my parents and my family like him very much. And secondly, I can't dance and the party isn't really my kind of thing."

"Ida, you are right." she said, "Don't go. You don't know these students. Tell your friend to stay in the nurses' home. There are enough parties here and we know who'll be there. Please tell her not go."

After going to college I began to understand English well. Bruna and I both passed the exams to become trainee nurses. Bruna had the most beautiful dresses and she was very excited because she was a good dancer. In Switzerland she had been to ballet school. She said,

"Come on, Ida, let's enjoy ourselves tonight."

"No, Bruna." I said, "Please don't go. How can you trust them? We might put ourselves in danger. We are foreigners and we don't know these people. I've been told by Pilar that the students are all up to no good. How will we be able to trust them after they've had a few drinks? Who knows what they'll do? Anyway, I can't dance, I don't even possess a dress, I've never been to such place in my life and I have no self confidence."

"I just don't understand you, Ida. How can you refuse such a kind invitation?"

"Look, Bruna, I can't go there with you for the reasons I've just told you."

"How can you let me go by myself?"

"Please, don't go there tonight. There's a nice film on television. We can enjoy that here just as well."

"It's a long time since I've had a dance. Tonight I shall enjoy myself. If you don't want to come because you haven't got a suitable dress, you can choose whatever you want from my wardrobe."

"Thank you, but no thank you! I just don't feel comfortable in that kind of environment. I'm not used to it."

"Ida, I must go."

"I will go downstairs to the lounge with the other nurses and watch the film and when it's finished I will go to my room and wait for you there. Then you can tell me all about your special evening."

I waited and waited for Bruna but she never came back. The nurses' home closed at ten o'clock but if you asked for special permission it could be kept open till eleven o'clock. But twelve o'clock,
One o'clock … I was out of my mind. Bruna never came home that night. I had no choice but to report her to the matron.

The matron said,
"Nurse Festa, will you please go on duty and I will find out what has happened to you friend." I went into the dining room and I noticed that some of the nurses were looking at me and then whispering to one another. I knew then something terrible had happened to Bruna. I left the dining room and went straight back to the matron's office. She said,
"Nurse Festa, you are a very close friend of nurse Rossa and I do understand that you must be very worried but it is against the law for me to give any information to you because you are not her next of kin. But I can tell you that she has been very badly hurt. At this time, I can't say anything more than that. Her parents have been informed and they will be here soon. You go to the dining room and have a cup of tea, please." Now I was very upset. I went to see Pilar, my Spanish friend, and asked if she knew anything about Bruna.
"Pilar, do you know what has happened to Bruna?"
"Ida, I heard from a doctor that she was found outside the nurses' home very badly injured and unconscious at about six this morning. I will try to find out more about what happened to her and where she is now. But please don't say anything."

Later on I met Pilar in the dining room and asked her for more news.
"Ida, I will see you in my room later on after lunch."
"Thank you, Pilar." A few hours later I went to Pilar's bedroom and said,
"Well, Pilar, please tell me everything you know about Bruna."
"There is a rumour that last night something terrible happened to her. Some of the students must have put some kind of drug in her drink and then she was sexually assaulted by many men. I've been told she is very badly hurt and she is in a coma."

I found it very difficult to come to terms with what happened to my friend Bruna. The fact that she was such a nice girl, full of joy, never reserved, made what happened to her seem even worse.

My friend Pilar gave me all the support I needed. But no-one ever told me if she recovered or if she died. I only know that I lost my friend that evening and that left me very sad.

My personality changed completely from then on. From being a very happy young girl, I became a very sad one. In one year I lost two people who I had had the privilege to know and love very much. I lost that smile I always had. The patients felt sorry for me. I refused to go back to the college. I couldn't look at any of them; to me they were all guilty. How can anybody do such a horrible thing?

Now I was in my second year and was sent for three months training to St George's Hospital which at that time was near Marble Arch. I was put on a private ward. There was a lady there who had just lost a baby and she was very low. Sister said,
"Nurse Festa, Mrs Brown has lost a baby and she is very sad. Will you look after her? She needs her hair washed and tender, loving care and I know you are quite able to do that." I said,
"Yes, sister." As I walked through the ward a patient said,
"Nurse Festa, why does a young girl like you never smile?" I said,
"I haven't anything to smile for." Mrs Brown said,
"I lost a baby and have been very sad, but I'm better now. I have been helped by special people and I know they can help you, too." I didn't say anything.

After a couple of days, the sister in charge of the ward called me into her office and said,
"There is a very smart young lady who has been asking for you." For a minute I thought it might be Bruna. She had recovered and now she had come looking for me. But I realised I was dreaming again when sister said,
"Nurse, this is the lady wanting to talk to you." I just looked at her and she said,
"I'm Miss Young. I've been to Hendon Isolation Hospital and was given a little clue as to why you became so sad." Once again I thought she'd come to tell me that Bruna was alive and well again.
"Have you come to tell me my friend Bruna has recovered?"
"No", she said, "I wish I could do that for you, but I'm afraid it is impossible. But if it is any comfort, the same thing happened to me as well and so I know how you must be feeling. You are in a foreign country, away from your family and just when you found a friend, tragedy struck. And I've been told that this was not the first

time."

"No, it's not the first one."

"My dear, life can be very cruel at times. I've been in the same situation. Away from my family, away from my country, nobody knew I even existed. That's the reason why, when you make a friend, you become so close to them. You think that this is the end of the world, but now is the time for you to take courage, put it all behind you and get on with your life. There is no other way, believe me. I know that."

"What happened to you, then?"

"When I was about twelve I was rescued from the Nazis by some English people, but unfortunately my family were all gassed during that evil time in Germany. So, by the grace of God, I'm here today but, like you, in a foreign country and with nobody to love. But life has taught me a lot of things: above all, to look ahead and to trust God." She went on talking to me for about an hour. Miss Young made me realise that I wasn't the only one and there were people in worse positions than me. The next day the lady who had lost her baby was also quite cheerful and we had a long discussion about life, and how to pick up the pieces and get on with it.

CHAPTER TWENTY-TWO – CHANGING FROM A NURSE TO A WIFE AND MOTHER

A few days passed and Mrs Brown, the lady who'd lost the baby, told the sister in charge she would like to have a word with me before she left. When I came on duty, the sister in charge said, "Nurse, Mrs Brown wants to have a word with you."
"Now what have I done wrong?" I said. Sister said,
"I don't know, nurse. You'd better go and see what it's all about."
"Yes, sister, I'll do that." and I went to Mrs Brown. My heart was beating as fast as it could. I didn't know what I had done wrong.
"Mrs Brown, sister said you wanted to see me before you go home."
"Have you have time now?"
"Not really, but maybe I could see you in my break time, if that is all right with you."
"Yes, of course."

In my break I met Pilar and told her I was worried about why Mrs Brown wanted to see me. Maybe I'd done something wrong and she wanted to discuss it with me.
"Oh, Pilar, I'm afraid." I said.
"Don't be so silly!" Pilar said, "Whatever could you have done?"
After I'd spoken to Pilar I felt a bit more confident about hearing what Mrs Brown had to say to me. I pulled myself together and went to her.
"Here I am, Mrs Brown!"
"I am going on holiday. Would you like to come with me to France?"
"Yes, I would like that very much but I must enquire if it's possible to do that without interfering with my nursing school." I was very excited. I went back to the ward and told the sister in charge what Mrs Brown had said.
"Make an appointment with the tutor and she'll be able to advise you," Sister said.
"Thank you, Sister."

I went to see the tutor and she said,
"Yes, but we must book the holiday a month ahead." I went back to Mrs Brown and explained the position. She said,
"All right then, book your holiday now and when I get back from my holiday, you can come and spend a week or two with me and my

husband in our house." Then I told her that I had a correspondence with a young Italian man from my village who was a friend of the family and maybe one day we would get married.

"His name is Aldo."

"Dear, we need a young man to work in our house. Why don't we get him to come to this country and work for us?"

"This is more easily said than done." I said, "My parents are very old fashioned. They will never permit him to come to this country without being married to me. And I hope one day to return to Rome and get a job as a nurse, if I ever manage to get my qualification here. If I can also learn to speak English well, there will be quite new possibilities for me to do what I've always wanted."

"Look," she said, "if you really love this young man, do what Sophia Loren did: marry him by proxy and when he comes to England you can get married in a church. Then your parents can't say a thing and, if you go back to the Vatican, they can't put any pressure on you to become a nun again."

"All that makes sense," I said, "but where will we live?"

"You can both live here. I will give you an apartment and if you like you can continue to be a nurse and he will work for us."

"I'll think about it and let you know when you are back from your holiday."

As I said before, I was at St George's Hospital for three months but after that my work shifted and I had to go back to Hendon Isolation Hospital Nursing Home, part of Edgware General Hospital. I told Pilar, my friend, what had happened to me and she thought that, as I had become very untrusting of people after the Bruna tragedy, maybe this was a good opportunity to settle down, put it all behind me and start a completely new life.

When Mrs Brown came back from her holiday I went to see her and talked about the future. I went to live in her lovely house not very far from St. George's Hospital at Chester Square, near Victoria Station. Mrs Brown was a young and beautiful lady. Her husband was much older than her and had a very important job. He worked for the royal family and the house was just behind Buckingham Palace. They had many more servants working for them. One of them was Mrs Aspel, the mother of the newsreader, Michael Aspel. At that time he'd just finished university and later he took a job at the BBC as a newsreader.

While I was there Mrs Brown took me to the theatre in the West End to see Mario Lanza. She let me wear a long, strapless, velvet dress with high-heeled shoes, my hair up and a lot of make up, which I wasn't accustomed to at all. I didn't enjoy it. I felt like a fish out of water.

The house had five storeys, about six bedrooms and five bathrooms. Some of the bedrooms had dressing rooms and en suite bathrooms. There was a very large sitting room with oil paintings on the walls, lots of armchairs, a big fireplace with a marble mantelpiece covered with expensive pieces of Doulton china and other ornaments, and a deep, fitted carpet. There was a long balcony a bit like Buckingham Palace's but with lots of plants which made it more like a small garden. It made the sitting room very pleasant and relaxing. There was a library and on the ground floor a very large hall from which a beautiful staircase lead to all the floors. The dining room had a sideboard, an oak table with twelve upholstered chairs on each side, another deep carpet and numerous watercolours on the walls. Next to it was a large kitchen with a big table, and electric and gas stoves.

Down in the basement was the flat she had talked about. It had an entrance at the front, down a few steps from the main door. There was a beautiful big bed, a sitting room and a kitchen-cum-dining room. But it wasn't a house I wanted to live in.

In the middle of the squares where rich and aristocratic Londoners live there are communal gardens. They are large, well kept and solely for the use of all the people living in that square. To enter the garden, you must have a key.

I know now that it seems absurd but at the time the only thing I wanted was to be safe, especially after what had happened to my friend Bruna. Mrs Brown said,
"Ida, the only thing you cannot do is to have any children here. The day you tell me you are expecting a child I will have to tell you to leave."
"I won't have any children." I said, which was a silly thing to say because at that time there wasn't any family planning.

On May 18th my husband and I were married by proxy. I was very silly. I never really understood what I was doing. It was so easy for me to get married. I thought nobody would ever do me any harm because I had a man beside me all the time. I knew all about babies because I'd studied biology but I thought I wasn't good enough for such a wonderful thing. I thought it happened only to special people, which was very stupid of me.

Pilar made me a beautiful wedding dress and everything was arranged at St Peter's Church on 16th June. It was the Italian church in North London. Mr and Mrs Brown got a permit for my husband to come to work in this country. I thought I was happy but I didn't really understand what I was doing. My husband arrived on 15th June and the next day we went to St Peter's. Everything went according to plan. Then Mr and Mrs Brown went away for a week and my husband and I had our honeymoon in London. Everything seemed fine.

Three weeks after I married Aldo, I became very, very sick. I couldn't understand why. I had never been sick before. I went to see a local doctor and he asked me lots of questions.
"Mrs Maddalena, how long have you been married?"
"Three weeks, doctor."
"Had you been sleeping with anybody else before you married Mr Maddalena?" I was very indignant at that question.
"Doctor, how can you ask such a question? What do you think I am?"
"I only ask what it is my right to know in order to make the correct diagnosis about your condition. I will send your urine sample to St George's Hospital and in a week you can come back here for the result. In the meantime, take these tablets with a cup of tea before breakfast."

I didn't take the tablets because I was too sick to bother making myself a cup of tea in the morning and I was too busy. After a week I went back to the doctor and he said,
"Congratulations, Mrs Maddalena, you are expecting a baby."
"A baby? What do I do with a baby?"
"You will look after him or her!" he said, "You young girls are all the same. You get married without understanding what it's all about. I think you'll manage somehow. Come back if you need more help."

Now what do we do? My husband was two years younger than me, he'd been three weeks in this country and he couldn't speak a word of English. I was in the middle of training for a nursing career. I knew we couldn't stay in that flat any longer. I didn't

know where to turn. Mrs Brown realised what was going on and said,
"Ida, I did tell you if that was the case, you can't stay here any longer." From being a kind lady she had become a very nasty one.

One evening at half past nine she told us to leave the flat and go back to my parents, so we took our belongings and went to a hotel nearby. Now our future was shattered. I had some money but it wasn't enough to stay in the hotel for long, so we decided to go to a bed and breakfast until we thought of what to do. We found a bed and breakfast at 99 St George's Drive, SW1. The place wasn't very nice but we had no choice.

CHAPTER TWENTY-THREE – LIVING IN OXTED

After a couple of weeks of uncertainty, I decided to leave my nursing career and to look for a job in a private house working for married couple or a family. Above all, a new employer would not have to mind about me having a child. It wasn't easy to find that sort of employer but I remembered what Sister Mary said to me, "Pray always and trust in God. He will never let you down."

In fact it took more than two weeks and by then our money had nearly all gone, but God answered our prayer. I do not how I found it, but it turned out to be the most suitable place for us to be in my condition. Oxted Place is about ten miles outside London. We arrived at the station where there was a Rolls Royce with a chauffeur to meet us. It was grand and for a minute it seemed as if I was in Rome again. Oxted Place was a beautiful mansion. All around it were magnificent gardens with beautiful flowers of all colours, hills, tennis courts, a lake and grounds stretching for miles around with several cottages for the people who worked for the old couple. There was also a farm nearby belonging to Mr and Mrs Wetter. They supplied all the food that was needed, like butter, milk, eggs and vegetables. In one of the cottages lived the chauffeur and his family. In others lived the gardener with his family, and the farm workers. We were allocated a flat in the mansion, which was very nice. There was also a nurse who looked after the old gentleman, a full-time housemaid and a daily helper.

I was the cook and my husband was the handyman, for which he was very capable. We enjoyed ourselves there and were very happy. Every time I had to go anywhere the chauffeur would take me. The lady of the house liked us very much. I enjoyed going round the grounds. There were lots of greenhouses and each one had something special in it. In September, fruit was abundant: figs, grapes, peaches and much more, which reminded me of Italy. We never knew anybody else there apart from the people who worked for them.

One day Mrs Wetter said,
"Ida, will you cook eggs, bacon, toast and marmalade and make coffee then tell Aldo to go room number eight, put it all on a chair and leave it there?" Well, we were curious and asked one another

who could be in there. One night we heard a noise downstairs. I say to my husband,

"Put on your dressing gown. Somebody is pinching the silver in the dining room. Get up and go and see!" My husband said,

"No, I won't."

"And why not?"

"What if he smashes something on my head?"

"Well, I'll go then."

"Oh no you don't!" But I didn't listen. I put on my dressing gown and went. But the person who was downstairs heard me coming down and ran away. I just managed to see somebody in a dressing gown running away from the kitchen. I went to bed very puzzled. In the morning, I went to see the lady and tell her what happened. She said,

"Don't worry. It must have been Mick."

"Who is he?"

"You know! You've been cooking breakfast every morning for him. Mick is my son." Mrs Wetter had a word with him and he came to see us. He was in navy uniform, a nice gentleman, proper and polite, and very big.

I was so accustomed to nobody understanding if I spoke Italian that I said in Italian,

"He is as fat as a pig." He must have understood me because the next morning, when my husband took his breakfast, he found a note on the door,

> 'Aldo, per piacere chiamami alle ore dieci. (Aldo, please call me at ten o'clock.)'

Aldo then realised that Mick would have understood what I'd said. What an embarrassment that was for me! I was very sorry. When I met him again I said,

"Mr Mick, I must congratulate you on speaking Italian so well." He said,

"Yes, Ida, I understand Italian and I quite agree with you. Now you've mentioned it, I will go on a special diet. From tomorrow on, don't cook me eggs and bacon. Make me special diet food to stop me looking as fat as a pig."

"Oh, I'm very sorry, Mr. Mick. It was silly of me to make such a remark." I said.

"It was a good thing and makes sense." He smiled. Later, his mother said,

"He speaks seven languages!"

Every month I used go for a check-up to Dorking General Hospital in preparation for the birth of my baby. They kept a close eye on me because I was quite a lot larger than normal. The doctor said, "Mrs Maddalena, you are large enough to be carrying twins." Sometimes I had to go more often because the doctors were concerned about the baby and me. It was a laugh. I always arrived in the Rolls Royce driven by Mr Marshall, the chauffeur. All the other mothers-to-be wondered who I was but I didn't say anything. I could see the women whispering to one another, wondering where I came from. I was just very pleased that God was looking after me.

On March 25th at seven o'clock in the evening, while I was serving supper to Mr and Mrs Wetter, I realised our baby was on the way. Mrs Wetter called Mr Marshall and said,
"Will you take Ida to Dorking Hospital because the baby is on the way?" At two in the morning my husband and I were blessed with a beautiful baby girl and we called her Luciana. She weighed nine pounds and eight ounces. She hardly cried, only just to let me know she'd arrived and then she was as good as gold.

At that time, people who had had a baby stayed in hospital for ten days afterwards. Everything was provided for you and your baby. It was the most beautiful experience a woman can ever have. She was my very own baby. Mrs Wetter was overjoyed and so was Mr Mick and everybody else.

But there were some problems which we did not know about. There was friction between the nurse and the old gentleman and the lady of the house. This nurse became very jealous of our baby and didn't like the fuss everybody made of her. I wasn't quite sure of this woman any more. I thought my child was in danger. The fact was that she couldn't have children herself. She didn't like to see anybody else with a child and she started to create all kinds of difficulties which everybody noticed. I was very sorry for Mrs Wetter and the situation she was in. She didn't like the nurse but she couldn't say anything because the old gentleman had become very fond of her and was very dependent on her. So, with much regret, we had to make a move.

The chauffeur said,

"My brother has just married a business woman. I'll speak to him to see if his wife can give you and your husband a job." So he did and an appointment was made for us to meet this lady. She offered us a job looking after old people in her care and also working in a nursery. There was a flat with the job. Well, I thought it was a good idea. I liked older people and it was a nursing job. I liked children and it would also be good for my child to be with other children. We gave notice to Mrs Wetter, which we were very sorry to do because we had been so happy there. Mrs Wetter and the rest of the staff were sorry to see us go, but not that wretched nurse!

We took the new position, which was not at all what had been promised. The poor older people were kept in disgusting conditions which were insulting for any human to live in. In another part of the house was the nursery for residents' children only. There was quite a pleasant room with at least a dozen cots, just for the benefit of the inspectors. To my horror I discovered what they never saw: down in the cellar there were at least another half dozen more cots. I heard terrible screams of children in the night so I went to investigate and found many more babies. In some of the cots there were two babies, one about six months old and the other much older. The poor things couldn't move. They were one on top of another. I was furious! No way would I work in those conditions. Poor old people! Poor children!

I confronted the woman and said,
"Mrs Webb we came to work for you because we thought you were a good lady and you were doing some good for the community. We came to do an honest job. But that is not what we found. In the little time we've been here we have seen things that are not right for any human. We will not stand for that. I have no choice but to report you to the authorities."

I met an Italian family and they offered us hospitality until we found a new position. I started to look for rooms and a job. I always wanted to go back to finish my nursing training.

We moved to Tunbridge Wells where Pembury Hospital was nearby. I telephoned the matron and she gave me an appointment. After my interview the matron said,
"Provided your references are all right, you may start work here and take up your career as nurse again. But we haven't got a job

for your husband. As soon as there is a vacancy, we will employ him." I was very grateful and said,
"Thank you very much. I appreciate it."

A week later I commenced work at Pembury Hospital. It wasn't easy to leave my lovely baby behind, but the one thing that comforted me was that my husband was looking after her and I knew he was quite able. Because he was one of six children, he had had plenty of experience - more than I had. Above all, he loved her very much. What about feeding the baby? This was a very painful decision. I had to go to the doctor and ask for advice about what I should do. She said,
"In your present situation you haven't got a choice. You'll have to put the baby on a bottle and you must have injections to take away your milk. I'm sorry but there is no other way."

Life wasn't easy. I looked for a house but rents were much higher than I could possibly afford. My husband had to look for a job and we had to get somebody to look after the baby. I didn't like that but, again, we had no choice. The work in hospital was fine and I enjoyed it very much, but I missed my baby. Our Italian friend said,
"When Aldo gets a job, there is a nursery nearby where our baby goes. We can book a place for your baby there." I said,
"I would want to meet the lady and see the nursery first, after the experience we've had. You can't be too sure." We went to see the lady. She only looked after a few babies, and we looked round everywhere. She was very nice and said,
"When your husband gets a job, I will look after your baby while you're both at work."

At the hospital everybody was very kind to me, especially the patients. I always liked working in Princess Elizabeth and Princess Margaret wards, both private wards. There was a kind sister there who tried hard to find a job for my husband, but without any success. The money I was earning as student nurse was not enough to make a living for us and it was absolutely essential for Aldo to get a job. Everybody wanted to help me with money but as a nurse you must never accept money or any gifts from patients. This was the hospital policy but in the private wards, when patients wanted to show their appreciation, it was permitted.

There was a doctor there who gave money to the Sister to give to me for my baby. I thought that was very nice of him. This poor doctor had cancer of the nose. He wore a mask so it wouldn't show. One day, when I'd been off for two days, sister spoke to me as soon as I came on duty.

"Nurse, the doctor has been asking about you. I think he'd be very pleased if you would take his breakfast in for him." I went to the kitchen, took his tray and went in. I'd never seen anything like it before. There wasn't a doctor in the bed but what appeared to me to be a skeleton! I dropped the tray on the floor and ran as fast as I could out of the ward, screaming my head off! Everybody wondered what was going on. The poor doctor must have felt awful. After they explained it to me I felt such a fool, and very sorry, but I couldn't help it. At the time it was such a shock. Not long after that he died.

One day sister called me into her office and said,

"There is a lady who would like to have a few words with you." There stood a tall woman, dressed very smartly with a big smile on her face. She said,

"Nurse Maddalena, my husband left this for you in gratitude for looking after him. I hope it will help you until your husband finds a job."

"Thank you very much. It was a great honour for me to look after such a gentleman."

My baby became unwell. She got an infection and needed antibiotics. The doctor couldn't understand why she was ill. Another difficulty arose which was that my husband needed a new permit to work in this country. I was hoping very much that the hospital would employ him but it was impossible, there was no vacancy. It was such predicament. I had a husband with no job, no house, a sick baby and maybe another one on the way. There was nowhere to turn. Once again I asked God for help. After I finished praying I felt as if I knew that God would not let me down and that somehow eventually everything would be all right.

CHAPTER TWENTY-FOUR – LIFE IN MAIDSTONE

In the *Kent Messenger* there was a job for a married couple at Linton Hospital near Maidstone. It offered accommodation with a nursery for children. I spoke to my husband and he was pleased with the proposition of working in a hospital. I was very sorry to leave Pembury Hospital but I had no choice. I telephoned to make an appointment with the matron of Linton Hospital, got an interview and, again providing the references were all right, was offered the job. But the matron said,

"The accommodation is for two and, because of your baby, it can only be temporary until you find something more suitable outside the hospital for the three of you. Now listen to me, young lady: you must make sure you have no more babies. I know you are a Roman Catholic but in your position it's impossible to respect what you believe." What could I say? 'But I'm already expecting another one.' I just nodded my head.

We started a new routine again. It was very hard work but we didn't mind. It was enjoyable. All the staff worked together like a big family. At Christmas, as always, there was plenty of food and lots of drink everywhere. After we had worked together for a while Nurse Mackenzie and I became good friends.

"Ida, we have done very well. We will soon be back at the nurses' home and then we can have a large drink!" When we reached the nurses' home she said,

"You look very tired, my dear, I'll go and fetch you that nice drink." She came back with a long glass of lemonade, at least that's what I thought it was. I took the glass and drank it all in one go. My goodness me, I felt sick! I didn't know what had hit me, I felt so ill. I had no choice but to go upstairs to bed and I was sick again and again. I thought I would lose my baby. Poor Nurse Mackenzie was very upset. She didn't know I was expecting a baby. What she'd given me was a glass of neat gin which I'd never drunk in my life before. I didn't even know the stuff existed.

The nursing job in those days was very different from what it is today. At that time we had to do everything manually, but today there is much more technology. Duty as a day nurse started at seven fifteen in the morning and finished at half past five in the afternoon. Sometimes we had a long day and at other times we finished at two o'clock, rested and came back at half past five. As soon as we came on duty we'd go into the office and read the night reports if we were day nurses, or the day reports if we were night nurses. There was a report for each patient and you made sure you knew the treatment and care required for each individual. We did TPR - temperature, pulse, respiration – and gave medication according to the doctor's prescription. Then we served breakfast. Afterwards the patients had a wash or bath according to their individual needs. We helped with dressing, made the beds and by ten o'clock all the wards had to be ready for the doctor's round with matron. We had to call all the patients by their surnames. The nursing care continued all the time and we only stopped for coffee and for lunch.

I enjoyed the job very much. After all, it had been my dream since childhood. We were mostly young nurses and sometimes we made our own entertainment by playing tricks on one another. On one night duty shift we were very short of staff and I realised I was on my own looking after thirty patients. This would never happen today but in those days it did. My duty before I started work was to read the day reports, which I did, but there wasn't anything special to note. I assumed the patients were all old people and as I went around and said 'Hello' to everybody I noticed a very young lady. She gave me a big smile. I was puzzled. Who is this lady? What is she doing here with these poor, old ladies? Surely she shouldn't be here. Is this a joke my colleagues have set up for me? I thought it was a stupid joke. How dare these nurses play jokes with other people's lives? But I wasn't going to let them worry me.

I saw to all the other patients and made sure the old ladies were well looked after. But after a while I was still troubled about the young lady. I went up to her and was shocked by what I saw. She was only about forty and suffered from MS, poor woman. How stupid of me to think it was a joke. She was in a lot of pain, was incontinent and had a very large bedsore. I was very sorry for my stupidity. I should have known better. The first thing they taught us in school was to check the patient first and I'd failed to do that. I felt very guilty and apologised to her. Then I gave her all the nursing and loving care she needed. She said,
"Thank you, nurse, you have made me comfortable."
"I'm very sorry if I took a long time to come to you." I said, "Tell me a little about yourself."
"I have two young children and I suffer from MS. I tried to manage but, as you see, I'm no longer able to do so. My husband left me

and my two boys have been taken into care." I felt very sorry for Cilla. Even when I wasn't on duty in that ward, I would still go there to talk to her and do what I could to comfort and help this poor young mother.

The hospital was mostly for geriatrics but C, D and E wards were an extension of West Kent Hospital and most of the time I was on duty on these three wards. One day I nearly lost my life and the baby I was carrying. After finishing my shift I was tidying the ward and took a sack full of dirty laundry downstairs to the pick-up point for the porter to take away. Instead of putting the sack first, I went downstairs pulling it behind me. It was heavy and toppled down on top of me, knocking me to the floor. It was about half an hour before another member of staff spotted me. The alarm was raised and I was very ill for a few days. The doctor said I was very lucky to be alive and so was the baby I was carrying.

At last we found accommodation outside the hospital in St Luke's Road. It was with a nice lady called Pauline who lived with her child in a big house. When she realised I was soon going to have another baby she said,
"Look, Ida, this accommodation won't be enough for you."
"Oh, Pauline, please don't say that! It is not at all easy to find somewhere better in my condition."
"Ida, have you got any money?"
"Well, we have saved as much as we can but with two children and nowhere to live the future doesn't look very bright."
"My mother is a very religious woman," Pauline said, "and she lets out her house to people in need. I'll see what I can do for you and your family. But you never go out! Tonight why don't I babysit so that you and your husband can go to the pictures? There is a good film on that I think you'll both enjoy."
"Oh no, Pauline, we can't go." I said.
"I insist! This isn't funny. You two only know one thing: work, work, work and nothing else. You must go!" I said to my husband,
"I think we'd better go, just for the sake of peace and quiet, otherwise she'll never stop. Right now we need her and she means well." So we went.

The film was all about Jack the Ripper. At the beginning of the twentieth century he went around the streets of London killing young girls. It was a horrendous film and scared me a great deal. When we came home Pauline said,

"Well, did you both enjoy the film?" We smiled and said,
"Yes, Pauline, thank you very much." But I couldn't sleep all night.

During that night it snowed very heavily. I had to get to Linton Hospital for the early shift. I dressed the baby up in a Father Christmas suit and with her in my arms and another inside me, I made my way to the bus stop. But St Luke's Road was covered with thick snow. It was dark and all the street lights were on. One light was by a small tree and the shadow it cast made it look to me as if the man from the film was lurking there. I didn't have the courage to walk past it. Eventually another lady came by and without saying anything I followed her. When I reached the tree I realised what a silly girl I was - the shadow was from the tree and not a man.

For a week or more I couldn't get that film out of my mind. Pauline came up again to our little apartment. For a minute or two I thought she was going to arrange for us to see another film. I was quite concerned about it. But no: she said,
"I've had a talk to my mother and I think she will be able to help you. I'll give you her address so you can talk to her about your situation.
"Thank you, Pauline." I said. A few days later I went to see Mrs Green, Pauline's mother. She lived at 6 Albion Place, not very far from her daughter. I knocked at her door and a lady opened it saying,
"Can I help you?"
"Pauline sent me here to see Mrs Green."
"Wait a minute." she said and went away leaving me on the doorstep. After a few minutes she came back and said,
"Mrs Green would like to see you now. Please come in." She took me into Mrs Green's sitting room and told me she wouldn't be long. After a few more minutes an old lady came in and said,
"My daughter has spoken to me about you and I will try to help if I can."
"I really need your help." I said, "I think Pauline has already told you about my situation."
"I have a vacant property which I wouldn't mind selling. It's worth about a thousand pounds." and she looked straight at me, "How much money do you have?"
"About three hundred pounds, Mrs Green."
"All right, you'd better come with me and I'll show it to you." She took me to a house in Marsham Street, not very far from her

house. I noticed it was just a few doors away from West Kent Hospital, which was good. It was a four-storey town house in a terrace. It had three bedrooms, a long corridor and with a door to the sitting room, a kitchen-cum-dining room and two large rooms in the basement. There was a small garden at the front, side and back with a lavatory in the back garden. It was partly furnished.

"I like the house but I only have three hundred pounds."

"That's all right," she said, "you give me three hundred pounds and I'll give you a mortgage of seven hundred pounds. Then you can pay me three pounds a week and with no interest. In less than five years you will have repaid the money I lend you. Because of your condition I will let you move in straight away and I'll ask the solicitor to get on with the paperwork. That will take three months and by then you will have saved enough money to pay the solicitor's fees."

"I can't thank you enough for this."

"Don't thank me, thank the Lord for His goodness and the mercy He has for His children. By the look on your face I can tell you are a child of God."

"Thank you, Lord, for such nice people." I said.

CHAPTER TWENTY-FIVE – A NEW BABY AND A NEW HOUSE

The matron and all the staff in the hospital were pleased for us. They came to see what we needed and gave us as much as they could to finish furnishing our home. It was the beginning of March and I had to stop work because of being in the later stage of pregnancy.

My baby, Luciana, had been catching infections since she was a month old but we didn't take any notice. The doctor usually prescribed some antibiotics and left it at that. But over time I began to worry and the doctor also became puzzled.

Luciana was one year and sixteen days old. It was six o'clock on Sunday morning April 10th that I realised the new baby was on its way. I alerted my husband and said,
"Take Luciana to Mrs Green. I need to go to the hospital. The baby is on its way." As I said before, luckily the hospital was only few doors away from us. He took Luciana to Mrs Green and then took me into hospital. Then he went to Linton Hospital to work. At about ten my lovely new baby boy arrived. He was a beautiful baby, just like his sister. He didn't cry much, just to let us know he had arrived. The hospital telephoned my husband's ward to give him the good news. The nurse in charge called him into the office and said,
"Congratulations, Nurse Maddalena, you have a baby boy. Please go home and see the new arrival." The hospital nurses had a collection and the new baby received lots of presents and I received lots of flowers. After three days I took my new baby and went home.

Mrs Green brought Luciana back and said,
"Ida, I have some news for you that I know will be very hard. Pauline and I are selling everything we have and plan to go to live in America. We have joined an Evangelical church. You can continue to pay the mortgage as arranged. Pauline will come to see you before we go." A few days later I heard a knock at the door. I opened it and said,
"Oh, Pauline, what a lovely surprise!"
"I think my mother has already told you our news about America." she said.
"Why are you and your family leaving the country?" I asked.

"Ida, it's a long story. Let me ask you a favour."

"You can have two if you like!"

"You know I have a couple living in my house. Because I'm going to sell everything, Charlie and Lydia will be homeless. I wondered if you and Aldo would mind taking them in. They said they wouldn't mind the flat in the basement. They know the house and Lydia loves children and wouldn't mind giving you a hand when you need."

"Oh! Actually Aldo has just decorated and insulated everywhere. He's put in a new ceiling and tiled the floors. The front room looks very smart. As you know, the back room was used as a kitchen. In fact the sink is still there and the gas point. It will be nice when it is finished. I'm sure we will be more than pleased to have them here with us."

A month later Charlie and Lydia came to live with us. Lydia was a great help and loved the children very much. Six weeks after the baby was born, I had to return to my job in the hospital. I went back as a night nurse and my husband as a day nurse. He started at seven thirty a.m. and finished at five p.m., or sometimes eight p.m. I started at eight p.m. and finished at eight a.m.. Lydia looked after our children in between times and paid no rent. Life was very difficult because I couldn't get much sleep and the children needed more and more attention. Also Luciana was getting ill more and more often. The doctor couldn't understand why this beautiful child was always getting fevers. She didn't look well but the poor child never complained. For that reason I couldn't take the children to the nursery.

Eventually I left my job at the hospital and tried my best to look after the children. The pattern for Luciana never changed: two weeks with antibiotics and four weeks without. With seven pounds a week to live on less three to pay the mortgage, it wasn't funny. Then Lydia and Charles left because the council found them a flat. I was very pleased for them but missed them a great deal.

One day my baby boy wasn't very well and I had to call the doctor. Because at that time nobody had telephones indoors, except very rich people, I had to go to the telephone box. Luckily there was one very near. I shut both children in the bedroom while I called the doctor and when I came back, went upstairs and opened the door: only Luciana was there. I couldn't find my baby boy anywhere! I was out of my mind. What had happened to my baby? I couldn't understand. I had only left for a few minutes. I'd shut the door and it was still shut when I came back. The girl was there but not the boy.

"Where is the baby?" I asked her.

"Baby!" she said. Then the doctor arrived.

"You rang saying your child wasn't well and now you tell me you have lost him!"

"I don't know, doctor. I left him with Luciana. She is here but my boy has disappeared!" The doctor looked very annoyed and said,

"I don't understand. These young mothers, they are all the same! They call the doctor out for their babies and then they lose them. Whatever next! When you find him, you let me know, will you?" I didn't know what to say. He went, leaving me there in desperation. I thought I'd better go to the police. Then I opened the wardrobe and there was my precious baby! He was fast asleep with his little finger in his mouth. I can't describe the joy I felt finding my baby. He was just lovely. When I calmed down I realised what must have happened. I must have left the wardrobe door open, he had crawled in and Luciana had shut it. Luckily there were pillows inside and he fell asleep on them.

Once an Indian doctor came to see my precious little girl but, like the other doctors, he couldn't find anything wrong with her. I knew this doctor because we had worked in the hospital together.

"I know your child isn't well," he said, "but I can't understand why." Again I felt desolate. I didn't know what to do. I had two children, very little money and above all nobody to talk to or get advice from. Who could help me? All the people I once knew seemed to have disappeared. I was in complete desperation. I needed more money to keep going. We made plans to build a bathroom and toilet inside the house and turn the two bedrooms into a little flat so we could let it. It was a lot of hard work but my husband managed to do it.

The Indian doctor came to see my child again.

"Mrs Maddalena, now you can't work any more and you could do with a bit more money, could I rent that little flat you've been talking about? My wife is coming to England."

"Yes, of course." I said.

"And how much will you charge?"

"Three pounds a week. Is that too much for you?"

"No, no. I think that is reasonable." So before long I had a young Indian girl living with us. She wasn't much more than fifteen years old. We became quite good friends.

"You are so young! In this country, children like you are still at school. How is it that you're already married?"

"I married my husband two years ago."

"Goodness me! How old were you then?"

"I was thirteen years old. You see, in my country there is a custom that the parents arrange their children's marriage even before they are born." I didn't understand.

"What are you trying to tell me?"

"It's like this: my parents are well off financially. They would never permit me to marry a man from a lower class than me. To prevent that, they promised me to another child from the same class as them. Before we could do anything about it, they married us, even without our seeing one another."

"It was not quite like that for me, but not far off. My parents also wanted me to marry my husband and we did so after a year of correspondence, but we did know one another."

She was very nice girl and we became good friends. One day she said,

"I'll make you an Indian dinner. I think you'll like that."

"Yes, please." It was very nice, so hot that I cried but I enjoyed it.

As usual my poor little girl wasn't well, complaining of a high temperature and being sick. I couldn't take her out to the shops which I badly needed to get to. I asked Mrs Sikh,

"I need to do some shopping but I can't take little Luciana with me. Would you mind looking after her? I can take little Nino with me."

"Oh, thank you very much. I will enjoy looking after her." she said.

While I was shopping I saw a young Indian lady with a child. When I looked closely I realised it was Mrs Sikh with my child! She'd dressed Luciana in Indian clothes. She looked beautiful but that wasn't the point. The fact is that I left her because she wasn't well enough to come out. I didn't say anything. I finished my shopping and it was time to go home.

One day it was quite warm and I was doing a bit of spring cleaning. I went into the bathroom, opened the window and sprayed some air freshener around. Not long afterwards Mrs Sikh went in there and came rushing out after a few minutes screaming and completely naked.

"Mrs Sikh, what is wrong? Stop screaming and tell me what is wrong! Cover yourself up and then tell me what is going on." But I couldn't make any sense of what she said. I thought it must be something very serious. Why else would an Indian lady, who was always modestly dressed, expose herself? The children and I became frightened. I had no other choice than to go upstairs to their flat and call for her husband, who was on duty in the hospital near by. Luckily the hospital put out a call for Doctor Sikh. That was a blessing because otherwise I don't know what I would have done. In the meantime I covered her up the best I could. A few minutes later her husband arrived.

"Doctor Sikh, whatever is wrong with your wife?"

"What have you been spraying in the toilet?" he asked.

"Air freshener." I said.

"Well, what has happened is that it has attracted an insect, perhaps a wasp, that has stung her in her private parts."

"Oh poor, poor Mrs Sikh! I'm very, very sorry. I'll never put anything in the toilet again, or anywhere else around the house." I said.

After what happened to Mrs Sikh, the problems with my daughter continued. She grew more and more ill and nobody understood what was wrong with the poor child. The worst thing was when a nasty doctor said to my husband,

"There is nothing wrong with your child. The problem is with your wife. I think the nursing job has affected her brain and she is imagining all these things and that is affecting the child." I thought it was very heartless to say such a thing. He didn't understand. In those days there wasn't much technology available to doctors - that has developed since. Then, when specialists didn't know why people were ill or died, they would accuse someone of being out of their mind. When I insisted that my daughter was ill, this doctor wrote a letter accusing me of insanity and threatened to take my children away from me.

I didn't have any support from my husband as he believed what the doctor had told him. I had nowhere to turn to and for that reason alone I made the most terrible, terrible mistake of my life, which will remain with me as long as I live. I loved both my children very much and I knew that if I didn't do something about this situation they would not be with me much longer. My daughter could have died and who knows what might have happened to my little boy? I think maybe I also began to believe that this doctor was right after all!

I wrote to my mother-in-law and explained what was going on and asked for her advice. She wrote back saying,

> 'Bring the children to Italy. I will look after them and you return to England, go back to work and send me money so I can pay for a doctor and for medicines and in few months Luciana will better.

CHAPTER TWENTY-SIX – THE TERRIBLE MISTAKE

I thought it was a very hard thing to do but what choice did I have?
My husband said,
"I agree with my mother. There is a good doctor in the village and
if anything is wrong with our daughter he will put her right." I didn't
like the thought of it but at that time it was my only hope.

So I went to our village and took the children to see Doctor
Shaldone. As soon as he saw my son he said,
"What a lovely child! Who does he belong to?"
"He is mine, doctor." I said.
"Oh, Ida, come into my surgery. How are you?"
"I'm all right, doctor, but my children are not."
"Do you know why your boy has so many nose bleeds?"
"I know he has many but I don't know why."
"I will give him a month's supply of concentrated vitamin C and that
will help him."
"Thank you, doctor. I would also like you to see my little girl. Let
me explain to you why I'm so worried about her: she is not well but
no doctor in England can find out what is wrong with her. She has
been catching infections since she was born. She's been on
antibiotics on and off. The doctors are now saying there is nothing
wrong with her but that it is just my imagination. Yet every time
she's ill, they give her antibiotics. If you can, I would like you to
examine my children. I will send money via my mother-in-law for
your services and for any medication needed. I do hope you can
make her better."
"Look, Ida, I can't promise you anything but I can tell you that I will
do what I can for her."
"Thank you, doctor." With a broken heart I left my children. I
returned to England ready to sell the house and go back to Italy if
we had to. But my lovely children didn't get any better in Italy and
indeed my daughter was getting worse. I missed them and was
having nightmares about them. I thought I could buy another,
cheaper house and use the extra money to help my children by
buying private doctors. I looked in estate agents and saw a
cottage just outside Maidstone for only seven hundred pounds.
So, I sold our house for two thousand three hundred pounds. We
could modernise the cottage and still have money for private
doctors for my daughter and for my boy, if he needed them. I
thought that was what I should do. I bought the house without

getting a survey done, without even seeing inside it. I just went there and saw that the other houses were all occupied, with lights on. I didn't look at anything else. I just went straight to the estate agent to say that I wanted to buy that cottage. I knew my husband and I could make it quite habitable.

To sell and buy took some time so we decided to go to Italy and bring the children back to England. When we came home, we would move into the cottage. We thought if we stayed in Italy for a month that would be enough time for the solicitors to do all the necessary things to complete the sale and the purchase and when we came home it would be all right and we would have the money.

CHAPTER TWENTY-SEVEN – THE CHILDREN COME BACK TO ENGLAND

After six months we saw our children again. I realised what a fool I'd been. Our beloved daughter wasn't any better but much worse. I went to see the doctor.

"Dr Shaldone, I see my child is not any better at all."

"I'm sorry, Ida, but you've got to take this girl back to London as soon as possible. She needs help which I can't give here in Italy."

"Doctor, I brought her here to Italy because the GP in Maidstone said he thought I was mad because I worried unnecessarily."

"Listen to me, there is no such thing as a mother who worries too much about her child. Every mother has a maternal instinct about her children. She knows when they are not well. So you are not mad at all. You are a good mother. They only said that because they don't know what is wrong with Luciana. I know a professor in London who will able to help your daughter. I will write to him and explain the position. His name is Professor Straight. Now I will prescribe some medicine to give to Luciana until she gets help from him."

We left Italy much earlier than we had planned. I couldn't get to see the professor even privately without going through the local doctor and he wouldn't write to Professor Straight to say that I had been recommended by Dr Shaldone. So I went back to my GP in Maidstone and said,

"Doctor, I've just come back from Italy where I was told that my daughter isn't well at all and needs to go to London to see Professor Straight at King's College Hospital as soon as possible."

"I can't see why your daughter has got to go to London." he said, "I think the local hospital will be good enough." So, I thought, here we go again! But I protested.

"I've been there before and they haven't done anything about it except call me mad and threaten to send me to a mental hospital and take my children away from me. My children need help, not to be taken away from their mother!"

"I will not write a letter to King's College Hospital." he said, "I know a very good child specialist at West Kent General Hospital and that is where she will go."

I was in desperation again. Even with money I was not able to help my daughter. Our cottage was two miles outside Maidstone at a place called Gidds Pond. There were eight cottages in a row and ours was the last one, number eight. Beside it was a large space that people used to park their cars on. It was a three bedroom cottage with a front room, dining room, kitchen and doors at the front and back. The cottage was in a mess. For many, many years an old couple lived there and their relatives occupied the other seven cottages. None of these people owned any of them. There was a landlord and they lived very primitively. They used the back gardens for parking and the rest as a tip, which was covered with stinging nettles about ten feet high. The children didn't like it but there was no turning back. Our house in Marsham Street had been sold and we had to move. We needed the money.

When we moved in we had another shock. We looked for the electricity sockets but there wasn't one. So the poor children couldn't watch television. How could we put on a light? I had to pull myself together and ask next door.

"I'm your new neighbour," I said, "and I would be very grateful if you can tell me how to put the lights on."

"We haven't got electricity." said the neighbour, "We only have gas for cooking. I'll show you how to get light."

"Thank you. My name is Ida and my husband is Aldo. We have two children, Luciana and Nino."

"My name is Mrs Wheeler. My husband's parents lived in your cottage for many years before they both died. The place is in a mess but they wouldn't have it any other way. You are both young and I hope you'll be able to make something of it."

The children were very disappointed because they looked forward to *Watch with Mother, Andy Pandy* and *The Flowerpot Men*! And, worse still, when we looked for the toilet we found it right at the back of the garden, full of stinging nettles.

I soon called an architect to try to do something and an electrician to see if we could get electricity. But the Electricity Board charged thirty pounds just to connect to the mains. Divided by eight, it wouldn't have been too bad, but the older people who lived there had no intention of changing. They said,

"Why we should change? We have lived here all our lives and we wouldn't want it any different."

I understood that they didn't want change; they were old and difficult. We began to make a lot of improvements to the place. I asked the estate agent if I could buy all the land at the back of the eight cottages so eventually my husband could build a bungalow there. The owner agreed and a deal was made. We cleared all the mess and the children began to like it a little better.

One day I was coming home from town after taking the children to school and, as I got off the bus, I smelt something terrible. I knocked at Mrs Wheeler's door and said,
"Mrs Wheeler, what is that terrible smell?"
"The council has come to empty the cesspool." she said.
"What is a cesspool?" I asked.
"You see, my dear; we don't have sewers here like in the town. We have a cesspool and every so often the council comes and empties it." Then I realised I had made a very big mistake and we would have to move away. It was not good for the children. I immediately looked in the *Kent Messenger* newspaper and saw that a gentleman had a house for sale. I went to see him and we made a deal like the one we had made before with Mrs Green. I put down a five hundred pound deposit and he gave me a mortgage of one thousand pounds to pay back in instalments of twenty pounds a month. In that way I still had money in my bank to be able to help my children.

The house was in Upper Fant Road in Maidstone. It had three bedrooms, a front room, dining room, kitchen and bathroom with all the amenities. The children were much happier with this.

My daughter was now in West Kent Hospital but she wasn't getting any better. I went to the hospital and said,
"Doctor, I demand a letter to take my daughter to King's College Hospital, privately." After many discussions I managed to get a letter and at last I was introduced to Professor Straight. He assured me he would do whatever was possible to put right what was wrong with my child.
"I will give you a flat in the hospital," he said, "so you can be with your daughter. Everything you need is on the National Health. You and your husband have paid your stamps and you have the same rights as everybody else."

CHAPTER TWENTY-EIGHT – MY PARENTS COME TO ENGLAND

In Italy my parents were getting old and frail and needed help. I was their only daughter. They knew my position very well and it was a difficult time for both them and me. How could I look after my children in England and them in Italy? I wrote to them,

> 'You've got to make a sacrifice and come to England and live here with us.'

They didn't like the idea but there was no choice. I wrote to the Home Office explaining the position we were in. They were in a financial position to live in England quite well without needing any help from anybody else. The Home Office investigated my parents and they were allowed to stay for as long as they wanted.

They arrived at the beginning of April 1965. It wasn't easy for them but they made the best of the situation. Now I was able to be with my daughter in King's College Hospital in London while my mother and father looked after my boy in Maidstone. At the beginning they settled down very well.

Our daughter was undergoing a lot of investigations and the poor child's life wasn't very pleasant. Nino, our son, missed his sister. I took him to London with me but it wasn't very nice in the hospital for such a young child. Next he started complaining that he felt sick and had pains in his stomach. Again, when I told the GP, he said he was imagining it and at his age it was impossible to have something wrong with his stomach. When we were next in London I mentioned it to Professor Straight and he said,
"We will give him a barium meal and find out what the problem is."
A few days later Nino had his barium meal. When the professor asked for me in his office, he gave me a chair to sit in and then said,
"Your son's X-ray shows that he appears to have caught some kind of infection but in two weeks on this medication he will get better. But our investigations of your daughter are a different matter. You were right all along that she has not been well. She was born with reflux in both kidneys and they are very badly damaged. If a doctor had recognised the problem earlier, a small operation would have saved her and you all the distress you went through and the

poor little girl wouldn't be so ill today."

"I knew there was something wrong with her but I never expected that." I said, "I would like to take that doctor to court."

"That is not possible." Professor Straight said, "If we were in the United States you might have been able to do that, but here in England there is no such mechanism. Tomorrow we will operate on Luciana. While we do that, you go to your chapel and pray."

It was a very difficult time for all of us and especially for my little girl. Yet she was so good, she never complained, she never made any fuss. She was a very special little girl and I loved her so that to see her suffer like that broke my heart. One day a doctor on duty at King's College Hospital said,

"Please, Mrs Maddalena, consider having another child. That would help you to bear this pain more easily."

"Doctor," I said, "another child won't make Luciana better. It wouldn't ease the pain because a mother loves all her children the same." Luciana heard what the doctor had said. Two days later she said,

"Mamma, I've been praying to our dear Lord Jesus to give me a baby sister." I just burst into tears.

It was April 1966 when Luciana had the first operation but I'd been told she needed much more surgery. The problem was still there and she had to take lots of medication. I was so upset to see my beautiful little girl suffer so much and not be able to go to school. Professor Straight told me,

"Mrs Maddalena, take the child home and continue with the medication three times a day. If at any time she needs help, bring her here at once."

Now I found I was expecting another baby and when I told the children Luciana said, "Mummy, I prayed to God to give me a baby sister."

One night Luciana was very ill. I called that terrible GP, who arrived smelling of spirits. He appeared to be drunk and said,

"Mrs Maddalena, have you any spirits in the house?"

"No, doctor, we don't drink and therefore we haven't any such thing in our house." He wasn't very nice at all.

"Why do you worry so much about this girl?" he said, "She's so ill. Don't let her suffer any more." This upset me so much that my husband called the police. They came, saw the situation and telephoned King's College Hospital for their advice. They told the police to call an ambulance and get her to London with a police escort. We were taken straight to the children's ward and the doctor on duty attended to Luciana immediately. In the morning the professor came and said,

"Your daughter is very ill. Tomorrow, when her temperature is down, we will operate to remove her left kidney. But I must tell you we can only do our best. You must pray to God because I'm only a tool for carrying out His will; if He wants her to live, the operation will be a success. Our lives are in His hands."

A couple of days later Luciana went into the operating theatre for the removal of her left kidney. It was a terrible time in my life. I was in desperation and the child knew and understood everything. She resisted the anaesthetic and they had to give her gas to make her to go to sleep.

"Mummy, don't worry, Jesus will look after me." she said. That was the worst and longest day of my life. As my precious child went into the operating theatre, I went to the chapel to pray for a miracle. After six hours, my daughter was back in an intensive care ward. I thanked God I could see my baby again. She was kept in hospital for a long time.

Then the professor had to go away abroad.

"The operation has been a success," he said, "but we will always have to look after her. However, I do believe that when God does something, He does it well. Her next appointment is with Mr. Reads who is a kidney specialist and he will take great care of her. He will be there when she needs him."

"Thank you very much for all you have done for us." I said, "Now at last we can be together at home and life can begin to look up."

One day I went to collect the children from school and Nino complained of pain in his ear. I had to take him to that horrible GP, who was very nasty, as usual. He told me he didn't want to see me or my family anymore because I was a fussy mother. Without examining my son's ear, he marched us out of his surgery. We went home very discouraged. My poor boy was in pain and I couldn't do anything. As he was getting worse I took him to the hospital. By now he had a very high temperature and he was admitted. His temperature went up and up but they couldn't find anything wrong. The children's specialist said,

"Why do you worry so much? He will be all right."

"You told me that before about my little girl," I said, "and now she hasn't got her left kidney and her right one is damaged."

"Yes, you are right but that was a very difficult case to diagnose. I'm very sorry for that."

My son was in there for two weeks and his temperature didn't come down. One day a trainee doctor came on duty in his ward. He was learning to examine all the children. When he examined my son he looked in his ears and said,

"You have a choo-choo train in your ear."

"What do you mean, doctor?" I asked.

"What I mean is that inside his ear there is something that shouldn't be there. I will speak to the other doctor about it and see what we can do." Before I knew it the ear, nose and throat specialist from the other hospital came and in no time the problem was solved. I didn't understand what it was all about, so the doctor explained to me what they thought had happened.

"Somehow a lead pencil had been put in his ear." he said, "It must have been pushed in by another child when playing. The poison in the lead had infected him leading to the pain and high temperature. But the problem is now solved and there is nothing to worry about any more."

At that time another problem arose: the church started to come after me because I was not attending Mass regularly. I couldn't go because of the problems with the children and I was expecting another baby. I was upset and it became too much for me to bear. When the new baby was born, it was almost impossible to take the children to the Roman Catholic school and I had no choice but to take them away. They started at St Michael's C of E school near our house instead. The children could walk there by themselves and didn't need to catch a bus.

We also had to look for another GP. My husband went to the Register Office and said,

"We need a new doctor because the one we had refuses to look after us any more." The official at the Register Office asked who this doctor was and my husband said,

My husband told the name of the Doctor.

"Of course he can't look after you any more," she said, "because he has died from alcohol abuse. It's not professional of me to tell you which doctor is best but, as you and your family are a special case, I would recommend Doctor Jean Mutimer. She is a wonderful, Christian young lady, very near to your home. It will be better all round for your family." My husband came home and said, "Ida, I've been advised to sign up with a doctor at 166 Tonbridge Road who is able to look after us."

When she got to know us, she understood and helped us a great deal. We thanked God for her. She had a wonderful family who were Christians and supported us like nobody else had. They welcomed us into their house and talked to us about God in ways that helped us understand like never before what it really means to be a Christian.

The doctor's father had devoted his life completely to God; he just lived to preach the word of God. We were told that he had lived in India for eight years until he became very ill and had no choice but to come home, but that didn't stop him raising money for the poor children of that country. Frequently people from India came to report to him how the money had been spent and often there were children's pictures to say 'thank you' for the help they had received. He opened his house to all sorts of people, those with drug addictions, the homeless, and even people from prison. He would give them his own name, like when someone adopts a child.

CHAPTER TWENTY-NINE – ANOTHER CHILD AND A NEW JOB

I had my baby and we named her Stella Angela. She was a beautiful girl. After she was one year old I thought I should go back to work again. I looked for a job as a nurse in a hospital with a nursery facility. I wanted to be near home. The hospital I used to work at before was too far away. I had to catch two buses to get there and now I preferred a job closer to my house. I made a few enquiries and found out there was a big hospital not very far away from us with a nursery facility. I wrote for application forms and a week later they arrived. I filled them in without reading anything about what kind of hospital it was, posted them and a week later I got an interview.

I caught the bus, got off and walked for about three minutes down St Andrew's Road to the big double gates on the right hand side. I was used to seeing beautiful gates, like those at the villa in Corso Trieste in Rome, at both entrances to the Vatican City and the ones in the garden between the Sistine Chapel and the Vatican gardens. I was impressed with these at the entrance to the hospital. When I went through them there was a park with big trees on both sides of a wide path that lead to the front of large and pleasant building. I went in and on the right was a glass window, above which was a sign, 'Enquiries'. I knocked on the window to ask where I needed to go and a man in uniform appeared.
"Good morning," I said, "can you please tell me where the matron's office is?"
"Yes, madam," he said, "but I will need to take you there as this place is very big and you'll never find it alone." He came out and took me down a long corridor until we arrived at a large door.
"This is the office you want. Good luck." he said and left.

For a minute I stood in front of the door and wondered what I should be doing. Then I pulled myself together and knocked. A voice said,
"Come in." I pushed open the door and went in. It was a very large office with two big desks. Behind them were two ladies in matrons' uniforms who interviewed me. They asked a hundred questions but it was never mentioned that this was not a general hospital but a mental hospital. I expect they thought I had read the papers they'd sent me and knew all about it. I got the job and they asked me to start there in a week's time.

On my first day I went to collect my uniform and only when I put it on did I notice that it was different from the usual ones. I reported to one of the matrons and she told me to go to Ward Seven. She gave me a big key and said,

"Make sure that you always lock the door behind you."

"Why ever should I do that?" I thought to myself, sighed and wondered what I was doing in this hospital. It seemed not to be what I'd been trained for. Anyway, I put the key in the door and the first thing I heard was a loud shout,

"I'm going to kill you!" Goodness me! I locked the door again, ran downstairs as fast as I could into the matrons' office and started to take off my uniform. Another woman started shouting just like the woman up in Ward Seven,

"Nurse, pull yourself together and go upstairs at once!" I protested that I never knew this was a mental hospital, I'd never been in one before and I had no intention of staying! She appeared even angrier than before and said,

"How dare you talk like that to me? You've signed a two year contract and can't just change your mind whenever you please. We sent you all the information. It's your own fault if you were too lazy to read it. I advise you, when you finish duty today, to go home and read the information you should have read before you signed." I was in shock. Whatever had I done? I had no choice. I had to try again so I went back upstairs and put the key in the door again.

It was worse than before! It was a very big ward full of people shouting. I was very frightened. I went into the office not knowing what I could possibly ever do there. I'd never been in that position before. The sister in charge realised and said,

"Nurse Maddalena, don't worry. It's not as bad as it looks. You will enjoy it when you get accustomed to this kind of nursing." I did very little that day.

When it was time for me to go the sister said,

"Do you see the lady that frightened you when you first came in this morning?"

"Yes." I said.

"Why don't you go to her and say 'hello' and then you'll see she wasn't shouting at you but at someone in her mind. In the past somebody must have hurt her very much and now it's playing in her mind." So I pulled myself together and said,

"Hello, Mary."

"Hello, my dear," she said, "and how are you today? You have a kind face. I hope you like it here and I didn't frighten you. You see that man over there? He is my husband and he is a very bad man. Please don't go near him because he is very dangerous." I looked to where she was pointing but there was nobody there. Then she said,

"Most people here are not bad at all. They are just people, like everybody else, and people like you come here and show us the kind of love we've never experienced in our lives before. I want to say 'thank you' from all of us." She smiled. I was so surprised that I didn't know what to say, I was lost for words. I just kissed her and said,

"Well, I'm privileged to be here."

It was time for me to go home so I went to collect my baby from the nursery and found the nurse in charge with a dressing on her head.

"What have you done to your head?" I asked.

"It's all thanks to your daughter. She smashed a cup on my head."

"She didn't!"

"Oh yes, she did." she said. Well, what could I say? When I got home I told my mother who said,

"Don't take her there any more. I can look after my granddaughter, thank you." So that was the end of that nursery for Stella.

I thought I'd better find out what I'd let myself into, so I took out the information that had been sent to me and, like a fool, I had signed without reading. I found out about the history of Oakwood Hospital:

> In 1825 the local court found that there were one hundred and sixty 'pauper lunatics' and fifty 'dangerous idiots' in the area (these were the names by which insane people were known at that time). The justices in Kent, along with Earl Romney, thought steps should be taken to house these people because they were a danger to the public and to themselves. For many years Oakwood was more like a prison than a hospital. The Mental Treatment Acts of 1930 showed that the attitudes towards these unfortunate people were changing and it was understood that they were suffering from mental illness. Specialist qualifications for both the medical and nursing professions were introduced for

the care for these patients. The importance of occupational therapy was recognised and opportunities for social interaction and communication were created: concerts, parties, weekly dances, football and cricket matches, and outings for patients to participate in. Their lives began to change from the restrictive conditions of the earlier years. More new Acts played an important part, the word 'lunatic' began to disappear and was replaced by 'unsound mind' and the institution in Maidstone was called the Kent County Mental Hospital. Suitable employment was found for patients within the hospital to provide a framework for the day, and create a sense of community and a sense of achievement. Men worked on the farm and in the gardens, in tailoring and bootmaking. Women worked in sewing rooms and helped with domestic duties on the wards.

After I read all these papers and realised what a mental hospital was, I thought it would be a good experience to spend two years there, as a new venture for me. Anyway it was near my house and the money was better than the pay from the General Hospital. So I decided to get on with the job.

My parents had settled as best they could in England. My mother liked being there because she knew how very much she was needed. She was very clean and kept the house spotless. She was a hard worker and because she had been brought up on a farm she liked growing vegetables and flowers. So I rented two allotments from the council and that was her hobby. At the allotments she was liked by everybody. She grew more vegetables than we were able to eat so she would give the excess to anybody who needed it. There was still plenty for us to freeze: peas, strawberries, raspberries, beans and many more. We also froze enough to give away to the old people we knew in the neighbourhood.

My father had a job in Leybourne Grange Hospital, West Malling as a nursing assistant. He had always liked to help people. When the war began and he was called up into the army, they tried to brainwash everyone with propaganda. His colonel insisted on how important it was to kill the enemy and, when he had finished, he asked his men if they had any questions. My father said,
"Yes, Sir, I have."
"Yes, Festa," said the colonel, "what do you want to know?"

"Sir," said my father, "you said it is so important to kill the enemy. Can you tell me why I have to kill people I've never seen before, when I have plenty of enemies in my business whom I can't do anything about?"

"Festa, what are you trying to tell me? If you go to war, are you going to let the enemy shoot you?"

"No. What I would like to do instead of shooting people is to help them in a medical centre, whether they are friends or enemies."

So they sent him to Ethiopia where they posted him in a medical centre. He liked to do his best for people less fortunate than himself. Every Sunday he went to the church and prayed.

Throughout his life in Italy he was a smoker. When he came to England our friend the doctor told him to stop because it was bad for him. He stopped immediately without any fuss. He would rise at five am and, after washing and dressing, would say his prayers, have a very light breakfast and go to East Station to catch the train to work. He enjoyed what he was doing.

The children began to settle down after a long and difficult time. I tried to learn a new way of nursing, which I didn't find very easy. At that time there wasn't much medication and it was very difficult to control the patients. You've got to know how to deal with that kind of patient and we had courses to learn how to look after them in right way and how to look after ourselves as well.

We were told to make sure you locked yourself in, in case of danger. One day I failed to do that. I went into the office to write my report and sat with the door wide open. A female patient came in with a knife in her hand and said,

"Now I'm going to kill you because you have failed in your duty. You should shut the door. I'm coming to put this knife in your back." As she began to approach the desk, I slipped underneath and ran out, shutting the door behind me and locking her in. Oh dear me! She had a knife and no nurses could go in. We all panicked and called for help from the fire brigade of the hospital. When she did come out she laughed and said,

"I knew she was new at this kind of work. I wouldn't have hurt her. I only wanted to give her a fright and make her learn the lesson that she should never go into a room without locking the door behind her." After that episode I certainly learned that lesson!

CHAPTER THIRTY – ON DUTY IN ROBIN WARD

After six months I asked if I could work in the geriatric ward because that was much more my kind of nursing. The matron accepted my proposal and I was posted to a female ward, Ward Two. There I could wash and take care of the women in the way that I was accustomed to in the general hospital. I would sterilise everything.

One day, after I had sterilised the large clinic which was a long job, I was feeling very pleased with myself. Then a fireman came and said,
"Nurse, there is a fire in the clinic room." By rights I should have evacuated the patients with the help of the other staff. Instead I turned round and said to him,
"I've just sterilised that room! You dare go and mess it all up!"
"You silly woman!" said the fireman, "Can't you see that this a fire drill? I will report you to Number Nine." (He meant the Head of Nursing; matrons were starting to be removed at that time.)

All hospitals were changing very fast but not for the better. If our patients needed operations or other special treatment they were sent to the general hospital and usually came back with big sores because they had been kept in bed for too long. The nurses in the general hospital did not have time to attend them individually and restore them back to health.

One patient came back to us with a big sore on her back. It was the size of a fist. Our job was to try to get it to heal before gangrene set in. It would have been impossible to save the patient otherwise. I myself spent a lot of time making sure our efforts were successful. At that time we didn't had the same facilities we have today. The antibiotics would stop the infection spreading but wouldn't replace the flesh that was missing. The only thing to do was to apply vitamin B directly onto the wound. We knew that Marmite had salt and vitamin B in it. Vitamin B was important for the flesh to grow and salt helped to heal the wound therefore, after we cleaned the wound properly with special instruments, we put the sterilization gauze into a Marmite pot and then back onto the wound making sure no germs could get in. We changed the dressing once a day until it was completely healed. That wouldn't happen in any hospital today because we have different technologies but in my old people's home I did it with very good results.

One day when I wasn't feeling very well the doctor on duty decided to perform a lumbar puncture on a patient who was paralysed, to find out why she couldn't walk.   He told me to prepare a sterilization tray in the clinic room and then assist him.
"Doctor," I said, "can we see if there's another nurse who could help you because today I don't feel very well and I'm frightened I won't be well enough to assist you?"
"Pull yourself together, nurse," he said, "and get on with it."

A lumbar puncture is when a doctor puts a patient face down on a sterilised bed and inserts a large needle with a tap into their spine. When it is properly inserted the doctor will turn the tap to draw liquid from the spine which will be sent to the laboratory.   The analysis of this liquid will tell the doctor what is matter with the patient.   I did everything I should have done but when the doctor put the needle in the patient's back and the liquid started to come out, I just collapsed on the floor. After it was all over he said,
"Why didn't you tell me you weren't up to it?"
"Doctor, I did tell you," I said, "but you told me to get on with it!"

I was growing very fond of the patients and in many cases felt sorry for them. It was so sad that these poor people had been put in a mental hospital because at that time it was the only way they could survive.   There were many cases of people who should never have been admitted but at that time if you did anything stupid you could be put in a mental hospital. For example, if you had a baby by mistake or if you stole something you could be admitted. If your relations didn't like you, they only had to fabricate a story against you, call a doctor and get you certified as a mad person, even if it wasn't true. Once a person was inside they might never come out again, unless a close relation took responsibility to care for them. That would never happen today.

But many people were there because they needed medical and nursing care. However, there were also people in mental hospitals who were not mentally ill but took advantage of the hospitality. It may seem absurd but that was the reality. In the geriatric ward there were many old, poor people who simply needed nursing care. Today they would be in residential homes or nursing homes.

Sometimes I got very tired, having three children, two older parents and a husband at home. Family life is not always what it might be. Often I faced great difficulties at the hospital but when I got home I just had to close my mind and get on with the family. Often I wished I could spend more time with my children, but my husband's income wasn't enough on its own to pay the mortgage and all the bills for running a five bedroom house and buying the children's school uniforms. We had some help from my parents but we had to feed seven and there was no other way. I had to go to work to help meet all our needs.

We did all the house decoration ourselves. One Friday afternoon I said to my husband,
"This week we must decorate the big sitting room. It doesn't matter who comes to the door, we will not answer it until we've finished." At about five p.m. the doorbell rang.
"Be quiet," I said, "whoever it is, we will not answer and they will go away." But the doorbell kept ringing and wouldn't stop. Oh dear! The house was all upside down. We didn't know what to do. Eventually we had to open the door, we had no choice. There stood a very posh, older couple with a lot of luggage. They said,
"Does Mr Maddalena live here?" I didn't know what to say.
"He doesn't live here." I said. Now this house had three gates. They went out by one gate and came straight back in another one. The bell rang again and my husband said,
"We must answer it again." But it was the same couple and again the same question,
"Does Aldo live here?" I couldn't say anything else, I had to say,
"Yes. But who are you?"
"We are his aunt and uncle from America," they said, "and we are very tired, need a bath and a bed." We were all gobsmacked. We didn't have any food in the house as we had already eaten and planned to go shopping the next morning. At that time there were no take-aways, so we cleaned ourselves up and took them out to dinner at the Star Hotel. That was the end of sitting room decoration for the time being.

They stayed a few days and I took some time off work. I couldn't say, 'I can't come to work because I have visitors' because the hospital rules were that you could only take extra time off if you were not well and for no other reason. So I told them a lie when I telephoned and said,
"I'm very sorry I can't come on duty because I'm unwell." After a

few days the Americans continued on their European tour and life began to get back to normal. I went back to work at the hospital as usual but before going onto the ward I had to report what had been wrong with me and whether I was well enough to start to work again. I did the best I could to convince the person in charge that I had been unwell but he wasn't totally persuaded by my story. I went back onto the ward and he went there secretly, by a back route, because he knew once I was on the ward I would talk about why I had been absent. When I arrived in the ward office I told my colleagues the real reason, without knowing he was listening to every word.

"I knew all along you were telling fibs." he said, "It would take more than a sore throat to keep you away from work."

When I started work again I was very saddened because a nice old lady who had been sent to the general hospital for a hip replacement had been sent back without having had the operation. When they opened her up they found it was impossible to operate because her bone was too far gone. This wouldn't happen today because with new technology they can see before they operate. Worse still, the wound wouldn't heal no matter how many antibiotics we gave her; the poor lady's muscle just wouldn't knit. The hospital is always a place of sorrow. There were so many cases it is impossible to write about all the poor, old people we had to look after every day.

When it was time for the summer holidays I asked for a month off but there were new rules that it was only possible to take two weeks at a time. We had been invited to Italy to my husband's brother's wedding. I thought one month would be better for the children. Soon they would start high school and a long holiday would be more beneficial to them. When I asked in the office I was refused so I took it higher and finally got permission.

We had a wonderful time in Italy except, as we left England on the train, we realised we had forgotten my daughter's blanket. She was only three yeas old and always carried a special blanket with her, no matter where we went. She started screaming and didn't stop for the whole of the holiday except when she slept. As always in our village there was a feast every other Sunday. One involved fireworks after the Mass. This screaming child just wouldn't stop and it was very difficult to do anything with her. I took her out of the church and said,

"You see that man lighting the fire? If you don't stop this noise you will get blown up on that fire." I know it was a very cruel thing to say but I just did not know what else to do. When we got home I took her to the bathroom to refresh her because it was such hot day and I noticed on my mother-in-law's bed there was a blanket a bit like the one we'd left at home. I went downstairs, found some scissors, cut a piece off and gave it to the child. That did the trick at last!

We really enjoyed the month's holiday, apart from the blanket. Back in Maidstone we all rejoiced at being at home again with my parents, our doctor and her family and all the people we knew. I went back to the hospital and had a not very pleasant surprise. I was moved to another ward which was not what I wanted. I liked working on the geriatric ward because it was what I was trained for. They put me on a ward with a very old sister in charge. There were only two of us and when she was on, I was off. The ward had people in it who should never have been in hospital but who, after so many yeas of institutionalisation, could not manage by themselves any more. My job was to come in the morning, take over from the night nurse, go into the office and read the report to see what had to be done. Most of the time I supervised breakfast, gave medication according to the prescriptions and then sent the patients to occupational therapy. Some of them weren't able to go anywhere for one reason or other.

One day I made a terrible mistake which gave me a shock and made me realise how easy it is to make silly mistakes. I will always remember it and I made sure never to make the same mistake again. There was a lady with a chest infection who was on a course of antibiotics by injection. It was time for her injection so I took a kidney dish and put the penicillin bottle in it and the sterile water. Before I could do anything else the emergency bell rang and I had to leave everything as it was, close the medicine cupboard and go where I was needed for the emergency. When I got back I went straight into the office, opened the medicine cupboard, took the kidney dish and prepared the injection as usual and injected the patient. After I'd done it I realised that I had injected the patient with the wrong thing. Instead of sterile water, I'd put a heart stimulant in with the penicillin. I can't describe the shock and horror I felt. I couldn't understand how I could make that kind of mistake. I assumed some silly nurse had played a joke on me by coming in when I wasn't there, opening the medicine cupboard, seeing what I was supposed to be doing by looking at the report, and then changing the sterile water for a heart stimulant.

The patient looked at me and asked if I was all right. She could see there was something wrong. I reassured her that everything was all right and asked her to go to bed and I would keep an eye on her. I didn't know what would happen to her but I was very frightened. At that moment the matron came round with a group of people. She told them all what a good nurse I was. If only she had known what was in my heart! I was very upset all day, imagining all kinds of things. What would happen if she had a heart attack? There would be an investigation and when they found substances in her body that shouldn't be there, whatever would happen to me?

I finished my shift and went home very concerned about this lady. I went to bed but couldn't sleep. Without my family knowing, at two o'clock in the morning I dressed and went to the hospital. When I got to my ward the night nurse spotted me and said, "Goodness me, what is the matter with you? Can't you sleep? What are you doing here at this time of night? Can't you leave the place alone?" I didn't answer but went straight to the lady's room. She wasn't there. Now I was really frightened but, as I turned round, I saw her come out of the toilet. She was very surprised to see me and asked what I was doing there at this time of morning. What could I say? I was very pleased to see her and asked how she had felt when I gave her that injection. She answered, "Fine, nurse." What a relief!

After working in this hospital for two years I began to understand this kind of nursing. It was challenging, sometimes great fun and sometimes very scary. Sometimes it was hard to understand and manage the situations you found yourself in. So I decided to stay for another two years. Now they sent me all over the hospital and I began to enjoy what I was achieving. I was sent to Farm Villa, a beautiful place with a large garden all around it. In this garden were all kinds of flowers and a tennis court for the nurses and doctors to play in. I was amazed to see such a beautiful garden. I'd not seen one like it since I left Vatican City and Oxsted Place in Surrey.

I thought it would be nice for my husband and my youngest child to come and see the place where I worked. When I mentioned it to my husband he said,

"Yes, Ida, I would like that very much." About a couple of days later they came. While we were admiring the garden, a lady patient came out from behind a bush and in a frightening voice said,

"This is the Garden of Eden and I'm the serpent come to tempt you!" I can't describe my husband's reaction. He took the child and ran as fast as he could, not turning back to see where I was. When he reached his car, he jumped in with our daughter, and sped away. I couldn't believe my eyes! I returned to Farm Villa, went into the lounge and there was Mrs Chester.

"Now see what you have done!" I said.

"I'm very sorry, nurse, I never meant to upset you." she said, "It was only a joke." I had a long walk home and that was the end of the fun for that day, if you can call it fun.

There was never a dull moment in that beautiful place. For a time I was in charge of night duty on the female side and Nick was in charge on the male side. When you came into the villa, you passed through the beautiful front garden, with its smooth lawn with rose beds, along the path to the front door. There was a big entrance hall with armchairs, many pictures on the walls, a small table with a pot of flowers on it and a bookcase filled with books so visitors could read if they wanted to. On the left was the nurses' and doctors' office. About fifteen feet away was the entrance to the female patients' sitting room and a music room. On the far left were many private bedrooms and straight in front was a big dormitory, bathrooms and other amenities. On the right side was the male ward, the clinic room, a sitting room and a dormitory. There was everything the patients could possibly need.

One night a young American patient came to me and said

"Nurse, I've taken two hundred tablets."

"Good for you." I said and went into the office to read the report, as you do when you come on duty. When I came out of the office this young man made sure he had plenty of witnesses so I would be responsible for anything that happened to him. He told me again and I still pretended to take no notice of him as I was busy taking over from the day staff. When I had finished, I went to see Nick and told him what was going on. He said,

"He might be calling your bluff but we ought to do something in case he really has done something silly and we will be held responsible." I went into the office and arranged for an ambulance to take him to the general hospital to investigate what he'd done. Because there was nobody else to go with him, I had to go myself. When we reached the hospital, as soon as the ambulance men opened the door, the young fellow jumped onto a motorcycle that was there waiting for him and said,

"Goodbye, nurse, I'm sorry if I've got you into a lot of trouble." Now the ambulance men couldn't take me back to my hospital. I had to telephone for a taxi. It was two in the morning when I got back on duty. I was very annoyed and got even more vexed when everybody had a good laugh at what happened.

You never knew what to expect when you went to Farm Villa. It was very mentally tiring and at the same time very challenging to look after people less fortunate than yourself. Often it was very hard to see people suffering from mental problems.

One night the police came to us with a very abusive, drunk man. The police said it was necessary to see a male nurse, so I went to look for Nick. When I found him he was very busy with another patient and couldn't come so I asked the police to take him into a room especially built for this purpose and I would see to him. But the police said a man in this condition was too difficult for me to manage. I explained to them that Nick and I were both in charge and when one was busy, the other one had to do what was necessary. It didn't matter whether we were female or male. So they put him in the room and I locked the door.

When I went back to the office and read the police notes, I realised who this gentleman was. As they say, the world is full of surprises. He was the headmaster of a school where my friend's son was a pupil. I couldn't believe what I'd seen. How can people in such a position lose themselves in that way? It was very bad. All night he was shouting,

"Nurse, give me some tablets, please, to end my life! Help me to get out of my miserable existence." The smell of alcohol came through the door. In the morning we called a couple of male nurses to help him have a bath to remove the smell of the alcohol and all the mess he managed to make. After we made him respectable again in hospital clothes, we called an ambulance to send him home.

At that time my daughter Luciana was offered a place at grammar school but she refused it. She preferred to stay where she was so she could be top of the class all the time and in that way build more confidence. My son, Nino, was at the boys' grammar school. I was and still am very proud of my children's achievements; they did what I would have liked to have done myself but could not because of the war.

One day I came on duty and read the day report. I saw we had a new patient. She was very young and a student of law but unfortunately it seems it was too much for her and she was not able to continue with her studies. She ended up with us and it was a great shame. I was very sorry for her and very frightened to see what too much pressure can do for some people. This girl was beautiful but she used to take all her clothes off and not realise what danger she was putting herself in, here in a mixed ward with men everywhere who were not in their right minds. We certainly had a job on our hands which was very difficult to deal with. Sometimes when you came on duty and you already had not had an easy day at home, it wasn't much fun to deal with so many problems of this kind. But that was the job, and you must do the best as you can.

One night I wasn't very well and telephoned the hospital to say I wouldn't go in.
"But," they said, "we haven't got anybody else. You must come in." I went in and after I read the report I called the doctor to see what we could possibly to do with this young lady. If nothing else, we might have to keep her in bed for her own safety. The doctor prescribed some sleeping tablets in the hope she would stay in bed. I gave her the tablets, said 'goodnight', made sure I closed the window and went to look after the other patients. Nick was always tired because in the daytime he had two grandchildren to look after and therefore he didn't get much sleep. It was always the same story: at about eleven o'clock he would go into a side room and settle down in a comfortable armchair. Once he'd sat down that was the end of him and unless there was an emergency I wouldn't bother him. It wasn't very fair but that was the situation. When I was ready to go and check all the patients to make sure they were all right before making myself a cup of tea, I saw the duty doctor come through the door with a very red face.
"Whatever is the matter with you?" I asked. Before he answered I'd realised what had happened. The young lady had gone out without any clothes on.   Luckily it was summertime but

nevertheless at twelve o'clock at night it can't have been very comfortable, not to mention the danger she was in. I called Nick but it wasn't easy to make him understand what had happened. We called for emergency support and started looking for her all over the hospital. Eventually we found her in Tonbridge Road, not very far from the hospital. What a night! I hadn't been feeling well before all this and so by the morning I was very tired and had a high temperature.

CHAPTER THIRTY ONE – ON DUTY IN FARM VILLA

There were young people in this villa and in particular a boy I'd grown fond of. He was very young and very ill. There was little that could be done for him. In his mind he believed he was an anti-Christ and must die because he was no good. He believed that when he died he would come back again as a better person. He was always waiting for me when I came on duty but this time it was different. As soon as I came in the door he asked for his medication.

"Look, Anthony " I said, "it's the weekend and it's much too early to go to bed yet. Why don't you go into the music room and enjoy yourself?" I went to Nick and told him that I was concerned about John because he wanted his medication too early. What could be going on in his mind?

"Don't worry." Nick said, "He'll be all right."

"Nick, if we give him the medication then he will go to bed." When I went into the male ward to see if everyone there was all right, because we had quite a few difficult cases, I could smell something funny. As I approached John's bed I slipped in a pool of blood. I shouted,

"Oh no, what have you done?" At that moment I realised what he had done. He'd cut both wrists. He had by him a bottle of white spirit and a box of matches. I think what he had in mind was, just before dying, to set fire to the place but then he realised that he wasn't going to die. I immediately took the spirit and matches away and called for emergency help. I was covered in blood. I ran to find Nick who was fast asleep and wouldn't wake up. I pushed his chair and shouted,

"Nick, please wake up!" He thought I was out of my mind and when he saw me covered in blood he was frightened, too. By then help had arrived and they took the situation in hand. I was able to wash myself and change my uniform.

Next we had to stitch John up and give him a blood transfusion but he wouldn't let anybody touch him unless I was there. I was very tired and didn't want to be there but the patient always comes first so I had no choice. My patience ran out when I saw the doctor stitch his wrists without using an anaesthetic.

"Doctor, why don't you give him an anaesthetic?" I asked, "Can't you see he is in pain?" The answer came,

"It didn't hurt him when he cut them, so why should it hurt him now?"

"You have no consderation! I said, "You should know that just because his brain didn't register the pain that it doesn't mean he is not in pain now."

"All right, but he doesn't deserve it!" the doctor replied, "we'll give him an anaesthetic because you are so soft with these people."

"I bet you'd be sorry if one of these boys was your son. You'd show more compassion then."

"I've heard enough from you, white witch! Let's go and have a cup of coffee and we can continue this discussion another day."

We had about twenty females and twenty males and they were all very sad cases. To us it was a job and I really put everything into it. My family was very important to me, too, and when I went home I left the job behind and concentrated on them. Our fellowship was also very important to me and my family. Every Sunday we went to church and there we met our God who gave us all we needed to get by. I wouldn't have had the strength to do the job and look after my family without that, because most of the time life was not easy. But with God everything is possible.

When I went on duty and read the reports, I was very sad to see what a mess these people had made of their lives, only because they never knew any better. There was a young girl, not much older than my daughter, who was brought into this mental hospital because she was on hunger strike. Why was she on hunger strike? The answer was that she'd fallen in love with a man much, much older than herself. He already had a family of five children and a beautiful wife. She'd managed to break up this lovely family. Now she wanted the government to give her and her boyfriend a caravan to live in together. Because the Social Services couldn't fulfil her desire, she came to us. She wasn't very easy at all and only God gave us the patience to look after her. She was on hunger strike and so we had to put her on a drip but every time we put it on, she'd take it off. When you have forty people to look after and only two staff it's a bit much to manage on a twelve hour shift.

One night we were very busy and this young girl didn't stop playing me up. The busier she could see I was, the more she tried. I didn't lose my patience very often but that night I did. I told her if she did not behave I would call the doctor to give her an injection to put her to sleep for the night. She said,

"Good. I'd like that." The night was very long and very busy. We had two more admissions and a lot of paperwork to do. This girl kept shouting and disturbing everybody else and then they all started. I went to her and said,

"Stop this noise otherwise I'll put you outside where there are security dogs and they will have you."

"Oh, I like the dogs." she said, "They won't do anything to me. I like them and they know who they like and who they don't." She continued to be very difficult and a trouble to everybody else. While I was attending to other patients, she took off her drip and ran out to the back of the villa. It was very dark out there and I had a job to get her back. When I finally managed to bring her in I gave her a big smack on her bottom like you would give to your child when you can't take any more. I said to her that that was what her mother should have done to her before she'd made a mess of everybody's lives. In the morning she said she would report me to the hospital authorities. I told her to go right ahead. I know I should never have done it but I had just had enough that night.

I also had a young mother with post natal depression with her young baby. I was scared to leave the baby with her and took it with me to the lounge. This baby was just beautiful but the young girl liked to make a nuisance of herself and I couldn't take any more. I asked God to forgive me, went into the office and wrote on her report all that had happened.

At last she fell asleep. When she woke up she asked for me and said,

"Sorry, nurse. Can I have a piece of toast, please?" I was surprised how this girl had changed. I thanked God for I knew I couldn't do any more without His help and the help was there when I asked for it. When I came in the next night the day staff told me what a good job I'd done. I said it wasn't the right thing to do but I was very tired and couldn't help it.

About ten years later, as I walked through the town, I heard somebody call me 'Nurse'. I turned around and saw a lady with a couple of children.

"Do you remember me?" she asked. I looked at her and her face was familiar but no, I didn't remember who she was.

"I'm that naughty girl who played you up so much that you had to give me a smack on my bottom to make me see sense."

"Oh yes. I'm sorry. I must have hurt you so much you can't forget it."

"No," she answered, "from that day I saw what a mess I'd made and did try to put things right. In fact now I'm married to a man my own age and these are our children."

"Well done!" I said, "I'm very pleased. You've made my day."

"I want to say 'thank you very much'."

After the incident with the young girl on hunger strike Farm Villa was as difficult as ever. It is difficult even to write about it. I had been there for two years by now and I wanted to go back to the geriatric ward because I had had enough of this kind nursing. However, it wasn't easy to make them understand that I couldn't take any more. I didn't want to leave because I still had to pay the mortgage, bring up three children and look after my parents as they grew older. I needed to work.

One morning when I was waiting to be transferred from Farm Villa, before I finished my shift the door opened and three men asked to speak to me in private. They showed their badges explaining that they were plain clothed policemen. I took them into the office and closed the door. They asked me if I was on the next shift and I said 'yes'. They said,

"Tonight there will be a police raid on Farm Villa. We do not want you to get hurt so when it happens we want you to get out of the way. Don't worry about the patients, we won't hurt them." I was very frightened, not understanding what was going on. When I arrived on night shift the police came in and again wanted to speak to me in private. They told me the raid was off. The person they were looking for wasn't there any more. When they left it was a great relief to me. I went to check the patients and found that one was missing. There wasn't anything about it written in the report so I didn't know what had happened to her. Later I found out that she was hiding under a false name. The people who had put her in realised the police knew, so they removed her. I never heard any more about it.

At this time I got very tired. My children were off school for the summer and my husband and I decided to take a long holiday, not to our village where we usually went but somewhere completely different. We looked in all the travel agencies and decided to go to Sorrento. We booked tickets including a very nice apartment in a hotel. I was hoping that when we came back I would be posted to a different ward.

We found Sorrento to be a very beautiful place. There was a lot to see and we enjoyed ourselves. Every day we went somewhere different. On the day we went to see Pompeii unfortunately there was a strike so we couldn't get in. Instead we went to see the new city of Pompeii which was interesting and very beautiful. We were amazed to see what the people of Pompeii had managed to achieve.

History tells us that in 79 AD volcanoes hurled out gases and molten rocks over the towns of Pompeii and Herculaneum. The inhabitants were victims of these powerful natural forces. Archaeologists found people's bones, buildings, ornaments, coins. The more they dug, the more they found. It is very interesting and visited by tourists from all over the world. It was a great pity that it was closed when we went there, though, as I said, we still enjoyed seeing the new Pompeii. We hope one day to go back there with all the family, especially our grandchildren who, I'm quite sure, will find it very interesting.

Sorrento was very nice but presented us with quite a few surprises. We were looking around the shops when our young daughter saw a pair of shoes she liked. We weren't really keen to buy them but she was making such a fuss that we had no choice but to go into the shop and enquire about them. The owner of the shop said to the assistant,
"Charge more because they are foreigners and don't understand."
"How dare you charge us more?" I said, "Foreigners are your bread and butter and you rob them. Shame on you! If this is how you treat people who come here from abroad to make your and our country a better place, wait till I go back to England. I will tell all the newspapers how people like you give a bad name to the rest of the Italian people who are trying to make an honest living!" She was flabbergasted! She didn't know what to say except to apologise again and again. She told us we could have the shoes for free. I said we would do no such thing; we would only do what was right and pay the right price for them. We were prepared to pay the amount of money we thought these shoes were worth. She agreed, we paid for the shoes and left. I'm sure this lady learned her lesson and didn't do that again for a long time.

The next day we were walking along the road past the shops when my husband stopped to look at some toys. The three children and I went into the shop and said,

"Please can you tell us where the fireworks are held?"

"You have the stomach to come here to ask me where the fireworks are held?" the man in the shop said, "You know where the fireworks are held! You really only came in here to show me your children and to see me, didn't you?"

"You've made a mistake." I said, "I do not know you. I'm not from round here. My family and I are here on holiday. We've never been here before." He didn't believe a word I was saying.

"Don't insult me! You know who I am. You've come here to show me your family. Well, I don't wish to see you or you family!" I realised that this man thought I was his ex-girlfriend.

"Children," I said, "let's get out of here. Don't let your father know that this man has mistaken me for somebody else." We found my husband and went into a bar but he followed us in there with a friend. He was asking his friend if he was right or wrong. The friend said,

"I'm not sure. She looks like Maria but I don't know." There wasn't anything we could do. I said to my husband,

"Aldo, let's go back to the hotel. I have a terrible headache." So we took a taxi and left.

The next day we went to Vesuvius, the volcano near Naples. While we were up there I began to get frightened by people lighting their cigarettes from the hot rocks; it made me aware that the volcano was still active so we went back to the hotel.

When we got there I realised my son wasn't at all well. I told the children to go upstairs, shut the door and not open it to anybody because there were a lot of thieves about. I spoke to the hotel manager to see if we could get a doctor. A doctor arrived so quickly that he got upstairs before us and when he rang the bell my eldest daughter answered the door to him and said,

"Thief!" The doctor said in English,

"I'm not a thief. I'm the doctor come to see your brother." By then we had arrived. The doctor was amused by my daughter's greeting but told us that our son had better be taken home to England as soon as possible. We were in England the next day and took our son to our friend the doctor and he soon recovered.

CHAPTER THIRTY-TWO – BACK FROM HOLIDAY

Back from holiday and back to the hospital again! I was expecting to be in the geriatric ward as I requested but it was not to be. Again I was posted all over the hospital on night shifts. It was a good arrangement because it meant I could be at home during the day. My mother was getting old, the house was big and the family required lots of attention from me. Being at home during the day was better for my mother and everybody else.

One night I was on duty in David Ward with what I thought were physically disabled ladies who were not mentally ill or dangerous. I soon realised things could be very dangerous if I wasn't prepared for them! I had a quite reasonable night but when the day shift was due to come on duty nobody appeared. I couldn't leave the ward without handing over to the day staff or the sister or somebody else able to take responsibility. There were about sixty patients in this ward and I was all by myself. That was all right when they were asleep but when they were all awake and you tried to make them get up and into the daily routine, if there were not enough staff on duty you could find yourself in for a big surprise.

Breakfast arrived from the main kitchen and I asked all the patients to sit at the table. I had already experienced some difficulty getting these ladies to follow the usual daily routine. Now I asked them to sit at their usual places. Most of them were on a diet which they didn't like. They didn't understand what was wrong with them anyway. The food wasn't much good, especially for those on a diet, and there wasn't much of it. It wouldn't have been enough for normal people let alone these poor women with low intelligence who, for no fault of their own, had been living in this institution since they were young. At that time this kind of institution was similar in many ways to the old workhouses. It wouldn't happen like that today as the world has changed, but sadly too late for these poor ladies. When they realised I was by myself, I sensed a time bomb ready to explode. I said to myself that I must be courageous and make them understand that I could handle the situation. I shouted at them,
"Look, ladies, sit down all of you and behave! If any one of you thinks because I'm by myself that I can't control you, you will have the surprise of your life. Kindly sit and eat your breakfast with no fuss and everything will be all right." At last they began to settle

down and the tension disappeared. Finally the day staff arrived and I was very cross with them because they'd put my life in danger. Staff should arrive on time no matter what. I told them I would make a full complaint to Mr Mulling about the incident. Sister said,

"Please don't do that! We apologise for what happened and we promise it won't ever happen again." At night we had full security and help on hand if we were in trouble but after eight o'clock in the morning all the night staff went off duty and the day staff took over responsibility for the wards.

My next shift was on Francis Ward which was more my kind of nursing. I liked old people and got a lot of satisfaction from looking after them. As always the first thing I did was to read the report from the day staff. It was particularly sad to read about a poor old lady with very bad scalding down below. It was painful and humiliating for the patient and difficult to understand how a nurse could ever have caused such a thing. The report said the lady had been very constipated and the nurse wanted to help her. The way this was done when there wasn't any medication about was to use an old remedy. But this nurse was really demented. How could anyone put a patient, never mind an old lady, on a commode full of boiling water and let her sit there hoping the steam would open her bowels? Even a stupid person would understand that if you sit on a pot of boiling water you will get very badly scalded. That is what had happened to this dear old woman. I felt very sorry for her and the only thing I could do was to make her as comfortable as possible and give her lots of loving care.

There was another nurse on duty with me and together we washed all the patients and gave them their medication for the night. We gave them night time drinks and put them to bed. At about eleven o'clock, when it was for time for us to have a break, this other nurse asked if I minded if she went to the bathroom before we had our drink. I said,

"Of course not. Do whatever you like." After half an hour, a young lady came and sat with me. She had beautiful, long hair and looked very elegant. I stared at her, puzzled. Who was she and where was the nurse who had been with me? I pulled myself together and asked,

"Can you tell me who you are?" She was very surprised and answered,

"Nurse Maddalena, it is me!" I couldn't believe it. How could this woman change so much in such a short time? I realised the long hair must be wig and her make-up was so well done it was deceptive.

That night we were very busy but the patients were all well looked after.

Nowadays hospitals aren't locked up like they were years ago. Everything has changed and now patients have more freedom to come and go as they please. Nurses still have keys but don't have to use them like before. You used to go into hospitals and find all the furniture attached to the floor or chained so that people couldn't remove it. It was a great shame, but that was what hospitals were like. Now the world has changed but not all for the better. People are greedier and have lost a sense of humanity. How can anybody dare to steal an indispensable machine from a medical ward, a machine bought with charity money?

One night I was in Francis Ward at about eleven or twelve o'clock when a big transport van arrived and two porters came and rolled up the new carpet which had been laid just the day before. We didn't take any notice because they wore the same uniform as our porters and had the same keys as we did. After they'd gone we began to be puzzled. How come night porters take away carpet that was only put there recently? This is not a night duty job. I was very troubled so I telephoned the night duty office and told them what had happened. They asked,
"Did you take the number of the van?"
"No we didn't," I said, "because we thought nothing of it at the time. Now we're wondering if we should have done something about it."
These terrible things began to happen more frequently in other parts of the hospital.

A couple of months later I was on a round of quite a few wards. I started on Martin Ward. My job was to see that all the patients were all right. All of us night nurses had a bleeper so that if we were in danger we only had to press it and help would arrive. In Martin Ward I couldn't help noticing a big colour television which at the time was quite rare because they had only just begun to come into the shops. They were very expensive and not many people had them. I went into the office and read the day report. I did what I was supposed to do and checked that all the patients were all right, then I looked in the paper to see what was on television. At about two o'clock in the morning there was a film on which I thought I might watch during my break time. But when I came back the television wasn't there any more. Did I dream it? Surely not! So I telephoned the duty office and told them what had happened. The nursing officer said,

"The thief must have known the television was there and knew your routine." So when I'd gone into the ward they must have waited until I went out again and then taken the television away. There must have been more than one person as the television was so big. Who knows, it might have been the men who delivered it in the first place? It was terrible. Worse still was that it had been paid for with money from the Friends of the hospital, in other words, charity money.

When I was on day shifts I would go in the ambulance to take patients to the general hospital for their cancer treatments. It was very scary because at that time they didn't have the same facilities and technologies as hospitals have today and results often weren't as successful as they are nowadays. I had many surprises, some of them very sad. One such was when I passed through a ward and heard my name called out. I turned round to see a very disfigured lady. I asked who she was and she answered,

"Nurse, but you know me!"

"I do not remember you."

"But I'm the lady you took to the general hospital for treatment to my face. You came in the ambulance with me every day for a long time. You looked after me!" Goodness me, I remembered! The poor lady! If she only knew what she looked like! What a disappointment to see her like that. My only hope was that she would never see herself in a mirror because the radiation treatment had eaten away half her face. I would never have recognised her if she hadn't told me who she was.

Another time a similar thing happened but not so bad. A lady called me saying,

"Nurse, do you remember me?" Again I said,

"No, I don't."

"When I came back from the general hospital," she said, "I had a big hole in my bottom which you managed to make better with gauze and Marmite."

"Come and let me see." I took her into her little bedroom, helped to put her on the bed and was surprised that all I could see was a big scar. I said,

257

"Thank God for that."

One night I was called to an emergency. It was in a ward of women who had all suffered some kind of abuse during their lives, mostly from their own families. Because they felt insecure they could become violent. One of the patients didn't like the nurse on duty and became abusive towards her. The nurse locked the patient in the padded cell. The nurse was alone, which shouldn't have happened because in these kinds of wards it was not permitted to be on duty alone. But it had happened and so the nurse had every right to do what she did to protect the other ladies and herself. Then the poor nurse had to open the cell to give the patient her medication and food, so I was called to help. As I went in the nurse was very frightened because the patient was shouting, "You bastard! When you open this door I will kill you!" I asked the nurse the patient's name and when she told me I knew who it was. She was one of Dr Jean Mutimer's patients. The doctor felt very sorry for her. Hers was a very sad story and you couldn't help but like her.

The nurse and I had a talk and decided I would speak to her because she knew me. Maybe that way we could handle her. So I went to the cell, called her name and said who I was, a friend of Dr Jean Mutimer. She was quiet for a minute and then answered,
"All right but I want the coloured nurse to come in first and then you." The nurse had the tray and I had the keys. I opened the door and the nurse went in. The patient caught the nurse's head and pulled her hair. The hair came off in her hands because it was a wig. The patient had never seen a wig before. She thought it was the nurse's head and was terrified.
"Nurse Maddalena, take this head away! I didn't mean to kill her! Please, nurse!" I felt very sorry for her and showed her it was just a wig.

When I next met Dr Jean Mutimer I told her what had happened. The doctor said,
"I don't know whether to laugh or cry. In one way it's very funny and on the other hand it's very sad."

Many, many times we came across sad and scary cases all because these young women had suffered abuse at the hands of their family or somebody else. There was a very beautiful young woman who harmed herself in her private parts with glass or anything she could lay her hands on. She felt unclean. On many occasions I had to take her to Casualty at the general hospital to repair whatever damage she'd managed to inflict on herself.

One night I was on a secure ward with about thirty patients who would have been a danger to themselves if they were left unguarded. There was a funny side to this night. At about eleven o'clock the doorbell rang. I opened the door and was confronted with five policemen.
"We want the male nurse in charge." they said.
"He is not available," I said, "because he is with another patient but I can deal with the problem if it concerns a patient."
"We have a man here who we think needs to be admitted to a secure ward."
"I will do whatever is necessary. Please hand him over to me."
"You must be joking! This man is very dangerous. It took five of us to handle him down at the police station. He managed to sabotage the electricity so we might all have been electrocuted. He is very violent and dismantled the door of the room he was in. It'll need a strong man to control him."
"There is no such man on duty here. There's only the two of us and as you can see we are not very strong. We are both small but we are trained to handle most situations we find ourselves in." The policemen looked at me and said,
"Are you sure?" Before I said anything the man said,
"I could kill the lot of you anytime but I won't touch that nurse or anybody else on duty here." The police left.

I asked the man to make himself comfortable and what he would like to eat and drink.
"Whatever you've got, nurse, will be very much appreciated." So I went into the kitchen and made quite a lot of ham and cheese sandwiches and a big mug of tea. I took them to him and he said,
"Thank you, nurse." After he'd eaten he asked if he could go to bed.
"Of course," I said, "I hope you have a good night."
"I will, nurse, thank you." He slept all night without any trouble.

On my next shift I read the day report as usual. It said he had been very quiet and cooperative. After the day duty nurses left I made sure the outer doors were all properly closed because it was a secure ward.
"Nurse, why do you lock the doors?" the man asked.

"I lock them up so people like you can't escape!"

"Do you think if I wanted to get out of here that door would stop me?"

"I'm quite sure it would. The doors are specially made for these wards and it doesn't matter how strong you are, you will not manage to open them."

"Will you dare me?"

"Yes, I will dare you." That was a very unprofessional thing for me to say. This patient had unusual strength and he began to remove the door from its frame. I had no choice but to activate my bleeper and call for emergency help. In a matter of seconds help arrived.

"Nurse, why did you that?" the man said.

"Because you removed the door!"

"But you provoked me."

"Yes, you are right. I should have known better. After all, the police did tell me what you are capable of."

CHAPTER THIRTY-THREE – PERMANENT NIGHT DUTY ON REDSTART WARD

Now I was working permanently on Redstart Ward. It was on the ground floor and was nice. There were two more floors above it, but Redstart was blessed with a garden all around with flower beds. It had about twenty-five ladies, mostly old. There were single rooms, a very large sitting room and a big dining room. It was very pleasant. Most of the time I was by myself. When I came on night shift the first thing, as usual, was to take over from the day staff and then read the report so I would know what had been going on during the day. I did my very best to look after the residents.

As I mentioned before, all the night staff had bleepers so we could call for help if we needed it. The first thing was to give all the residents a drink of coffee, Horlicks or whatever they wanted and their medication as prescribed by the doctor. By about ten o'clock all the residents were in bed except one or two who sometimes watched a film on television.

One of the women had at one time been a nun. I became very fond of her. One night I was very sad to read in the report that she had gone into the chapel at the hospital and while she was praying had been sexually abused by a horrible, old, long stay mental patient. She was very badly hurt and needed medical attention yet she didn't say a word. She suffered in silence. I gave her all my tender loving care but it left me with deep thoughts about how humans can sometimes behave little better than animals.

This poor ex-nun began to be very dependent on me, like a young child. Not long after that she died. I was called into the office and found out that she'd left me her treasures: her prayer book, rosary and a few more personal things. I was very sad for the poor, old nun.

Sometimes when I came on duty the patients were hungry, not because there wasn't enough food but because they were too slow to eat it and the domestic staff were in too much of a hurry to finish and go home. Consequently the patients went without food and couldn't sleep. The only thing I was able to prepare in the kitchenette was bread, milk and sugar and I gave this to one hungry woman as a sweet meal.

I always liked working in general hospitals but fourteen years at Oakwood gave me much more experience than just looking after sick people. They taught me how to love, understand and have a positive approach towards people less fortunate than myself. Redstart patients, elderly, confused and ill, needed a lot of care and understanding which I enjoyed giving. I accomplished what I'd always wanted to do.

A sad time was waiting for me. One morning I came home from hospital and my husband said,
"Ida, tell your dad not to go to work because he doesn't look well."
I went into the kitchen where he was sitting at the table reading his bible and saying prayers. He saw me and said,
"Ida, come here and listen to the bible." I sat on a chair and listened to him read. When he had finished I said,
"Dad, please don't go to work today."
"Why not?"
"Because you don't look well."
"Ida, please don't make a fuss. I will be all right." But he only got as far as the front garden when he collapsed. At that time not many people had telephones in their houses and I had to go to the telephone box to call my doctor. When she arrived we had already taken him to his bedroom. After she examined him she said,
"Ida, your dad has had a cerebral stroke. He looks well but every day you will notice the difference. He needs absolute rest."

We persuaded him to stay in bed but after a day or two he insisted on going back to work at the hospital. At the beginning we didn't notice very much change but after a while we began to understand what the doctor meant. It was very sad, such a lovely man. Everybody liked him in Italy and in England. He really enjoyed working at the hospital and he always told me it was a privilege to look after people less fortunate than himself. I couldn't agree more.

I wanted my children to be well educated, that was more important to me than anything else, so every Saturday they attended Italian lessons and every Sunday they went to Sunday School. It was important for them to know who Jesus was, to obey the law and to be taught that there is a God who is Our Father and is there when we need him.

'Call upon Me,' He said, 'and ask anything in My name and it shall be given to you, if it is good for you.'

At that time there weren't as many distractions as nowadays. It was easy to get the children to read and take an interest in the church. They were more obedient to their parents and school teachers in those days.

My youngest child would see her brother and sister doing their homework and scribble anywhere, on their homework or any piece of paper she could find. The older ones would get very annoyed. Before we knew it she could read Italian and English.

It was very difficult looking after my poor father. Mr Mutimer, our doctor's father, was a wonderful Christian and used to take my father out for long drives and tried his best to help him and us. This man opened his house to everybody who was in need of help. He and his family dedicated their lives completely to preaching the gospel.

They used to live in a very beautiful house called 'Maranatha' which means 'Everybody is welcome'. It was in Tonbridge Road and had a big garden all round it. There was a lawn in front with beds of roses and other beautiful flowers. On the right was a large driveway with a car park for visitors. The rest of the garden was lawn with very large cedar trees. At the far end was an orchard with a variety of fruit trees. The house had four bedrooms, a bathroom, and a beautiful sitting room and library downstairs. There was a patio door leading to a hall where the Fellowship used to pray on Sundays from ten till twelve. This was followed by Sunday School and then more prayers between six and seven. On Wednesday evenings it was just used for prayers. The money they collected was given to children's charities in the UK and abroad.

On the right side of the house, next to the dining room, was the doctors' surgery. The doctors in the practice were Dr Chaming and Dr Jean Mutimer. They were very good doctors. Adults and children loved Dr Jean and she loved them.

Mr Mutimer's son, Paul, was a wonderful person with a beautiful family. In summer they organised a holiday for all the local Sunday

School children. All the schools closed on 22nd July and soon after that they would take the children away. Mr Mutimer and Paul had negotiated with a farmer in Hastings that they could use his land free of charge. It was close to the seaside, an ideal location for the Sunday School children.   This would become the summer campsite for the Maranatha Sunday School every year. Paul's wife and Dr Jean, with help from members of the Maranatha Fellowship, made sure all the children were well fed and looked after.

One year I had not been well and Mr and Mrs Mutimer thought it would be nice for me, my children and my mother to have a week's break in Little Switzerland in Folkestone. It was called 'Little Switzerland' because it was on a cliff side. I spoke to my mother and she agreed. Mr Mutimer drove us there in his car on a beautiful day. It was a very nice campsite with a restaurant, a shop, an outside water tap and all the amenities we required. After one day there my mother said,
"Ida, when are we going home?"
"In a week's time, mother!"
"And you're expecting me to stay in that caravan?"
"Yes, mother!"
"I prefer the comfort of our own home." Without speaking a word of English she managed to call a taxi and go home to Maidstone all by herself. We stayed for the week and really enjoyed it. Mr Mutimer and Mr Apps came to collect us and the caravan and took us to the campsite in Hastings where all the others were due to arrive the next day.
"You and the children can spend the night here," said Mr Mutimer, "and sometime tomorrow everyone else will arrive." and they left.

The children had been there before and knew all the camping procedures and were quite relaxed. We had our evening meal and then settled for the night. At about eleven o'clock I heard a loud noise. I kept quiet because I didn't want the children to get scared. Minutes later I heard the noise again, much nearer the caravan: a loud 'moo'. I was terrified, opened the curtain and right up against the window were two big eyes looking at me. I can't describe the shock. I tried not to wake the children. At last morning came and I looked out of the window again. There was nothing there except green fields so I opened the door and stepped out. In doing so I lost my slipper and trod in a great cowpat with my bare foot!

My children went to camps every year until there were eighteen. They only stopped when they went to university.

My father died on 20th March 1977 from an embolism. Three years later my mother died. It was a very sad time for all of us. My parents' deaths left an emptiness in our lives. Even the house seemed to miss my mother's tender loving care. My son Nino was at London University, my daughter Luciana was working for Kent County Council and studying part-time at college and my youngest daughter Stella was at grammar school. My husband then worked at the Marley Factory. It was a big house for just the four of us.

One day Dr Jean Mutimer said,
"Ida, you miss your parents and are left with a big house. Why don't you take a couple of old ladies in? You won't need to go out to work, you can work at home that way. It might suit you better." I asked Mr Mutimer's advice.
"I think it would be a good idea!" he said, so I started to enquire with the Social Services. Everything seemed to go in my favour for this new project. The government required references for all my qualifications and hospital experience since I had been in the UK. Now there was no more time to feel sorry for myself!

The Social Services thought my house was adequate for eight people but I had to fulfil the regulations according to the law. With the cooperation of my bank I raised enough money and applied for change of use from a private house to a residential home. I would have liked a nursing home but my house wasn't big enough for that. I promised myself that I would provide the best nursing care and the best food to any old person coming to live in my home. I was committed to the best in everything for the comfort of the residents. Above all, it would be a Christian home.

While I was preparing for this new venture I was still working at the hospital. The registration was granted at the beginning of April. I renamed the house 'Shalom' which means 'peace'. I gave in my notice at the hospital and was thanked for my many years of service. The nursing officer in charge emphasised that, if at any time I wanted to go back, there would always be a job for me. They organised a party and I was presented with a big card signed with good wishes from all the hospital staff.

I decided to go back to Italy before opening the new home and collect some of my late parents' money that was still in their bank. At that time it was impossible to take money out of the country but I was determined to because I needed it for security. I told my husband to unscrew the base of a flask so I could hide the money in it.

At the end of April I took a 'plane from Gatwick to Rome where I stayed to visit Natalino and his family and the Vigenzino and Gianni families. It was a joy to be reunited with my beloved cousin. We had a beautiful dinner and a lot of fun. When I confided my intention to my cousin he said,
"Look, Ida, you've done a lot in your life. It's time for you to take it easy. It's not fair on you or your family to take that kind of responsibility on your shoulders!"
"Natalino," I said, "this is my last challenge."

Soon I left for the village where my in-laws, my dearest Aunty Nicolina and her family and my cousin Elisa and her family still lived. This was where my late parents' bank was. I left Termini station on a direct train to Mignano Di Monte Lungo. My husband's cousin was waiting for me at the station. It was nice to see my cousins, their children and my family-in-law.

Two days later I went to the Italian Credit Bank to take what I believed was rightfully mine. The bank manager asked me,
"What will you be doing with that amount money?"
"I will spend it all in Italian shops," I said "and then arrange for the goods to be shipped to England." He looked at me and I knew he didn't believe a word I said.

I took the flask my husband had prepared for me to hide the money in. The bank notes were big. I rolled them all into the flask and kept it with me at all times. When I was in my mother-in-law's house she saw the flask and filled it with red wine for my journey home, without me knowing. I made sure I put it in my hand luggage.

I left the village in the early hours of 29th April to go to Leonardo Da Vinci Airport in Fiumicino. When I arrived the loudspeakers were announcing that there had been a bomb scare but if passengers wanted to go through at their own risk they could do so. I thought I would take that chance. I checked in with British Airways, knowing the risk I was taking. Before I boarded the 'plane I thought it was a good idea to visit the toilet. Because of the hot weather, the wine had fermented. I ran downstairs to the toilets. There was a loud explosion which caused panic and confusion among all the ladies in there. They started to scream and I realised red fluid was streaming from me. At first I thought I'd been hit by an explosion and then I realised it was wine. I looked in my travel bag. Everything was saturated in red wine. The flask was in a hundred pieces. For a minute I was terrified. I knew if the police arrived I would be in serious trouble because I was trying to take money out of the country.

"Please, ladies," I said, "there is nothing wrong. It's me. My flask exploded. There is nothing to be frightened about." I had some beautiful figs my cousin Gianni had given me to take to Maidstone. I offered them around to keep everyone quiet and this seemed to work. I threw the remains of the flask away in a sanitary wastebin and put all the money loose in my bag. The loudspeaker announced the last call for my flight and I ran to Gate Ten. When they asked me if I had anything to declare I said,

"No, I haven't anything to declare." and miraculously I went straight through. What a relief when the 'plane took off! When the bank manager in Maidstone said,

"Mrs Maddalena, what happened to this money of yours?" I told him the story. It was a laugh!

CHAPTER THIRTY-FOUR – THE BEGINNING OF THE RESIDENTIAL HOME

Our house had been the family home for ten years but now my parents had both died and my son was at London University studying law. It was a detached house about thirty miles from London in Maidstone, Kent. It had about twenty feet of stone walls around it with three gates. The main entrance was in Tonbridge Road, an iron gate about twelve feet wide and twenty feet high, another was in Bower Lane and a third, small one between the garage and the house. There was a big garden all around it. In the front garden were about thirty conifer trees screening the house from the road, a beautiful lawn, flowers and many varieties of fruit trees. At the back of the house was another lawn, more fruit trees and vines.

There was a large, dark, oak front door. Inside on the right was a coat rack and on the left a mirror. Along a corridor was a door on the right to the sitting room and farther along one to the dining room. Past the staircase was a door to the basement and at the end of the corridor was a good sized kitchen. On the left was another room, a shower and toilet, a double bedroom, a utility room and the back door to the garden and garage. Upstairs were two more double bedrooms and three singles. There were wash basins in every room, plus two showers, two bathrooms and two toilets.

The sitting-dining area was quite large with a thick carpet, a couple of watercolours and a few interesting oil paintings that the residents brought in. There were about eight comfortable armchairs, a large television and a long bookcase. I arranged with Maidstone Library to refill the shelves every three months for the benefit of the residents. In the middle of the sitting room was a coffee table where all the daily newspapers were placed. In the corner by the window was a large plant which made the room look very pretty. The dining area was pleasant with a dark, oak dining table, eight chairs, a sideboard and a red lampshade which gave the room a warm light. There was an archway leading through to more sitting space.

'Shalom' was registered on April 20th 1982 but I didn't open it until 2nd June. The first resident was a widow, Mrs. Janet Hughes from

London Road, Maidstone. She only had one adopted daughter who lived far away. She came to 'Shalom' because she was no longer able to look after herself. She was very pleasant and appeared very appreciative of our hospitality. The fee was £90 a week for full board, the best food I could possibly give to her, as much nursing care as she needed and whatever entertainment and occupational therapy she wanted. Her speciality was knitting squares for blankets for Oxfam.

I had my two daughters to help me. Luciana was in charge of all the books and correspondence and organised the running of the business. She bought herself a flat in London Road. At 9 a.m. she 5 p.m. Then she would come to me until 11 p.m., Monday to Friday. On Saturdays and Sundays she spent all day at our residential home and did the best she could for the benefit of the old people. Stella, my younger daughter, helped me to look after the ladies in the mornings between 7 and 8 before she went to the grammar school and in the evenings. I also employed a care assistant recommended by Doctor Jean Mutimer, Nicola who worked from 8.30 a.m. to 3 p.m., Gladys Shrubsole who did general duties from 9 a.m. to 1 p.m., and Judy, an SRN, from 10 to 12.

'Shalom' was registered to care for seven old people. The second resident, Freda Bennett, came from Sidcup. She had two grown up children who loved their mother very much. The daughter was abroad and the son had an estate agency in Maidstone. Freda was tall, very pleasant and had a birthmark on her head which made it look as if she had been hit, though luckily her hair covered it up. She was with me for less than a month.

Her son came on Sunday evenings to take her out for a meal. One evening he didn't bring her back until eleven o'clock.
"My mother has had a very big meal," he said, "and I think the only thing she wants to do now is go straight to bed." I took her upstairs to see she had a wash, attended to her teeth and asked if she wanted a night time drink.
"Freda, is there anything you'd like before going to bed?"
"No, nurse. Like my son said, I only want a good night's sleep." I made sure she was in bed, gave her a goodnight kiss and left her. I would usually go to check the ladies were all right every two hours. At three o'clock both ladies were OK. At five o'clock when I went upstairs to Freda's room I realised she was no longer with us.

It was a shock. I called an emergency doctor and he confirmed what I already knew.

"Because she wasn't ill," he said, "there needs to be a post mortem." I telephoned the son and he was also shocked. Later in the morning the coroner came to investigate and found she had had a brain haemorrhage. She had died instantaneously.

The next resident was Mrs Roger, who had been the Mayor of Maidstone. She was a short stay resident, visiting often for respite care. Later, Mr Jenner brought his mother to 'Shalom' while he and his wife went on holiday abroad. Her name was Beatrice and she seemed a sophisticated, well-educated lady. She couldn't understand why she had been brought to 'Shalom'. She used to say,

"Matron, why has my son brought me here?"

"Look, Mrs Jenner," I said, "you are only here for very short time. You will go home as soon your family returns from abroad."

"But I don't want to go home. I want my friend Caroline to come here and share the room with me. When my son gets back from holiday he can arrange it all and I can spend the rest of my life here in comfort with my friend Caroline, under your care."

"If that's want you want, but what about this friend of yours? Does she want to share a room with you? Do you think she is ready to leave her home to be looked after?"

"She will be delighted."

One day the receptionist from a doctors' practice rang and said,

"Mrs Maddalena, Dr Barr would like to speak to you. Can we make an appointment at your convenience?"

"Yes, Dr Barr can come to 'Shalom' any time." I said, "It will be my pleasure to meet him."

"Thank you. I will tell him. Goodbye." A couple of days later Dr Barr came to 'Shalom' and said,

"I have a very nice patient who I would like to come under your care."

"Yes, Dr Barr," I said, "do I know her?"

"Yes, you have nursed her before at St Michael's Nursing Home. Mrs Johnson was very sad when you left there. She always thought she would stay there permanently but now she lives two doors away. She heard that you had opened your own home and has asked me if I could see you about taking her in."

"Doctor, it is my policy to assess potential residents and decide their needs."

"I think that is very wise."

At this time Mr and Mrs Jenner returned from holiday. They spoke to Mrs Williams, the daughter of Mrs Caroline Page, and it was arranged for me to visit Mrs Page. She lived in a beautiful, detached bungalow in Queen's Road. It was the first week of July, a very beautiful day. As I arrived I couldn't help admiring Mrs Page's garden. I thought she must employ a professional gardener. I knocked on a very dark, oak door that reminded me of 'Shalom', except that mine was much older and more carved than Mrs Page's. A frail little lady opened the door and I soon realised she was in need of help.

"Mrs Page, I come from 'Shalom' and bring greetings from Mrs Jenner."

"How do you know my friend Beatrice?"

"Because she lives with me."

"Ah, you must be the Italian lady my daughter spoke about. Come in, will you?" I went inside and saw her neediness even more clearly.

"Beatrice would like you to come and live with us and share a room with her. What do you think of that?"

"Beatrice has always been a very good friend of mine and her suggestion makes me feel very honoured. Tell Beatrice I will be more than happy to spend the rest of my life with her."

"I must go back now to my lovely ladies. Soon you will be one of them."

"I look forward to that."

Three days later Mrs Jenner and Mrs Page were reunited in a nice big double room which had a smaller room beside it. After they had breakfast in bed, they would sit in the little room, read the newspapers and enjoy cups of coffee and eventually they would come down for lunch. We nicknamed them 'Hinge and Bracket' after the television characters. My goodness, they were so happy together!

But I had a problem: I wanted to help Mrs Johnson but I was well aware of her needs. She was a very large lady and needed full-time nursing care. She needed a double bedroom because she wanted her own furniture with her. She was an aristocratic lady and liked her privacy. The only room I had that could be adapted for her was upstairs but she was a fire risk. I promised Dr Barr I would consider it but I was in a predicament about how to resolve these problems. I had a meeting with my family to discuss the matter carefully and we decided I should take a week to assess her.

It was the beginning of August. On a very hot day I went to her home in St Michael's Road. I knocked on her door and a domestic opened it.

"I have an appointment with Mrs Johnson this afternoon."

"Come in." she said and took me to a waiting room, made a sign for me to sit and left. A few minutes later she returned and said,

"Mrs Johnson is ready to receive you now." I followed her through a door but I couldn't see anything because the room was full of clouds of smoke. I said to myself, 'I promised the social services 'Shalom' would be a smokeless home.'

"Mrs Johnson," I said aloud, "it's good to see you again. How are you?"

"I would be all right if I had someone to look after me." she replied.

"Mrs Johnson, it would be a great honour to have you as a resident in my home but I don't think you will be very comfortable because my house is non-smoking."

"That won't be a problem because I will stop at once when come to 'Shalom'."

"That will be impossible! You have smoked nearly all your life. You can't give up just like that!"

"Yes, I will! In my situation stopping smoking will be a very small effort in exchange for the care and attention you and your staff will give me."

"There is another problem, Mrs Johnson. The room you require is upstairs."

"I will make a declaration to the social services," she said, "taking full responsibility for myself once I am a resident of 'Shalom'."

"I will have a word or two with Dr Barr and we can arrange for you to come as soon as possible." A couple of days later I had a meeting with the doctor who offered to help with her move.

About the same time I had a 'phone call from Dr Jean Mutimer who said,

"Ida, you've got to help me out! I have a patient who has to go into West Kent Hospital for a special investigation. She will have a general anaesthetic and afterwards the hospital will send her home. But she isn't well enough to be by herself. If you have an empty bed, can you look after her until she gets better? It would have to be an act of charity, although Dr Michael Price and I will help you in every way we can. After she gets better she can go back to her own home."

"Yes, Dr Jean, I will take her."

"Oh, thank you, Ida. I knew I could count on you." I went into the lounge and said,

"Janet, smile! In a couple of days you will have company in your room, but only until she gets better and returns to her home."

"Oh, thank you." Janet said, "Now Beatrice has her friend Caroline with her, I don't have anyone to chat to."

"But remember, Janet, this lady is very ill."

"Well, I will be able to call you when she can't manage to ring the bell herself!"

"That is very good of you, Janet."

Now I thought I'd better go to Bower Mount Road to see this lady. I knocked at number seventy-nine and a very tall, elegant lady opened the door. It was Mrs Hope.

"Oh, I know you! Aren't you Mrs June Hope?" I said.

"I know you, too, Nurse Maddalena. You nursed me at Linton Hospital."

"Oh yes. So many years ago and you still remember me!"

"How could I ever forget you? Do you remember when you were on night duty and used to feed me poached egg on toast? The funny thing was that I was on a diet but by the end of the week instead of losing weight I had gained pounds!"

"Yes," I said, "and I had a good telling off from the sister. Of course it was my fault for not reading the report when I came on duty. But if I had read it you wouldn't have been any different."

"Why are we talking on the doorstep?" she said, "Come in, will you?" I went into her sitting room, which was large and well decorated with fine furniture. There were pictures of her sons in uniform and beautiful grandchildren. She made a sign for me to sit in one of the armchairs and said,

"Dr Mutimer said you may be able to help me by having me in your house until I recover from the operation. Is that right?"

"Yes, it is the least I can do for such a lovely lady as yourself."

Two days later she was admitted into the general hospital under the care of Mr Percival. As soon Jean told me, I thought I'd better go to see the sister in charge so she could tell me what kind of nursing June would need when the ambulance brought her to 'Shalom'. I went to the ward and asked a nurse if I could I have a word with the sister in charge.

"She is very busy at moment," the nurse said, "but if you care to wait I'm sure she will speak to you as soon as she can."

"Thank you, nurse." After a few minutes the sister called me into the office.

"The doctor has already told me you are going to look after Mrs Hope." she said.

"Yes, sister."

"Dr Mutimer had a word with me and she thinks Mrs Hope will be much more comfortable in your home. Otherwise the ambulance would take her back to Bower Mount Road where there is nobody to look after her."

"Sister, my staff and I will do whatever we can to see Mrs Hope is well cared for and comfortable, with the help of our doctors."

"When you read her notes you will be fully aware of her medical condition, but let me tell you now that Mrs Hope hasn't got any idea what is really wrong with her. But she is not a fool and understands that she is very ill. I know you will do the best for her but in time she will be readmitted to hospital."

"Thank you, sister, I very much appreciate your encouragement."

"I have already arranged for the ambulance to take Mrs Hope to 'Shalom'."

Later that evening Mrs Hope arrived as planned. She was indeed very ill. Dr Michael Price stayed by her all night and did what he could to make her feel comfortable. After a couple of days she was getting better but she refused to go back to Bower Mount Road. That pleased Janet no end!

Dr Barr telephoned and said,

"Ida, I am arranging for Mrs Johnson to come to 'Shalom'. Are you ready?"

"Dr Barr, my staff and I are prepared for her." It was 10th August when Mrs Johnson arrived. Her room was already arranged with her antique furniture. The ambulance men refused to take her up because they weren't insured under the National Heath Service, so poor Dr Barr and my husband were very nearly left with broken backs. But the lady was very happy to be in her new home.

'Shalom' now had five residents and life became very busy. I had an SRN on duty and together we organised the home so the residents would be comfortable, have the best food and the best nursing care. We were helped by the doctors and my two daughters. The residents and staff together created a nice ambience but for me it was very hard work with a lot of responsibility. The telephone never stopped ringing with enquiries for beds but I wasn't in any rush to fill the vacancies. It was important for me that the staff and residents had time to settle in.

I always bathed the ladies and washed and set their hair myself, unless I was attending a meeting in the hospital or another important engagement. I was doing the cooking with the help of my husband and I took all the responsibility for whatever happened in the home.

Like everyone else, Mrs Johnson had a wash and a cup of tea first thing in the morning and at about eight thirty had breakfast in bed. Later on I would bath her, dress her, make her comfortable and help her to sit on a special chair which had a table in front. There she had coffee and biscuits and read her newspaper, *The Daily Telegraph.* Lunch was a meal of her choice, for example, melon with Parma ham followed by roast chicken, roast potatoes, peas and carrots and after that a pudding of her choice. She could have a glass of Amontillado sherry or tea if she wanted. The menu would change daily for all the residents. In the afternoon they rested until three when they could have tea, cakes or biscuits. Occupational therapy was knitting, drawing or whatever else they liked to do. June and Janet always sat in the lounge. Mrs Jenner and Mrs Page ('Hinge and Bracket') would spend the mornings upstairs but came downstairs for lunch and stayed there until bedtime. Visitors were welcome any time of the day.

'Shalom' was a Christian home. The ladies settled in very well and enjoyed each other's company. Mrs Johnson stayed in her room all the time because of her incapacity. Earlier in her life she had raised a lot of money for charity. She had also appeared on television (*Call My Bluff* and other programmes). There wasn't a day she didn't have visitors. Father Gibson, the vicar of St Michael's Church in Tonbridge Road, would visit her every Friday and administer Holy Communion. Mr and Mrs Ainsley visited her. Mrs Ainsley was her adopted granddaughter and they were very fond of each other. Often they would throw a party for her charity in 'Shalom'. Mrs Johnson enjoyed a very colourful life despite her health. She had a younger sister who lived far away from Maidstone and was not in good health, but would still come for long weekends. She also had many aristocratic friends and sometimes she couldn't help showing her superiority. In a kind way, I had to remind her that at 'Shalom' there were no class distinctions.

You only had to start a conversation with Beatrice to realise that she was a very special lady. She had been educated in a private school in York. Very often she would talk about how sad she felt at seeing poor children in Newcastle with bare feet and frostbite. Yet she would never disclose who she really was. She lived in a very modest semi-detached house in Square Hill, Maidstone. She had two sons, Philip and Stephen. Philip was the one who took great care of his mother. He and his wife lived locally and would come every Sunday to take her out for the day. Stephen would only come occasionally. My staff and I were puzzled by who she really was.

I had an antique wall clock in the lounge and very often she thought it belonged to her family. She would say,
"Matron, how did you come to own that clock?"
"I bought it in an antique shop."
"I remember when the servants cleaned that old thing."

Sometimes she would forget where she'd put her wallet and we had a job to find it. After looking everywhere we would find it under her mattress. I would say,
"Beatrice, why under the mattress?"

"To stop the servants taking it."
"But, Beatrice, we haven't any servants."

Philip applied for Attendance Allowance, which in her case was the right thing to do. When the doctor came to visit her she said,
"Doctor, who applied for this Attendance Allowance?"
"Your son did, on your behalf."
"He hasn't any right to do that."
"Yes he has. It is to help you pay Mrs Maddalena."
"But I have lots of money to pay the matron. I could even buy a bigger nursing home for her." The doctor wrote in his notes 'Senile dementia' and Beatrice got the Attendance Allowance.

Beatrice also had many friends. A special one was Mrs Bartlett from the Conservative Club. She owned a big farm in East Farleigh and used to bring beautiful fruit to the home. She always came in a big car driven by a chauffeur. She was very well dressed and every time she came to visit Beatrice it was as if the Queen of England was visiting. They would talk about the old times when they were young and beautiful and spent a lot of time abroad in places like Rome, Amalfi and Capri.

June Hope was also beautiful, outside and inside. Despite her illness she always had a smile for us. The entire neighbourhood came to visit her. She had two sons, one was of high rank in the army and the other was in South Africa with his family.

Caroline Page had only one daughter, Jean Williams. She and her husband were public figures in the country. They supported many charities and had a beautiful family. They also lived in East Farleigh, a lovely area, and were Church people. Caroline herself was a nice lady whom we all loved very much.

Janet was a Londoner, not from Golder's Green or Chester Square but from East London. She had married a Maidstone man and came to live down here. Her husband had been a representative for the TGWU. She never went to work but accompanied him to all his meetings. She never had any children but in the war they adopted one and went to live in the north. She would say to people,
"My husband loved men and there was one he couldn't bear to be apart from, night or day. His name was Jack." She didn't meet many people down here but her sister decided to move to be near

her. I arranged with the Social Services to get a visitor on a voluntary basis to take Janet out when she wanted.

'Shalom' was ready to take a new resident. As I said before, I had a long waiting list of people who wanted to come in and be looked after. Dr Talbot was waiting for his mother to come in. He and his wife both worked in London hospitals and found it impossible to look after his mother. They lived along Tonbridge Road so it wasn't far for me to go to assess her needs. They had a big, detached house but it wasn't suitable for the old lady. I found her pleasant and appreciative. I thought she would fit in well with the 'Shalom' family. My policy was to take only one lady at a time and let her settle in before taking another. In the meantime I promised the other single room to Ella, who again lived not very far away, but not for two weeks.

Then I received an urgent call from Dr Jones who said,
"Mrs Maddalena, I need to ask you a big favour."
"Yes, Doctor," I said, "you can have two, if I can be of help."
"I need my mother to come to 'Shalom' for two weeks for respite. It is very important and I would much appreciate it."
"The house is fully booked but I can help you out for two weeks." So she came in. She was very nice and 'Shalom' was a busy and happy home.

Everything was just fine, two weeks went by but then Mrs Jones didn't want to go home. I was stuck! The room was already booked. What could I do? My daughter said,
"Mother, you can't let Ella down. You must keep your word no matter what. I know it isn't easy but you have promised."

Well, Mrs Jones became unwell. I called the doctor to see what was wrong and she said,
"There is nothing wrong with her. She just doesn't want to leave you." Now what? I called her son and explained the situation. He agreed she had to go home for the time being and I promised that when I had a vacancy I would take her in. Ella was then able to come in. She was also very nice and all the residents were happy with the newcomer.

I bought a house just opposite 'Shalom' – in Bower Lane - for my family use. It was a terraced house. Inside was a long corridor with a sitting room on the left, a dining room farther down and a large kitchen. In the corridor was a staircase to three good sized bedrooms and a nice bathroom. There were gardens front and back.

I had been told by Dr Mutimer that Mrs Hope needed much more help and only the hospital could provide her medication. The illness was progressing rapidly and she was taken to Linton Hospital. Two days later she wrote me a beautiful letter saying,

> 'The nursing I received at 'Shalom' was the best nursing care I ever had. I want to thank you. May God bless you for all you did for me and for your other residents.'

Two days after that I received a call from Linton Hospital to say Mrs Hope wasn't with us any longer. Our staff and residents were all very sad at her death. It was my duty to go to the funerals of everyone who had been a resident. I met her two sons who took me to one side and said,
"We very much appreciated what you did for our mother. She wanted to give you this envelope." I didn't know what to say. With tears in my eyes I said,
"Thank you."

Janet was alone again and I had to choose another lady to go into her room. I had a long waiting list but my home was only small. It was impossible to please everybody. I decided Miss Winters would be the next one to assess, so I telephoned and made an appointment to see her. It was in early spring 1984 and the garden looked its best with daffodils everywhere.
"Judy and Gladys," I said, "tomorrow I have to go to see Miss Winters so can you both take charge of 'Shalom' for a few hours?"
"Of course we can." they said, "Take your time. We will do our best." Gladys only lived a few doors away and always obliged me anytime I needed her.

Miss Winters lived in a very nice house called 'Rose Garden', about two miles from the centre of Maidstone. It was at the end of a cul-de-sac, a modern, detached house in a posh area. I pressed the bell and an old lady holding onto a walking frame opened the door and said,
"Are you the lady from 'Shalom'?"
"Yes I am. Pleased to meet you, Miss Winters"
"Come in." She took me into the back kitchen and asked me to sit

by a small table.

"You see, my dear, I've been living here with my sister who is much older than me. I used to look after her but the time came when I couldn't help her any longer because I needed help myself."

"And where is she now?"

"She is in Loose Valley Nursing Home but she doesn't like it there. You see, she isn't a very easy person to live with. I should know as I lived with her all my life. It's not always been easy."

"Would you like to go to the Loose Valley Nursing Home?"

"No, for many reasons. Your fees are much more reasonable and besides you have all my old friends there."

"Oh yes? Who are they?"

"Mrs Page, Ella, Beatrice and I believe Mrs Bartlett also comes to visit. You know those two ladies were inseparable? We all went to the grammar school and belonged to the Conservative Club."

"Miss Winters, I haven't got a single room. What I have is a shared room."

"That will be fine. When will it be possible to come in?"

"Oh it won't be long, as soon as I can arrange transport for you. But remember, you will come for two weeks trial and after that you need only stay if you find it is right for you, and that also goes for 'Shalom'." I always advised people to keep their own home until they were quite sure they liked the place. A week later Miss Winters was with us and all the residents knew one another.

CHAPTER THIRTY-SIX – I KNEW I HAD A GOOD MASTER

Before July 1986 there weren't many residential homes but soon after they appeared everywhere, like mushrooms in fields. For some it was just a profitable business. My home was small but, since I'd been little, my only ambition was to be able to look after people and here in England I achieved just that. I also wanted to run a Christian home where I could give elderly people the love and care they deserved.

In the hospital geriatric wards it was necessary to start washing the patients from five am to be able to get the job done. It was demanding for us nurses and very stressful for the patients. It wasn't restful for them and they didn't always receive the care they needed. We did our best in the little time we had.

I knew I would have to work very hard and take a lot responsibility in running my own home but I also knew I had a good master to serve who would not let me down. I relied completely on Him. He was with me at all times and He showed me the way to love and care for the most needy people.

Mrs Johnson had been stuck in her room upstairs for two years when I thought the time was right to give the ladies of 'Shalom' and the staff two weeks holiday in Hastings. It was the least I could do for them all after two years of hard work. I booked a hotel in Warrior Square in Hastings and at the same time booked a painter and decorator to give 'Shalom' a freshen up. The residents and staff were all excited at the thought of being by the seaside. Gladys stayed behind because she had a husband to look after and she kept an eye on the house while the decorators were there. With the help of Age Concern transport was arranged.

Beatrice was the most excited but unfortunately she became very ill. Dr Reoch came and examined her and said,
"Ida, this lady is very poorly. You must take her to Preston Hospital to see Dr Mackroyd. You know how it is with very old people."
"I know, doctor" I said, "and I will do my best to see she is comfortable." Immediately I booked an appointment with the hospital and before long she was taken in for an investigation. It was a very worrying time for Beatrice and for me. She looked at me and said,

"Ida, I wasn't secretary to a consultant in Newcastle for nothing. I know what the matter with me is but I don't want to be in hospital."

"Beatrice, I will do whatever I can to look after you at home." The hospital sent a letter saying they wanted her to stay in Allington Ward. I took her there but no way would she settle down. The doctor said,

"Ida, go home to the other ladies. We will look after her." I was very worried as I knew it would be a problem to her. As I tried to leave to go home she grew very restless and shouted,

"I know how the other half lives! I don't want to stay here!" So I asked my husband to get a wheelchair and we got her out of the hospital, into our car and took her home. We were all very concerned and Caroline was especially upset to see her beloved friend so poorly. I was with Beatrice night and day. I gave her all the care I could. The doctor came regularly and said,

"She would not get this nursing care in hospital."

Two days later a letter came for her from Newcastle but she was too ill to understand what was going on so I had to open it and read it to her. In doing so I discovered who Beatrice really was. I wasn't at all surprised as I'd always thought she was different. The letter ran,

> 'Dearest aunty, I have been searching for you for a long, long time but until now without success. I would like to meet you very much. I have been to the castle and seen many photographs of you when you were a little girl, some in school uniform, and others. I would love you to come to the castle. It would bring back many memories.'

It went on to say that Duke Percy had never forgotten her; unfortunately he wasn't there any longer but he would have loved to see his beloved sister again and embrace her for the last time.

Just before Beatrice died a big car decorated with a royal crest parked in our car park. A very tall lady emerged and asked for Beatrice. I realised who she was and took her to Beatrice's room and left her there. The lady wept.

"Oh, aunty, why? Why?" she cried. After a while she came out and thanked me for looking after her aunt. I took her downstairs to her car where the chauffeur was waiting for her. She thanked me again and left. Beatrice died soon after. We all missed her and poor Caroline was inconsolable. A week later the funeral took place at Vinter's Park Crematorium, Maidstone.

For a few months the holiday went on hold. Then it was on again but with one less. I thought to myself: Janet has a sister, she is poor, old and lives alone, maybe it would be nice for her to have a holiday with us and it might please Janet. When she came to visit Janet, I asked her,
"Mrs Brown, would you like to come on holiday with us?"
"Yes, I would," she said, "but I can't afford it."
"Don't worry. It will all be paid for."
"Are you are sure you can do that for me?"
"Yes, I can, providing when we are there that you stay with us. In that way we can keep an eye on you." I said.
"Oh I will!" she said.

August 1st was a beautiful day. Just the thought of being by the seaside would make anyone relax. Age Concern arrived with a small bus equipped to take Mrs Johnson's wheelchair. One by one we helped the residents onto the bus. The driver made quite sure the wheelchair was well strapped in and secure in case of any bumps on the road. We said 'goodbye' to Gladys and to my precious girls and off we went. On the way we sang popular, old songs. We were all excited. After just an hour we arrived in Warrior Square, Hastings. The hotel manager came out and welcomed us and the hotel staff helped us to our rooms with all the luggage. Then we were served with tea and sponge cake which was well received.

The place was as beautiful as the weather. All my ladies seemed happy to be there. We had nine single rooms on the second floor and my husband and I had a double room. The lift was big enough for the wheelchair.

Nicola, my husband and I used to go into the ladies' rooms first thing to see if they were all right and wait for the domestic to bring the tea tray. Then one by one we helped them wash in the hand basins, did their hair and then gave them medication. By then it was about eight thirty. With the help of the hotel staff they were taken one by one to the lounge where we waited for Mrs Johnson to arrive in her wheelchair. In the dining room a special table awaited us with a big sign, 'Shalom Residential Home'. On the table was a breakfast menu and I ordered what they wanted. At about ten o'clock we took them round Hastings to have a look at the town and the shops. At twelve thirty we would return to the hotel for lunch. We had already ordered what they wanted. I thought it was very good; for once, I didn't have to cook and that for me was a holiday in itself! Afterwards we would go into the lounge for tea or coffee. At two o'clock, if the weather permitted, we would go to the beach or onto a verandah specially reserved for residents of Warrior Square. Seven thirty was suppertime and again I ordered what they wanted. After supper all the hotel residents were invited to music and entertainment and everybody could buy drinks. Mrs Johnson, Caroline and a few others were accustomed to this kind of life but not Janet or her sister. I had to pay for them when it was their round, although they were the first to order drinks when it wasn't their turn! For me, evenings were quite an expensive time but I didn't mind as long as everybody was happy.

A few days passed and everything was going fine until Mrs Brown decided to walk away from us when we were going round the shops. Without being noticed she went by herself to the beach and fell over something, gashing her left leg. I was immediately informed and went to her aid. It wasn't serious enough to go to the hospital and there was a chemist's nearby where I bought bits and pieces to stop the blood running down her leg. Back at the hotel I got out my first aid box and attended properly to her leg.
"Mrs Brown," I said, "what did I tell you when I offered you this holiday?"
"Yes, I know," she said, "but I thought I could manage."
"But you didn't manage. But that's beside the point. You didn't keep the promise you made to me. I have insurance for the residents of 'Shalom' but not for you and I have broken the law by bringing you along."

After ten days the ladies began playing me up. Ella said,
"Ida, somebody came into my room in the night and stole my necklace."
"First, I told you, no jewellery on holiday," I said, "and second, when I put you to bed I locked the room so nobody could have come in. So what you just said to me cannot be right."
"I do not know what happened but the fact is I haven't got my necklace."
"Let me wash you and get you ready for breakfast. After that we will have a talk about it."
"I want you to call the police now."

"One thing at a time, Ella." After I washed and dressed her, I put my hand in her jacket pocket to see if she had a handkerchief and there was the necklace.

"Oh, Ella, how could you do that?"

"I must have forgotten that I'd put it in my pocket!"

Then the ladies began to complain that the food in the hotel wasn't any good. I realised they have had enough. It was time to go home. I telephoned home and asked Luciana if the house was ready for us to return.

"Mamma," she said, "the decorators finished yesterday and Gladys has been just wonderful. She's put everything back as it was. You wouldn't think anybody had been here at all, except the house looks much brighter and cleaner."

"Luciana," I said, "I will telephone Age Concern tomorrow and ask them to take us back to 'Shalom' as soon as they can." After just twelve days we were back at 'Shalom'. We were all very tired but glad to be home. The residents said,

"We never want to go on holiday again. We like our home better."

St Michael's Road was lined with elegant, Victorian, detached houses now converted into hotels and old peoples' homes. On one corner was St Michael's Church and on the other a large hall used for prayer meetings. Mr and Mrs May were members of a Christian fellowship that used the hall and they needed a Christian home for another member. Knowing that I ran one, they introduced me to Mrs Olive Weston. She had been well educated in her youth and after finishing her education she'd become a royal nanny. Every year she received a card and a calendar from Buckingham Palace and a very affectionate letter from one of the royal family. She had married Mr Weston, a devout Christian. They were blessed with a daughter who later emigrated to Australia.

Mrs Weston was about eighty years old, five feet seven inches tall with dark brown hair, brown eyes and of medium build. She didn't want to come into a home but she needed help. After her husband's death it was too much for her to be alone in her own home and she was in very poor health.

"Mrs Weston," I said, "come in for two weeks holiday and then go back to your own home and think about it." After two weeks she realised she couldn't manage on her own any more.

"Ida," she said, "I would like very much to remain in 'Shalom' with you."

"Mrs Weston, if that's what you want I'm quite sure Mr and Mrs May will be very pleased to know you are being looked after properly."

CHAPTER THIRTY-SEVEN – THE JOY OF LOOKING AFTER ELDERLY PEOPLE

When Mr and Mrs May came to 'Shalom' to take Mrs Weston home she told them her decision. They were pleased and reassured her that they would never abandon her and she would always be part of the Fellowship. Every Sunday morning they would come at ten to take her to the hall at the corner of St Michael's Road where their worship took place. When my children and I used to pass by on our way to Maranatha for our Fellowship in Dr Mutimer's house, I always admired the little girls wearing hats and beautiful dresses and the little boys with their suits. Many from their congregation visited Mrs Weston regularly along with Mr and Mrs May, their grandchildren and their mum and dad. It was a blessing to her and the other residents to have such kind people in our midst.

Mrs Weston shared a room with (Caroline), taking the place of the late Beatrice. Before Caroline went to bed it would take her half an hour to brush her teeth before I could help her wash and settle down for the night. Once she was in bed it was her custom to have a very small glass of whisky to help her relax. Mrs Weston held the strict belief that alcohol was bad for your health so this went against her spiritual conviction. I realised she didn't really like to be associated with anybody who had a drop of whisky.
"Mrs Weston," I said, "I will provide different accommodation for you as soon as possible." She was so sweet, she gave me a smile and I knew she understood.

But I had a problem downstairs between Janet and Rose. These two had very different upbringings. Janet, as I said before, came from the East End of London and was not as well educated as the rest of the 'Shalom' ladies. She hammered on all the time about the money she paid which was keeping everybody else as well. None of the others took any notice, but Rose used to get very upset about Janet's attitude and they argued. I didn't approve of this as we were a Christian family and should be able to live in perfect harmony with each other. It was difficult to make Janet understand that she was creating friction in the home. I began to be concerned about these two sharing a room. In the back of my mind I always thought something might happen when they were by themselves.

One night the bell rang from Janet and Rose's room. I ran there immediately and, as I opened the door, I heard voices. My heart felt as if it would come out of my chest. I saw Rose near the hand basin with blood on her face. I immediately thought Janet must have hit her with a stick. I attended to Rose and found it wasn't as bad as it looked. I made her comfortable and then questioned them. Janet said,

"Ida, I rang the bell because Rose woke me up with a shout. I realised she'd banged her head on top of the basin and was hurt."

"You hadn't any right to call Ida out of her bed for such a little thing as this," said Rose.

"Ida would rather I called her to investigate what happened," said Janet, "than find you hurt in the morning and I'd done nothing about it."

"Well done, Janet!" I said and helped Rose to her bed. I went to the kitchen, made myself a cup of tea and thanked God it wasn't what I'd thought.

In the morning it was the usual routine. I went into each room to check everyone was all right. I looked again at Rose's head and had a shock. It looked like a split watermelon. Her hair was pure white and there was a very thin line from the top to the bottom. I was very frightened and called Dr Ricci.

"Dr Ricci, there's been an accident with Rose. At the time it was nothing to worry about, just a little scratch, but this morning her whole head is cracked."

"Don't worry," she said, "I will come right away." A few minutes later she arrived and I took her to Rose. After a thorough examination she said to me,

"You silly fool! Can't you see the line is congealed blood and not a crack?"

"What a relief, doctor." I said.

"The trouble with you, Ida, is that you worry too much."

"Well, doctor, I'm responsible for all these people while they are in my care."

"I know you are and you do a good job. Let me tell you, these people are very fortunate to have you."

"Thank you, doctor, for those kind words."

The home ran beautifully and the ladies had all they needed but Janet and Rose continued to argue which made me feel sad. It was not good for the home. I worked very hard to stop this bickering but it was no use. Janet kept saying it was her money that paid for the luxury of 'Shalom'. Sometimes she could be nasty to the other residents as well. I needed to take action but it was very difficult! I was in a quandary with two old ladies who both needed love and attention. It didn't matter what I said, Janet wouldn't stop picking on Rose. 'Shalom' was too small to keep them apart.

I took Janet to her room and explained that I wasn't pleased with the atmosphere she caused and if it carried on I would have no choice but to call her adopted daughter and tell her she must find different accommodation.
"It's not my fault," she kept saying, "it's Rose's fault. I've been here the longest and it's my right to stay here. If anybody has to go, it should be Rose."
"I'm a better class of person than you are," said Rose, "and I have the right to stay here because all my friends are here. We are the right sort of ladies for this home, not Janet. She is not one of us."

I called a staff meeting and discussed the matter to see what we should do. I didn't like seeing these two old ladies unhappy but I didn't know how to deal with the position they were in. After the meeting it was decided that both must leave 'Shalom' and go to two different homes. This was heartbreaking for me but for the sake of the other residents we had to take action. My daughter wrote to Janet's daughter and explained the situation and that it would better for her mother to move nearer so she could benefit from family visits. Then my daughter wrote to Rose's representative and explained that for Rose's sake it would be better for her to have different accommodation. This was the most difficult thing we had had to do in running our home thus far. Everything else was hard work, a lot of responsibility but nothing to compare with having to turn people out of the home because they didn't fit in with one another.

The whole affair made me feel very unhappy but I was determined to run 'Shalom' as a Christian, happy home with all the amenities of nursing care. I prayed to God every day for the happiness and wellbeing of my residents and that I might never again have to turn anybody out of 'Shalom' until God Himself took them to His home.

Now Janet and Rose were no longer with us, I decided it was time Mrs Johnson took up residence in the big room downstairs as I had promised when she first came. It was the front room and had two large windows, one facing the front garden and the other the entrance with the big gate. Mrs Johnson was very happy to be downstairs at last. It was better for her in many ways: it was easier to get her out in case of fire, she liked the garden and now she was able to hear the birds sing in the early morning. Her adopted granddaughter Jean with her husband John often arranged parties for her and it was easy for her old friends to visit her without having to use the stairs. It was better all round for Mrs Johnson and for us.

One day Maidstone Hospital 'phoned and said,
"Mrs Maddalena, we have a patient called Catherine in need of nursing care. She refuses to go anywhere except your home. Will you come to assess her and see if you can take her in, please?"
So I went to Maidstone Hospital. I was very familiar with the place, went straight to the ward office and said,
"Sister, I've come to assess Catherine."
"Oh, Ida, that is good." she said, "The Social Services have already spoken to Catherine 's niece and both agree that your home would be best for her needs." Sister took me to Catherine 's bed and said,
"Catherine , this is the lady the Social Services spoke to you and your niece about."
"Pleased to meet you." said Catherine .
"Catherine , I'm pleased to meet you, too." I took a chair, sat beside her and said, "I've been told by the sister on duty that you had an accident. How are you now?"

While she was explaining what had happened to her, I realised Catherine was an intelligent woman. She was eighty years old and until the time of the accident she was still working as an accountant for a local firm in Maidstone. The accident happened when she was returning from a business trip to Canada. She had had an operation to her knee but caught an infection. Because she refused to take antibiotics the operation wasn't successful. Now the only way she could walk was with a frame. I realised she didn't really want to go into a home but unfortunately she didn't have any choice. She did need care.

She wasn't very tall, had brown hair and brown eyes and wasn't an easy character to deal with. She had married Mr Farmer , a bank manager, and they had lived in a detached house in Bearsted, near Maidstone. She was a business woman. She told me she would have liked children but unfortunately she and her husband never slept in the same bed because he wasn't interested in that kind of relationship so she hadn't had the chance.

Catherine came to our home two weeks later without any things at all, just herself. She had spent a lot of time in hospital and while she was there her house had been put up for sale and all her clothes sent to charity shops. I asked her niece which shops the clothes had been donated to and Valerie said,
"To the British Heart Foundation shop." Fortunately when I went there everything was still in black bags. In one was Catherine 's handbag full of traveller's cheques, money, personal belongings and a legal document with hundreds of names on, all still inside. I realised the document was her Will. I had to pay the charity shop for the clothes but I didn't say anything to Catherine because it would have been very distressing for her.

I decided to put Catherine in with Olive in Mrs Johnson's old room because I thought they would be good company for each other. I hadn't predicted that Catherine would keep Olive up all night by demanding help from her. I couldn't allow that. Mrs Weston (Olive) was a gentle lady, full of love and compassion, but she was in 'Shalom' because she wasn't well herself. So I moved Catherine in to share with Caroline.

Catherine knew Caroline well from the Conservative Club. She was intrigued by why Caroline had a small glass of whisky and she didn't. She rang the bell and I responded, asking in what way I could help her.
"This is not fair." she said, "Why does she get whisky and I only get Horlicks?"
"Catherine ," I explained, "you can ask me for whatever you want but not alcohol. Caroline buys a bottle of whisky each month for herself. I usually don't permit it in 'Shalom' but because it's a very small amount and it's her money I bend the rules. So if you want you can do as she does, but not at my expense."

The second night Catherine rang the bell every few seconds for my attention. The next night, after I'd made them both comfortable for the night, I went next door to look after Ella and when I was out of the room heard Caroline say,
"Catherine , please don't call the matron every five minutes. Don't you think she deserves a little rest after working all day for us?"

As usual I did the round every two hours to make sure the ladies were all right. Catherine slept all night. In the morning I said,
"Catherine , you didn't call me once all night. I see you're beginning to settle down."
"I wanted to call you," she said, "but Caroline gave me a big lecture about you needing a rest because you work all day."
"I'm telling you I'm as near to you as that bell is." I said, "If you need me I'll always be there for you."
"Yes," said Caroline, "but only for an emergency, not otherwise."
Catherine went quiet.

Every time I checked on Catherine during the night she was fast asleep again. At seven o'clock in the morning when I went in as usual I said,
"Catherine , you've had a very good night again."
"What choice have I got?" she said.

Olive and Catherine became good friends and I thought what a good thing it that was for them to have found one another.

One day Dr Ferry, an eye specialist at the ophthalmic hospital in Church Street, telephoned me and said,
"Ida, I need a favour from you."
"Dr Ferry," I said, "you can have two if you like! What is it?"
"A friend of mine's mother urgently needs accommodation in a home. If you have a bed for her it would be greatly appreciated."
"Doctor, I have a bed but it's in a shared room."
"That will be fine. I will tell the daughter to contact you."
"That will be fine, too, Dr Ferry!"

The next day while I was writing the daily report, Gladys came in and said,
"Ida, there's a very nice lady at the door asking to see you.
"Gladys, please bring her in, whoever she is."
"Her name is Rosina Desantis," said Gladys, "and she has been recommended by Dr Ferry." Mrs Desantis came in. She looked very distinguished, about five feet eight inches tall, of medium build with blue eyes and light brown hair. She told me that her husband was a chemist in Lenham, near Maidstone, she was an opera singer at Covent Garden, and her daughter Helen was an actress in television plays.
"My mother," she went on, "is very old and she needs residential care. Dr Ferry is a friend of my husband and he highly recommended 'Shalom'."
"My policy is to assess people before they come in." I explained, "When do you think I can visit your mother?"
"Look, Mrs Maddalena, it would be much easier for me to bring my mother here for you to assess her."
"That's a good idea. When can you bring her?"
"Would tomorrow afternoon be all right for you?"
"That will be quite all right. Tomorrow afternoon it is."

The next day Mrs Violet Cook came to 'Shalom' with her daughter, Rosina Desantis. Violet was over six feet tall and so thin she looked like a walking skeleton. It was quite scary to look at her. I didn't know what to say. In all my years in hospitals I had never, ever seen anyone like that before. I had mixed feelings about accepting her, but on the other hand, she was desperately in need of help and as a Christian I was obliged to help her and not worry what she looked like. But I was concerned for the other six residents. While I was assessing Violet I realised more than ever how much she needed help.

"Mrs Desantis," I said, "bring your mother in next week and I will do my very best to give her all the love and care she needs."

"Please, Mrs Maddalena, call me Rosina."

"My name is Ida and my husband is Tony. With us are Gladys, Nicola Judy and my two daughters: Luciana is responsible for the office and Stella, my younger daughter, helps when she can. Although she's young, she is an excellent carer. To make things more homely we all use our Christian names."

"As I soon I set foot in your home I sensed the lovely atmosphere you've made. It's very different from any of the other homes I've visited."

"This is not just because of me, it's also because it's a Christian home. My staff and I try to do what God commands us to the best of our abilities and that means giving loving care to all our residents."

"I have to confess," Rosina said, "I also go into lots of hospitals as a voluntary worker for young people who can't communicate in the usual ways. I've been blessed with a musical talent and these young people respond better to music therapy than anything else. It's more rewarding for me when a young person responds to music than all the applause I get in the opera house."

"What you're doing is just beautiful," I said and realised more than ever that I must try to do my best to help Rosina's mother for His glory.

"Mother, it's time to go home now." Rosina said.

"But I am home!" Violet replied.

"No, mother, you'll be coming back here next week!"

"Why waste time?" Violet said, "Why don't you go home and fetch all my belongings?" It took quite a long time to persuade her she must wait a week before becoming a resident at 'Shalom'.

In the meantime I had to speak to Mrs Weston (Olive) about making Violet welcome. After all, they would have to share a room and Mrs Cook (Violet) looked like a scarecrow. But I knew Olive was a nice lady and very much a believer in the Christian faith. She would get on with anybody. I also went round to the others and explained the situation.

A week later, on the day Mrs Cook was due to be admitted, I asked Judy and Nicola to stay to do some overtime. The bell rang, Nicola opened the door and said,

"Ida, Mrs Desantis here."

"Please let her in." I said. It was four p.m. and I'd just finished the daily report.

"Good afternoon, Ida." Rosina said, "Thank God for today. I have had such a difficult time with my mother. She has been so eager to come to 'Shalom' she hasn't given me a moment's peace." A few minutes later the ambulance arrived with Mrs Cook. Judy and Nicola got the ambulance men to take Mrs Cook upstairs to Mrs Weston's room because she was on the National Health. In Mrs Johnson's case they wouldn't do it because she was a private patient so Dr Barr and my husband had to do it. While Judy and Nicola settled Violet in, I talked to Rosina.

"What food does your mother like best?"

"Well, you only have to look at her to see that she's not been eating much."

"Every afternoon I go around with a pencil and paper and write down what they want to eat. Most of the food comes from Marks & Spencer."

"Oh, Ida, that's so expensive! How can you manage to do that on social security benefit?"

"My policy is 'buy little and buy good'. I only buy what the residents enjoy so there is not much waste."

"Let me tell you, you've got to be very careful with my mother. She might take advantage of your goodness. Also, she doesn't get out of bed easily."

"Don't worry, Rosina. If she prefers to stay in bed, she can stay in bed. As long as we give her a good wash all over every morning and wash her hair once week that's all that matters. She's got to be looked after properly."

"The only way I can get her out of bed is by putting a bottle of sherry in the cupboard. Then you'll see how she shoots out of bed!"

"In 'Shalom' I don't allow smoking or drinking but we'll turn a blind eye if it's just a little and we can control it. Mrs Johnson buys her own sherry because she entertains a lot and it's her custom to offer guests a glass of Amontillado. And Caroline is used to having a little glass of whisky with Perrier water before going to sleep. It would be cruel to deny them something they've had all their lives and simply by coming into a residential home are not allowed any more."

"How do you manage to get them out of bed in the morning?" Rosina asked.

"I don't get them out of bed. I have my routine and I explain it to all the relatives. Let me tell you now. At 7 a.m. I go into each of the rooms to see if everyone is all right. When I'm quite sure they are all right I will wash their hands and face, comb their hair and make them comfortable for breakfast. Then I go downstairs to the kitchen and cook the breakfast of their choice."

Mrs Johnson always had a cooked breakfast of eggs and bacon with toast and marmalade and a pot of tea with milk and sugar. Olive Weston might have porridge, toast and marmalade. Ella had a very small bowl of cereal with toast and marmalade, tea or coffee. But not everyone had the same thing each day. Caroline Page changed her breakfast every morning. Mrs Talbot might have a very light one depending on how she felt. They all had a choice. I supervised breakfast to make sure they ate it and helped them as best I could.

When breakfast was over by 8.30 I collected the trays and put all the crockery in the dishwasher. Nicola would have come on duty by then and she started washing the residents. I would do their medication. At 9 a.m. Gladys came in and she and my husband would clean the house and help where necessary. After that I would go and help Nicola bath and dress the residents and once a week I personally washed and set their hair. Once every two weeks a professional hairdresser came in to cut or perm their hair if they wanted. I made absolutely sure above everything else that they had individual care. If anyone needed a doctor it was dealt with. At ten thirty I would go into the kitchen and prepare coffee, tea and biscuits. One of the staff would take them round to the residents. Meanwhile I started cooking the lunch.

As I said before, most of the food came from Marks & Spencer. While I did the cooking the staff would come into the kitchen and have coffee or tea and chat. Lunch was always served at twelve thirty and by one thirty it would be finished. All the residents sat together and had coffee or whatever afterwards.

In the afternoon some of them would knit and most had visitors. Every afternoon I would write the daily report. Twice a week my husband and I would do the shopping. I would arrange for two staff to be on duty while we were out. Supper was served at six thirty, again the food of their choice, and after that they would watch television until it was time for bed.

Mrs Johnson stayed in her room most of the time but she was an active lady, writing, reading and knitting. She was very popular and had visitors nearly every day. A special friend came three times a week to play Scrabble and have supper with her. Her sister lived away from Maidstone so when she visited a friend, Joyce, who lived two doors away, put her up. She would spend all day in 'Shalom' and have meals with her sister. When we had a garden party we would wheel Mrs Johnson out into the garden to join the other residents, and she would join them for other entertainments.

The day after Violet arrived, when Gladys came on duty I said,
"Gladys, we have a new resident. Her name is Violet and she is upstairs in Number Two. Please go and see if she is all right."
Gladys went upstairs, opened Violet's door, shut it immediately and ran back downstairs. From the look on her face I knew she was in shock. She couldn't speak.
"Whatever is the matter with you?"
"What is the matter with *me*? Whatever is the matter with *you*, Ida?"
"Why?"
"You have a live skeleton upstairs!" I laughed and said,
"Oh, Gladys, you're in shock! Sit down and I'll make you a cup of tea. I expect you've never seen anybody like that before, have you? But now you have. We have to work very hard to make her better."
"I know you will."
"And will you all help me?"

After the death of her friend, Caroline wasn't herself any longer. She became very confused and disoriented needed attention at all times.

CHAPTER THIRTY-NINE – JEAN AND *THE LAST OF THE SUMMER WINE*

Mrs Jean Talbot was a small lady of medium build with brown eyes and a cute face. She was a good Christian who very much appreciated the love and care she received in 'Shalom'. There was a television programme called *The Last of the Summer Wine* and because she came from that part of the country and her friend was coincidently named Nora Batty as the character as on T.V. She thought the programme was about her dear friend who had passed away. She would say,

"Please, Ida, don't let anybody watch that programme. It's not fair that my friend has been portrayed in that way. They were a very respectable family."

Ella Smith was a very nice, thin, of medium height with beautiful white hair and brown eyes. She was also very appreciative of the love and care she received. She and Mrs Talbot became good friends and spent many hours talking about their families. Ella was very proud of her daughter, Brenda , and her son-in-law and their children.

One evening at about nine o'clock Caroline asked to go to bed. I took her upstairs to her room and as usual it took her half an hour to brush her teeth. While she was doing this I poured a little whisky in a glass, filled it up with Perrier water and left it on the bedside cabinet. Then I went to attend to the other residents. Catherine said,

"I'm also ready to go to bed. As Caroline is using the hand basin, I don't mind going to the bathroom to wash." I helped her to wash and took her back to her bedroom then helped her into bed while Caroline was still at the hand basin. Then I went next door to Ella's room. I heard a crash and realised it was from Catherine 's room. I ran in and found Catherine on the floor by Caroline's bed. I couldn't understand how she'd got there. I examined her and realised she needed a doctor so I made an emergency call. Dr Christmas from The College Practice came and said,

"This lady needs to go to the hospital to X-ray her arm."

"I'll call one of my staff to come on duty to look after the rest of the ladies," I said, "while my husband and I take Catherine to casualty." Catherine always resisted going to hospital but we had no choice. I said to her,

"Look, I don't want to take you there but we haven't got any choice.

You've had a fall and the doctor said I must take you to hospital. That is an order." I asked Tony to get the car and he brought the ambulance chair upstairs for Catherine to come down in.

By now it was ten o'clock in the evening and it was a long time before we were seen. The receptionist took all the details. She knew who I was and tried her best to get us seen by the doctor on duty as soon as possible. It was eleven by the time Catherine had her X-ray which showed that she had a fracture. The hospital admitted her because they also thought she was suffering from an infection which needed further investigation. Catherine was very angry that she wasn't allowed to come home. I wasn't very pleased myself but that's life!

When I went home it was three o'clock in the morning and Caroline was still awake, complaining that she hadn't had her whisky. That puzzled me because I was quite sure I had poured the whisky myself with the Perrier water and left it on top of her bedside cabinet. Then I realised what must have happened. Catherine had been thinking for a long time about Caroline having a whisky before she went to sleep. While Caroline was brushing her teeth she must have drunk her whisky and that's why I'd found her on the floor near Caroline's bed. Poor Catherine, I thought!

Violet wouldn't get up from her bed at any time and she wouldn't feed herself. She was fed just like a baby by one of the staff. The reason she gave was that she couldn't stand up, so we did what her daughter had suggested: we put a bottle of sherry in her cupboard and sure enough she got up. I came to terms with her. We helped her get up, gave her a good wash all over, dressed her and she lay on top of the bed. We fed her, brought her newspapers and asked if she would like to have a television. She declined the television. She was very happy with those arrangements. Her daughter came as often as she could and so did her granddaughter when she wasn't working for television.

The Maidstone Hospital telephoned and asked me if I could go and discuss Catherine 's situation. I made sure everybody was all right and there were staff on duty, put my suit on and make sure my hair was presentable, got my husband to get out the car and went. Ten minutes later I went into Pye Oliver ward to see Catherine. When she saw me she said,
"Ida, why have you put me in here? Is it because I took Caroline's

drink?"

"Now you're talking nonsense, Catherine." I said, "How could an intelligent person like you even think that? You are here because you had a fall and fractured your arm."

"Hospitals don't usually keep people in for fractures unless something else is terribly wrong."

"That's what I shall go and find out. The hospital telephoned me to ask if I would come and have a talk with the doctor. But please don't worry, you won't stay a minute longer than you have to, I promise." Catherine began to calm down. "I'll go to the office to talk to the doctor now," I said. I knocked on the office door and a voice said,

"Come in."

"I've come to find out what Catherine Farmer's situation is."

"The doctor in charge of Catherine is out of the ward," the sister said, "but he won't be long." About ten minutes later the doctor came in. We shook hands and he said,

"I know you."

"I know you, too." We both laughed.

"I believe you have Catherine in your home," he said.

"Yes, I have," I said.

"Well, besides the fractured arm she has an infection called Hepatitis A." Before he'd finished I said,

"What?"

"Calm down, will you?" he said, "I will explain. Hepatitis A has an incubation period of between fourteen and forty-two days. It is most common in children and young adults. The virus is found in patients' faeces and is transmitted by contaminated food or water. Isolated cases are usually due to person to person contact but epidemics are generally caused by flies spreading the infection." I was in shock and after a while I said,

"And what is the hospital going to do about it?"

"We'll keep her in because as yet she hasn't shown any symptoms. We'll keep her under observation."

"What are the symptoms?"

"'Flu-like jaundice. We will make sure she gets better and then she can go back to 'Shalom'," he said.

"The district nurse came to the home to give 'flu injections to all the residents when I had an important meeting with the social services. I left a message for the nurse that she could inject everybody but not Catherine because she is allergic to the injection and it can seriously affect her health. But the silly nurse misunderstood and did inject her. When I came home and found out what happened I

was annoyed. Do you think that could have caused this problem?"
I asked.

"It looks very likely to me."

"And now what can be done for her?" I said,

"The jaundice might increase over a week and then fade away."

"Are there any complications?"

"Relapses can occur though very rarely with Hepatitis A, and slow recovery." I was speechless. Now what was I to say to Catherine ? I had no choice but to tell her she couldn't come home until she got better. I went back to her and said,

"Catherine , you are not well enough to come home but you soon will be. I will come in every day to see you are all right. Goodbye, I'll see you tomorrow."

Catherine 's case frightened me. Instead of going home I went to Somerfield Hospital and I demanded an Aids test. The doctor laughed and said,

"Ida, you are joking, of course."

"No, no, I'm not joking. I mean it." He looked at me and said,

"Ida, what is wrong?" I told him I had a lady with Hepatitis A, which is very infectious and she had been with me for two years in which time I washed her and embraced her every night as I do all my residents. What if I had caught something from her?

"You haven't caught anything but I will give you an Aids test just to shut you up."

"Thank you, Doctor." I went home and all the ladies asked how Catherine was. I didn't know what to say. I got all the staff in the kitchen and said that when Catherine came home everything she needed would have to be sterilised and that all of them needed to wear gloves and white coats.

The next day I went to the hospital. Catherine needed attention so I put on a white coat and gloves and I gave her a good wash all over. I made her comfortable and she looked much better. There was no sign of jaundice yet. I began to wonder.

I noticed that they had catheterized her and in the bag was blood, not urine. I questioned the staff but they weren't able to give any explanation. I was puzzled. I asked for more blood tests to be done on Catherine and the results came back quite normal. Then I said,

"Catherine has been here for a few days and there are no signs of jaundice. I would like to take her back to 'Shalom' and care for her

there."   The doctor said,
"Ida, I think you are right. Catherine will be better looked after at 'Shalom'."
"Can the hospital make arrangements for today, please?"

At last she came home. I put a white coat and gloves on and I took her catheter off and found the tube wasn't inserted into her bladder but into her uterus. Poor Catherine ! From that day on she made good progress and had no more health problems for a long time. The result of my test was that I had nothing wrong with my blood.

CHAPTER FORTY – I NEED TO EMPLOY MORE STAFF

For four years 'Shalom' enjoyed the good fortune of having three good part-time staff. Now Nicola was sixty and it was time for her to retire. Judy's children were old enough to go to secondary school. Her husband was a mathematics teacher and he was offered a job with a school where his children could go and Judy could become an assistant matron. I was very pleased for them but sorry for myself and my residents. Word went around and two new ladies came forward. My daughter Luciana made appointments for me to interview them on the 1st and 2nd December.

After the residents had had their breakfasts, washed, dressed and been made comfortable, my policy was that the care assistant or myself would not leave their rooms until the beds were made and the rooms were clean and tidy. Only then would we take the residents out. The reason was that in an emergency if a resident needed to go back to their room everything would be in order. After ten thirty I would go down to the kitchen and begin to prepare lunch while the care assistant continued to look after the residents.

When I made coffee, tea and biscuits my husband or the care assistant would take them around to the ladies and I continued to prepare lunch with my husband's help. About eleven o'clock we all had coffee and a chat about the residents. Sometimes we had a good laugh about Violet Cook, she was good entertainment.

On the day of the first interview the doorbell rang at eleven o'clock and Gladys opened the door, as she always did.
"Ida, there's a lady here saying she has an appointment with you."
"Bring her to the kitchen, please." Gladys brought her. She was middle aged, good-looking and very pleasant.
"Please sit down and tell me all about yourself and how you knew I needed a care assistant," I said.
"My name is Elisabeth and my aunt Maisie is, I believe, a friend of yours. It was she who told me you had a vacancy for a care assistant."
"Have you done this job before?" I asked.
"Yes, all my life."
"Have you any references from your previous employers?"
"Yes, I have."

"Did your aunt tell you that this is a Christian home?"

"Yes, she did. I'm a Christian myself."

"I have quite a few rules which must be observed. They are:

(1) The residents are the most important thing. This is their home and we are to do whatever is needed for their wellbeing. They are here because of their circumstances but we are here because we want to do this job. It is also our living, but they always come first.

(2) Tender loving care above everything.

(3) Staff must report any kind of problem to me and I'm the one to see it is dealt with.

(4) In all circumstances the residents' wishes must always be respected.

(5) The home must be kept clean and tidy at all times.

(6) Always approach the residents in the right manner.

(7) The home is no smoking at all times.

(8) Visitors are allowed at any time of the day.

Now I'll take you round and introduce you to the residents. Come with me and we'll start with Mrs Violet Cook. She is in Number Two upstairs."

So we went upstairs to Violet's room and I said,

"Violet, this lady will be coming to help me to look after you." Violet didn't say anything but just gave Elisabeth a funny look.

"All the other ladies are downstairs," I said, "Caroline, Mrs Farmer, Ella, Mrs Jean Talbot and Mrs Olive Weston. They've just had their coffee and at 12.30 lunch will be served. Now, Elisabeth, you have met all the ladies in the lounge but we have one more in Number One. She is Mrs Johnson. You'll soon get to know her. She is very nice." Elisabeth said goodbye to the ladies,

"I'm looking forward to being here with you all." They all waved to her and we left the lounge and went to Mrs Johnson's room. We knocked and Mrs Johnson said,

"Come in." We went in and there she was, all dressed up, sitting in her mobile electric armchair with her special table in front, enjoying her coffee and biscuits. Before she said anything I said,

"Mrs Johnson, this is Elisabeth and she will soon be joining our little family."

"Well, Elisabeth, we all welcome you!"

"I'm looking forward to working here," Elisabeth said, "and I will do my very best to please you all." We left Mrs Johnson's room and went back to the kitchen where I said,

"Elisabeth, I will take your references and you will hear from me very soon."

"I'll be waiting," she said, "Goodbye for now."

"Goodbye, Elisabeth I said as I took her to the door where we waved at one another and she left. I went back to cooking lunch for my lovely ladies.

That day lunch was either pork chop or breast of turkey. I cooked the pork in the same way as the turkey by crushing two tablespoonfuls of fresh sage and rosemary into four tablespoonfuls of flour, adding salt and pepper to taste and lightly dusting the pork chops and the breast of turkey on both sides with the seasoned flour. I had already prepared potatoes, broccoli, fresh beans and carrots. At twelve o'clock I put the potatoes on to boil and put two dessertspoonfuls of butter in a big frying pan with extra virgin olive oil in which I cooked the meat for six or seven minutes on each side. Then I kept them warm while everything was made ready to serve. For pudding there was apple pie and cream or something else of their choice.

After lunch my husband helped me to settle the ladies for an hour's rest before the occupational therapist came in for a couple of hours while I wrote the daily report. I checked all the drugs making sure I had the right quantities and that everything was locked up. I had sole responsibility for the medicine cupboard which was kept safe and ready for any social services inspection. They could come in at any time of the day or night. I was also always prepared for the fire service, holding a regular fire drill with all my staff every two weeks. The health inspector also visited the home to make sure it was tidy and clean and that the food was fresh, hygienically stored, properly cooked and of the best quality.

As I mentioned, my daughter had made two appointments for me to interview new staff. The first was easy but the second looked as if it might present a dilemma. Luciana left me a note saying:

'Dear Mum, remember you have an appointment with Mrs Ann Mackenzie at three o'clock this afternoon. Much love, Luciana.'

I looked at the note. I knew two Mackenzies, one at Linton Hospital and one at Oakwood. Which one would it be? If it was the one from Oakwood Hospital I didn't think it was worth having the interview because she wouldn't be suitable for my home. But if was the one from Linton Hospital it would be a miracle. I made myself a cup of tea, sat down and thought about the old days at Linton. We had a big ward with many patients to look after and we used to work tirelessly. Mrs Mackenzie was kind to the patients and her nursing care was of the best.

Three o'clock came and the doorbell rang. I ran to the door. I didn't recognise her but she recognised me. She also knew my name and the house.
"Nurse Maddalena, you haven't recognised me," she said, "but we knew each other at Linton Hospital."
"Oh, Mac! Please come in." I took her to the kitchen and asked her to sit down. "Before anything else I'll make you a nice cup of coffee. Then we have a lot to say to one another. Mac, you are just the lady I need."
"I retired from nursing a couple of years ago but I miss it so much, the patients, the nurses and the money. My world is upside down."
"Not for long, my dear Mac. You are the person I need most. I don't need to interview you. When can you start?"
"Whenever you want me to."
"If you can write down the days and hours you can work, I will give them to my daughter who will put you on our roster. I'd like to show you around the home and introduce you to our residents."
We went around, like I had done with Elisabeth
"I'm impressed," said Mac, "Looking after people is part of your make up. That's why you've been successful. I'm ready to come on duty as soon as you need me."

All the ladies were happy that we would soon have two new members of staff to help me. Elisabeth's references were excellent. Luciana put Elisabeth and Mackenzie alternating with each other on the roster so I always had one of them with me. Often I needed to go to the hospital to assess people or to attend meetings but I didn't need to worry with three good staff, Gladys,

Elisabeth and Mackenzie, available with my husband any time we needed them.

When I had sent Janet and Rose away I promised I would never do that again. I received a letter every week from Janet begging me to have her back. She was moved around from pillar to post but never settled anywhere. She was longing to come back to 'Shalom' but unfortunately there was no coming back, no vacancy for poor Janet.

As I mentioned, after the loss of her friend, Beatrice, and because of deep mourning of her friend Caroline became very difficult to look after. I was getting tired. Tony and I needed a holiday badly. Working night and day began to affect my health. The doctor advised a holiday.
"Ida, you can't leave Caroline here It's not fair on the other residents."
"I manage her well," I protested, "and this is her home."
"Yes, you manage her well," said the doctor, "but your health is beginning to suffer. You and Tony need a holiday and it is not fair to leave such a responsibility to your new staff and your daughters." So I had to take a decision and it was a difficult one. We loved Caroline and Caroline loved us but because of her mental condition she had for some time become a danger to herself and the other residents, through no fault of her own. When I told Caroline's daughter, things didn't go well. There was a lot of upset because Caroline had been with us for years and she was very fond of us, as we were of her.

Caroline went to another home but sending her away wasn't good for her or me. I had a staff meeting to explain the position. If Caroline didn't settle down in her new home I would take her back again.
"When I leave here nobody will do my hair like you do," Caroline said. She had long hair and I'd always done it in a French pleat which she liked very much. She wouldn't accept anything else. As soon as she moved to her new home I went to visit her. Her hair had been cut and she was very upset. I promised her that as soon we came back from our holiday we would have her back in 'Shalom'. I was told that she stayed near the door all the time saying,
"Ida and Tony will be here soon and I can go back home." But when we came back Caroline wasn't with us anymore. She died

after a few days in the new home. It was a sad time for all of us.

'Shalom' now had a vacancy. Looking at the long waiting list I had
I saw Patricia Brown, a name very familiar to me but I couldn't
remember who she was. I telephoned and a lady answered.
"This is Shalom Residential Home," I said, "I'm Ida and I have
Patricia Brown on my waiting list and wonder if she still needs
help."
"Oh, matron," a voice said, "I'm so pleased you rang. Patricia
needs your help very much. She won't go anywhere except your
home. She says she knows you and is looking forward to seeing
you."
"Patricia Brown is a name I know but I can't put a face to it. Maybe
when I see her I'll recognise her."
"When do you want us to come and see you?"
"Tomorrow at three o'clock would be fine," I said.

The next day at last I was able to put a face to this name that was
so familiar to me.
"Miss Brown, how are you? Please do come in." I took her and
her friend to the kitchen and sat them down.
"It is a long, long time since I've seen you. After I sold the house I
had in Bearsted I didn't go there again but we did miss your little
Post Office. Maidstone General Post Office is always very busy,
with long queues and it doesn't offer the friendly atmosphere that
you did for your customers."
"I'm now retired and miss the contact I had with the public. Then
my neighbour went to Canada and when returned she'd had an
accident and never came back to her home again," Patricia said.
"What was her name, Patricia ?"
"Catherine . She was a good neighbour."
"Patricia , Catherine is living here with us!"
"You must be joking!"
"No, I'm not. I'll take you to her. Come with me." I took her to the
lounge where Catherine was. Before I said anything Catherine
gave a shout,
"Patricia ! Fancy seeing you here!"
"Oh, Catherine , I wondered where you were. How have you
been?"
"Well, as you see, I walk with a frame. I've been here for more
than two years and Ida and her staff look after me well."
"I'm hoping to become a resident."
"Good. There is an empty bed in my room. I do hope you can

come. I've made a friend called Olive, so if you come and stay in my room I won't just have a daytime friend but one for the night as well!"

"Patricia ," I said, "come for two weeks at first and then you will know if you like it here or not and I will be able to assess your needs and if we can meet them, then you will be able to stay permanently."

"Thank you, matron, for giving me this chance."

"Don't call me 'matron'. Call me 'Ida', it makes the place more homely."

Patricia was a petite old lady. I knew her when she was much younger and always admired her. She just wasn't pretty on the outside but inside as well. She always had a lovely smile for her customers. I took her around the house and she met all the other residents who liked her very much. Two days later she was sharing a room with Catherine which pleased them both.

Olive Weston had now been a resident for two years and she began to get very poorly. I called the doctor who told me she must see Dr Mackroyd at the hospital again, so an appointment was made.

"I don't know how long we'll have to wait before we see the doctor." I said to my husband, "You'd better drop us here and when we're ready I'll call you to come and fetch us."

"I would rather wait here with you," he said, "in case you need help with Olive."

"No," I said, "there's too much to do at home and the staff need you there. Violet is playing up because her daughter hasn't visited lately. She needs one of us there."

"Yes, you are right." Tony said, "If she realises we're not there she'll get upset and the staff will find it a job to make her behave." So Tony left and we went to the ward and checked in at reception.

The receptionist said,
"Mrs Maddalena, Dr Mackroyd is not here because he's been called out to an emergency but I don't think he'll be very long. His nurse is here and you can talk to her." I left Olive sitting in the waiting room and went to talk to Dr Mackroyd's nurse to find out what the position really was.

"He won't be long, Maddy," she said, "take a seat and have a bit of a rest while you can." All the doctors called me 'Maddy', short for 'Maddalena', which I didn't mind. While we were waiting another nurse came in who I knew.

"Hallo, Maddy, how are you?" she said, "It makes a change to see you sitting down!"

"I'm worried," I said, "I have a new occupational therapist visiting my ladies and if I'm not there you know what old people can be like: if they see different staff on duty they can be very funny. I want to be there and introduce her to them. It would work better. The last occupational therapist said she couldn't manage them if I wasn't there. They said, 'Why on earth should we want to do that?' so the therapist said, 'All right, what about singing old songs?' and they all said, 'Oh yes! We like that.' One of them said, 'I have a piano at home. I'll ask my son to bring it here and then I can play and everybody else can sing and we can enjoy ourselves, if the matron doesn't mind.' The lady here with me today, Olive, has a beautiful voice. Her friend from the Fellowship she belongs to comes every Sunday to take her to the service. One Sunday while she was there, instead of joining in with the congregation, she stood up and sang the whole of *It's a long way to Tiperary*. You can imagine the Fellowship's surprise! When they told me I said, 'Yes, of course Olive is not well, she is an old lady and at times she gets a bit confused and doesn't know where she is.' That therapist left us because of family difficulties and today a new one is starting. I would really like to be there but I also need to be here."

"You never change, do you?" said the nurse, "Always working. Now you have your own business, you should relax."

"You must be joking! Now I have my own residential home it's much harder work. I'm responsible for the ladies in my care. It's my job to be there, care for them, love them and meet all their needs. They didn't ask to be there with me. I asked them to come to me. More than anything I have an obligation to God to make sure everything they want is provided for them."

"You employ people to do that for you, don't you?"

"Yes," I said, "I do have part-time carers and nurses to help me and they are very good. I couldn't manage without them but I like to look after the ladies myself as well. I like being there twenty-four hours a day."

"You are silly." she said, "You have a dog but you bark yourself!" She left and Doctor Mackroyd came in.

"Oh, Maddy, not you again!" he said, "It seems you bring all your residents to me to look after."

"That's because I know you are a good doctor and you will do your best for them."

"Ah, now you're trying out your psychology on me, aren't you?"

"No, no. I speak the truth," I said.

"I will do whatever you say, if we share the nine million pounds left to you by that rich lady I helped you to look after!" he joked.

"I tell you, doctor, I'm willing to share the sherry decanter that was presented to me by the sons!"

He laughed and said,

"As I don't drink any more I'll leave all the decanters to you. You see how generous I am?"

After he had examined Mrs Weston he said,

"Maddy, she is very poorly. I'm afraid there is very little I can do for her. What she needs is a lot of love and care and I know she'll have that from you. I will write to her GP and he will give her and you all the support you need. When you can't manage any longer, we'll be here to help you."

I was very sad to hear what he said about Olive. I thought what a brave lady she was, never complaining or making any fuss. I knew she was a good Christian. Even though her illness must cause a lot of pain, she always had a smile for everyone. I telephoned Tony and he came to fetch us about ten minutes later. He looked at my face and knew I didn't have good news. He took us home and I took Olive to the kitchen and gave her a nice cup of tea and big slice of sponge that I had baked earlier.

When she had finished I took her to her room and said,

"Olive, it has been a long day for you. Now you need a rest and when it's supper time, if you're feeling well enough, you can come down. Otherwise I'll bring whatever you want upstairs."

"I'll feel better after I've had a little rest then I will come down." This lady just amazed me. She was so ill yet she never moaned or made any fuss. It must have been her faith in God that helped her manage her illness so well, I thought. I decided that when Mrs May next visited I would ask if she had any relatives for me to contact.

I left Olive's room and went to Violet's room where she was lying on her bed as usual. She looked at me and said,

"Where have you been? I haven't seen you all afternoon. Helen has been and told us that Rosina is going to buy a flat not very from here so she can be near us."

"That is good news, Violet! So I will be able to take you to visit her."

"No, you won't."

"And why not?"

"I will never get out of this bed. I'm too ill," she said.

I went downstairs to see how the other ladies were and what they thought of the new occupational therapist.

"All right, ladies, what do you think of the new occupational therapist?"

"We don't need anybody. We enjoy being by ourselves," they all said with one voice, "We like chatting to each other and we feel we have enough entertainment here with all your family. Why do we have to have somebody else?"

"Right," I said, "I will arrange to go to the Hazlitt Theatre once a week when there is a dance on. You can have a good time and maybe find a partner, who knows?"

"We don't want go to a dance. Maybe a play sometimes but only when it's a good one."

I left and went to Mrs Johnson's room. She didn't need any therapy because she was always busy, had visitors, played Scrabble with her friend Joyce, read or knitted. She often held parties in her room for her aristocratic friends from the Conservative Club to raise money for charity.

It was Christmas Eve 1986 and I was busy preparing Christmas lunch. We had already had carol singers round from St Michael's Church when we heard beautiful music. Next we saw a cameraman and didn't know what was going on. Then we realised it was Rosina, Violet's daughter, and Helen, her granddaughter, come to give all of us a surprise with a television crew.

Since I'd opened we had always had wonderful Christmases and so it was to be this year, but Olive was very poorly and I was concerned about her. With the help of the staff and my family we tried to make everything just like last Christmas. In the morning it was the usual routine but with a special breakfast of orange juice, eggs and bacon, toast and marmalade and a pot of tea or coffee. My daughter Luciana and my husband prepared Christmas lunch in the kitchen while I did the medications. Elisabeth washed the ladies and dressed them in the clothes we had prepared for that special day. As I said before, we never left a room until everything was tidy. Some ladies watched the service on television and some were taken home by their relatives for the day.

Olive needed a doctor and I had no choice but to telephone for one. I dialled the number and Doctor answered.

"One of my ladies requires a doctor urgently. Will you please come to visit her?"

"Ida," he said, "you know today is Christmas day!"

"Yes, doctor, I know but this lady isn't well and she needs you."

"What about if I don't come today but come tomorrow?"

"Doctor, Mrs Weston needs you now, not tomorrow! Unfortunately you are on duty. You must come now!" He didn't like it but he came and said,

"Yes, Ida, you were right to call me. She needs help." and he prescribed special medication that was strong enough to keep her settled throughout the seasonal holidays. I thanked the doctor and Christmas passed without further incident.

Soon after the holiday I found out from Mrs May that Olive had a daughter who lived in Australia. Her name was Margarita. Mrs May told her about her mother's condition and before long she was in England. The doorbell rang and the lady at the door said,

"I'm Margarita Weston. I believe you are looking after my mother."

"Yes, please come in." I took her to the kitchen because, although I had an office in the basement, I felt more at home with people in the kitchen.

"My name is Ida." I said, "First I'll make you a cup of tea or coffee, whatever you prefer, and explain your mother's condition." While I was talking to her I realised she understood the situation very well. I could see her mother in her: tall with black hair, brown eyes and very polite. I couldn't help noticing what perfect English she spoke. It reminded me of when Mrs Weston used to correct me when I said, 'innit' instead of 'isn't it'.

We had a good talk about her mother's health then I said,

"Now, Margarita, I will take you upstairs to your mother's room." We went upstairs to Olive's room.

"Look, Olive, who is here to see you!" But Olive was too ill to take in that her beloved daughter was beside her. Again I said,

"Olive, it's Margarita, all the way from Australia."

"Margarita? All the way from Australia? But you are Margarita!" Olive said, unable to recognise her own daughter. Margarita wept.

She came every day all the time she was in England. When it was time to go back to Australia her mother was still alive but only just.

Margarita said,

"Ida, I'm a matron in a hospital in Melbourne and I couldn't look after my mother better than you do. It is God's blessing that she is with you and I've seen her with my own eyes." She went back to Australia without her mother recognising her but she was comforted to know she was being looked after and was in God's hands. Before she died Olive said,

"I thank you for all you have done for me and will go and wait for you."

"Olive, where will you wait for me?" I asked.

"At Jesus's feet." I immediately called the doctor. Dr Timothy Ireland came, who was a good Christian. We said a prayer and sang *The Lord Is My Shepherd*. Soon after that she went home to the Lord. I missed her very much.

CHAPTER FORTY-ONE – MY HUSBAND AND I NEED A HOLIDAY

Tony and I were very tired and we decided that, before we took on another resident, we'd better have a holiday. We had a flat on the Italian Riviera on the Adriatic coast in a place called Viserbella. The address was 59 Via Port Palos, Rimini. I asked my friend Maisie if her daughter, Margaret, who was a SRN, would come for two weeks to live and work in 'Shalom' while my husband and I were on holiday. Margaret was a wonderful nurse, a committed Christian and a very caring lady. Elisabeth was a relative of Margaret and together they made a good team. They never let me down and were always ready to help in every possible way. Gladys was a trusted friend and a good and conscientious worker. I could always rely on her for any help I needed. I also had Nurse Mackenzie, my friend for more than thirty years and a very good nurse, and my two daughters. Shalom Residential Home was well covered.

However, there was one thing: if Violet found out that my husband and I were not there, she would play everybody up. We had a staff meeting and I emphasised to all the staff that Violet must not know that we were going on holiday. Violet was not stupid but if she didn't know, it just might stop her from behaving badly towards the staff or anybody else.

Every time we went away I put a poster on the kitchen wall with details of the daily routine according to which I wanted the home to be run. It was written up by my daughter, Luciana, and dictated by myself.

(1)   7 am. The care assistant on duty needs to check all the residents one by one to make sure they are well.

(2)   Make sure they all have their hands and faces washed and comb their hair.

(3)   8.30 a.m. Elisabeth goes downstairs to cook the breakfast they order and takes it to their bedroom and puts it on their special breakfast table, sits the residents up in bed and serves the breakfast.

(4)   Collect all the trays and put the crockery in the dishwasher.

(5)   9 a.m. Nurse Mackenzie and Gladys have arrived. Nurse Mac does the medications, already left in each individual's box for each day I'm away.

(6)   All the residents have a wash all over and two ladies have a bath every morning and their hair is washed and set by whoever bathes them.

(7)   Gladys and Mac continue to look after the ladies, come downstairs and prepare coffee or tea and biscuits. Gladys takes these around to the ladies, and after that the staff have a break

(8)   While Elisabeth prepares the dinner, Mac and Gladys carry on looking after the ladies.

(9)   12.30 p.m. Lunch is served and the ladies are helped to the table, except Mrs Johnson and Violet Cook who remain in their rooms at all times.

(10)   The staff help the ladies to the toilet and then to sit in the lounge where they chat to one another.

(11)   When all the residents have settled down, the staff have their dinner.

(12)   2 p.m. Mac goes off duty. Elisabeth and Gladys remain, Elisabeth writes the daily report and Gladys does some ironing.

(13)   3.30 p.m. Tea and cake in the lounge for residents and visitors. The cakes are either from Marks & Spencer or made by me. Gladys goes home and Lorraine comes in to help Elisabeth.

(14)   6.30 p.m. Supper of their choice. After supper they sit and watch television.

(15)   The residents are asked what they would like for lunch the next day. There is always a set menu prepared,

but the residents can make their own choice.

(16) Always remember to take food out of the freezer for the next day.

(17) 9 pm. onwards. Residents are helped to wash, undress and get into bed with a night time drink, again of their own choice.

(18) By 10.30 p.m. all the ladies are in bed. Elisabeth has a bell where she sleeps. If any resident rings their bell she will immediately go and attend to them wherever they need her.

(19) During the night always go round to see everything is OK, until 7 a.m.

With the help of my daughter, Elisabeth Gladys and Mac we were able to have our holiday and know that the residents of 'Shalom' were well looked after.

On August 15th we went from Gatwick Airport to our flat in Rimini. As I said before, August is a holiday month for the Italians, and the fifteenth is a special day because the Catholic faith celebrates the Assumption of the Mother of Jesus to Heaven. The whole country is in holiday mood. While we were on the 'plane we could see the fireworks down below. It was very exciting for us. When we reached Rimini Airport we realised how hot it was. We took a taxi and in twenty minutes we were in our flat and enjoying the comfort of our own home and the beautiful view of the lovely sea.

Our flat was very beautiful: one double bedroom, one bathroom, a big kitchen, dining and sitting room all in one, two French doors onto the terrace around the flat. One side faced the sea and the other faced the square. In the square was a beautiful church with shops all around and the bus stop was right by our front door. There were buses every two minutes to Rimini centre. Viserbella was and still is a beautiful and posh part of Rimini. From there we travelled to all parts of Italy: Perugia, Rome and to my village.

In the first week of September we were back to the most precious things in our lives: the children and the ladies of 'Shalom', my beautiful ladies of 'Shalom'. As soon as we entered the house, I left the suitcase in the corridor and telephoned my family.

"We are back in England." I said. Elisabeth gave me a full account of what had happened every day. I couldn't thank her and Gladys, Mac and our two daughters enough for looking after the ladies so well.

I went to Mrs.Johnson's room and she said,

"Ida, the staff looked after us ever so well, but we did all miss you and Tony and we are glad to see you back." When we went in the lounge, all the ladies clapped their hands for joy, but the joy was mine and Tony's to be back where we belonged.

I went upstairs to Violet's room. Violet wouldn't speak to me, so I pretended to go away, but I was behind the door to listen to what she would say to her imaginary friend. She said,

"Do you know that b***** left us for three weeks and now she comes back home and expects us to talk to her! But, you know, I'm glad they are back, aren't you?" Her imaginary friend was herself and she answered herself,

"Yes, I'm glad they are back and that's a call for a celebration." I was astonished: under her bed she had a bottle of sherry and a small plastic cup. She poured out a small amount of sherry and looked in the mirror and said,

"Violet and I welcome them back home." I was speechless and didn't know what to make of her behaviour. Helen said she'd given the bottle of sherry to her grandmother, or Rosina had. If she kept the sherry under her bed, surely the staff would know about it because they always cleaned under the beds. I couldn't resist any longer and went in the room.

"Violet, who is your friend?" I said.

"Violet is my friend," she said.

"And where she is now?" I asked. She pointed her finger at the mirror and said,

"There she is, Violet." I wanted to laugh but I didn't. It took me back in time to when I was small and once had an imaginary friend. I felt very sorry for her and thought, 'This poor lady is here by herself all the time and it must play on her mind'. On the other hand, I was pleased for her that she had an imaginary friend. I put my arms around her and gave her a kiss on the cheek.

"Oh Violet, I'm so happy to be back here with you and you friend." I said, "I'm sorry if we left you and your friend for three weeks, but we were very tired and needed a rest. But now we are back, so will you forgive us?"

"Of course," she said, "My friend and I forgive you both. The important thing is you are both well and you are back with us."
"Thanks very much to you both you," I said.

Around this time I began to feel inadequate about what I could do. I was always going to the hospital and assessing the situations people were in and, when I could, I would help in any way. But I had such a small home there was a limit to what I could do. If I had a larger house I could begin a business but that wasn't what I'd intended to do. I liked looking after the elderly myself and being responsible for them.

One day the hospital rang and said,
"Mrs Maddalena, we know you have a vacancy and we have so many emergencies and not enough beds. Please come in and see if you can take this lady." So I went to the hospital and asked the sister on duty which patient it was that she wanted me to assess. The sister pointed to a little lady sitting in the corner of the ward. I said,
"Thank you, sister." and she went back to her office. I went up to the lady and noticed how sad she looked. I took a chair and sat near her and said,
"My name is Ida. What is your name?"
"My name is Joanna Wilson
"Well, Mrs Wilson how are you?"
"I'm much better. In fact, the hospital want to send me home but I haven't anybody to look after me at home. I have two sons and a daughter. My daughter doesn't live in Maidstone and neither does my son, Paul. He has a wife, Margaret who isn't well herself. Steven lives with me but isn't young and he has a job. I can't be left alone."
"Would you like come to my home for two weeks holiday?"
"And what will happen after two weeks?"
"If you like it and I manage to give you all the tender loving care you need, you can stay. Otherwise, we will make other arrangements to try to make you comfortable wherever you want to be."
"I'd like that very much."
"Mrs Wilson I will go to the office now and see sister and we'll take it from there. Is that all right?"
"Oh yes, please do, and then sister will tell me what you have decided."

319

I went to the office and said,

"I have been assessing Mrs. Wilson and I can see no reason why I shouldn't be able to help her. I told her she could spend two weeks holiday at my home and we'll go from there. Can you tell me about any conditions she may have?"

"There's nothing to tell except she is an old lady," sister said, "and she can't be left at home alone and needs someone like you to look after her."

"Can you make arrangements with the doctor and the ambulance for Mrs Wilson to come to 'Shalom'?"

"I will do it as soon as I can."

I left the hospital and went home. As soon I walked in the telephone rang. Rosina Desantis had had an accident and needed help. Rosina Desantis was Violet Cook's daughter. It was a mystery what happened to her husband. We only knew that she had bought a flat in London Road, not very far from us, to be near her mother. Now she needed help. Tony immediately took the car and drove to her flat. Rosina had had a terrible accident: while she was settling in she had fallen and the dressing table mirror had tumbled over onto her, cutting her face. Tony took her to Casualty at Maidstone Hospital.

I went upstairs to Violet's room. She looked at me and said,

"You know, Ida, my daughter hasn't visited me for quite a few days. Do you know why?"

"Your daughter," I said, "has just bought a flat not far from here, so you must her give time to settle in. She will come soon, don't worry." But inside I was very concerned for Rosina Desantis's future.

Not long after that the doorbell rang and it was Violet's grandaughter, Helen, with her dog, Princess. She knew I didn't like dogs in house so she used to tie it to a tree near the door. I took Helen into the kitchen and told what had happened to her mother.

"Tony is with her in casualty. He'll be home soon then he can take you to her, but please don't say anything to your grandmother because she would worry and there is nothing she can do." I could see Helen was very upset.

"Sit down," I said, "and I'll make you a cup of coffee." While I was doing that Tony walked in and looked at Helen. He could tell that I had told her what had happened to her mother.

"Helen," he said, "it's not as bad as I thought. Your mother is already back home and I can take you to see her after you've visited your grandmother."

"Oh thank you, Tony, for helping my mother," she said.

Helen went upstairs and I went outside to see the dog. She looked at me in such a way that said it all. I untied her and said,

"Go upstairs, Princess." The dog ran upstairs like a shot and I went up after her. She went in and you should have seen the happiness at being reunited with her owner! After a while I said to the dog,

"Princess, you can't go with Helen today. You've got to stay with me downstairs." The dog looked at me then looked very sorry for herself.

"Go with your Helen, then," I said and the dog ran as fast as she could after her owner.

Just after Helen went, Jean and John and arrived. Jean was looking astonishingly beautiful: very tall and slim with her blonde hair and blue eyes and a blue dress. They both came in to the kitchen and said,

"It is time Mrs Johnson held another party."

"Well, Jean and John I said, "right now I have too much going on to be able to organise a party, but in a few weeks time we can think about it."

"Oh don't worry," they said, "we will organise it all and bring the food. You don't have to do anything."

"That's very kind of you."

"Don't mention it. We are only too pleased to be able to do something for that special lady. By the way, Ida, I am going to go back to university to take another degree."

"Jean" I said, "you already have a degree; you are a doctor of science. "I said,

"Ladies, tomorrow we will have a new lady. Her name is Joanna Wilson."

"We will all welcome her to 'Shalom'," they said. I went upstairs and told Violet,

"Tomorrow you will have a new companion to share your room with."

"I don't want anyone else. I have my friend here already. Her name is Violet, like myself."

"And Her name is Joanna, she is a very nice lady," I said.

"I don't care what name she has, I repeat, I'm happy as I am." I left her and went into Helen's room and told her what Violet had said and we both had a good laugh.

Everything was going fine: we really enjoyed looking after the ladies and the ladies enjoyed every second of their lives. One day the doorbell rang and I opened the door to be confronted with half a dozen firemen.

"Matron," they said, "your residential home is on fire!" It reminded me of when I was in hospital and the fireman said, 'The clinic room is on fire!' and I'd answered, 'Don't be silly, I've just sterilised that room. Don't you dare make a mess in there!' I was reported to the head of the hospital for that, so this time I took action immediately.

In three minutes, with the help of my staff, all the ladies were out of 'Shalom' and at the meeting point in the garden. The firemen congratulated me and the staff on the efficiency with which we had evacuated the residents. After the firemen left, I emphasized to the staff the importance the fire drill we had done so often.

The next morning the ambulance arrived with Mrs Joanna Wilson on board. She was helped out by the ambulance men and they brought her inside. I thanked them for their service and took Joanna straight into the lounge and introduced her to the other ladies. I let her sit down in an armchair and told her she could soon have coffee or tea and biscuits with the other ladies. She appeared very tranquil and relaxed - a very pleasant old lady. All the others chatted to her and made her welcome. Elisabeth took her belongings upstairs and put them in her drawers and wardrobe and later on I took her upstairs to meet Violet. I explained to Joanna about Violet's imaginary friend. Violet looked at Joanna and said,

"Well, she isn't anything like my friend." Joanna and I laughed and said,

"Of course not, your friend is just like you. But she is a very nice lady and I'm assuring your friend and you will be come good friend. Violet said, " but Mrs Joanna Wilson she is a an old Lady."

" Joanna she is the same age as you are, but at one time you were both beautiful young ladies. Now you are both very nice old ladies, so be glad about it."

That evening I took Joanna near the hand basin, pulled the curtain and gave her a good wash all over. Then I put her nightdress on her, put her to bed and asked what she would like to drink. It was the same routine for all the ladies every night.

A week passed and Jean Mrs Johnson's granddaughter, telephoned to say,

"Ida, John and I have been arranging the party for Mrs Johnson for next Saturday. Because of her condition we have sent invitations for two couples to come at a time, from two p.m. to three p.m. and so on until seven p.m."

"That will be fine as long you will both be here to arrange everything and make sure it all goes well." Saturday came and it was nearly time for the guests to arrive. There was no sign of Jean and John. So I took two loaves of bread, butter, ham, lettuce, tomatoes, cucumber, a tin of red salmon, two tins of anchovies and two of mozzarella.

(1)   I buttered all the bread. On one slice I put a slice of ham, a lettuce leaf, two thin slices of tomatoes, salt and pepper, and then put another slice of bread on the top. I cut the crusts off all around and cut the whole twice to make four little triangular sandwiches. I repeated this until one loaf was finished. I put the sandwiches on five serving platters. Then I buttered slices from the other loaf. I opened the tin of salmon and mixed it with salt, pepper and a drop of vinegar. Again I cut them into little sandwiches. I boiled six eggs and mashed them with mayonnaise, and added salt, pepper and cucumber. I finished the rest of the loaf and put these on another five serving platters.

(2)   I cut the mozzarella cheese into twelve sticks, each three inches long. From the two tins I made two dozen sticks. I removed the fat from the ham and sliced it into twelve strips. Carefully I wrapped each strip of ham around twelve sticks of cheese and put them neatly on a serving platter.

(3)   I opened a tin of anchovies and carefully wrapped an anchovy around each remaining stick of cheese and also arranged these neatly on a serving platter.

(4)   I opened two tins of artichoke hearts and cut each of them in half.

(5)   I cut twelve figs into quarters and arranged them on a

serving platter.

(6)   I peeled two mangoes and then sliced them down each side of their large, flat central stones. I sliced the flesh into strips and arranged them so that they formed a fan shape, again on a serving platter divided into five servings.

(7)   I made dressing and pared the rind from one orange, using a vegetable peeler. I then cut the rind into small strips and placed them in a bowl.

(8)   I added *passata* (sieved tomatoes), mustard, yogurt and seasoning to the bowl and mixed them together. I shredded basil leaves and mixed them into the dressing.

(9)   Again, I divided this into five little dishes and served them with the Italian Platter accompanied with bread sticks.

So every hour we served up the three serving platters and there was enough to go round all the people that had been invited to Mrs Johnson's party that day. The doorbell rang and one of my staff opened the door. It was John without Jean.
"John, where is Jean?" I asked.
"She is unwell," he said and then took over the party so I could get on with the rest of the residents.

The next day began with the usual routine at seven o'clock. At nine o'clock I was doing the medication when nurse Mac called me,
"Ida, quickly, come into Ella's room. She's having a terrible nosebleed!" I went into Ella's room and realised that it wasn't just a nosebleed; it was much worse. It was like an open tap. I immediately called Tony and asked him to get the car out of the garage.
"Ella needs to go to hospital immediately. This is an emergency," I said. Then I told nurse Mac to take as many towels as she could to help Ella to mop up the blood. I telephoned the emergency number at the Ophthalmic Hospital and told them my husband was on his way with a patient with much more than a nosebleed. Later I telephoned again and said,

"I'm Ida Maddalena. About an hour ago I sent one of my residents to you with a severe nosebleed. Can you please tell me what has happened to Ella?" The hospital doctor said,
"We checked her blood pressure for hypertension and we think that was the cause of her nosebleed. It was necessary to cauterize the blood vessels that are prone to bleeding. She lost so much blood she is having a blood transfusion and will need to remain in hospital for treatment." Tony and nurse Mac came home and I informed Brenda, Ella's daughter, about her mother's condition and that she had been admitted to the Ophthalmic Hospital for treatment.

After two weeks in hospital, Ella came back home and I realised she needed more nursing than I could give her. It was very sad for both of us. Ella liked me and my home and after five years with us it wasn't an easy thing to do, but the doctor said that's what we must do so we did as we'd been told. Ella was readmitted to the Pilgrim's Way Nursing Home in Bower Mount Road. Gladys and I often visited her. She always expressed the desire to come back to 'Shalom' but, much as we all would have liked that, we knew it was impossible.

CHAPTER FORTY-TWO – OUR RESIDENTS ARE VERY HAPPY

It was necessary for me to look at my waiting list again. A long way down was a nice little lady who Elisabeth knew. I called her daughter, Jackie, to see what the situation was. She told me she would much appreciate it if I would accept her mother as one of the residents of Shalom Residential Home. I made an appointment to visit her mother who was called Mrs Aileen Brown. After the visit I was able to offer her a home and the tender loving care she needed.

Aileen was very small, lady-like and had four children. Rosina and Jeny were both in the Salvation Army but not in Maidstone. Mary went to live in Australia and unfortunately died a few years back leaving behind a young family. Then there was Jackie and Charley. Jackie was a civil servant working for the government and Charley had a young family and his own business.

When Aileen arrived she was welcomed by all the residents and staff. She soon made friends with Joanna and they chatted about their families all day long. I discovered Aileen suffered from psoriasis, a recurring scale eruption of the skin. It usually begins between the ages of five and twenty-five, is not infectious and the sufferer has to learn to live with it. The symptoms are:

(1)   A red spot slowly develops, covered by a scale. About one third of patients complain of slight itchiness.

(2)   Several spots merge together to form patches which may be two to three inches long.

(3)   The patch is deep red covered with silvery scales which can be scraped off. The centre of the patch may revert to normal skin, leaving an oddly shaped rash.

(4)   Sometimes, especially in children, the onset of the rash is on the trunk and the limbs with many circular patches. The face is rarely affected. Such an attack, called *mutate psoriasis,* may follow any general illness.

(5)   Pitting and destruction of the nails.

(6)   The scalp may be affected with severe crusting and some hair loss.

(7)   Psoriasis may develop in scars or in recent wounds.

(8)   Although the skin may heal it is common for psoriasis to recur throughout life. The cause is unknown but in some people it is hereditary.

(9)   Surgery to the skin, streptococcal infections, worry and some drugs may trigger or aggravate an attack.

(10)   Complications: arthritis usually affecting the hands may arise in five per cent of sufferers. The arthritis is similar to rheumatoid arthritis but less severe.

There is no effective treatment for psoriasis without a doctor's advice so I called a doctor at King Street practice who came and explained that Aileen's' psoriasis was a recurrence of a condition which had not responded to previous treatments. If there was soreness, discomfort or moistness he recommended using dithranol ointment and he prescribed coal tar dithranol as the most effective, but warned that it is very messy and stains clothes and bedding. Although the patches of psoriasis persisted, Aileen accepted her condition and I made sure I looked after her myself and made her life as good as possible.

One evening at supper Mrs. Wilson (Joanna) appeared to have a heart attack. I immediately called 999 for an ambulance to take Joanna to the hospital, and then the doctor, explaining Joanna's condition. Before the ambulance arrived I realised that Joanna hadn't had a heart attack but an epileptic fit. This is what I did:

(1)   I laid the patient on her side without a pillow.

(2)   I loosened the clothing around her neck.

(3)   I made sure there was enough space around her so she couldn't harm herself on anything. I didn't give her any fluids or put anything in her mouth, but I removed her dentures.

(4)   I didn't restrict her movements.

Once the movements had stopped and Joanna was asleep, the ambulance and the doctor arrived. The ambulance men said this was not the first time they had attended her. When she was in her own home, her son had rung many times for exactly the same thing. With the help of the ambulance men we managed to get her upstairs to bed and let her sleep it off. The next day the doctor came back and put her on medication. I was very cross with the hospital for having failed to disclose her condition.

A few months passed and the local police threw a party for the senior citizens to which we were invited. All the residents were excited about the occasion, especially Joanna.
"I know a lot of people and most of them will be there," she said. Somehow I knew that Joanna was showing all the signs of being about to have one of her epileptic fits. I wanted her to go to the party very much because all week she'd talked of nothing else but this alarmed me. I said to my husband,
"I'm very concerned about Joanna. She doesn't look herself. I may need you tonight and will call you if I do."
"I'll stay here if you want me to."
"That won't be necessary because you're just over the road. I'll ring if I need you."
"Well, make sure you do if there's anything out of the ordinary."
"I will. Goodnight."
"Goodnight and remember, I'm there if you need me."
"Go now then, Aldo." Aldo is his first name but everyone in the hospitals and at 'Shalom' called him Tony, from Antonio, his second name.

I put Joanna in the sick room so if anything happened Violet wouldn't be disturbed. I put an armchair near her bed and sat there. From there I could hear if any emergency bells rang for my assistance. At about two am Jean Talbot rang her emergency bell and while I went to her, sure enough Joanna had her fit. It was so violent it threw her from the bed to the floor and the impact damaged her face. I went immediately to her aid and this time I knew exactly what was wrong. I felt very sorry for her as there was nothing I could do to prevent the terrible fit but, as always, I tried to do the best possible for her. All my staff went to the police party but Joanna wasn't well enough to go anywhere.

Susanna Westmancott was a SRN but didn't go to work because she had three children, Benjamin, Oliver and little William. They didn't live far from my residential home and she always came to help when I needed her. If the children were off school they would come with her and go down to the basement. She was a good, trustworthy Christian lady and her children were well behaved.

Many of my residents had been with me a long time and were very old and now some of them began to get very poorly. Violet Cook had been with us for five years and we'd loved every minute. She was a funny character. You couldn't pass without going into her room and coming out in stitches. In the autumn of 1989 she was ninety-five years old and I realised we couldn't have her for very much longer, no matter how hard we tried. She was just an old, old lady. I could tell when she was really ill and when she put it on. When she was well, she would go to the cupboard and fetch the bottle of sherry that her daughter or granddaughter had put there. They thought we didn't know about it, and we pretended not to because it wasn't enough to worry about. Mostly Violet talked to the mirror with her imaginary friend, but when she felt poorly, she would pray to the Lord to take her to heaven.

One morning I was very concerned about her and called the duty doctor. Doctor came to see her and said,
"You know, Ida, there is not much we can do for her."
"I know, doctor," I said, "but at least we can say to her daughter that you have been to see her." He went into her room.
"Who is he?" asked Violet.
"Violet, he's your doctor." I said.
"He isn't my doctor. You are my doctor." Doctor left the room and I went after him saying,
"Doctor, please come back to see her. She needs you. She doesn't know what she said. She is an old lady." But he left and I went back to her room where she was praying,
"Lord, I can't take any more. Please prepare a place for me and also prepare a place for Ida."
"Violet, please don't say that! I have a lot to do and I'm not ready yet!"
"Well, I can't go alone. St Peter will not let me in by myself, but with you it will be different. He'll let us both in." I looked under her bed and said,
"Look, Violet, you have a bottle of sherry here. Take it with you. If you give that to St Peter, he will let you in." She laughed, and after

that laugh there was no more sign of life in her. I didn't know what make of it. Many times she had fooled me but this time was different. I took her hand and couldn't find any pulse. I put my head on her breast to hear a heart beat, but again there was no sign of life. I still couldn't believe it.

"Violet, stop, this is not a joke. Talk to me at once." But Violet wasn't with us any longer. She had gone to our Lord. I telephoned the doctor again and said,

"Doctor, you didn't visit her before but you will have to visit her now because she doesn't appear to be with us any longer." He came immediately, examined her and said,

"You are right, she isn't here any longer." Before he went, he left the death certificate. What I didn't like about my job was when one of my residents died. After looking after them for so many years I became very attached to them. It was worse still when I had to break the news to their family that their loved one had passed away.

I telephoned Rosina and told her to come to 'Shalom' as soon as possible. After half an hour she arrived and I took her to the kitchen and said,

"Rosina, I'm very sorry but your dear mother passed away about one hour ago." Rosina looked at me and said,

"My mother is not dead. She's playing you up as usual."

"I'm sorry," I said, "please come up and see for yourself. Here is the death certificate left by the doctor." We went upstairs and Rosina said,

"Ida, I told you my mother wasn't dead. She's playing a game with you, not for the first time. I will go now and telephone you later on." I thought, 'Rosina Desantis is a strange woman. Despite the doctor's certificate she still thinks her mother is alive and playing a game with me. I'm mystified that this clever woman can't accept that her mother's time has arrived.' Two hours later Rosina telephoned and said,

"Ida, any news?"

"No, Rosina, nothing has changed."

A week later the funeral of Violet Cook was held in Tonbridge Cemetery. There were a lot of famous people from the opera house and many more from television. After the service, we were invited to Rosina's beautiful home where she made a speech telling all the guests how well we looked after her mother and all the residents of 'Shalom'. Then she presented me with a beautiful, porcelain Royal Doulton jar, one of many things that have been given to me by various relatives of the residents I have had the honour to look after, which I treasure.

CHAPTER FORTY-THREE – MRS JOHNSON MOVES TO BETTER ACCOMMODATION

Mrs Johnson was very happy in the front room but I thought she deserved better accommodation. It was time for her to have her own room with en-suite bath and shower. Mrs Johnson was not pressing me. She liked what I did every morning which was to take her to the hand basin and wash her all over. I thought a proper shower would be better for her and in time she would get accustomed to it and be pleased. I got the builders in and made a special room just for her. Outside her new room was the utility room, where all the washing and ironing was done, and the back door to the garden. Here were two steps which I asked the builders to remove and put in a ramp with a rail so I could wheel Mrs Johnson in and out of the garden and anywhere else she wanted to go. When it was all finished she came to terms with her new accommodation and enjoyed having a proper shower every morning.

One day I took her into the garden and very strong wind blew up. It was so strong it reminded her of the 1987 hurricane which caused such destruction in the south of England. Mrs Johnson knew, or wrote, a poem about this:

> I saw you toss the clothes on high
> And blow the birds about the sky;
> And all around I heard you pass
> Like ladies' skirts across the grass.
> O wind a-blowing all day long,
> O wind that sings so loud a song!
>
> I saw the different things you did,
> But always you yourself you hid.
> I felt you push, I heard you call,
> I couldn't see you at all.
> O wind a-blowing all day long,
> O wind that sings so loud a song!
>
> O you that is so strong and cold,
> O blower, are you young or old?
> Are you a beast of field or tree?
> Or just stronger than me?

O wind a-blowing all day long,
O wind that sings so loud a song!

"Oh, Mrs Johnson," I said, "you are clever. I know your background gave you a good education and you're able to do good things. I have a great admiration for people like you who don't forget about those less fortunate than us."

"My dear Ida," she said, "we are all born the same. Some people, like me, find a shirt to put on but that doesn't make me better than anybody else."

"I heard that before in the Vatican from Lady Rossi, but sometimes it's difficult to take in when you look around the world and see so much suffering, especially among children."

"You're right and that's why there are so many charities. Ida, you always tell me you were born at the wrong time because of the war. You say you didn't have much education, but do you realise how blessed you have been? All the things you have done! Surely, you've had a more colourful life than some rich people."

"Mrs Johnson, I have had to work hard for everything I have but I thank God for looking after me. I overcame many problems in my life but God has been with me all the time so, yes, I count my blessings."

"Ida, I'd better tell you that tomorrow some special people are coming to see you and Tony. It will be a big surprise. I can't tell you more now otherwise it will spoil the fun."

"Oh dear me, who are they? I have so much to do tomorrow. I really can't squash any more into my diary."

"Don't worry. Nurse Mackenzie is going to stay on until it's all over." she said. I gave up asking questions. I just had to wait for tomorrow to see whatever this surprise would be.

The next day Joyce came in with a lot of flowers for Mrs Johnson's room. She arranged them beautifully so the room looked very nice. Then she put an embroidered tablecloth, which was kept for special occasions, on Mrs Johnson's portable table. She laid on a spread of cakes, sandwiches, cheese biscuits, little sausages, olives and all sorts of things. There were two or three bottles of sherry and fruit juices. Tony and I had been told to dress smartly and not to worry about the residents as they were being looked after by the staff. I didn't know what was going on. The doorbell rang and Mac opened the door to the Mayor of Maidstone and a few others who said,

"Mrs Johnson is expecting us." Mac took them to Mrs Johnson's room and Joyce let them in. About ten minutes later Tony and I were asked to go there. We knocked as always and as we went in Mrs Johnson and all her guests clapped their hands. We both wondered what would happen next. Then the Mayor made a speech saying we were the best home in the country and presented us with The Grand National Care Award 1988 for Residential Home of the Year. We weren't expecting it and we were overjoyed but lost for words!

As Mrs Johnson was no longer in the front bedroom, I needed to look at my waiting list again. My eyes stopped on a lady called Sylvia Woodland. She lived in the Royal British Legion Village at Aylesford in Kent. Her late husband had served in the army and the village was just for old servicemen and their wives. We made an appointment and my daughter, Stella, and I went to meet her. She lived in Admiral Moore Drive, if I remember rightly, in a second floor flat. We knocked and a lady came to the door. She was tall and skinny, even worse than Violet Cook. It was scary! My daughter said in French,
"Mum, let's get out of here, I'm frightened." But the lady replied in French,
"Please don't go. I know I look like a witch but I can assure you I'm not! Please come in." When Stella heard the old lady speak French she felt more confident about going into the flat. Sylvia and my daughter engaged in French conversation and I could see they both enjoyed it. When they finished Stella said,
"Mum, please take this lady in. She is in need of help and above all tender loving care."
"Stella, tell her in French we will do whatever is possible to offer her a place in 'Shalom'." Stella reassured her we would do our best as soon we were able.

We went home and told the staff about how Sylvia Woodland looked like Violet and spoke French and Spanish as well as English. We emphasized that she looked very skinny and poorly and by taking her in we would be performing an act of charity. The staff understood her position and prepared a place for her.

Three days later we went to tell her but the place was lifeless. We thought she must have died and that was the end of the matter. But next day we had a message from Sylvia's friend telling us she was in Pilgrim's Way Nursing Home, where Ella was. I went to visit her and as soon as I arrived she told me not to speak because the place was bugged. I realised she was having delusions, maybe because she was so ill or because of old age.

A week later Sylvia was brought to 'Shalom' to live in Mrs Johnson's old room. She soon made herself at home. Everyone in 'Shalom' had their own television, their own telephones with individual lines and all the amenities of their own homes. Sylvia had three dear friends: Mrs Grant, a long-standing family friend and business associate, now widowed; Mrs Jill Parkinson, the wife of her local doctor; and Ruth McAllen. All three took care of Sylvia as best they could but the death of her husband had left Sylvia bitter and confused.

Sylvia and her husband had emigrated to Spain in 1965 and they both enjoyed life there very much. At that time Spain was still under the Fascist General Franco and the country's economy was in poor condition. For Mr and Mrs Woodland living in Spain at that time was very comfortable. They bought a flat in Alicante, a town in a beautiful part of the country. They could afford a full-time domestic, plenty of fine food and a good social life with other English couples in similar circumstances. She told me Alicante was a seaside town and she and her husband and friends would swim in the warm sea after breakfast. At that time the beaches were almost deserted and often they would swim naked, which was prohibited but nobody saw them. Then more and more people began to visit the beaches and one day they were reported to the authorities. The police asked everyone to clear the beach and they erected a screen behind which they made them get dressed. Mr and Mrs Woodland and their friends thought it was all a bit of a laugh, but they didn't swim naked any more.

They enjoyed every day there for twenty glorious years before returning to England because he was suffering from stomach cancer and wanted to die in his own country. Sylvia resented coming back and after his death she soon went downhill. She said they should both have died in Spain.

Joanna Wilson's epilepsy occurred more and more frequently until her poor heart couldn't take any more. She was a very good lady and much loved by her children. Paul and Steven were devoted to her. Two weeks after her last epileptic fit Joanna passed away. It was very sad for her children and all the residents.

I had become very attached to Joanna Wilson, as I was to all the residents. They were my life. My faith in Christ and my family always supported me in everything I did. I couldn't have done without them.

Sylvia Woodland said,
"Now the room above me is free, I would like to have a look at it. Because I lived in a flat for a long time in Spain, I'm accustomed to being high up. It makes me feel more at home than being on the ground floor. Besides, sometimes the gate is left open and children come into the garden. Once I went to the French window to shush them off and they called me an old hag."
"All right, Sylvia, if that's what you want I'll show you upstairs." She was expecting a bigger room so I converted it from a double bedroom to a single one. Before long Sylvia took up residency there.

Now I had two vacancies downstairs and I needed to look at my waiting list again. Before I did so, a nice couple arrived at the door and said,
"We've been recommended by Charley Brown He said you have two vacancies on the ground floor and we might have a chance of booking our mother in here." I was taken by surprise and said,
"Will you come in, please?" I took them to my kitchen and sat them down to tell me about their mother's needs.
"Our mother's name is Jacqueline. She lives in London but we live down here. I can't look after her because of an accident to my knee."
"What are her needs?"
"She walks with a frame and needs to be on the ground floor with everyday care like you provide."
"What did Charley say to you about 'Shalom'?"
"He said his mother has been with you for quite a long while and she couldn't be in a better place. You give her all the loving care she needs and more."
"I have a shared room downstairs. Would she mind sharing with another lady?"
"I don't see why not. She has to share in the hospital with other ladies and men, too."
"Then bring your mother here so we can see if I can help her. Remember, to begin with your mother stays for two weeks convalescence and after that, if Jacqueline likes it and we can manage her, she can stay. Otherwise you'll have to look for a

better place for her."

A week later Jacqueline arrived with her daughter and son-in-law. As soon as I saw her I thought what a lovely lady she was. She had a big smile and spoke in a London accent. I knew she would be the right sort for 'Shalom'.
"You must be Jacqueline."
"You must be the Italian lady everybody is talking about."
"I hope they're not saying bad things about me!"
"Oh no, they say you are kind to your ladies and spoil them by making them eat all the good food you provide for them."
"Please come in." I took them all to the lounge, asked them to make themselves comfortable, turned to the other residents and said,
"This is Jacqueline. She is from London and has come to join the gang at 'Shalom'." The residents all laughed and welcomed Jacqueline into our midst.

After two weeks with us, Jacqueline seemed very happy and comfortable. Her daughter and son-in-law visited often and created a lovely atmosphere for the residents, which gave a lot satisfaction to the staff.

Not long after that a dear lady from an Evangelical church came to see me on behalf of her mother, Mrs Mary Preston, who lived in the north of England. The daughter, Mrs Ashby, lived Maidstone and the only way she could help her mother was to move her closer to be able to visit and keep an eye on her wellbeing. As always I explained the rules of 'Shalom'.

Mrs Mary Preston was a nice, Christian lady. She was about eighty years old and had a fracture of the thigh which had been operated on without success. She needed a lot help, but was very independent. She wouldn't ring the bell and always tried to help herself, but unfortunately that was impossible in her condition. Often I found her on the floor. It was difficult to look after her and I wasn't having much success. I was very sorry for her and would have liked her to stay with us to give all the love and tender care she needed, but it was very difficult as she didn't give us a chance. But we tried. Eventually, with a broken heart, I had no choice but to tell her daughter we couldn't look after her. We recommended a nursing home and she went to Loose Valley, where I visited several ladies that had left us. Deep in my heart I would really have liked to help such a lovely person.

When I came back from Loose Valley, I went straight to Mrs Johnson's room and somehow she didn't seem well. I became very concerned about her, telephoned Jean and said,
"Mrs Johnson doesn't look well."
"What do you think is wrong with her?"
"I don't know. She hasn't anything I could put a finger on, unless she has a pain she isn't telling us about."
"Telephone Dr Barr." Jean said, "As you know, he's a good friend of hers. He'll find out what the matter is."
"Good," I said, "because Sylvia belongs to the same practice and she needs to see a doctor. She hasn't slept well for the last couple of nights and seems very confused." I said goodbye to Jean put the telephone down and five minutes later rang the doctor.
"I'm Ida from 'Shalom' and I need Dr Barr to see two residents. They are both his patients." About two hours later there was a knock at my door and I knew it was the doctor.
"Good afternoon, doctor."
"What's good about it?"
"Well, you have two ladies to see and they are both great admirers of yours."
"I didn't know I was so popular. Who are these ladies?"
"Mrs Johnson and Mrs Woodland. Can you please see Sylvia first because Mrs Johnson always has a chat and, if you're not in a hurry, a glass sherry with you?" So I took Dr Barr to Sylvia's room. While he was examining her my telephone rang and he said,
"You go to answer your telephone. I will be all right with her."
When I'd dealt with the inquiry I went back upstairs. Dr Barr was just coming out of Sylvia's room and said,
"Ida, I'm very surprised at you." He had a big grin on his face.
"Why, doctor?"
"Because you made so much noise when you were in the cupboard with the Japanese soldier that your poor residents can't get a wink of sleep! That's why she is so tired." We both burst out laughing and I took him to Mrs Johnson's room and left him there, as she always liked.

After half an hour he came out and said there was nothing much wrong with Lola (Mrs Johnson), that she felt a bit down at the loss of her sister and a few friends, but that's how it was when you live as long as her. Mrs Johnson asked me many times to call her Lola but I would have had to call all the other residents by their

Christian names as well. I saw the doctor out and went back to Mrs Johnson. I could see she and the doctor had enjoyed a good laugh about what Sylvia told the doctor about the Japanese soldier and me in the cupboard.

"Now you know what I get up to in the night!"

"Oh, Ida, fancy you being like that! But I can't understand why he was Japanese?"

"Poor Sylvia is getting very confused. I think Mr. Woodland was a commander in Japan and told her stories of his wartime experience and now they're playing in her frail mind. Do you know, Mrs Johnson, it reminds me of a story from an old nun I had the honour to look after? In a short time we became good friends. I told her the story of how I came to England and then she told me her story. Her name was Aileen, she was born in Ireland. She said,

> 'As a little girl I was brought up in a convent and always wanted to be a nun. In my country it was an honour if one of your family became a nun or a priest. So when I was twenty I took the veil and my family rejoiced with me. I became Sister Teresa and not long after was sent to Japan to be a missionary with several other nuns. I enjoyed looking after children and old people and I thought life was grand. I missed my home country and especially my family but the joy of what I was doing compensated for that. But soon the war started and we were put in a concentration camp. It was infested by cockroaches but it was a good job they were there because that was the only food we ever had. We were abused by the Japanese soldiers in the most humiliating ways a nun or any human could be.'

Then she showed me a picture of her and the other nuns taken when they were liberated. I was frightened just looking at it: they looked as if they had been kept underground for twenty years and then brought out to walk about. I never could get that image out of my mind." Mrs Johnson was horrified to hear the story.

"Those poor nuns!" she said, "I wonder how many stories like that poor Sylvia may have heard from her husband, and now they play in her mind."

As Sylvia had three beloved friends, I thought it would be nice if one of them, Ruth McAllen, could come and help her. I would pay for her services. When I put the idea to Sylvia she was over the moon. Not long afterwards Ruth walked in.

"Ruth," I said, "I know you looked after Sylvia in her home. I wonder if you'd like to come and work here for a couple of hours a day?"

"Oh, Ida, I would like to."

"Well, you can start anytime you like. You know how Sylvia likes being looked after and I'm quite sure she'll be happy about it." Ruth was nice, happy person and made 'Shalom' much brighter.

Time was passing, 'Shalom' was a happy home, everything was going beautifully but good things don't last for long. Patricia Brown became very disorientated. I called her doctor who said,

"She has a bad heart condition and at her age things don't get any better. There is very little we can do for her. I know you give your residents the best attention possible, but don't be surprised if she isn't with us for much longer." I took the doctor's comments with a pinch of salt. I knew she was getting confused and that she had a heart condition but she could last a long time like that.

How wrong I was! Two days later, after I'd washed her all over, done her hair, brushed her dentures and given them back for her to put in her mouth, she went crashing to the floor. I immediately dialled 999 for an ambulance and telephoned her doctor. Then I did the following:

(1) I laid her flat on her back and tilted her chin up so her neck was not constricted.

(2) I put my ear to her mouth to feel and hear her breathing. I put my hand on her chest to check its rise and fall.

(3) I used my finger to clear her mouth and pulled her chin up so her neck was fully extended.

(4) I gave artificial respiration to make her restart natural breathing.

(5) I couldn't get the air into her lungs so I checked that her neck was fully extended and checked for blockages in case she'd swallowed her dentures.

(6) Patricia was still not breathing so I began to make chest compressions three or four times and then tried

340

mouth-to-mouth resuscitation again.

By that time the ambulance and the doctor had arrived but Patricia had died. The doctor said,
"I'm sorry, Ida. I did tell you not long ago that she was very ill. She's had a massive heart attack. You just have to accept it." But I didn't take it very well when one of my ladies died. I can't get it out of my mind that Patricia might have swallowed the top set of her dentures because I never found them anywhere.

Now Catherine was again left alone in her bedroom and she said,
"Ida, I do hope you fill that bed very soon and I do hope it will be somebody I know."
"Don't worry, Catherine, the right person will come long. I have a long waiting list but I need time to get over Patricia's death."

The next day Mrs Herriott rang the doorbell and Gladys let her in.
"Gladys, tell Ida I would like to have a word with her."
"Mrs Herriott, at the moment Ida is in a meeting with the social services and it will be a couple of hours before she'll be free."
"I'll wait a while in Mrs Johnson's room and if she isn't free then I'll come back again because this is very important." An hour later the social services went and Gladys said,
"Ida, Mrs Herriott would like to have a word with you urgently."
"Where is she?"
"She's with Mrs Johnson. Shall I tell her you are free now?"
"Wait, we'll have a cup of tea first."

Elisabeth was coming down from upstairs and met Mrs Herriott in the corridor who said,
"I actually came to see Ida but Gladys said she was with the social services. I wonder how long it will be before I can speak to her."
"The Social Services left just a few minutes ago. I'll see what I can do, Mrs Herriott."
Elisabeth came into the kitchen and said,
"Ida, Mrs Herriott needs to have a chat with you."
"Tell Mrs Herriott to wait in the lounge and I'll be there in a few minutes." I finished what I was doing, went to the lounge and said,
"Mrs Herriott, I hear you would like a word with me. Here I am. Are you going to tell me something exciting?"
"A little bird told me you have a vacancy."
"Yes, sadly I just lost Patricia. It won't take me long to fill her bed. Nevertheless, there is a lot of stress when I lose a resident. I get

so attached to them that every time I lose one of them, I lose part of myself."

"Why I came here today was to ask if, before you fill the bed, you would consent to visit Maidstone Hospital where my sister Dorothy is in need of help. I know she would be very pleased to see you there."

"Oh dear, what is the matter with Miss Wickendon?"

"You know she is about ninety-five and the time has come when she's finding it difficult to manage by herself. Mr Herriott and I are also getting on, I'm not well enough to look after her and my poor husband is losing his sight so it is difficult to have Dorothy with us."

"Mrs Herriott, I quite understand. You've been too poorly and it would be impossible for you and your husband to look after Miss Wickendon. I know your feelings but it would be just impossible. I tell you what, I will go to the hospital, assess the situation and do whatever is possible for your dear sister."

CHAPTER FORTY-FOUR – A VISIT TO MAIDSTONE HOSPITAL

The next day I went to Maidstone Hospital to see Miss Wickendon. First I went into the ward office to have a word with the sister.

"Good afternoon, sister, I believe you have Miss Wickendon here."

"I knew you would come to her rescue sooner or later. She's already spoken to me about you and I told her that we know you well."

"Sister, please tell me about her medical needs."

"She's an old lady who can no longer manage by herself. She needs your tender loving care and Marks & Spencer food, like all your residents."

"Thank you, Sister."

"Come, I'll take you to her."

When we got to her bed she wasn't there. Sister asked the other patients where she was and they said,

"The nurse took her to the bathroom quite a while ago. Maybe she needs help to get back again." I said I'd go to help her and sister said,

"All right then, I leave her to you." I went to the bathroom where she was waiting. When she realised who I was she was very pleased to see me.

"Your sister Rachel told me you were here so I came to see you. Let me help you back to bed and then you can tell me all about yourself." Slowly we walked back and I helped her to sit on the armchair beside her bed. I fetched a visitor's chair for myself.

"Well," I said, "how are you and how long have you been here?"

"I've been here about a week because I had a fall. I realise that I can't stay in my bungalow any longer because I can't look after myself. I can't go to my sister and brother-in-law's because she isn't well herself and they're also getting old."

"Dorothy, I've already had a word with the ward sister. When the hospital discharges you, come for two weeks to 'Shalom' to see if you'd like to stay there. Then if you think you'll be better in your own home, you can go back to your bungalow. What do you think?"

"What I think is that if I come to you, I'll stay with you."

"Let's take one step at a time. Now I've got to go and see what's going on at home. I'll tell your sister Rachel I've been here and explain what we've discussed. I can assure you everything will be all right."

When I got home the residents were having tea and cakes.

"I'd like to have a cup of tea with the ladies in the lounge." I said to Elisabeth

"OK, Mrs Maddalena, you will be served."

"No more of this 'Mrs Maddalena', Elisabeth you can call me 'Ida' like everybody else."

"I'm only joking," said Elisabeth and we both laughed.

Mr and Mrs Herriott rang the doorbell and Gladys opened the door.

"Hello, Gladys. Is Ida in?"

"Yes," Gladys said, "she's upstairs with Jean Talbot. Come in, will you, and I will call her." Gladys took them to the lounge so they could talk to the other residents while waiting for me. Gladys came to Jean's room and said,

"Mr and Mrs Herriott are downstairs wanting to speak to you."

"I will come downstairs very soon." I went downstairs and asked them to come to the kitchen, the place I most liked to do all my work in, including the staff meetings and chatting with the residents' relatives. They sat at the big kitchen table.

"Mr and Mrs Herriott, I have been to the hospital and assessed Dorothy's situation. I agree with the hospital that she does need full-time care. I told Dorothy she could come to 'Shalom' for two weeks convalescence. After two weeks it's up to her if she wants to stay permanently or go back to her bungalow."

"We are very pleased that Dorothy can come here to be with you, your staff and your family."

"We will do what we can to make her comfortable when she is here."

A week later I received a telephone call from the hospital telling me Dorothy would arrive in the ambulance some time the next morning. I telephoned Mrs Herriott with the news. The next morning at about eleven the ambulance arrived with Dorothy on board. I went out and welcomed her. She was very frail and needed help. The ambulance men brought her into the lounge and sat her in a comfortable armchair. All the ladies welcomed her. Not long after, her sister and brother-in-law arrived. They had a long chat and then came to the kitchen and thanked me for taking her in. Then they went to Mrs Johnson's room to tell her the good news.

Nurse Mackenzie was there and called me upstairs.

"Ida," she said, "Catherine seems to be in pain."

"What sort of pain? Explain it to me."

"Well, she suffers from piles."

"Don't worry, Mac. I'll get the doctor to prescribe an ointment that will help to relieve the pain." I rang Dr Mutimer's surgery and spoke to the receptionist.

"Please tell Doctor Jean that Catherine needs some asshole."

"Asshole to you to, Ida!" she said.

"Don't be silly, Catherine is in a lot of discomfort and it's my job to make sure she gets this ointment."

"Say it after me, 'Anusol'," she said.

"Asshole," I said and heard everybody laughing. What silly people, I thought. I ask for some ointment and they all laugh at me. I'd better ask my staff what that word means and why it's so funny. When my daughter Luciana came back from the office I asked her.

"Luciana, today I needed ointment for Catherine 's condition and the doctor's receptionist laughed when I asked for some asshole."

"Oh, no, Mum! It's a very rude word. I'm not surprised they had a good laugh at you."

"Tell me what it means."

"Mum, I'm not prepared to swear. I can only tell you never to say that, but when you want the ointment, try to say 'Anusol'."

"Oh, I'm sorry to make myself such a laughing stock."

"You can't help it. It happens when the language you speak isn't your native one." When the staff got to know they also had a good laugh.

That evening at nine o'clock I took Dorothy upstairs to the bathroom, washed her and then took her to her new room. When Catherine saw her she said,

"Oh, Dorothy, fancy that! We meet again and we're going to share a room."

"Well, well! They say even mountains meet sometimes, but this is a big surprise! I never expected this." And they both laughed.

"Well, Catherine , this is the third lady you've had in your room who you knew before you came here. It is a surprise for you and it will be for all the staff when they get to know about it." Catherine and Dorothy talked and talked until late. I thought they had so much in common they would never go to sleep, but eventually they did.

The next day Dorothy said,

"Ida, I know the history of this house well. Two well-known families have lived here. I was associated with them both before Mr Small bought it. I always liked the house and the people who lived here. I knew you and your children. I often met them going to school."

"And I knew you, too. How can I forget that pretty lady with white hair, blue eyes, and always a smile on her face? You were smartly dressed and always wore shoes with very high heels, marching up and down Tonbridge Road."

"Yes. I was a private secretary to Colonel Stile Winch for more than forty years. They were gentry and I felt very honoured to be employed by them. After I retired, I went to college and did sewing, which I'd always been interested in. I love my sister and my brother-in-law. They are very dear to me but they can't look after me because they're too old and not well enough. I know you told me I'd be here for two weeks and then we'll review the situation, but I can tell you now I want to be part of this little residential home. It's like a big family which I will enjoy very much. My dearest sister is only few doors away and she can visit me any time she likes." I thought, Catherine has what she's always wanted, a good companion to share her room with.

Time passed and the home ran smoothly until one night when I was putting Aileen Brown to bed. After I'd done everything, I realised Aileen didn't want me to leave. She kept saying,

"Ida, I love you and Tony, ten thousand times. The Lord above sees how you look after all of us and He will bless you and your family because you are good people. You work from morning till night, night till morning and you never moan. No matter what we demand, you are always there for us."

"Aileen, whatever is the matter with you? I only do my job the way I should. I don't always get it right but I do the best I can, and I love you all. Now I must go to the other residents. If anything worries you, ring the bell and I will be here for you." I helped her into bed, gave her a goodnight kiss and went to attend to Sylvia.

When I'd settled all the residents, I went back to Aileen's room to see everything was all right. I opened the door very carefully. I didn't want to disturb her if she was asleep. There she was, well gone in a deep sleep. I went downstairs, had a shower and tried to go to bed but for some reason I was up all night.

As always I went into each room every couple of hours to check the residents and at seven am I went in to wash their hands and face and make sure they were clean and comfortable before breakfast. Aileen was still all right. At eight o'clock I served her breakfast and she was extremely happy, continued to thank me for the tender loving care I gave to them all, and said how God would reward me in heaven. I thought it was a bit strange but I then thought no more about it.

At about nine o'clock Mac came in and said,
"Good morning, Ida. Have you had a good night?"
"Not really. For some reason I was up all night."
"Ah! The residents kept the bell going?" she said.
"No, it was me; I felt as if something would happen."
"You silly woman, you should relax and go to sleep when you can."
Mac went upstairs, straight to Aileen room and ran downstairs again.
"Ida, Aileen is not in her room!"
"That's impossible. I took her breakfast in and she was all right."
"Yes, the tray is on the table with nothing on it. It seems as if she ate all her breakfast but she isn't there."
"Well, I don't understand. Let's go up together."

We went up, opened Joanna's door and she wasn't there.
"Let's look in the wardrobe to see what clothes she's put on." As I went to the wardrobe, there was Aileen behind the armchair. While she was taking off her dressing gown she'd had a heart attack and there she lay. I told Mac to call 999 and then tried compression to her chest to see if I could bring her round. But it was no use. Aileen wasn't with us any longer.

Later the doctor said,
"Sorry, Ida, there wasn't anything anybody could have done. She had a massive heart attack and died instantly. She suffered no pain, she died before she knew."
"This job is beginning to get me down," I said, "It is too upsetting for me to carry on."
"Now, Ida, you always knew the nurse's job is all about life and death. You have done for so many years. You must pull yourself together and get on with it. You think, what would the others do if you gave up?" I kept quiet. The doctor patted my shoulder and left. I went to the kitchen and had a good cry. After a while I went to the bathroom, washed and changed my uniform and told Aileen's daughters what had happened. Of course they were very upset but they understood. Later I received a presentation clock inscribed, 'I love Ida ten thousand times Aileen xxx'.

CHAPTER FORTY-FIVE – A VISIT TO LINTON HOSPITAL

It took more than two weeks before I started to look at my waiting list. As always the social services from the hospital rang me and said,

"We know you have a vacancy and we have a lady who lives very near you and needs your help."

"What is her name?"

"Amanda. She lives in Bower Place only few yards away from you. She keeps mentioning your name so she must know you well."

"Right, where is she at the moment?"

"She is in Linton Hospital."

"As you know, I've got to assess her needs first. I will visit her and then we can decide what is best for her." The next day I went to the hospital to assess her. As I entered the ward I heard a lady calling me. I recognised her.

"Oh, please come and help me! I know you and your husband well. We call you the Angels of Tonbridge Road."

I knew Amanda and her husband. She always told us she was a London girl and met her husband when she came on holiday in the summer, hop-picking near Maidstone. She married Mr Brookfield and had lived in Maidstone ever since. She was a dressmaker and had been in my house many times to work for the previous owner.

I went into the office to look at her notes and began to understand what had happened to her. They both lived in Bower Place in a terraced house with no heating, no bathroom and a lavatory outside in the garden. They had a tin bath down in the basement where they bathed and where she did her weekly laundry. That year the winter had been very cold and they both got acute bronchitis. Without a telephone they could not call for help. The house was cold and damp and, being elderly without any treatment, pneumonia set in. They both stayed in bed and eventually her husband died beside her. She fell into unconsciousness. They had a son, married with two lovely daughters. It was her daughter-in-law who discovered what had happened and raised the alarm. Now she was in hospital and didn't know anything about the death of her husband. I went back to the ward and assured her I would do my best to help her.

"Thank you, I knew you would help me when you knew where I was. But please go to my home and tell my husband where I am.

You see, he's also been very poorly and he hasn't any idea where I am." I was speechless. How could I tell her that her dear husband was no longer at Bower Place, but lying in Sutton Cemetery? I went away with a lump in my throat.

My husband was outside the hospital waiting for me. He realised I couldn't speak, helped me into the car and tried to find out what had happened. When I managed to speak, I was able to tell him the story of poor Amanda.
"I'm very sorry to hear that. I knew her husband well. He was a very nice man and she is a very nice, London lady. I was very fond of both of them."
"She will come to our home and we will do our very best for her, like we do for all the other residents. But how can I tell her that her husband didn't leave her but he died and the funeral is all ready over?"

A week later the ambulance men brought Mrs Brookfield to 'Shalom' and we put her in Pat's old room. With a lot of tender loving care, after two weeks she began to feel better, but she never stopped asking about her husband and why he'd left her.

Over the previous few weeks I'd had a lot of meetings to attend and inspections from the social services and by that night I was very tired. After I'd put all my ladies to bed and prepared the trays for breakfast it was about ten thirty. I had a nice shower and went to bed. I thought to myself; everybody seems to have settled down so I might manage to get a couple of hours sleep.

When the bell rang I looked at the panel and saw it was Number Six, Jean Talbot, upstairs in the left wing of the house, next to the bathroom. I ran there, opened the door and realised Jean wasn't at all well.
"Jean, stay in bed. I'm going downstairs to get one of the tablets the doctor prescribed for you." While I was opening the medication cupboard Jean became very confused. She got up from her bed and went to sit in her armchair but she lost her balance and smashed her face on the side of the chair. When I returned there was blood on her face and hands, all over the chair and everywhere. It was very frightening. For a minute or two I was very disconcerted, then I pulled myself together and gave her First Aid.

Her son lived in Tonbridge Road, not very far from us at all ('Shalom' was in Tonbridge Road). I thought, her son is a doctor, he'd better come to see his mother. I telephoned and said,

"Dr Talbot, your mother has had an accident. I know it is eleven thrity at night but it is important for you to come."

"Give me five minutes and I'll be there." Just after five minutes later he was at the door. I explained what had happened. He rushed upstairs to her room and I was right behind him. He looked at his mother, turned to me and said,

"I'm sorry, Ida, but my mother is getting very confused. She can't help it. She's just had a very bad nose bleed. She may have a black eye but no more than that. She is ninety-five
e years old and things will only get worse."

"Well, doctor, I will do my best for her as long as I can and then we will see what the future offers us."

"I very much appreciate what you have done for the five years my mother has been with you. I will understand if things get too difficult for you. You know I'm here." He said goodbye to his mother and left. I sat in Jean's armchair and stayed there all night.

As time wore on Jean Talbot slowly but surely grew very ill. Her age caused a lot of confusion and I wasn't able to keep her in bed or in her chair. The law was that you must not restrain a patient in any way, so she needed a nurse at her bedside twenty-four hours a day and this was impossible in my small residential home. The time came when a decision, however painful, had to be taken. I discussed it with her son and the social worker. Again a place in Loose Valley was found and Jean was transferred there. Not long after that she passed away.

Before I took another resident, I wanted to take the ladies out. I couldn't take them on another holiday like before because they'd made me promise not to do that again. They liked 'Shalom' better than anywhere else. They weren't all the same residents but Mrs Johnson was still here and she wouldn't accept leaving 'Shalom' for another holiday in England. So then I thought, what about if I took Catherine Farmer to Rome? She kept saying that the only holiday she'd like would be to go to Rome. So I had a word with her niece, Valerie Sutton, and she said,

"If that is what my aunty wants to do, why not, as long as you will be there with her?"

"Of course, I will be there." So she arranged the flight, the hotel as well as trips to the theatre and places to visit. We talked about the posh shopping we would do (where Lina took me all those years ago). We were all excited but at the last minute Catherine wasn't well enough and everything was dropped. Catherine and I were very disappointed. Mrs Johnson said she'd like to go to Florence, where she used go with her parents, but she was too old. It would involve too much risk and responsibility, so that was out of the question.

I made a few inquiries and found out that the Hazlitt Theatre still held a weekly dance for old people so I booked for the ladies who were well enough to go. I would accompany them. I knew Dorothy had been a dancer when she was young but I never thought for a moment that at ninety-seven she would still go on the floor and dance. Well, she was one of the best! I nearly lost her to a much younger man!

Christmas 1988 was drawing near and we were very busy shopping for presents and cooking. The hospital kept ringing for me to go and assess people because they knew I had two vacancies and they wanted to get as many patients as possible out for the Christmas holiday. But I didn't mind having a couple of empty beds until the holiday was over. Social services always knew when I had a spare bed, and in their eyes to have two just wasn't allowed. The winter months were the most difficult time for hospitals, busy with young and old requiring extra beds, and with staff wanting time off for Christmas. The telephone kept ringing and I had no choice but to take more residents.

Linton Hospital urgently wanted me to help a poor gentleman. Just before Christmas there'd been a 'flu epidemic and their beds were full of poor, old people. They needed help. I didn't usually take gentlemen because my home was too small, and I felt more comfortable looking after ladies only. I went to Linton Hospital, saw the gentleman and felt sorry for him. I looked at his notes and read he was wounded in the battle of Monte Cassino. Now here he was with no relations and nobody to take care of him. I made arrangements with the sister to transfer Mr Thomas Smith to 'Shalom'. I accommodated him in Room Six, in the left wing of the house, where Jean Talbot used to be. It was just two weeks before Christmas when the ambulance men brought him.

He was overjoyed to spend the last days of his life being looked after by an Italian family in this country. It brought back old memories of that momentous battle.

"We were near Cassino," he said, "and there were ferocious attacks on the Germans. It was an appalling sight, bodies scattered everywhere, German, English, American, Italian. It was a massacre and all you could hear was a long lament. I felt someone pulling me and he put me over his shoulders. It was an Italian partisan. He rescued me and took me to a shelter where there were hundreds more, mostly women and children. The conditions there were very poor but I stayed until Monte Cassino was liberated. And now, here I am being looked after with tender, loving care by an Italian family again, in my own country!"

"Mr Smith," I said, "your story brought back to me some of my childhood memories. Now we won't talk more about those awful times. The war is long gone and we can look forward. Think, soon it will be Christmas time and we will enjoy it together."

Ivy was brought to 'Shalom' by one of her daughters who regularly visited. She was a nice lady. She and Jacqueline got on well together and enjoyed each other's company. Ivy had many daughters and they all visited frequently. One day one of them was there while her mother was eating lunch. After she'd finished the daughter said,

"Mother, have you had a good meal?"

"Perhaps one day, when you are old like me," Ivy said, "you might find a good cook like Ida to prepare your meals for you."

Christmas came and we were very busy. Some of the residents would spend Christmas Day with their families but most of them stayed in 'Shalom'. We always did our best to give the ladies and (this year) gentleman a good time. Lunch was served in the lounge and even Mrs Johnson and Sylvia joined us. Thomas sat at the table with the other residents and all my family. We all enjoyed our meal and rested afterwards. Some stayed to hear the Queen's speech in the lounge. They all liked to hear what she would say and see how well she looked.

That day everybody was excited. We had a lot of visitors. Mr and Mrs Herriott came to wish us a Merry Christmas. Mr Herriott was such a nice gentleman and he entertained us all, including Mrs Johnson, which pleased Dorothy immensely. They sang old fashioned songs, played games and nibbled food all day long so when it came to supper nobody wanted any. By about ten o'clock I was very tired. After I put everybody to bed, I was hoping for a good night's sleep, but no such luck!

At about one in the morning Thomas rang his bell. I ran upstairs, went to his room and asked,
"Thomas, are you not well?"
"I'm quite well," he said, "but I wanted to tell you what happened when I was rescued by the partisan at Monte Cassino."
"Thomas, wait and listen: that bell is there for you to call me if you are not well. What you want to tell me is not for this time of night. It is a daytime story. Please do understand, I work all day and I'm on night duty only for emergencies. Good night." I closed the door and went downstairs to bed but I felt sorry for the old man.

The holiday was over. It had been very nice for the residents but a lot pressure for me. A worrying time lay ahead. Thomas had been with us a very short time when he was diagnosed with cancer of the bladder. He didn't have long to live. I was very sorry for him. He needed urgent treatment so was readmitted to hospital and not long after he passed away.

One evening Jean and John and arrived at the door. Jean always looked beautiful and elegant but that night she seemed extra special. She was wearing a burgundy dress which suited her blonde hair very well. She came to the kitchen, we had a little conversation and she left to go to Mrs Johnson's room. After an hour or more they left Mrs Johnson, came back to the kitchen again and said,
"Mrs Johnson looks very well. We would like to hold another party for her."
"Look, Jean," I said, "it's only a month since Christmas. Can we wait for Easter? It will be spring then and a better time for her and her guests."
"Well, Ida, I do understand. You are very busy and we shall do as you say."

Some time after that I had a call from Mackenzie, sounding very upset.
"Mac, what's happened?"
"Ida, I'm very sorry but I can't come on duty for a week or two because …. I just lost my husband."
"Oh, no! Mac, don't worry, you take all the time you need and if there's anything I can do, just ask, please."
"No, Ida, there is nothing you can do. My son and daughter will do

whatever is necessary. It's just the shock. Think, Ida, now I'm a widow." Mac couldn't stop sobbing. I was very sorry for her. Poor woman, I said to myself.

There was nothing around me but sadness and death. What a life I've made for myself! I went to the kitchen and started making the morning coffee. After I'd taken it around I went back to the kitchen and called for Elisabeth and Gladys to join me for a chat. When they arrived they could see I was very upset.
"Ida, what is the matter with you?"
"It seems I've made a right mess for myself. I'm surrounded by work and death all time."
"That's not true, Ida! Look at your husband and family all around you, and all the ladies who love you. Only last year you had the Care Award, not many people have that. And besides, isn't it the job you always wanted to do? Unfortunately in every job you get ups and downs."
"Now you have both given me a lecture, I'll tell you what the news is." I took a deep breath and said, "Mac can't come to work for a couple of weeks because she's just lost her husband."
"Oh, no!" they both said, "We are very sorry for Mac. Is there anything we can do?"
"Not really, she has her children to help her."

Sylvia rang her bell and Gladys went upstairs to her.
"Gladys, tell Ida to come upstairs at once,"Sylvia said. Gladys ran downstairs and said,
"Ida, Sylvia is very agitated. She says she wants you upstairs." So I went upstairs and said,
"Sylvia, are you all right?"
"No, I'm not!"
"Why? What's happened?"
"Tony has been putting wires everywhere all morning so he can communicate with the Japanese soldiers. But of course you won't say anything to him because one of them is your boyfriend." I didn't know what to say! I looked at her and gave her a kiss, realising she was hallucinating about Japanese soldiers again. I wondered how many tales that husband of hers had told about those soldiers and how bad they must have been. If he saw her like she is now he would be very upset.
"Don't worry, Sylvia, I will do something about it. They are not always my friends, you know."
"Don't kid me! I know what you get up to all night." I went

downstairs, a bit upset and the other residents noticed. One of them said,

"Ida, you look upset. What is the matter?"

"There are some things in life you can't help," I said.

Ivy wasn't well and the doctor couldn't understand what was wrong with her so she was admitted to Maidstone Hospital. I realised it was very serious and was sorry I couldn't help her. After a short time in hospital she passed away. We were all upset. Jacqueline couldn't understand why she died, and neither could I.

To hospital again to assess another lady! This one was in Cornwall Ward. As usual I went to the sister on duty, who said,

"The social worker told me you would come today to assess this lady."

"I'm sorry if I'm a bit late but I couldn't come any earlier as I had a meeting to attend and it took longer than I expected."

"Don't worry, Louise couldn't run anyway!"

"Before I see her, may I look at her notes so I can assess her needs better?"

"Of course you can." She handed the notes to me and after a while I gave them back and she said,

"I will take you to meet Louise."

"Thank you, sister." We both went into the ward to meet her. She was in the third bed on the left, a nice, tall, good-looking woman who smiled at me.

"You see the lady smiling at you?" sister said, "She is the one who's been waiting for you." I went to her bed and said,

"I'm Ida and I'm sorry if you've been waiting long for me."

"You have a beautiful smile," she said.

"Oh!" I wasn't expecting that. I took a chair and sat by her. "How do you do?" I said and gave her my hand.

"I'm LouiseBaxter and I'm pleased to meet you." We began to talk. I thought she was very bright, the sort of person Jacqueline would like to share a room with. She was about eighty years old. She told me she'd been a smoker all her life but a couple of years ago the doctor had said, 'Louise, if you continue to smoke, you won't last long.'

"Of course, I knew the doctor was right," Louise said, "so I stopped at once. But it was too late, I already had emphysema. Now the hospital doctor has explained what emphysema really means. Do you know anything about this disease?"

"Louise, I'm not a doctor but what I learnt in hospital is that emphysema is usually part of another condition, bronchitis. The symptoms are breathlessness and blueness of the lips. Most cases are diagnosed when a chest X-ray is taken to assess the condition of the lungs. Because the blood flow through the lungs is slowed down, the lung tissue is destroyed and added strain is put on which sometimes leads to heart failure. When emphysema is established, there is little that can be done."

"You say you are not a doctor but you seem to know all about emphysema!"

"Oh, I've been a nurse for a long, long time. I have a lot of experience but I'm not a doctor. I wanted to be one but studying medicine needed many years and unfortunately I never had that privilege."

After I'd been there more than an hour I understood Louise very well and it was time for me to go.

"Well, Louise, if you like you could have two weeks convalescence in 'Shalom' and then we will take it from there. What do you think?"

"What do I think? I hear so much about your home I would like to come very much, thank you." I gave her my hand and said,

"Well, I'll be seeing you soon, Louise." As I left the hospital I remembered my husband had been waiting for me all this time, poor man. As I got near the car I saw he wasn't there after all. He'd met a friend in the car park and they were both in the hospital restaurant having a coffee and a chat. Just as I was wondering what to do they both appeared. At last I went home to see my dearest ladies.

As I came in one of my staff said,

"A lady and gentleman have been here looking for you."

"Did they tell you who they were and what they wanted?"

"No, they wouldn't say but they will ring and make an appointment with you."

"Well, that will be fine. Has everything been all right here while I've been away?"

"Oh, everything is fine!" I went around and said to the residents,

"Ladies, we are home."

"Where have you been?"

"Well, all the homes had a meeting with Ann Widdecombe at the Great Danes Hotel and after that I had to make an assessment of a lady in Maidstone Hospital. Now here I am, glad to be back with my ladies."

Soon after that I answered the telephone.

"I'm Mr Wilcox and I need to make an appointment with you."

"Yes. May I ask what the purpose is?"

"I have a dear old aunty who needs to be taken into care and your home has been highly recommended by numerous people."

"Well, I have a single bed which needs to be filled but not before the end of this month. After six o'clock my daughter Luciana will be here and she'll be glad to book you an appointment."

"That'll be fine, I will telephone later on." Mr. Wilcox rang soon after six and made an appointment.

Not long after that the telephone rang again. It was the hospital saying Mrs Baxter would be discharged the next day.

"Fine. At what time?"

"You know as well as I do the ambulance men can't ever tell you the time, but I expect it will be in the afternoon."

"That will be all right, Sister."

The day next the ambulance arrived with Mrs Baxter on board. The ambulance men stopped in front of the gate and one of them came and rang the doorbell.

"Here we are again with another lady for you to look after."

"Thank you very much," I said and they helped me bring her in. We took her to the lounge where all the other residents welcomed her to her new family. They felt we were just like a big family.

Louise Baxter settled down very well. She and Jacqueline became very good friends and all day long they engaged in long discussions about everything that was going in the world. Many of them liked to talk about the good old days, but not wartime when they had to live on food rations. They enjoyed today's food, especially Marks & Spencer food, and ate as much as they could.

About two weeks after Louise was admitted a new lady came into Room Six and joined the family at 'Shalom'. She was full of fun. Mr Wilcox and his wife also became part of 'Shalom' by visiting their aunt regularly. Their visits contributed to the nice atmosphere which all the residents and staff enjoyed during her stay with us.

CHAPTER FORTY-SIX – THE STAFF KEEP THE RESIDENTS HAPPY

The summer of 1989 was full of fun for all of us. With eight residents, my family and staff and visits from the residents' relatives every day, life was just fine. Ruth McAllen, Elisabeth Gladys Sharbsole, Ann Mackenzie, my two daughters, the occasional visit from my son and all the other visitors kept 'Shalom' very much alive. There wasn't a day without a surprise or a laugh or something happening. Mrs Johnson had her charity parties. Catherine and Dorothy kept up their non-stop chat about office life and their working days, the aristocratic people Catherine had met, her holidays abroad and their romances. Amanda Brookfield talked about the holidays she and other Londoners used to enjoy in Kent during the hop-picking season, and how they met their boyfriends there and how some of them married.

Sylvia never stopped talking about the lovely life she had when she was little, the only daughter of rich parents who spoiled her. She boasted about how well she had been educated. It all came to a brutal end when her beloved mother died of tuberculosis. Her father was young enough to marry again and finally had the son he had desired since he married his first wife. That made Sylvia very bitter and unhappy because she was no longer the apple of his eye. She grew up to rebel against him and even more against her stepmother, who had taken her mother's place in her father's life. She left home and went to live in a bed-sitting room outside Maidstone. She married a very well-off, army man. He was the source of all the stories about Japanese soldiers. They spent a wonderful time in Spain, but now that was all over. Sylvia had grown very old and had senile dementia, but underneath you could still see the lovely little girl she once was.

Then we had Dora with her stories of working in a factory canteen. In her youth she was a very beautiful girl, and when the men came for their lunch break, the things they used to say to her! It's not possible to repeat them, I can only leave it to your imaginations! Jacqueline and Louise, in Room One, were full of fun. There wasn't a dull moment and we all enjoyed a very happy and interesting time.

We went on holiday again to our apartment in Viserbella on the

Adriatic Riviera, and then travelled through Umbria and Tuscany to Rome, back to our flat, then back to our beloved residential home, where we felt we belonged with our dear old people.

The summer passed, autumn was upon us and before long Christmas would arrive. When Mrs Johnson asked me to buy fifty Christmas cards I said,

"Mrs Johnson, surely it's bit too early?"

"Not for me, Ida. I'm nearly ninety-six years old. Everyone I once knew has died. I must send these Christmas cards early as who knows what will happen to me? My dear Ida, those cards have to go to all my charities. They each contain a special gift and, no matter what happens to me, you must see they are sent to the addresses written inside."

"Of course I will, Mrs Johnson, but please don't speak like that or I'll think you are not happy with us any longer."

"Oh no, Ida. You must understand I have been very happy here with you all. You have done your best for me and I couldn't be better looked after anywhere else. But I'm nearly ninety-six and none of my family is left alive. I only have my beloved adopted granddaughter and my nephew who, as you know, has already had a heart transplant. Oh dear me, I feel my age now. That's why I had the solicitors here and asked them to put all my business affairs in order before anything happens to me." And with a smile she pointed her finger at a big chain which she asked me to put around her neck every morning and said, "That will be yours, along with many more jewels, but this precious ring on my finger belongs to my dearest Jean."

"Mrs Johnson, I just can't take any more of you talking like this. I need to go to the kitchen and make your supper. By the way, what do you want for supper?"

"You know, Ida, Joyce 'phoned to say she'll be here later to play Scrabble with me. She has always appreciated your cooking. Could we have scrambled eggs on toast with grilled tomatoes on top and for seconds an Angel Delight each? And I'm sure Joyce wouldn't mind having a glass of sherry with me."

"What about tea or coffee?"

"Later on, please, Ida."

"Of course, Mrs Johnson." All the others ladies had smoked haddock, bread and butter, grilled tomatoes, cheese soufflé and tea or coffee.

The next day Mrs Johnson didn't seem very well. I was concerned and after giving her a bed bath I telephoned the doctor.

"Dr Barr, I don't like the look of Mrs Johnson. Will you please come to visit her?" He arrived later and said,

"She is an old lady. Just do your best for as long as you can." Then he came to the kitchen, sat down and said,

"Look, Ida, I know you are very concerned about Mrs Johnson and you have every right to be. She is having continual small strokes. There isn't anything a doctor can do because her age is against her. Strokes can cause a sudden loss of function to one side of the body due to an interruption of the blood supply to part of the brain. They affect mostly old people and are very uncommon in people younger than fifty. There are three types of stroke: one is complete; one causes very serious loss of function that may be recovered slowly, but in many cases the patient will always be paralysed and need help. Mrs Johnson's one is a transient ischaemic attack which results in mild loss of function that disappears within a few minutes, but it keeps recurring and because of her age it will be unlikely that she makes a complete recovery. I must go now. Out there are many more people in the same condition as Mrs Johnson but they haven't got Ida to look after them." And he left.

For two weeks my staff, my husband and I managed to look after her the best we could. When she developed a high temperature and had difficulty breathing I telephoned the doctor again. After he'd examined her he said,

"I'm sorry, Ida, Mrs Johnson needs to go into hospital, on to strong antibiotics and on to a ventilator."

"Is there any chance she might make a full recovery?"

"There is no chance. She is too old. Even if she gets a little better it won't last long." When I heard that I was very upset. The ambulance arrived and I went with her to Chaucer Ward, which at that time was a mixed ward. I visited her every day and her condition remained very serious. Even so, she could still see the funny side of life, like one day when she noticed a man without a stitch on!

After a month the hospital called me in and the doctors and sister said,

"We are very sorry, Ida, but Mrs Johnson hasn't any chance of recovery. We can't keep her here because there's nothing more we can do for her. Before you say anything, we won't let her come back to you because she will be far too much for you to manage."

"I promised her I would never, ever send her anywhere else. I want to look after her."

"Never mind what you have promised. When you made that promise you didn't know she would be in this condition. If she were in her right mind she wouldn't demand that amount of work from you."

"What will you do for her?"

"We will find her a nursing home. You can visit her anytime, day or night, as you wish." I was very sorry. I always wanted to look after the residents until the last day of their life, but many times I had to come to terms with situations I didn't expect.

Mrs Johnson went to a nursing home, very poorly but aware of what was going on around her. One evening Jean and John visited her and then came to me. Jean always looked astonishingly beautiful but that night she was lovelier than ever. She was worried about Mrs Johnson.

"I do understand that the hospital put her there because she was too much for you to look after."

"I also understand that," I said, "but I would have done everything for her if they had let her come back to 'Shalom'."

"I know you would have done." They said goodbye and left. She was a bit tearful because she knew her beloved granny soon wouldn't be with us any longer.

The next morning at about ten the telephone rang.

"Ida, I have very bad news for you."

"Who is speaking, please?"

"I've been told to let you know that this morning at nine o'clock, after John went to work, Jean died. The domestic found her. Everything that could be done was done, but unfortunately her life couldn't be saved." I was shocked. Oh no! How could that be? For a minute I thought it was a sick joke being played on me. Then I thought who in their right mind would do that? I went around the kitchen like a headless chicken. I just couldn't take it in. Then my thoughts went to her beloved husband. He idolised his wife. Now what? Poor, poor John! And then I thought of Mrs Johnson. How was anybody going to be able to tell her that her beloved granddaughter was not with us any longer? Mrs Johnson must never know, I thought. She will find a surprise when they meet on the other side. They can both rejoice in the presence of the Lord. Mrs Johnson had been a good Christian. All her life she had worked for charities. Every week we took her to Holy Communion with Father Gibson in St Michael's Church in Tonbridge Road, where she had worshipped for many, many years.

The next day I went to visit her in the nursing home. I wasn't happy about the nursing care she received there but there was nothing I could do about it. It was out of my hands. She looked at me and realised I was very upset.

"Ida, don't get upset! I know this is not the way you would look after me. It's not your fault I've been put here. I understand why the hospital did this. I can only say 'thank you' for all your love and care over the eight years I was with you. My only hope is you will get your reward in heaven." I burst into tears. I couldn't take any more. I put my arms around her and said,

"Oh, Mrs Johnson, my heart is with you at all times. Please pray for me." We both had a good cry and I ran out of the nursing home into my husband's car. He tried to comfort me but it was no use. I couldn't take any more. By the time we reached home I realised I had no choice but to pull myself together, for the sake of my family and the ladies in my care.

About a week later the matron of the nursing home telephoned and said,

"Ida, Mrs Johnson is very poorly and she wants you and Tony beside her now." I called the staff and said,

"Elisabeth, take over in the kitchen. Tell Mac to stay here for as long as you need her. If you need more staff, Gladys is only a few doors away and you know she'll come and do her best to help. Tony and I must rush to Mrs Johnson now." Elisabeth looked shocked.

"Whatever is the matter?"

"There is no time. We must go now." We both sped to the village where the nursing home was. The matron was right. While we were there Mrs Johnson passed away very peacefully. I thought now she is in the presence of the Lord where she will meet Jean We returned to 'Shalom' and broke the news to the staff and everyone concerned.

After a week the funerals were held in St Michael's Church. I met John with his mother. He looked very poorly. My heart went out to him. He must miss Jean very much, I thought.

A little while later the nursing home rang to ask me to go and collect Mrs Johnson's property.

"I don't really need the electric armchair here. I wonder if you have any use for it?" I said.

"Oh yes, it will be good for one of my residents. What about the little antique table and the drinks cabinet?"

"John always liked those two pieces. I'll ask him if he wants them. I'm sure Mrs Johnson wouldn't mind. She liked him very much and it would please her immensely if he had them in his house."

"Right, I'll put them in store and when he's ready he can come to collect them."

"Thank you very much. If you can make any use of anything else, please do so."

"You know as well as I do, in these places you can make use of anything. Thank you for your kind offer."

Now Mrs Johnson's room at 'Shalom' needed to be cleared. There wasn't much left after her nephew had a good look around. After a couple of days he came back with Mrs Johnson's jewellery and said,

"Ida, this is your property. They were left in her will for you to have. Thank you for what you did for her. We feel you and your family are part of our family. We'll keep in contact and if any time you and your husband would like to visit we'd be honoured to have you both as guests." I thanked him saying that for the time being we were very busy, but in future we might like to accept his generous offer.

After a time I looked in the jewellery box. Among the bits and pieces there was the chain I spoke about. I put it in the rubbish bin but my husband saw me, fished it out, took it to the jeweller's shop and found it was a fine piece worth quite a lot of money. When he told me I was quite shocked.

It was time to stop grieving for Mrs Johnson and get on with the job. The hospital never stopped ringing, all because there was a vacancy in 'Shalom'. I went to assess quite a few ladies but they were too ill to be admitted to 'Shalom'. The hospital needed beds and I had a vacancy and the pressure was building up for me to take someone. One day the sister said,

"There is a lady who knew Mrs Johnson well. She has her mother here and is eager for her to come to you. What do you say?"

"Well, you know I don't take anybody without assessment."

"You'd better come to Culpepper Ward and see what you can do. We need the bed." So I went to Culpepper Ward, where the staff

recognised me and took me to this lady. I sat by her and said,
"My name is Ida, and what is your name?"
"My name is Charlotte, why do you want to know?"
"Well, I come round to talk to the patients and see if there's anything I can do for them. I try to help them if I can."
"That is very nice of you. You have a kind face."
"How long have you been here?"
"I don't remember but I think it's a long time."
"Do you want to go home?"
"Yes, but my daughter said I can't."
"Charlotte, your daughter says you can't go home because you are not well enough yet." I carried on talking to her about various things and realised she was a bit confused. She couldn't walk without a frame but nevertheless I felt sorry for her and decided to take her in. I did say that if she got worse eventually it would be necessary to find her different accommodation.

Charlotte arrived at 'Shalom' and we put her in the late Mrs Johnson's room and, like her, she stayed there all the time. Her family came to visit, including an older sister with a much younger husband (Amy and Henry). After a little while Charlotte settled down so well that she didn't realise she was in a residential home but firmly believed it was her own home and that her sister and brother-in-law lived there with her. If she needed anything she wouldn't ring the bell but, day or night, she would call,
"Amy! Henry! I need you to help me now!" The staff were marvellous with her; they always did their best for all of them.

For me it was still the job I'd always wanted to do. I felt privileged to be able to look after people in this country, where I'd been given the chance to realise my dreams. Nothing was too hard, whatever was asked of me, as long as it made the residents happy and comfortable. They had individual care at all times. We all had a lot of pleasure looking after the ladies and most of the time they were sensible. Now and then Sylvia would say her room was covered with red ants. We had to pretend to spray it with ant killer. Of course there were no ants, so we put water in an insecticide container and sprayed the room. After that she would eat the food she had asked for.

CHAPTER FORTY-SEVEN – NURSE MAC GOES ON A CRUISE

In 1990 the summer holiday season was approaching when Mackenzie said,

"Ida, you know I have booked a cruise for my holiday."

"Yes, Mac, I know. But I've noticed that you don't look as well as you usually do. Before you embark on this adventure, you should go for a check up with your doctor to make sure your health can take the strain of getting on and off a ship for two weeks."

"After the death of my husband, I've not been the same the person. But I think this trip will do me the world of good and I need a change."

"Please see the doctor and see what he says, then you can do what you like. But I'm concerned about you."

"I'm concerned about you, too. The strain of running a home is beginning to make a mark on you."

Dora's body was riddled with osteoarthritis, a degenerative disease affecting the protective, shock-absorbing cartilage between the bones of the joints. It affects more women than men and is very painful. Deformities appear in the hips, knees, spine and fingers. Dora began to move about with more and more difficulty. I administered the painkillers the doctor prescribed but with little effect. It upset me to see her suffering. It became impossible to move her about, and she had to stay in her own bedroom. That wasn't Dora; she liked company, she lived a very social life and being shut in a room wasn't what she enjoyed. She needed other people. Her beloved nephew and his wife did all they could, visiting her as much as possible, but it wasn't enough for her. She needed much more stimulation for her brain, and lacking that made her begin to hallucinate. She used see men in her room threatening to take advantage of her vulnerable condition.

"Ida," she said, "you must do something about this. It's not nice at my age. It's your job to call the police and get these men arrested."

"Dora, who are these men? Can you point them out to me?"

"Yes, they come from the club down the road. When the club closes at eleven o'clock, instead of going home they come here and verbally and physically abuse me."

"How that can be?" I said, "All the doors are closed. Nobody can ever get in here without me opening the door."

"They don't come through the door, they come through the windows."

"But the windows are double glazed and I make sure they are locked every night."

"That doesn't matter, they still get in through the glass." One time she said,

"Do you know pigs came flying into my bed last night?" I was very sorry to see her afflicted with such pain and so tormented by senile dementia, like Sylvia with the Japanese soldiers in her cupboard and the red ants. Yes, the strain did begin to affect my health.

"Yes, Mac," I said, "the job I love is beginning to have an effect on my health."

"It's about time you did something to help Dora." Mac said, "Why don't you tell Barry and his wife that their aunt needs to be somewhere downstairs with more people around, and with more nurses who can lift her in and out of bed. You can't do it all by yourself, it is not good for you or her.

"Barry and his wife wouldn't like it. They know their aunt has been happy here and besides they'll have to look for somewhere else and that it isn't easy. I haven't the courage to break the news to them. If one of the rooms downstairs came free, that would resolve the problem."

"But you know that's impossible for the time being."

"You're right. I do have to speak to them, for Dora's sake."

"You work night and day. It's like having a dog and barking yourself! Do you want Elisabeth or me to speak to them and explain the situation?"

"No, no, I must do that myself. I took the responsibility and I must speak to the people concerned when it comes to the wellbeing of the residents."

"You need more time for yourself, Ida."

"But can't you understand? Finding people like you and Elisabeth and Gladys is not easy. When we go on holiday, Elisabeth works like I do, night and day, until we come back. Gladys is always at hand. I know that the ladies of 'Shalom' are well looked after by all of you. That is what matters to me more than anything else. Mac, I hope you feel well enough to go and have a nice holiday."

A month later, Mackenzie left Maidstone for Portsmouth where she boarded a cruise ship to sail around Europe. Two days later, I received a telephone call from her daughter.

"Mrs Maddalena, I'm Ann Mackenzie's daughter and I have very bad news. My mother died at two o'clock this morning." For a minute I thought it was a joke.

"But your mother is on holiday on a ship," I said.

"They are the people who 'phoned me and told me."

"And now what will happen? When will the funeral be?"

"Not for two weeks. They will keep her body on board in a special, cool place until they finish the journey. In the meantime, we will arrange the funeral. She will be buried with our father in Maidstone Cemetery."

That did upset me. She wasn't just someone who worked for me. I got to know her in Linton Hospital in 1959. We worked together, enjoyed looking after people and had so much in common. Now what would I do without her? But I had no time to grieve. I had to get on with the job. She would have understood.

I had a word with Barry and Cathy about their aunt's condition but they didn't want to move her anywhere else. They thought if they bought her a television she would get better but that proved not to be the case. They didn't want to move her and neither did I, but it was necessary for Dora to be with other people. After a couple of weeks she was moved to another home where that was possible.

The rumours soon went round that I had a vacancy and the telephone never stopped ringing, but I had Mackenzie's funeral on my mind and wasn't interested in the vacancy. After the funeral I was left with only the memory of the friendship I once had.

I needed another nurse to take her place. I spread the word around and before long I found one. Her name was Mary Pilkington and she worked the same hours as Mackenzie. I thanked God because Mary was also a good nurse who loved looking after the ladies. She was very much loved by the residents when they got to know her.

The telephone kept on ringing about taking a new resident. There was a lady just down the road in need of help. I thought I would be doing a good deed if I took her in. Most of the people in my home were privately funded, but it made no difference to me as I charged the same money to the social security, who paid for non-private people. In 'Shalom' everybody was treated the same, whatever their background. Once they joined us we did the utmost to see they were happy and comfortable in every way.

The new resident was Georgina Parkinson. There was nothing much wrong with her, but she was old, lonely and had nowhere to live. Her son had died and left some grandchildren but they didn't want anything to do with her. We tried hard to get them interested in their grandmother but for some unknown reason they didn't want to know. She preferred to stay in her room and liked to read a lot. Maidstone Library supplied and delivered books to our home and every three months renewed them. She also liked watching the television and settled in quite well. Maybe because she had no friends or relations she became very attached to me. If she knew I wasn't in, she would play the staff up. I took her out to the shops and for walks wherever I could, but when I was attending hospital meetings it was impossible to take her with me. Once she threw herself on the floor and dislocated her shoulder. I had to take her to casualty and it pleased her to have my undivided attention. But I had another seven people who also needed my attention, even more than she did.

In Room One were Jacqueline and Louise, bless her heart, didn't ask for anything. So long as you washed her properly, made her comfortable and gave her the food she liked, she was happy to sit and talk to other residents. Her daughter Maureen and her husband came as often as they could. Louise, as I said before, suffered from emphysema and, as time passed, found it more and more difficult to breathe. I had to administer oxygen from a big bottle beside her bed, supplied by the hospital. She was very happy to chat all day long, when she could.

In Room Two was Sylvia who needed full-time attention. The hallucinations never left her, but she was easy to look after. After you'd washed her all over, did what was needed and let her eat the food she'd asked for, she wasn't any bother. She kept us in stitches with the things she used tell her visitors. Sometimes the doctors came into the kitchen in fits of laughter about what Sylvia had told them about me and the Japanese soldiers in the cupboard. I didn't mind, as long as she was happy that was all I cared about.

In Room Three were Catherine and Dorothy who both needed attention at all times. Catherine had been with us a long time and enjoyed the loving and care she received. She was easy to look after her. Dorothy loved me very much. Sometimes she would be difficult with a member of the staff after breakfast when it was washing time. Then I would go upstairs and begin a conversation about her past and take her mind back. She would go back in time so that she didn't realise I was bathing her. Because of her dry skin I had to apply aqueous cream for tropical use to soothe it. After bathing, as she dressed and the conversation about the past was almost finished, she would say,

"Ida, why is it that when I've had a long chat with you I feel so much better?" What could I say? Because I've given you a good wash but you didn't realise it because you were so busy telling me about Colonel Winch and how wonderful he was? No, of course not! I would just give her a big kiss and say,

"I'm pleased you're feeling better."

Room Four was where Amanda was. She was the Londoner that fell in love while hop-picking in the summer holidays. She needed a lot of attention but was easy to look after. Room Five was Charlotte Gates, always calling for her sister and brother-in-law because she thought she was in her own home. This was the picture of my residential home in 1990.

Life was active: we had visits nearly every day, we took out those residents who were able and wanted to come, we had social services come to inspect us. They never found anything to complain about but now and then wanted me to change the design of the house, even though they registered it how it was. They never found any trouble. Some of them were very professional and some of them didn't appear to know what they were talking about. We had fire drills and everything was kept according to the law. In all that time we never had any complaints and the doctors who visited always complimented us on the way we looked after the residents in our care.

CHAPTER FORTY-EIGHT – THE YEARS MADE THEIR MARK

Time passed by and the years made their mark on me and the staff and residents. Charlotte complained of tummy trouble all the time so we took her to hospital for investigations but the results were always the same. The doctors said,
"Ida, we can't find anything to explain her pains." The poor lady became more distressed than ever and it was difficult for me to continue to care for her. It was hard to talk to her son about his mother's worsening condition and explain that she needed to go into a nursing home. It didn't go down well with her son, who said,
"But my mother is very happy with you here. I can't see why she should move."
"Yes, your mother is very happy but she is not well and I find it very difficult to look after her. You see, Sir, my home is only small and that is the way I like it. But the drawback is that when a resident needs full-time attention and I can't leave them even for a minute, we can't cope. I would like to look after all my residents from the time they come in until the day they are no longer here, but now and then I have to take very difficult decisions for their own safety."
He began to come to his senses and to understand that I ran a residential home and could not look after people like a nursing home could. Sometimes I already did take on more than I could manage by myself at night time. Charlotte was moved into Pilgrim's Way Nursing Home, where Ella was. I went to see her and Ella a couple of times. They both asked me if I could take them back to 'Shalom' and it distressed me that I couldn't help them any longer.

In the summer of 1993 a friend of mine said,
"When you have a vacancy, let me know. I really need your help."
"Actually I have one now. Why do you ask?"
"My friend is seventy eight and she's in a home she doesn't like very much."
"What is wrong with your friend?"
"She suffers from Parkinson's Disease."
"Joan, I've just had to send a resident to a nursing home because she was too much for me, and now you want me to take on someone in even greater need!"
"I know what you're trying to say, but Cilla is my friend. She does suffer from Parkinson's Disease but drugs control it and I can assure you she is very sensible and wouldn't call you unless it was

absolutely necessary. She told me she would like to spend the rest of her life in 'Shalom'."

"You know I don't take anybody in unless I assess their needs to see if I'm able to meet them. Take me to see her." She took me to the home, pointed her out to me and said,

"Now I will introduce you to her." As we approached Cilla, her face lit up and she said,

"Joan, is this the lady from 'Shalom'?"

"Cilla, how did you guess?"

"She has a kind face, just like I always imagined!"

"I'm pleased to meet you, Cilla," I said.

"I've been looking forward to this. I've heard so much about your home."

"I've been looking around here," I said, "and I can see that this is a big home with all the amenities."

"Yes, it's big, it's a big business. Some of the people who run these homes haven't any feeling for the residents. To them it's just a money-maker. You can't get attached to any of the staff because they're continually changing."

"Ida, I'll leave you with Cilla." Joan said, "I'll just go outside for a cigarette so you can have time together."

"Well, Cilla, tell me something about your life and how you see your future."

"I had a very important job which I enjoyed until I was struck with this illness. I'd been in my own home as long as I could and eventually my relatives brought me here. Here we are just a number, you don't feel as if you are a person, just a number, and the food is nothing to speak about."

"Cilla, you said, 'since you had been struck by the illness'. In what way does it affect you?"

"I was diagnosed with Parkinson's Disease when I was about fifty-eight, just before I retired. Now it's controlled by drugs."

I had a long chat to Cilla before Joan came back. My feelings were mixed. I saw a poor old lady sitting in a chair with no hope whatever of a better future. Parkinson's Disease affects the nerves and muscles causing stiffness and tremors which get progressively worse. The first symptoms are in the hands, arms and the legs. I could see she'd already had it for quite a number of years. She was confined to a wheelchair and I could see she was uncomfortable. I realised she was very poorly and in need of help.

For a moment my mind went back to when I lived in Bearsted and I helped out at the Cheshire Home in Mote Park where there were many people like Cilla, some with Parkinson's Disease and many more with Multiple Sclerosis. One of them was also called Cilla. I'd met her first in Linton Hospital. The residents in the Cheshire Home had all kinds of genetic and incurable diseases but they were well looked after. They had the best food, donated by Marks & Spencer and other shops around the town, and plenty of nurses to help make their lives comfortable in every possible way. They had entertainers from all over the country, including Maidstone Theatre. There were cheese and wine parties to raise money for the Cheshire Homes.

I can't forget one occasion when I was helping at one of these parties. To be sociable I had a glass wine. I'd never drunk since I left Italy and it affected me very badly. I felt very tired and later on, when I put Cilla to bed, I fell asleep on her bed beside her! Because she wasn't able to speak or move, she couldn't raise the alarm. When I didn't arrive home, my husband came to find out what had happened to me. Nobody knew and a search party went looking for me all around the park and beyond. Later on I woke up and found myself beside poor Cilla. I got up and looked at my watch: it was three am. I ran out of the room and called for the night nurse. Everybody was happy to know I was safe but I felt very embarrassed by the incident and the trouble I caused.

What was most amazing how well they were looked after in the Cheshire Home. They lived almost happy lives. Now I looked at poor, dear Cilla, so ill and suffering neglect. While I had this thought in my mind, Joan came in.
"Sorry I took such a long time but while I was smoking my cigarette one of the carers came out and we had a long chat."
"Just as well because I also had a long chat with Cilla and told her we would see each other again." Joan and I went back to 'Shalom' and she said,
"Now you have seen Cilla, what do you think?"
"Cilla is very poorly. I don't think she has years to live, but months. I will take her into my care and try to give her tender, loving care for the rest of her time. I would like her to go to a Cheshire Home but they don't take people over sixty."
"Bless you, Ida, for having such a kind heart. Cilla will be happy."
Two weeks later Cilla arrived at 'Shalom'. She stayed in her room and we lavished all the loving care on her that was possible (the same as all the other residents).

The life I'd made for myself was most enjoyable but at the same time the pressure was building up. It began to affect my health.

One Sunday Cilla was watching the church service on television, as usual. I went in and waited until it was finished.

"Cilla, what do you think? Shall I take you in the shower and then make you comfortable? I can make you a nice cup of coffee and then I'll get on with the Sunday roast."

"Ida, I'm ready when you are." I went to call Elisabeth to help me put Cilla in her wheelchair. As we both returned to her room Elisabeth said,

"Here I am, Cilla. Ida's going to give you a lovely shower and you'll feel like a new woman."

"Yes, I will feel better when it's over." We put her in the wheelchair and while I was wheeling her into the shower, she just passed away. It was a tremendous shock for all the staff. The doctor said she died from heart failure. It was very sad but we all knew she was very poorly. I felt I had given her, in her last few months, love and comfort like that in the Cheshire Home.

It was our custom to decorate each room every time it became empty so it would be nice and fresh for the next resident.

As I said, Louise was getting more and more breathless and became more dependent on oxygen. One winter evening, before I started putting the ladies to bed, I thought it was necessary to administer oxygen to Louise who appeared to need it urgently. First I put her nightdress on her, let her sit up in her bed with pillows behind her and made sure she was comfortable.

"Louise, I'm putting the big bottle of oxygen beside your bed. I'll put the mask on you and turn it on for ten minutes. I'll put the timer on and when it rings the gas will turn off automatically. I'll give you the bell and if for any reason you need me during the next ten minutes, ring it and I will come immediately. Now I'm just going upstairs to Sylvia to see if she is still in bed." As I went upstairs I heard a noise loud enough to frighten anybody. I ran back down straight into Louise's room. She had knocked the two big bottles of oxygen together and it looked to me as if she was having a heart attack. I called Tony to stay with Louise while I rang for the duty doctor.

"Doctor, I have a patient who urgently needs your assistance."

"I can't come to see your old lady. Wait until tomorrow and then you can call her own doctor."

"She can't wait for her own doctor, she needs a doctor now! Tomorrow may be too late."

"I have too much on and I can't come."

"Right, Doctor, I've done my duty. If anything happens to this lady tonight, you'll be responsible." He put the telephone down.

I called for Susanna to come and help to put the ladies to bed while I kept a close eye on Louise. By about ten o'clock Susanna had finished, with the help of my husband, and she came into Louise's room.

"Ida, all the ladies have had their night time drinks and we've put them all to bed. Everyone seems well."

"Thank you, Susanna, for coming in at such short notice."

"You know I don't mind giving you a hand when you need me. Good night, Tony. Good night, Ida."

About half an hour later the doorbell rang. I was a bit worried about opening the door at that time of night. I put the chain up and opened it a crack. In the shaft of light I could see a very tall man, wearing what looked like dirty clothes.

"Who are you and what do you want?"

"I'm the duty doctor. You called me about three hours ago." I was surprised. The way he was dressed he didn't look as if he was a doctor. I let him in. As soon as he went into Louise's room, before he got near her bed, he said,

"Ah, you are a smoker! We have to pay the price for people like you. Goodbye." Before I could say a word, he was out of the door, into his car and away. I was upset. He had no right to treat a poor, ill lady like that, I thought. I went back to her room and realised Louise was having a heart attack. I immediately called 999 for an ambulance to take her to Maidstone Hospital. She was in shock. She had severe, constricting pain in her chest, shortness of breath, and her pulse was very irregular. I began to give her chest compression and mouth-to-mouth resuscitation. When the ambulance arrived they took her but unfortunately she died just as we reached the hospital. Inside the hospital they did all they could, but it was too late. I was very upset. I had to make a report and in it I complained about the way the duty doctor had behaved towards the patient and I referred him to the medical committee. It took me a long time before I could come to terms with what happened to Louise.

The telephone kept ringing and I had to make a decision about Room Six. A little lady was recommended to me who I thought would be the next resident. Her name was Doreen Slater. She was very old and wasn't able to look after herself. She had a nice daughter who had done the best for her mother. She'd got someone to help to look after her mother, but Doreen needed much more than that. She needed twenty-four hour care and the daughter just couldn't manage it. But, like Sylvia, Doreen wanted people she knew around her. She asked Oriole to come in to help her and she also wanted her own hairdresser. We already had two hairdressers visiting 'Shalom', one for the late Mrs Johnson and another for all the other ladies. But Doreen wanted her own private hairdresser.

She was very happy in her way. She'd never been in hospital in her life but she did appreciate the care we gave and the companionship of the other residents. Unlike the other inhabitants of that room before her, she would come out, sit at the table and enjoy her food and surroundings. She was much loved by everybody. Her daughter and son-in-law came as often as they could and were happy to see their mother well looked after.

It was time to put someone in Louise's bedroom. Jacqueline needed a companion. The social worker said,
"Mrs Maddalena, I have the right lady for you. She would suit that room beautifully." For the first time I didn't follow the usual routine of assessing a future resident before she came in. It turned out to be a bit of a distraction for our happy home. I had never met a character like this before, except in Oakwood Hospital where we were well equipped to care for such people.

Her name was Bertha. The war was nearly fifty five years ago but in her mind the Germans were still dropping bombs on British soil. She was very distracted and it was a job to maintain the lovely atmosphere we'd always enjoyed. At times it was good entertainment for us. One day Mary said,
"I can't see Bertha anywhere." We searched the house but Bertha wasn't anywhere to be seen. I told Tony to go down Tonbridge Road to look for her and I ran down Bower Lane. Tonbridge Road was the main road and I was worried because many accidents happened on it. We were responsible for Bertha and something like this had never happened before. It put immense pressure on me. Bertha couldn't be found anywhere. I decided to ask the police to look for her. It was lunchtime and I was laying the table when I heard a voice from under the table say,

"Ida, come down. There's room for you." I lifted the tablecloth and there was Bertha, taking refuge from Second World War bombs that had ended at the beginning of May 1945!

Life at 'Shalom' continued to be very busy. Georgina always had her head in a book. She would still become very difficult if she knew I wasn't in. She would throw herself on the floor and cause herself injuries. What with the suffering she went through and the visits in and out of hospital, it became an embarrassment for her and for me. I tried everything to distract her from this attention seeking. She was a good artist so, in addition to the occupational therapist, I employed another lady to come in and have discussions about painting. She was interested in taking her to an adult education centre and we hoped that would provide her with a different outlook.

Eventually I found out why she behaved in that way. She had had a son who died when he was in his early fifties and that upset her so much the only thing she wanted to do was die so she could be with him. Now I had taken her son's place and if I wasn't there, she could see no reason to live.

Well, with Bertha living in wartime, and Sylvia with Japanese soldiers in her cupboard and red ants all over her floor, there was never a dull moment! Sometimes we had a lot of fun, sometimes life was very busy, and sometimes very sad. Often I lost a best friend.

If Bertha was in her right mind, she would say at lunch time,
"I've been a cook all my life but the best food I've ever eaten is what Ida cooks." or "This food is so good I must eat it, even though it's too much for me. It just tastes too delicious to leave on the plate."

Doreen had never been ill in her life, but now she wasn't well. Her doctor, Dr Brawn, said,
"This lady has been my patient for a good many years and I've never needed to give her tablets. Now she is old and I'm afraid she is ill and, because she's never felt like that before, at times she can be very difficult."
"Poor Ivy! She is such a nice little lady it is a pity she isn't well." I said.
"Yes, that's so, but we all have to die sometime. Doreen has been

blessed with good health in her long life. As you know, some of us have to go through a lot of pain before we die."

One day Doreen wasn't feeling well. The incident with Bertha and the table must have played in her mind. Lesley, a friend of the home who used to visit Janet one of my first residents, knocked at the door. I asked her into the kitchen and sat her down.
"Lesley, I'm sorry, today the road is very noisy."
"Ida, it's not the road, it is inside here," she said, "It sounds like it's coming from Room Six." We ran to the room and found Doreen shouting,
"The doctor said I'll soon be dead, but come and tell him he is wrong!" It took a long time to calm her down.
"Lesley, I'm very sorry. Doreen must have heard what her doctor said."

The time came when Doreen was too ill and all the love and care didn't help any more. Dr Brawn came nearly every day but there was little anybody could do. Eventually she passed away very peacefully. Again, as always, we all were very upset.

A couple of weeks passed and a voice on the telephone said,
"I'm Derek Hurdle and I want to speak to Mrs Maddalena."
"Derek, I'm Ida Maddalena. What can I do for you? By the way, how is Mrs Hurdle?"
"That's what I have to discuss. When can I see you?"
"Come tomorrow about eleven am, will you?" The next day just about eleven he arrived and said,
"Ida, you know my mum better than anybody else. It's true you have been very busy and she's not been well, so you haven't able to see one another. That's what I wanted to tell you: she is not well at all and she needs care. Who could be better than you? You've known each other for so long. I know she's always liked you. At one time she did jobs for you. Now you can do one for her."
"Derek, your mother has been a very dear friend to me, and to my parents. Whatever she needs I will be more than happy to look after her. Luckily I have just the room for her. She can come for a holiday or whatever she likes."
"Wait till I go home and tell her! She'll be very pleased to hear this news."

He left and the staff came in for coffee.

"Ida," they said, "you look very happy. Have you won the pools?"

"No! Mrs Pamela Hurdle has been a good friend of mine. When I needed her she was always there for me and my parents. I've known her for years, since I worked in the hospital and she was the domestic in the same ward. She is coming to 'Shalom'."

My husband got to know her husband and they become good friends. They had a lot in common. They both repaired watches. One day in hospital while we were having our lunch break I said to Mrs Hurdle,

"I do not know what to make of my husband. When he comes home from work, after he has his tea, he disappears and comes back much later in the evening."

"Don't you know?"

"Mrs Hurdle, what should I know?"

"He comes to see my husband and they spend long hours together repairing watches."

"Now I understand! For a while I've been thinking he has a lady somewhere."

"You should know your husband better than that!"

When my dad was ill and my husband was working all hours of the day, Mrs Hurdle was there for me and my parents. She came and picked my dad up to take him to hospital every time he had an appointment with the doctor.

She also gave lifts to my daughter Stella who went to school at Benenden, near Tenterden. It was the most expensive school in the country and only very rich people could afford to go there. Stella used to go to Maidstone Grammar School for Girls and was studying languages – French, German and Italian - but because the Grammar School didn't do Italian and Benenden did, I had no choice but to send her there. The day Stella had to sit Italian exams Mrs Hurdle wasn't well enough to take her in. I didn't know Mrs Hurdle wasn't well. A friend of her daughter had a Rag-and-bone business and she asked him to take Stella to Benenden instead. So on Monday morning a scruffy van stopped near 'Shalom'. I thought it must be one of the gypsies that come round to ask if you've got any rubbish for sale, but no. A man came to the door and said,

"Hello, madam. I believe you have a daughter who goes to the posh school where Princess Anne went."

"Yes, and what is that to do with you?"

"It's lot to do with me. Mrs Hurdle is not well and there is no taxi available to take you daughter there. I'm the last resort to make sure she gets to her exam. After all, it's important for her to get there, how she travels doesn't really matter."

"Elisabeth! Gladys! Mary!" I said, "A change of plan for today! I will explain it all to you later on. Do the best you can, as always, and I will see you later." Stella and I jumped into the scruffy trailer and off we went. Bumpety bump!

We were nearly there when I said to the driver,

"Look, stop here! Here is some money. Buy yourself something to eat. Come back here in three hours time, not a minute before. We're going to walk to the school."

"No, no! I will take you right to the front of the school."

"That is absolutely impossible."

"Why is it impossible?"

"Can't you understand? This is a very posh school. What will all the girls say when they see Stella arrive in a scruffy van?"

"That it is different from their Rolls Royces, of course. But the important thing is that she is there in time for her exam."

"She would be laughed at all day long." At last he understood that Stella would be embarrassed by the van. We walked for about ten minutes and arrived with all the posh girls in their graduation gowns.

It was a very big, old mansion with large windows at the front like Tudor houses, and an oak door something like 'Shalom' but much larger and beautifully carved. We went into an enormous hall with a very, very long staircase. Stella mingled with the other girls and went up it. One of the staff showed me to the waiting room. The walls were decorated with carved wooden panels. There was a big table in the middle with chairs around it. There were magazines and later on a member of the staff brought me coffee and biscuits.

Three hours later Stella finished her exam and we said goodbye to the head mistress. After ten minutes walk we found the Rag-and-bone man waiting for us. A rough ride home and then back among the people we loved. I paid the man well and thanked him for taking us, even if it was in a trailer full of old scrap metal. In the end what was important was that Stella took her exam. When I told the staff and residents about the Rag-and-bone van they all had a good laugh.

"It is all right for you to laugh, but you don't know how

embarrassing it would have been if the snobby girls had seen us arrive in the Rag-and-bone van."

CHAPTER FORTY-NINE – OUR DEAR FRIEND MRS HURDLE

Mrs Hurdle came for two weeks convalescence to our home. I said to Derek,
"Your mother has been and still is a dear friend to us. She helped my family when I needed it most and now it's my turn to help her as much as I can. She can stay here for two weeks on the house and any time she needs more rest she will always be welcome." After two weeks she said,
"Derek, I can't manage in my own home by myself. If you and Zoe don't mind, I would rather stay here with Ida and Tony." We felt privileged to have Mrs Hurdle with us and did our best for her wellbeing, as we did for all the residents in our house.

Now I was fifty-eight years old and began to feel unwell. I realised my heart wasn't what it should be. Since the death of my dear friend Ann Mackenzie I hadn't ever felt well. Things started to get worse and I knew it. My heart was strong when I took on my responsibilities and I was so happy in what I was doing and achieving. The satisfaction of looking after people was great and it fulfilled my life's ambition. I was prepared to work at all costs.

Amanda became unwell. It didn't matter how much the doctor tried to help her – and he did try his best – her illness didn't give in. Dr Minnie said,
"This lady has lasted so long because you look after so her well. But now she's beginning to get very poorly and I'm afraid it doesn't matter what we do, we can't help her any longer."
"What is the matter with her?" I asked.
"I think you know what the matter with her is, and you also know we've done what we can for her. I'm here if you need me at any time. In the meantime, I'll give you some medication you can administer to make her comfortable."
"Thank you, doctor."

I was on duty night and day with little rest. Amanda needed twenty-four hour nursing. She was very appreciative and, like Aileen Brown she told me how God would bless me for my work and dedication. She surprised us, lasting longer than the doctor expected. She continued to be thankful for the care she received and even kept her sense of humour.

Most of the time I worked long hours without any break and the stress began to show on my face. Catherine understood and would get upset. I would take a chair, sit by her and ask,
"Catherine , tell me why you are upset?"
"Ida, my heart is crying for you. I have been here a long time, nearly since you opened, and I can see you are not as well as you make us believe. You work far too much, harder than your health can take."
"Catherine ," I said, "you must not worry about me. I will be all right as long you are all right."

Georgina always played up when she thought I was too busy looking after other people and not her. She would seek my attention and try to cause herself some kind of injury. At times she was very difficult to manage but with the help of the staff we tried our best.

Sylvia was pampered by Ruth and the rest of the staff. She kept everybody in stitches with her stories about me and the Japanese soldiers, and many more. She kept the staff well entertained. Sometimes I'd walk into her room and she'd say,
"Oh, Ida, I know what you've been up to!"
"If you do, Sylvia, please tell me!"
"I can't tell you because you know it is too embarrassing for me to talk about such things."
"Well, Sylvia, it doesn't matter if you can't tell me, as long you tell the doctor when he comes to see you."
"Oh, I will, it's much easier to tell the doctor in confidence." I would go downstairs and have a good laugh with the other members of staff.

Mrs Hurdle settled in well in her room. She liked to be with the other residents and enjoyed the homely atmosphere. Of course the home wasn't new to her. She had been many times before I opened as a residential home and many times since. Now she was one of us and enjoyed it.

Bertha amused Mrs Hurdle a great deal with the things she used to say and do. One day Mrs Hurdle said,
"Ida, don't you think Bertha is very clever?"
"In her time she was, yes. I don't think she is very silly now, it is just old age that makes her mind play up."
"All this nonsense about the war, I think she makes it up for

something to say."

"It is a lot to make up. If she was a bit more sensible, I do not know what we would know about Bertha."

"One thing is that she does keep us all amused," said Mrs Hurdle and the other ladies laughed. Jacqueline said,

"She is always on the move. That's how she can eat so much and still keep her figure."

"Jacqueline," I said, "it's a nice day today. Would you like to go and sit in the garden with Mrs Hurdle, Dorothy and Catherine ?"

"Yes, please, but I think my daughter and son-in-law will be visiting."

"That doesn't matter, you can come back inside then if you want to. In the meantime you can sit with the other ladies and play games out there. Later on I'll bring tea and sponge cake out to you."

"And me?" said Bertha.

"Yes, Bertha," Jacqueline said, "as long as you behave yourself."

"It's not me that has to behave! It's the soldiers who should behave themselves. I think they should fight among themselves. Why should we pay the price of their war games?"

"At last Bertha has said something sensible," they all said.

My husband and I took five ladies outside. They all sat in garden chairs and played games on a garden table, supervised by Gladys, who also served them tea and cakes.

I went upstairs to have a look at poor Amanda. At last she was having some rest.   The medication the doctor had prescribed seemed to do some good. I went into Sylvia's room and she said,

"Ida, for supper tonight I want a Spanish omelette and a *shambosi*."

"What is that? And what is a *shambosi*?"

"A very thick omelette cooked with plenty of sausage, and *shambosi* is a chocolate mousse."

"But a thick omelette with sausage would be too heavy for you in the evening. I don't mind making it for you at lunchtime but not at night."

"All right, make me an English omelette then, and a chocolate mousse."

"I'll make you a cheese omelette with grilled tomatoes, bread and butter and a chocolate mousse, is that all right?"

"Fine, I look forward to it. I'm sure it will be very nice," she said. This surprised me and then I thought she had forgotten she was now an old lady and was remembering the days she spent with her beloved husband in Spain. They must have had very happy times there. I felt very sorry for her.

Amanda had been very poorly for the last two months. She was a wonderful woman and never complained. Her daughter-in-law and her two lovely granddaughters had just visited and you could see on her face how pleased she was. A few hours after they left, Amanda passed away very peacefully. We all loved her and she was very sadly missed.

Catherine was now very old and wasn't able to come down any more. She was confined to the small sitting room next to her bedroom where she had her own television. She was well looked after there. Elisabeth made sure she had every attention at all times.

Often we took the opportunity to give comfort to people in the neighbourhood by offering respite care if they needed to go on holiday. We had a room to spare and always obliged them if they wanted to leave their relatives in our care while they were away, as we had done for Mrs Jones, Mrs Roger, and others.

Jane (had joined us as a part-time domestic helper).
"Ida," she said, "Room Four is empty. I know a lady in need of help. I wonder if we can do something for her."
"Jane, I'm not feeling very well. I'd like to slow down for the time being and keep that room for short stays. It is less responsibility than our long term commitments to permanent residents. "Please, Ida, you can do that in the future, but for now please help this poor lady."
"All right, Jane, tell your friend I'd like to have a meeting to discuss the situation with them."

A few days later the lady's family came. They were all very nice people and I asked them to bring their mother to 'Shalom' for assessment. She appeared very nice but in need of care. Her name was Janet and I believe she had grown up children, but they all lived away it was impossible for them to look after their mother. A week later Janet settled in with us and it pleased Jane to see that she had been helped. The family visited her regularly and seemed very close.

After a few months, I realised Janet was very poorly. Not feeling well myself, I knew what it was like to be ill. With the help of the staff we did the best we could for her. One day I went in her room and found she was very ill and telephoned for the doctor.

"Doctor, Mrs Janet Baily is not well and requires your assistance immediately." I went back upstairs to her room to look after her and Mary brought the doctor up when he arrived.

"Ida, what is the problem?" he said.

"She is complaining of severe and constricting pain in the chest, sometimes radiating down her left arm and up to her neck, shortness of the breath, and a weak and irregular pulse." He examined her and said,

"You are right. This lady is ill and needs hospital attention. I will call the ambulance now and it will be here in a few minutes." He then said goodbye and left. Not long after, the ambulance arrived and took Janet to hospital. I went with her. She was admitted to an upstairs ward and I went home to inform the relatives. I went every day to see her and she seemed to get better.

"I would like to come back to 'Shalom'," she said, "because I feel much better, if you and your staff can look after me."

"Janet I'll go and see what the doctor says about you coming home." After a long wait at last I saw the doctor who'd been looking after her.

"May feel better," he said, "but she isn't better. There need to be more investigations done."

"Janet," I told her, "the doctor said you have to be here for a few more days."

The family said, "she should never have gone to hospital. She was better off in your home."

"It wasn't my decision," I explained, "it was the doctor's. If I hadn't called the doctor and something had happened to your mother, then what?" After a few days, the hospital telephoned me to say Janet had passed away with heart failure. It was a sad time for me her and her poor family. It seemed to me most of my life I loved people and then had to bury them.

I began to feel more and more ill and it worried me immensely because I was responsible for other people's lives. I decided that when someone died I wouldn't replace them any more, because old people need loving care and if I wasn't able to look after them properly, what was the point? Time was passing by and I felt lifeless. I realised why when I took my pulse I found it was very irregular and slow.

When I first started the old people's home, I had taken out medical insurance with BUPA because my responsibilities meant that I couldn't afford to be ill and away from the job I loved. It was a good thing because I didn't have to wait long to see a heart specialist, Dr Holt. After the investigations were done she said,

"Mrs Maddalena, you need a pacemaker. It will set your heart rate, speeding it up during exertion and slowing it down during sleep. Your natural stimulation is impaired and your heart's pumping action has slowed down, which is why you need an artificial pacemaker. Drugs can't control it and there is nothing much else we can do. In a couple of days you will feel much better." In fact after the operation I did feel much better.

Now Catherine was getting very ill. She had been in 'Shalom' for ten years and was very old. All the care and attention couldn't take away the years. Like the ladies before her, she was very appreciative of what I had done for her. She thanked me. I called the doctor to see what else could be done for her. Dr Christmas came and said,

"We can't do very much more for her."

"Do you think she will be better cared for in hospital?"

"Certainly not! You give your residents first class nursing! She will never be cared for better anywhere else. Catherine knows that and I've made sure she won't go anywhere else. Goodbye for now." I went to the door to see him out and then back upstairs again to Catherine 's room. I felt very sad to see her so poorly.

Dorothy was very concerned about Catherine 's condition. Room Four was now empty and before the pressure started from the social services I thought it would be better for Dorothy to move into her own room. Next day while I was washing her I took the opportunity to talk about the idea.

"I know you like Catherine , but at the moment she is far from well. Because of her condition I'm in and out of your room all night. I thought, if you don't mind, you might like to go into Room Four. It is a good sized single room, very pleasant with French windows onto the flat roof. It has the same amenities as all the other rooms. When I have a minute or two I'll take you there and you can see for yourself."

"Since I have been here with you," she said, "I've noticed that when someone is very ill, like Catherine , you put them in the sick room. Why not this time?"

"Because she is so ill it is too much to move her about. Anyway, it would be nice for you to have a single room. We do not know if you will like the next person to share your room as much as you liked Catherine ."

"You know best. If you think it's better for me, so be it." That night Catherine hallucinated, her mind going back to the first years of her marriage. She became very distressed, arguing with her later husband saying,

"I do my very best to provide you with a decent meal and you don't come home before the early hours of the morning! Are you telling me you've been working in that bank for all this time? We've been married for two years and our marriage is not consummated yet. Derek, what is going on?" She was getting more distressed. I was beside her bed but there wasn't very much I could do for my beloved Catherine .

In the morning Dorothy said,

"Yes, Ida, you are right. I think I'll move to the room next door if it's free. It doesn't make any difference to Catherine if I'm here or not! She is too ill to understand. I will be happier in a single room." Not long after that Catherine passed away in her sleep. Every time one of them died, I felt deep pain inside which lasted a long time. Even now there is not a day that passes without one of them coming into my mind.

Life carried on very much the same in 'Shalom'. Mrs Hurdle was well settled in and felt part of the place. Dorothy was visited daily by Mr and Mrs Herriott. They were pleased that she was in a single room. Mr Herriott was a well educated man with a good sense of humour. He kept us all in stitches of laughter. The hospital continued to ask for beds but I wasn't ready to fill them before we had a good holiday, which we really needed.

We were very fortunate to have good staff who we trusted: Elisabeth, Mary and Gladys. We also had our two daughters on standby for the staff at all times. We left Maidstone in the spring of 1993 to go from Gatwick Airport to Rimini, to our flat there. From this base we went to Tuscany and from there to Rome. We always visited the Vatican and our relations.

While I was there I had a fall and injured both my knees, one more than the other. I was taken to St John Lateran Hospital in the centre of Rome, which brought back memories of my visit there many years before when I was much younger. They gave me a strong painkiller and told me to go straight to hospital once I got back to England. I made an appointment with Mr Tassel at Somerfield Hospital when we got home, who said,

"Mrs Maddalena, because you belong to BUPA I will operate on you straight away."

"Yes, doctor. You know I have a small residential home to run. Before you operate, I want to know how long the operation will take, what is involved and how long it will be before I will be able to look after the residents again."

"It is necessary to replace your knee cap," he said, "and to do that I use a tool like a Black and Decker saw to remove the injured one, and I then replace it with a plastic one. You will need to spend a week or two in hospital and you won't be able to do anything for a minimum of three months."

"I'm in a lot of pain but at the same time I have a lot to sort out. I'd rather take strong painkillers until I've dealt with all my responsibilities."

At this time I was still under Dr Holt for my heart condition, who continually told me my health couldn't take the stress of managing the home any longer. I didn't take any notice and continued look after the residents, without taking any more on until my health improved. Social services, knowing I had a vacancy, wanted to know why I refused to fill the empty bed. It was the most difficult decision of my life. I had had many difficulties in the past but this was different. This concerned my own health and the old people I had in my care. I had to decide how best to resolve the problem without disturbing the residents. For the time being I had no choice but to take painkillers and get on with the job as best I could.

It was a hot summer and as usual the residents spent time enjoying afternoon tea in garden. Sylvia remained in her room and every day was hallucinating more. She was seeing all kinds of things, sometimes very frightening. It was necessary for me to call the doctor and see what could be done to make her more comfortable. I rang the surgery and said,

"I need a doctor to see Mrs Woodland and would very much appreciate it if someone could come today." Dr McLean came and said,

"There is nothing we can do for this lady. She is very old and frail and not enough oxygen is reaching her brain. I don't think she will be with us very long." I was very sad but knew what to expect.

After a few days Sylvia passed away very peacefully. It must have been a relief for her, but it was very sad for all of us.

Now I had much more time and had long chats with Georgina. She used tell me her life story and a very colourful one it was.

"Ida, you feed me too well," she said, "When I came here I wasn't half the size I am now."

"I don't think you have put any weight on."

"I have!" she said, pointing to her chest.

"There's nothing wrong with your bust."

"No, there's nothing wrong with it now. I only I wish it had been like that when I was in Australia."

"Why is that?"

"I was in love with a great man who had lived in Australia since his youth, though he always felt his home country was England. He was a very good cricketer and played for Australia. He was known all around the world."

"How did you meet him?"

"My brother emigrated to Australia. He wasn't there very long when he joined the police force. He liked his job and did very well, becoming the Chief Inspector in Sydney. Every time this man played cricket, because he was so famous, the police would get involved and my brother was in charge. They became friends and he often visited my brother and his family, which is how we met."

"Did he have any family?"

"Oh yes," she said, "he had a wife and children."

"And you still went out with him?"

"I would like to have married him, but only if he left his family. But no, he said his wife had better breasts than I!" I couldn't help but laugh.

"I was so disappointed," she continued, "I felt as if my whole world caved in. I decided to come back to England and try to forget all about him, but that was very hard. Every time I bought a newspaper he was there on the front page. It took me a long time before I could put that man behind me."

The next day she rang her bell and I ran upstairs to see what she needed. She had in her hand a newspaper with a picture of an old man on the front page.

"What is it?" I asked. She could hardly speak.

"Remember what I told you yesterday?"

"Yes, you told me your love story."

"Ida, this is the man who made me suffer so much! I nearly took my own life because of him." I looked at the paper and recognised a face I had seen many times before. The story was about him, his fame as a cricket player and how, at ninety years old, he was returning to his beloved home country.

"Oh, Georgina, it must be very hard for you to see him again and not be able to have a word with him."

"Well, after all this time he might not recognise me - after all, my bust is much bigger now! But I don't think it's much good to him these days!" We both laughed.

Then she told me her last story. When she was very young she had had a child but never married his father. At that time there wasn't any government help for unmarried mothers and, without support from their family, it was impossible to survive.

"What did you do with your baby?"

"I put him in a Dr Barnado's Home and when I came back from Australia I looked for him. I found out he was married with two children. His family never accepted me, but he did and we became very close. He died aged fifty-four. I did get over my love affair but I never, ever got over the loss of my dear son and the only place I want to be is where he is." Now I knew why she was so depressed at times and why she wanted to die.

Georgina was doing well with her painting therapy. As time went on, she demanded more and more attention from me and the staff. I could hardly go out anywhere without taking her with me and when I didn't take her with me she behaved like a spoilt child. While we were out she would throw herself on the floor for no reason and often injured herself. We were in and out of hospital with her. All that pressure wasn't doing my health any good. Under the doctor's order I was told to let social services deal with her, so the next time she threw herself on the floor I told the hospital that I couldn't be responsible for her any longer. It was too much of a strain on my health.

Georgina was sent to a nursing home, not a very nice one. I used to get messages from her that she wanted to come back home and I was very sad for her. After a few months I received a call from the home saying Georgina had passed away that morning. As always, we attended her funeral. It was sad. There were only a few people to see her off to the place she most wanted to go.

Good news came our way: my daughter and my son had both been married for quite a few years without children, but now at last

Luciana and Nino's wife were both expecting! That was a great joy for all of us. It was now time to decide what I was going to do. I could hardly walk for the pain in my knees and it was impossible for me to take on more responsibility. I asked the Social Services for advice. When they came to inspect 'Shalom' they said,

"Mrs Maddalena, everything is fine but why do you keep four beds empty when you know there are many people who want to come to your little home?"

"The reason is I'm not well enough. My health is not what it should be. I haven't the right to take old people into my home, who pay to be looked after, if I'm not able to do so."

"But you could employ more staff and still run the place."

"The home is very small and the income wouldn't be enough to pay for more staff and still give the residents the standard of care I set. I would have to put the fees up much too high and that is not what I want to do. Most of the residents here are private but they don't pay anything because Social Services pay for them."

"Why don't you sell 'Shalom' and buy a bigger house, then you could take more residents and afford to have a manager."

"I've been a nurse for twenty-five years. In hospital there were too many people to look after. With limited staff, we couldn't give the patients the care and attention they needed. For me, opening a small home meant I could do just what I'm doing now: give them the best food and the best nursing in a homely atmosphere. My family helped me achieve this but now my daughter is going to have a baby and has a full-time job. It's too much to ask."

"We are very pleased with the way you look after people and wish you would continue. May we suggest you take on a partner and for two years you become a sleeping partner to give yourself the chance to recover your health?"

I spoke to my family about this idea and they said,
"Mum, you must make sure you draw up a legal contract to protect your home and the residents. You also need to set up a contract with the bank to protect your interests."
"Fine, I will do just that."

Eventually I found someone I thought would be right. I asked social services about her and they said,
"We know her and we think it will be all right but only for two years."

I went to the bank to see the manager, who said,
"Mrs Maddalena, let your family draw up a contract and then make sure it is legal and we will abide by what it says."

We had already sold our family home to our daughter Stella so now we had to look for another one. We had the flat in Italy but I needed to be in England for many reasons: my old people's home, my health and above all my family. The thought we would soon be grandparents was the most beautiful thing we were waiting for. On 9th June our first grandson was born to my son in Essex and our second was born on the 19th!

I said to my husband,
"The first thing is to look for another house and then I'll take it from there." We looked everywhere but couldn't find what we really wanted. Because we liked 'Shalom' so much we were looking for something similar but smaller. But there wasn't a house like 'Shalom'! One day we went to the College Practice to collect the residents' repeat prescriptions and noticed a detached house for sale. It was a small house but in my condition I didn't want a big one. We made an appointment with the owner, liked it and started the procedures for buying it. I was still taking painkillers for my injured knees and continued to look after the ladies until the contract for the new house and the contract for 'Shalom' were finalised.

We couldn't go to the new home until everything was completed and we wouldn't leave 'Shalom' just before Christmas. I was in terrible pain but that didn't stop me making sure our few residents would enjoy a merry Christmas, just like all those in years gone by. On Christmas day my family joined them and sat around the table to enjoy lunch. We were all one big, happy family. But inside me was a terrible sadness. I couldn't stop thinking about the job I loved so much now being put in someone else's hands. Never for a moment would I abandon the residents and leave them to the mercy of strangers.

My husband also wasn't well and he didn't want to leave the home either. The residents were very dear to both of us. 'Shalom' had been our family home for thirteen years and our residential home for twelve. Now we were heart broken, but we didn't have any choice. One thing I was happy about was that the contract specified that the home should be run just as I had run it with no differences. At the beginning of 1995 we left 'Shalom' for a property just off College Road in Maidstone.

CHAPTER FIFTY – OUR NEW SMALL HOME

Our new home is a small house situated between College Road and College Avenue, very central yet without the disadvantages of the town centre. It is behind All Saints Church and we enjoy beautiful views of the River Medway at Lockmeadow. It is surrounded by beautiful gardens. The market is just the other side of the river. I don't need to catch a bus or drive the car because it is only five minutes walk to the middle of town. It is a very desirable area and the Baptist church, where I like to worship, is just on the corner of nearby Nightrider Street.

Soon after we moved I contacted Mr Flitcroft to arrange the operation to my left knee.
I spent three months on crutches, and then needed to walk with a stick. During this time I found that my residential home wasn't being run according to the legal agreement that was made and it troubled me much to visit my lovely home and the ladies I'd left behind there. After two years the contract ended and I was left with lots of debts and a very dirty house. Only one resident remained, Dorothy. All the rest had died. It was very sad for me and my family. I tried to start again but it was impossible. The house needed complete renovation and, with my poor health, it wasn't worth doing.

I made sure Dorothy had somewhere to go and I sold the house as a family home. I continued to visit Dorothy Wickendon in her new home. On her hundredth birthday she showed all her party guests the physical exercises she used to do at 'Shalom'. She was a lovely little lady, but not long after her birthday she had a fall and died. She was sadly missed; it was a very great loss for Mr and Mrs Herriott.

I continued to work, mostly voluntarily in hospitals and a residential home, until one day I fainted while on duty. Now I go around and visit old people and help them as much as I can.

Not long ago I received a telephone call from the person I sold 'Shalom' to, who said,
"Mrs Maddalena, please come over, there is a very important letter for you." I went there and he handed me the letter.
"It arrived yesterday," he said, and when I opened it there was a cheque for eight thousand pounds from St James's Palace and a

note thanking me for the service I had rendered to a member of the royal household. I didn't understand. I had cared for a couple of people from a royal background but they had died a long time ago. Why this now? It was clearly addressed to me at Shalom Residential Home with the right address and postcode. I was mystified.

I had a word with my bank and they said,
"This cheque is made payable to you and you should put it in your account because it is rightfully yours." I didn't feel it was right and waited for my family to come home to discuss it with them. They said,
"Mum, send it back. It's a mistake. Send it back at once! Don't accept it. You closed the home years ago now and that was the end of it." But curiosity got the better of me and I telephoned St James's Palace and explained the position and that I wanted to know exactly what it was all about. They said,
"There is another woman with your name and she uses the same business name, but she lives in Tower Gate in London. There must have been a mistake with the computer. We want to thank you for your honesty." So the money went back to St James's Palace. I said to myself,
"Wow, what a funny coincidence! Another person with my name and my business name! It seems extraordinary that could ever happen, but I have no choice but to believe what I've been told."

Now I had almost succeeded in all my ambitions and I hadn't anything more to do but take the advice my teacher gave me all those years ago.
"Ida," he said, "one day you will be a writer." So, this is my life story!

Ida Festa in Maddalena